Psychology
or
A View of the Human Soul, Including Anthropology
(1841)

By Frederick A. Rauch

A Facsimile Reproduction
with an introduction
by Eric T. Carlson, M.D.

Scholars' Facsimiles & Reprints   Delmar, New York, 1975

Published by Scholars' Facsimiles & Reprints, Inc.
P. O. Box 344, Delmar, New York 12054

© 1975 Scholars' Facsimiles & Reprints, Inc.
All rights reserved. Printed in the U.S.A.

Library of Congress Cataloging in Publication Data

Rauch, Friedrich August, 1806-1841.
  Psychology: or, A view of the human soul,
including anthropology.

  (History of psychology series)
  Photoreprint of the 1841 ed.
published by M. W. Dodd, New York;
with new introd.
  Includes bibliographical references.
  1. Psychology — Early works to 1850.
2. Man. I. Title.
BF111.R2 1975   150   74-22335
ISBN 0-8201-1142-2

Introduction

Frederick August Rauch was instrumental in the introduction of Hegelian philosophy and psychology to the United States in the 1830's. Born at Kirchbracht, Germany, on 22 July 1806, the son of a clergyman of the Reformed Church, Heinrich Rauch (1778-1853) and Fredericke Karoline Hadermann (whose father was also of the same clergy), Rauch spent the first twenty-five years of his life within fifty miles of Frankfort-on-the-Maine.[1] He lost his mother just after birth and, being of a sickly nature, was not entered in the Hanau Gymnasium until twelve years of age. After three years there, followed by two more at the Budingen Gymnasium, he entered the University of Giessen where he continued his extensive classic education and developed a professional identity as a philologian. Then, at twenty, he accepted a teaching position with his uncle at the Hadermann Institute of Education at Frankfurt and started his campaign to obtain a doctorate. It is unclear why he did not do this at Giessen but instead submitted applications in January 1827, plus copies of his dissertation (*Observations on Sophocles' Electra*)[2] to Heidelburg and Marburg where he had never studied. Rejected by Heidelberg, he pressed his case at Marburg using the plea that his uncle was ill and anxious that he be prepared with his advanced degree to assume the directorship of the Institute. Encouraged by the Marburg faculty, he made the suggested changes in his treatise, had the required one-hundred copies printed, and received his degree on 6 March 1827.

There is no evidence he ever assumed control of the Hadermann Institute, for by the same December he had enrolled as a student of philosophy at Heidelberg. Six weeks later, he petitioned for the right to lecture as a step towards becoming a Privat-dozent and, in support of his application, submitted his doctoral publication. After various machinations on both sides, Rauch evidently withdrew his petition, and in November 1828, we find him back at his original university, Giessen, attending classes and taking his oral exams the following month. This time he was successful and was made a provisional Privat-dozent in December 1828 but still subject to state approval. An altercation with one of his professors at Giessen involved him in a series of lawsuits that were finally resolved in his favor by the Ministry of Justice and the Interior, which decided that Rauch should lecture to have the opportunity to show his value in open competition. One may question his likelihood of success, for he had to prove himself locally in what undoubtedly had become quite a hostile atmosphere.

During these stressful conflicts and negotiations, Rauch continued his academic endeavors. Although his provisional permission to teach was in history, his true interests were revealed in a provocative petition in which he proposed to give lectures in psychology, logic, and natural law based on Hegel and Goethe's *Faust*. He continued to teach at Giessen until the summer of 1831. Early in 1829, he applied his anthropological and linguistic interests, which reflected a German trend[3], to a study entitled *Hindu, Persian, Pelasgian, Germanic and Slavic Identity as Expressed in Language, Religion and Customs*.[4] The following year, he published his lectures on Goethe which showed the influence of Hegel's *Science of Logic*.[5] Another work which may have been a product of his two years at Giessen, *The Clarification of the Universe or the Density of Mankind*, did not appear until 1833.[6]

The summer of 1831 arrived with the Ministry still not having made a final disposition of his case. This undoubtedly played a part in his decision to emigrate to America. He embarked on 30 September 1831, leaving his lawyer unpaid and owing money to the University of Heidelberg. Landing in New York six weeks later, he went on to Easton, Pennsylvania, with its considerable German population, and he initially supported himself by giving music lessons. The people of Easton had been striving for nearly six years to establish a college. Their efforts finally came to fruition in May 1832, when Lafayette College opened with a staff of two, a president, and Rauch as professor of literature and the German language. That this classical scholar also knew Sanskrit impressed the board of trustees. There was little security in this position—at least five other men had declined it—so it is hardly surprising that Rauch resigned two months later to accept an appointment as professor of Biblical Literature and head of the Classical Department of the Theological Seminary of the German Reformed Church in the United States at York, Pennsylvania, a position both secure and in accord with his religious beliefs. Although offered the presidency of Pennsylvania College at Gettsyburg the next year, he declined probably because of his warm current acceptance and his forthcoming marriage to Phoebe Moore (1813?-1846). The school had financial difficulties, however, and the trustees resolved to broaden its acceptance of students beyond those seeking the ministry and to seek a community vitally interested in such a school. They found such a place in Mercersburg, Pennsylvania, where the school was moved in November 1835, under its new name, the "High School of the German Reformed Church." Within the year an act of the state legislature had granted a charter to convert this school into Marshall College with Rauch as its head and professor of Hebrew, Greek, German Languages and Evidences of Christianity. Three years later, Rauch was able to speak optimistically about the future of the school. In 1841, he was joined by a congenial colleague, John W. Nevin, who lightened Rauch's teaching load. But Rauch's health broke soon thereafter, and his early promise was terminated when he died of unknown causes on 2 March 1841, at the age of thirty-four.

In the last year of his life, Rauch published his volume on psychology and made the revisions for the second edition.[7] Having expressed a desire to teach psychology as early as 1830 in Giessen, he was able to bring this to fruition at Marshall College where psychology joined Ancient Languages, Mathematics, Natural Philosophy and Christian Ethics to form the curriculum. He recognized that his book was "the first attempt to unite German and American mental philosophy" and wrote it in such a style as to make "this noble and delightful science accessible to all classes of readers." Although he makes many classical allusions, his acknowledged references are to the more contemporary British and German authors. He mentions Locke, the main force in American philosophy and psychology until the Revolution, and various members of the Scottish school (Thomas Reid, Lord Kames, Dugald Stewart, and Thomas Brown). The Scottish School of Common Sense dominated American psychology at the time of his arrival; but for Rauch, the German philosophy was primary. He patterned his book after the works of Karl Gustav Carus, Jr., Karl Rosenkranz, and Carl Daub. Daub's influence was critical in the development of his psychology. It is likely that Rauch attended Daub's lectures on Hegelian Theology at Heidelberg, for in his literary remains there is an extensive collection of student notes on Daub's lectures. Rauch's arrangement follows that of Daub, which is, in turn, modeled after Hegel's *The Philosophy of the Mind*. Rauch's book, thus, is probably the first in English to present Hegel's mental philosophy.

Rauch's human behavioral science is divided into two parts: the first, anthropology, studies the effects of the seasons, racial and national differences, temperaments (the classical four), and the state of the body on the mind; the second forms his psychology proper. Here, in this discussion on reason, he continues to show his earlier interest in language and introduces the term semeiotic, largely in its physiological and psychological sense.[8] His book received mixed but generally favorable reviews. The Harvard philosopher, Francis Bowen, gave the most unfavorable opinion, while James W. Alexander of Princeton gave it his qualified approval. The *New Englander*, a journal that served as the organ of the Yale Divinity School, praised it, and Orestes Brownson proclaimed it "a work of genius."[9] How widely it was adopted as a text is unknown—records indicate its use at the University of Vermont, Dartmouth College, and Marshall College. It had its greatest impact in the Transcendentalist Mercersburg Theology that developed at Marshall College and was exemplified in the writings of its leaders, John W. Nevins and Philip Schaff. (Less important are Theodore Appel and Emmanuel V. Gerhart.[10]) Jay Wharton Fay says Rauch's is the first book in English to have "psychology" in its title; of far greater significance, however, is the role it played in introducing into the United States the German psychology that would become so important after 1865.[11]

Eric T. Carlson

New York Hospital—
Cornell Medical Center
New York, New York

Notes

1. Howard J.B. Ziegler, *Frederick Augustus Rauch-American Hegelian*, Lancaster, Pennsylvania: Franklin and Marshall College, 1953. This book is the main source of biographical information about Rauch and gives his complete bibliography.
2. Friedrich August Rauch, *In Sophoclis Electram Observationes*, Frankfurt-on-the-Main: Naumann, 1972.
3. R.H. Robins, *A Short History of Linguistics*, Bloomington, Indiana: Indiana University Press, 1967.
4. Friedrich Augustus Rauch, *Die Identitat der Hindu, Perser, Palasger, Germanen und Slaven, dargethan aus Sprache, Religion und Sitte*, Marburg: Christian Garthe, 1829.
5. Friedrich August Rauch, *Vorlesungen uber Göthe's Faust*, Bogen, Budingen: Heller'schen Hofbuchdruckereri, 1830.
6. Friedrich Augustus Rauch, *Die Verklarung Des Weltalls oder die Bestimmung des Menschen*, Bogen, Budingen: Frankfurt-a.-M., 1833.
7. Friedrich August Rauch, *Psychology or a view of the Human Soul: including Anthropology*, 1st ed. New York: M.W. Dodd, 1840. 2nd ed. New York: M.W. Dodd, 1841. Reprints Boston: 1844, Boston: 1846, New York: 1850.
8. For current usage see Thomas A. Sebeok's "Semiotics and Ethology," *The Linguistic Reporter*, October 1969, Suppl. 22, pp. 9-15. Rauch was in error saying that it had not been used in English, for semeiotics in medical writing since the seventeenth century had signified the branch of medicine interpreting symptoms.
9. Robert Clemmer, "Historical Transcendentalism in Pennsylvania," *Journal of the History of Ideas*, 1969, *30*: 579-592.
10. James Hastings Nichols, *Romanticism in American Theology: Nevin and Schaff at Mercersburg*, Chicago, Illinois: The University of Chicago Press, 1961.
11. Jay Wharton Fay, *American Psychology Before William James*, New Brunswick, N.J.: Rutgers University Press, 1939.

PSYCHOLOGY;

OR,

A VIEW OF THE

HUMAN SOUL;

INCLUDING

ANTHROPOLOGY,

ADAPTED FOR THE USE OF COLLEGES.

BY REV. FREDERICK A. RAUCH, D. P.
LATE PRESIDENT OF MARSHALL COLLEGE, PENN.

SECOND EDITION, REVISED AND IMPROVED.

NEW YORK:
M. W. DODD,
BRICK CHURCH CHAPEL, OPPOSITE THE CITY HALL.
BOSTON:—CROCKER & BREWSTER.
PHILADELPHIA:—THOMAS, COWPERTHWAIT, & CO.

1841.

Entered according to Act of Congress, in the year 1841, by M. W. DODD, in the Clerk's office of the District Court of the Southern District of New York.

STEREOTYPED BY SMITH & WRIGHT, 216 WILLIAM ST. N. Y.

Printed by D. Fanshaw.

PREFACE.

"*Know thyself*" was the inscription on the temple of Apollo. The meaning of this terse admonition was either a *practical* one: Know thy frailties, thy human weakness, thy sinful nature; acknowledge thyself what thou art,—and amend thy ways; or it was a *theoretical* one: Man, the highest being in nature, who studies every thing below himself, who knows the soil which he cultivates, and the stars that regulate the seasons, and the laws of crystallization, vegetation and animalization—should not he desire to know himself? a being, who stands midway between the kingdom of nature and that of immortal spirits? who is the measure of the earth and all it contains, who unites what is dispersed in nature, every power and every beauty in himself? But *how* shall man become acquainted with himself both *practically* and *theoretically*? This is the question, which the great Apollo did not answer. Shall he merely observe himself? But man is inclined either to place too high or too low a value upon himself; he has not a proper measure for his judgment in himself. Shall he watch others? He that will understand himself must observe those around him, but to understand them, he must look into his own heart. Thus he may indeed obtain a knowledge of man, but one, that is without systematic connection, incomplete, partial and imperfect. While we cannot do without such a knowledge of man, the admonition of Apollo will only be listened to fully, when we connect with this experimental knowledge a *systematical* development of all contained in man, especially of his *reason* and *will*. These are the basis of all the thoughts and actions, of all the sciences and practical pursuits in man, and without a knowledge of them, it will always remain difficult to understand man, as we meet him in life. *Theory* must here, as every where else, assist *practice*.

The principal object of the author in writing this book, was to render this noble and delightful science accessible to all classes of readers, for as the inscription on the temple of Apollo was not only intended for some, but for every one approaching it, so the knowledge of man is desirable for every one and not for a few only. The author flatters himself, that he has effected this purpose by using plain language, by following a simple course of thought, by taking all his illustrations from nature, and by comparing constantly the activities of mind with those analogous to it, in nature. With the exception of a few divisions, it is hoped therefore, that the present work may be read by all.

A *second* object of the author was to give the science of man a direct bearing upon other sciences, and especially upon religion and theology. Psychology and theology are connected by their common subject, which is *man*. Religion, of which theology is the science, is intended *for man*, and for him only; psychology treats of man and not of any other being. Man as the subject of psychology, is created for religion and cannot do without it. Religion is not a mere *quality*, but the *substance* of man. He remains what he is, though he has no learning, no beauty, no wit, neither a strong memory nor an acute judgment; but he ceases to be man in the full sense of the term when he has no religion;—he is then only an animal, more cunning, crafty and prudent, than all the others, one that can invent machines, but he is no longer the lord of the earth, the image of his Creator. Now religion has for its soul, *faith*; this contains thoughts and ideas, as for instance, those of providence, of sin, of sanctification, of regeneration, of repentance, &c. Psychology develops the nature of reason and consequently that of its productions, which are thoughts; and without understanding the nature of reason and its capacities, that of faith will not be clearly known; for if *faith* and *reason* differ, as they do, how can this difference be exhibited, unless the being of each is manifest to us? Again: Faith must be active by love, or else it is dead. It must therefore affect our will and fill it with love and animate it to good works. If so, the being of our will in its state of nature, and previous to its regeneration, ought likewise to be known. But as such it exists in the form of desires, inclinations, emotions and passions, and these are the subjects of psychology; hence the study of the latter again is indispensable to a thorough study of theology. While, therefore, the first section of the second part will assist the science of dogmatics, the second has for its remote object to be auxiliary to that of christian ethics.

It will scarcely be necessary to show the influence which a

good, systematical knowledge of man, of his reason and will, and their union with his body must have on the practice of medicine; and if the physician studies human and comparative anatomy, physiology and somatology in general, he will find it much to his advantage, to know the whole life contained in the body which he dissects. And how will he manage cases of mental disease without psychology? The basis of all pathology is certainly a knowledge of health, and this must be the same in the sphere of mind.

The lawyer, on the other hand, who protects our rights, will be the more successful in doing so, the better he understands human nature; for all rights are those of man, and when disputed, passions and desires have darkened our knowledge of them; and the lawyer in addressing the court, in developing the case before him, must well understand the nature of the passions, to make his case clear. The greatest lawyers and public orators, Pitt, Sheridan, Fox, &c., were also the finest psychologists. Many actions are committed under the influence of vehement emotions or passions: to value the guilt of such actions, their moving springs, the passions must be known.

But above all is the study of psychology useful to parents and teachers; they have to draw out, what is in their children, and how can they do this well without knowing the nature of what they are expected to cultivate? Hence the study of psychology and especially of desires, inclinations and emotions, is indispensable to them.

Yet why should we speak of the mere usefulness of a science, which if well represented, is one of the most entertaining and interesting, which the human mind has produced? Who would not feel anxious to see his portrait, drawn before the eye of his mind? Psychology is not only intended for the *wants* of man, whether sensual or intellectual, those of life or of social intercourse; its highest design is to make man *conscious* of the subjects of which it treats, *reason* and *will*, and give him full possession of both. Man possesses only that of which he is conscious; an inheritance of which I know nothing, may be mine in law, but not by possession. Unless I know my *reason* and *will*, I possess neither fully, but only partially.

The present work is, as far as the author knows, the first attempt to unite *German* and *American* mental philosophy. This design has not been executed by bringing together two separate systems or by forming an *eclectic compound*, which is neither the one nor the other, and the parts of which do not grow forth from one spirit, but are brought together from different sources and united by the writer—a real sphinx in the sphere of science. The author was rather anxious to have whatever the work contains, bear witness of one and the same *objective* spirit, which formed all the parts into *one* life, as the specific life of a tree changes all particles into one juice.

The author feels himself under obligation to acknowledge fully the use he has made of the following writers: *Locke, D. Stewart, Reid, Brown, Rosenkranz, Carus,* Jr., *Carus,* Sen., *Daub, Stiedenroth, Suabedissen, Eschenmayer, Heinroth, Hegel, Kant, Wirth, Steffens, Herbart, Hartman,* and others. He has used these authors with more or less freedom, and especially Carus, Jr., Daub and Rosenkranz, whose general arrangement he has adopted not without some improvements, however, as he hopes. The work was to be of *one* spirit; whatever has been suggested by others, had to become a part of the whole by receiving this spirit and by representing it. Hence to save space, a general acknowledgment has been thought sufficient.

As to the language, the author has particularly to beg the indulgence of his readers. He hopes this will be granted, as in philosophy *beauty* of speech is less desirable than *clearness*, and as in this science we desire less to be entertained than to be enriched with ideas. The terminology of mental philosophy in the English language, as in almost all others, is difficult and not perfectly agreed on. Thus, to mention one instance instead of many, the difference between *sensation* and *perception* is by no means clearly established; as yet it is still disputed. The author has therefore used *sensation* indiscriminately both for the perception of the object and the feeling connected with it in the sense by which it is perceived. Simplification has been his great object; yet the signification once given to a word, has been strictly adhered to.

MERCERSBURGH, APRIL 21ST, 1840.

PRELIMINARY NOTICE

TO THE

SECOND EDITION.

The amiable and highly gifted author of the following work, had not quite completed his revision of it for the second edition, when it pleased God in his wise and righteous sovereignty, to take him away by death. In the circumstances, it seems proper to prefix here a few statements with regard to his life and character. Dr. Rauch was a native of Kirchbracht, in the Grand Dutchy of Hesse Darmstadt, born July 27, 1806. His father, a minister belonging before the "Union" to the *Reformed Church*, still lives to mourn over the tidings of his son's untimely decease. He is an orthodox and diligent pastor, in the neighborhood of Frankfort, on the Maine. At the age of eighteen, Dr. Rauch entered the University of Marburg, where he took his diploma in the year 1827. Afterwards he spent a year, as a student at Grissen; and subsequently to this another year still, at Heidelbergh. Here he enjoyed, as it would seem, the special regard and favor of that aged giant in the sphere of mind, *Charles Daub*, since dead; a man, who had followed Kant, Schelling, and Hegel, to the farthest bounds of speculation, without surrendering for a moment his firm hold upon the great objects of faith; resolutely facing the billows, as Tholuck has expressed it, and forcing his way *through*, where even Schleiermacher could save himself only by retreating towards the shore. For the memory of this man Dr. Rauch entertained always the highest veneration. Daub had fixed his eye upon *him* as a young man of more than common promise, who might be expected to do good service to the cause of science, in the department to which he wished to consecrate his life. On quitting Heidelberg, he spent a year again at Grissen, as *professor extraordinarius;* at the end of which time, he received an appointment to a regular professorship in Heidelberg. Here however his fair prospects were suddenly covered with a dark cloud. In his lectures, he was supposed to have expressed himself with too much freedom with regard to government. Jealousy was awakened; and it was considered necessary, in the judgment of his friends, that he should quit the country. With a sorrowful heart accordingly, he came in the year 1831 to the United States. His first year was spent at Easton, in the State of Pennsylvania. In the summer of 1832 he was invited to take charge of the classical school, in connection with the Theological Seminary of the German Reformed Synod, then located at York in the same State. On the removal of this institution to Mercersberg in the year 1836, and the establishment of Marshall College, he became the President of the College, retaining his connection with the Seminary still as Professor of Biblical Literature.

It is not saying too much to affirm, that Dr. Rauch was one of the finest scholars belonging to this country. His mind was of the first order, and his education had been complete. In the whole compass of the German Philosophy he was most perfectly at home. By a ten years residence in this country, he had become, at the same time, sufficiently *Americanized* to be able to enter without difficulty into the modes of thinking and feeling, which are here prevalent. He had ceased indeed to think of himself as a foreigner, and loved to identify himself entirely with our institutions and our character as his own. Thus might he be considered as qualified, beyond most if not all others, for transferring into the English sphere of thinking, the true spirit and life of German thought in a useful and intelligible way. This requires more a great deal, than mere translation or report from our language into the other. It can be properly accomplished only where the mind has become thoroughly pervaded with the life of its subject itself, so as to be able to give it out naturally and easily in a new form. That German Philosophy must, in the end make itself deeply and extensively felt upon our system of thinking, in one way and another is not to be doubted. It ought to do so; for it embodies elements which are needed to give tone and vigor to our inward life. At the same time, it is immensely important that the medium through which the one form of mind is made to flow over into the other, should be pure and clear. Under this view, Dr. Rauch was eminently fitted to transact between the mind of Germany and the mind of this country. He understood and honored Hegel as a philosopher; and *because* he did so, he found himself in no danger of following him blindly into his errors. He was secured against all transcendental, pantheistic dreams, by knowing familiarly the boundaries of this enchanted ground, rather than by mere blind prejudice. He was moreover a firm believer in the truth of the Bible, and in the great doctrines of grace which it teaches.

As he seemed to be thus specially qualified for such a service as has now been mentioned, so did he feel himself powerfully drawn towards it, as his proper and congenial vocation. Enthusiastically attached to his favorite studies, he cherished the lively hope of making himself useful, on this field, in a permanent and extensive way. His *Psychology* was only the beginning of what he wished and expected to accomplish, as an author. Of much more account, in his own estimation, was to have been his *Moral*

PRELIMINARY NOTICE TO THE SECOND EDITION.

Philosophy; a work on which his heart was greatly set, and which he hoped to be able to publish in the course of the ensuing summer. A treatise on *Aethetics* was intended to carry out and complete the scheme.

His system of Moral Philosophy is expected still to make its appearance, in substance at least, after some time. A course of lectures which he has left behind him on this subject, embody the principles and main thoughts of his contemplated treatise, though they may not exhibit fully the form in which it was designed that all should finally be comprehended, before going to the press.

As it regards the present work, its character may be considered as already fully established. No work of the sort in this country, has ever been so favorably received. The first edition was exhausted in a very few weeks after its publication. In this second edition, the author will be found to have made some material improvements upon the first; not by changing or modifying his views at all, but by throwing them occasionally into a more perspicuous form, and guarding here and there against misconceptions, to which they were before exposed. He has moreover paid special attention to the phraseology, which here and there sounded too strongly of a foreign idiom, and to the occasional errors in typography which had escaped notice in the first edition. In this accurate revision due regard has been had to the opinions expressed in different reviews, in relation to the work, so far as they were considered to be worthy of attention. In the case however of most of the strictures which had been made upon it, he felt that he had no reason to yield his own judgment, as it had influenced him at first, to that of his reviewers. That he might not seem, at the same time, to have overlooked or despised such criticism, and for the purpose also of apologizing for his own views, he had expected to notice certain points thus animadverted upon, in a new Preface, more full than the first, and designed to stand in its place. This has been prevented by his death.

JOHN W. NEVIN.

MERCERSBURG, MARCH 23, 1841.

For " Grissen" in lines 13 and 27, page vii, read " Giessen."
For " Aethetics" in line 3, page ix, read " Aesthetics."

INDEX OF CONTENTS.

	Page.
INTRODUCTION.	
CHAPTER I.—Difference between man and the animal,	13
(1.) Man has the same physical functions as the animal,	14
(2.) The psychological difference between man and the animal,	15
CHAPTER II.—Life.	22
§ 1. Life in general,	ib.
§ 2. Of the plastic power, or the principle of all individual life,	25
§ 3. Instinct,	34
§ 4. On the ingenuity of animals,	39
§ 5. Relation of instinct to man,	48
PART I.—ANTHROPOLOGY.	
CHAPTER I.—Modifications of mind produced by the permanent influence of nature,	55
§ 1. The influence of nature upon the mind of man,	ib.
(1.) Highlands,	61
(2.) Plains and valleys,	ib.
(3.) Coasts,	62
§ 2. The different races of mankind,	66
National differences,	68
(1.) The French,	73
(2.) The Italians,	74
(3.) The English,	ib.
(4.) The Germans,	76
Remarks,	78
§ 3. Qualities of the mind produced by sexual difference,	80
(1.) Physically,	ib.
(2.) Psychologically,	81
Woman.	
(1.) Moral disposition,	ib.
(2.) Mental qualities,	ib.
Man.	
(1.) Moral disposition,	83
(2.) Mental qualities,	ib.

INDEX OF CONTENTS.

	Page.
§ 4. Temperaments,	85
The sanguine temperament,	88
The choleric temperament,	89
The melancholic temperament,	90
The phlegmatic temperament,	91
§ 5. Mental capacities,	92
(1.) Docility,	ib.
(2.) Talent,	94
(3.) Genius,	ib.
§ 6. Idiosyncrasy,	100
CHAPTER II.—Of the transient influence of nature upon the mind,	103
§ 1. Age,	ib.
(1.) Childhood,	105
(2.) Youth,	107
(3.) Manhood,	108
(4.) Old age,	ib.
§ 2. Sleeping and waking,	109
(1.) What is sleeping and what is waking?	110
(2.) Where is sleep met with?	111
(3.) What is the design of sleep?	113
(4.) What are the conditions of sleep?	115
(5.) What is a regular sleep?	116
(6.) What is falling asleep?	117
(7.) What is awaking?	118
§ 3. Dreaming,	119
(1.) The form of dreams,	125
(2.) Causes of dreams,	127
§ 4. Prophetic dreams, presentiment, vision and deuteroscopy, or second sight,	129
§ 5. Magnetic sleep,	141
§ 6. Health and diseases of the mind,	149
Division of the diseases of the mind.	
(1.) Melancholy,	151
(2.) Insanity,	152
(3.) Mania,	ib.
CHAPTER III.—The power of the mind over the body,	160
(1.) The mind has an influence on the form of the body,	ib.
(2.) Mind exercises a power over the health of the body,	161
(3.) Power of the mind over the body may be seen from the formation of habits,	164
(4.) The power of mind over the body is perceived in the art of representing the emotions and thoughts of the mind by the emotions of the body,	166
(5.) The power of the mind over the body leaves its traces and impressions on the face, on the forms of its single parts, as nose, lips, eyes, forehead,	168
(6.) The power of the mind over the body is indicated too by the formation of the skull, which must bear witness of the life of the mind,	170

PART II.—PSYCHOLOGY.

INTRODUCTION.

§ 1. Self-consciousness, ...
   (1.) Self-feeling does not enable the animal to distinguish between the subject that feels and the object that is felt, ... 178
   (2.) The animal having self-feeling does not distinguish between itself and its members, ... ib.
   (3.) The animal having self-feeling does not distinguish between itself and its race, ... ib.
§ 2. Mutual relation of body and soul, ... 180
§ 3. Personality, ... 186
   (1.) The *person* is not only the centre of man, but also the centre of nature, ... 189
   (2.) Our personality is the centre of the whole human race, ... 190
   (3.) Our personality is complete only when we are conscious of God and our relation to him, ... 191
§ 4. Division, ... 192

REASON.

CHAPTER I.—§ 1. Sensation and the senses, ... 204
   (1.) Matter in general, ... 207
   (2.) Its chemical qualities, ... ib.
   (3.) Its light and sound, ... 208
General remarks on the senses, ... ib.
§ 2. Of attention, ... 216
   (1.) Attention in general, ... 217
   (2.) Difficulty of comprehending attention in its origin as it exists in a child, 218

CHAPTER II.—§ 1. Intellectual conception, ... 223
§ 2. Of conception, ... 225
§ 3. Fancy, ... 229
§ 4. Imagination, ... 233
Characteristics of imagination, ... 240
Semeiotic imagination, ... 249
§ 5. Language, ... 251
   (1.) Without language there can be no knowledge, ... 253
   (2.) If God taught Adam language, he of course taught him but one, ... 254
Its etymological elements, ... 261
First,—in the vowels, ... 262
Secondly,—in the consonants, ... 263
   (1.) They are altogether imitative, ... ib.
   (2.) Symbolical, ... ib.
The grammatical and syntactical elements, .. 264
Written language, ... ib.

INDEX OF CONTENTS.

		Page.
§ 6. Memory,		268
(1.) When memory is productive it is a general conception,		269
(2.) Mechanical memory,		ib.
CHAPTER III.—On pure thinking,		274
(1.) How thinking differs from the other faculties of the mind,		276
(2.) The contents of our sensation are dark and little understood before our thinking penetrates them,		283
Comprehension or apprehension,		284
Judgment,		ib.
Syllogism, or conclusion,		285
Who is qualified for pure thinking,		287
Remarks,		290

OF WILL.

	Page.
CHAPTER I.——§ 1. General nature of will,	293
Desire,	296
Inclination,	298
Emotion,	300
Passion,	302
§ 2. Relations of desires, inclinations, emotions, and passions to the will,	304
CHAPTER II.——§ 1. On desires,	310
Sensual desires,	ib.
Sensual-intellectual desires,	311
Rational desires,	312
Remarks,	315
CHAPTER III.—On inclination and passion,	317
§ 1. Inclinations arising from the relation in which man stands to himself,	319
Self-love,	ib.
Love of life,	320
Self-hatred,	325
Self-love as a passion,	327
Self-love as a passion in a negative form,	328
§ 2. Inclinations arising from the relation of man to his fellow man,	330
Love of property,	ib.
Love of property as a passion,	334
(1.) Covetousness,	335
(2.) Avarice,	336
(3.) Prodigality,	337
Love of honor,	340
Love of honor as a passion,	345
(1.) Ambition,	ib.
(2.) Pride,	346
(3.) Vanity,	347
Love in general,	349
Sexual love,	352
Sexual love as a passion,	353
Parental and filial love	355
Fraternal love,	356

	Page.
National love,	358
Love of mankind,	359
Remarks,	360
CHAPTER IV.—Emotions,	364
§ 1. Simple emotions,	ib.
§ 2. Mixed emotions,	366
Hope,	ib.
Fear,	367
Remarks,	370
§ 3. Compound emotions,	ib.
Depressing emotions,	371
Anxious expectation,	373
Despondency,	374
Patience,	375
Awe,	376
Strengthening emotions,	378
Wrath,	379
CONCLUSION.—On religion,	383
§ 1. General nature of religion,	ib.
(1.) Religion is not the mere knowledge that there is a God,	384
(2.) Religion is not mere morality,	ib.
(3.) Religion does not proceed from a feeling of dependence in man,	ib.
§ 2. True religion,	388
§ 3. Religions of desire,	389
(1.) The lowest of all superstition is enchantment or feticism,	ib.
(2.) Buddhism,	390
§ 4. Religions of imagination,	391
(1.) Brahmanism,	ib.
(2.) The Persian religion,	392
(3.) Religion of the Egyptians,	393
(4.) Religion of Beauty, or the religion of Greece,	394
§ 5. The religion of understanding, or cool reflection,	396

INTRODUCTION.

CHAPTER I.

DIFFERENCE BETWEEN MAN AND THE ANIMAL.

Simia quam similis turpissima bestia nobis!—Ennius.

It is a very general remark, that man is the highest order of animals, or that he is an animal gifted with reason. Were this correct, we might say with equal truth, that the animal is man without reason; or that some of the plants, which seem to form a transition from the vegetable to the animal kingdom, are animals without sensation. Though man has, physically speaking, many things in common with the animal, he nevertheless differs from it in his whole constitution. Man is no more a mere continuation of the animal, than the animal is merely a continuation of the vegetable. The difference is perceptible, both *physically* and *psychologically*.

1. Man has the same *physical* functions that the animal has, but they are more perfect and more delicate. The body of the animal is either covered with scales or feathers, with fur, wool, or bristles. All of these approach more or less nearly to the nature of vegetables; and some of them, as for instance, the shell of snails and the tortoise, to inorganic nature. These insensible substances, interposed between the skin and the elements that surround and affect living beings, deprive animals of the more tender and delicate sensations, at the same time that they serve to protect them from the inclemency of the seasons. The body of man is covered with a thin, highly sensitive, and beautiful skin, which is not concealed under a vegetable and lifeless veil, but unveiled exhibits the presence of

the blood, the pulsations of the heart, and the utterance of animation over the whole body. Everywhere sensitive, the swelling life shines forth from within, and the fresh, blooming color of the skin is but the expression of the internal power, the mirror of its healthy or sickly state. Over the face of man are shed beauty and spirit, and even animals are said to gaze at him with mute wonder. The complaint, that man alone is born without raiment, is silly, for this apparent helplessness is the source not only of the most various and delicate sensations, and knowledge derived from them, but also of much ingenuity. Man has not claws, but hands, that are susceptible of many different positions, by which he handles the chisel, which pours life and beauty over the hard, cold marble, the pencil that animates the canvas, the instrument from which he draws forth sweet melodies, and the iron, from which he forms the weapons denied him by nature. His body is so fashioned that he must walk upright; for while no animal is intended to walk otherwise than on all-fours, the proportions of the human frame are such, as to render any other than an upright position almost impossible. His legs are much longer than his arms, his knees bend forward, his eyes are in front and not at the sides, the ligaments of the neck are weak and incapable of supporting the head when hanging down, the arms are at a great distance from each other, and the breast is broad and full. A horizontal position would drive the blood into the head with such violence as to cause stupor. Man is made to turn his head from the earth to the sky, from the right to the left, to view now the crawling insect beneath his feet, and now the millions of stars above his head. To the fish it is natural to swim, to the bird to fly, to man to walk upright. The Greek word for man, ($ἄνθρωπος$) a being that can look upwards, indicates the difference between man and animals in this respect. It influences our whole being and nature. Even the bees, when they have lost their queen-bee, cause the larva of a future laboring bee to be transformed into a queen by changing its horizontal to an upright position, and giving it different food.

The same superiority is visible in the human face, its proportions and features. With the animal, the most prominent part is the mouth; with man, the upper part of the face. With the animal, the mouth, jaws, and teeth are to serve only physical purposes; they are formed to pluck the grasses and twigs, or to seize and carry their prey, and thus to perform at the same time the service of the hands of man. The human mouth, with its beautiful and sensitive lips, its regular rows of teeth, serves not only the body, but the soul; nourishes not only the stomach, but also the understanding. Its muscles are so movable, that according to Haller's calculation, it may pronounce in one minute fifteen hundred letters. The contraction of a muscle forming the letter must consequently take place in in the three thousandth, and the vibrations of the stylopharyngean muscle in pronouncing a letter, in the thirty thousandth part of a minute. 'No bird flies as fast as the winged words fall from the lips of man.'

Comparing the animal physiologically with man, we cannot but perceive a great difference in this respect also. The lower the animal in the scale of being, the more it is confined to one and the same food. To this food it is directed by instinct, by constitution and appetite, as the magnet to the pole. Man, on the contrary, selects his food and drink from all the kingdoms of nature, from the salt of the ocean to the mushrooms of the forests, from the oyster and the amphibious turtle to the lofty sailors of the air and ibex of the High Alps. He prepares his food by fire, and the story of Prometheus is not a mere fable, but contains a deep truth. The laws of his digestion differ widely from those of animals, the functions of assimilation penetrating more thoroughly the elements of nutrition. The flesh of the fish, when compared with that of the bird, is found less formed and solid; that of the bird less so than that of the quadruped, but the flesh of man is more perfect than that of any animal. This shows itself externally on the whole surface of the human body, and especially in the "morbidezza" of the skin, the trial-point of all artists.

2. The *psychological* difference between man and animals is yet more striking. The animal has in common with man, Sensation and Perception. By sensation we understand an internal motion or activity, produced in a sensi-

tive organ by something external. The organ may be seen externally, but this internal activity or motion cannot be observed; it can only be felt. The eye, for instance, is the organ of sight; the fluid surrounding it is constantly in motion, and this motion may be seen, because it is an external one. But when the light falls upon the eye, it causes a sensation, which as an internal motion, is invisible to the eye of the observer. He may notice the dilation or contraction of the pupil, but cannot see sight itself, nor hear hearing. Comparing the vibrations of a string of the piano with those of a nerve, subject to sensation, we shall find the former altogether mechanical and external, the string moving away from itself. The nerve, when affected, trembles within itself, and self-touched in its motions, it has sensation, or feels. The vibrating string of the piano gives a sound, but the sound is not felt by it; the nerves of the ear, on the other hand, receive a sensation from it. These trembling motions of the nerves are called *sensations*, because they are peculiar to the senses. Now, the animal has these sensations in common with man, but with this difference. In the animal *one* sense prevails over all the others, and these are subservient to it. In the eagle, for example, it is the eye that is predominant; from immense heights he observes the mouse creeping on the soil, and darts upon it, certain of his prey. Yet this one sense has always reference to the means of subsistence, which the animal seeks under its guidance; so that while it may be extremely acute and successful in discovering the food, it may be dull and stupid in respect to other objects, of which man receives the most accurate sensations through the same sense. The ear of the wood-cock is acute in perceiving any rustling noise, as that in the fallen leaves of the forests, but shrill and clear sounds it does not notice. The eye perceives only such objects as reflect the light upon it. The eye of man may, however, direct itself to the different parts of these objects, to their color, proportions, size and form, motion or rest, and inspect each by itself, while the eye of the animal, for want of reason, is forced to admit a sensation from all these parts at once, and consequently receives but a confused impression. As one sense prevails in animals, the others are found less active. The lion has an excellent scent, but his sight is weak. Hence the animal is under the dominion of one sense, while the harmonious and equal strength of all the senses places man above them, and makes him master of them all. Which of the senses prevails in an animal, depends always upon the species to which it belongs. In the eagle it is sight, in the mole hearing, in the vulture scent; but wherever one sense predominates, the others must subserve and be directed by it. In man, no sense being more acute than another, none reigns, but all are co-ordinate with each other, and subordinate to the understanding. The animal is *vis sentiens*, man *natura intelligens*. Hence it is, too, that we do not speak of *insanity* or *derangement*, but of *madness*, when animals can no longer distinguish one object from another, but like infuriated elephants or horses, trample under their feet every object that opposes their course. And, finally, man sees not only with his eye external objects, but is also able to examine the eye, by which he sees; the animal can neither see its eye nor itself.

Perception, however, is more than Sensation. The latter is and remains in contact with the object, by which it is called forth, and is consequently dependent on it. The sensation of hearing is impossible without the vibration of the air; that of seeing is impossible without the presence of light. Sight and light, hearing and sound, are so inseparable, that the one could not be without the other. Without light the eye could not see, without an eye, there would be an eternal night. And if there were no ear, the brooks might continue to murmur, the waving trees to rustle their branches, the winds to roar, but to earthly beings nature would be silent as the grave. Nor can man avoid admitting a sensation, when the element that excites it, acts upon the organ. As we cannot have a sensation of light unless it falls upon the eye, so we must have it, when the eye is affected by it. We cannot taste salt unless it lies on the tongue, but when once it is brought in contact with the tongue, we must have such a sensation, as its specific nature is capable of exciting. In sensation, therefore, we depend wholly on the presence of external objects, and are determined by them. But after we have once had a sensation, we may have perceptions of the objects of sensation, and these perceptions are possible without the presence of the objects. This appears from the fact that one, who in the latter part of his life becomes blind, may have perceptions of all he once saw. Yet perceptions are impossible without previous sensations, for one born blind can have no perception of color or form. Another distinction between sensation and perception is this. Sensation always exists in an organ; perception not. When I hear a fine melody for the first time, I have a *sensation* of it; but when afterwards, without hearing it, it floats in my mind, I have a *perception* of it. Or when I experience hunger, I may have a perception of food, though it be not present, but when I eat, I have a sensation of it. The animal has perceptions as well as man. The hunter's dog dreams, and pursues in his dream the hare or the stag. The dog, when near to his master, has a sensation of him by scent, or sight; but when seeking him for days in succession, he can have only a perception of him. The animal is confined within the sphere of sensation and perception, and as its sensations are limited to its natural wants, so must be its perceptions. But the perceptions of man are as much more numerous and accurate, as his sensations are more various and acute. And in addition to sensations and perceptions, he has what the animal has not, and which we may express by the term *apperceptions*, or *thought*.

As the animal is separated by sensation from the plant, so man is elevated by apperception above the animal. Perception and apperception differ widely. The objects of perception are always such as are single and met with in a certain place and time. The eagle, that builds his nest on a high rock, has not the least idea of the nature of the stone on which his nest is placed, nor of the region in which it stands, but he carries with him the image of this single rock, as it stands in a particular place, and noticing no resemblance between it and other rocks, he would find it among thousands of others, its peculiar features being strongly and solely impressed upon his eye. The objects of apperception, on the other hand, are the kind, the species and individuals of things. It is by apperception, that man distinguishes between his perceptions and the objects perceived; and again, that he classifies nature and its productions, by discovering union in the greatest variety, as when he says: these bushes are rose-bushes; and by distinguishing one class from another, as pears from apples, and these from peaches. This the animal can never do. It sees, it perceives the grass, but it never arranges it according to its botanical classes. The dog universally will pursue the hare, and it may seem that he does so, because he knows this class of animals, and distinguishes between it and others; but the truth is, that all hares being exactly alike in size, form, and scent, will produce the same sensations in the dog, and these will always set him in motion. This then is the broad difference, the chasm between man and the animal: the former can *think*, the latter cannot, for it is *glebae adscriptus*. It lives, but acquires no experience; it eats its food daily, but never knows what this food is. Some indeed have gone so far as to say, that animals not only judge, but draw conclusions from causes to effects. To draw conclusions is the highest power of human reason, and if they could do this, they would be able to *think*, and to *will* like man, and to have apperceptions like him. If animals had the power of thinking, and could not express their thoughts by language, but only by barking, like the dog Berganza in Hoffman's novel, they would be worse off than Shakspeare's Lavinia, who had lost both tongue and arms, and while full of the deepest emotions and an ardent desire to express them, was unable to communicate any thing, either by language or signs: or than Saintine's "*Le mutile*," whose breast was surcharged with a poetical spirit, the productions of which, in his opinion, would have surpassed those of Dante and Ariosto, and yet he had to be mute. But the fact is, that men who ascribe these high and noble powers to brutes, generally speaking, do not know what thinking is, or what is to be understood by judging and drawing conclusions. Animals have no idea of power, of capacities, of energy, of proportions, of beauty, of truth, and consequently none of cause and effect. None of these are visible or accessible to the senses, but only to thought, which it yet remains to be proved, that animals possess. The process by which we arrive at conclusions is simply this. We have three thoughts; each differs from the other, and each is included within a certain limit. But while all differ, one is capable of uniting the two others, and of removing this difference. Thus two thoughts are reduced to one class by a third one connecting them. To make use of an example frequently adduced, the dog once whipped, fears as soon as he sees his master take the cane with which he has been beaten on a former occasion. The cane is one thing, the master's intention another, and the pain proceeding from the whipping, a third. Now it would be foolish in the extreme, to say, that the dog connects the idea of pain with the cane by the intention of the master. He has but a *confused* impression, and without any conclusions or judgments, he darkly connects things as they formerly were connected, and anticipates consequences, without being conscious of such a connection, or without having any thing like an idea of cause and consequence. Hunters, it is true, tell many anecdotes about the acuteness and ingenuity of animals, as do sailors also voyaging to distant countries. The fact, however, is, that unless their game were bound by the invariable laws of instinct in all its actions, unless one fox would dig its hole as the other, and all stags would go to the water, and seek food at regular hours, and live in certain places at different seasons, the hunters would not be able to entrap them.

Animals, finally, cannot have any emotions; neither joy nor grief, neither hope nor fear. The external expressions of these emotions are *weeping* and *laughing*, neither of which has as yet been observed in animals. We indeed all remember from Homer's Iliad, that when the noble Patroclus, alone and at a distance from his true friend Achilles, fell by the hands of the Trojans, his horses shed big tears and refused to obey, because they missed the well known voice of their beloved master. But these tears belong to poetry; they are the tears which Homer himself wept at the death of the hero his fancy had created. So poetry attributes innocence to the lily, because it is of the purest white; modesty to the violet, because it blooms and exhales its fragrance unseen; love to the rose, because the cheeks of the maiden blush like it, when for the first time she feels this noble emotion. What is *joy* in man, springing from a feeling that connects itself with some thought, in animals, is but a physical sensation or bodily pleasure, the agreeable re-action of the muscles against some external influence, the satisfaction of some want. And so what is *grief* in man, is but a physical pain, or suffering in the animal. The dog, that lays himself upon the grave of his master and remains there until he dies, does so not from deliberation and free choice, but being forced by the chain of habit, which he is unable to break. Nor do animals *fear* or *hope*, for neither the future nor the past is known to them. A dark anxiety which they do not understand, a confused anticipation, is all of which they are susceptible.

CHAPTER II.

§ 1. LIFE.

It is not my intention, in this Chapter, to show what life is in itself, but only to exhibit some of its most striking phenomena, and the different stages of its general development throughout nature. Thus only can we gain a clear idea of the rank occupied by man among animated beings.

Of Life in general.

In the following three points, the living differs from the dead or lifeless, the organic from the inorganic.

1. Whatever is alive, must be a union, a totality of many organs or members, and so united with them, that they cannot be separated from each other, nor from the whole, without being destroyed. The crystal, however transparent, and beautiful, and regular in its form, is not alive, for it is not an individual being, nor a whole, whose parts are *organs* or *members;* it is not *organized* at all. The many forms of the crystal are not indeed produced by a power foreign to its matter, not by an external contrivance, but by a plastic power, which, resting in its matter, always calls forth the same symmetrical forms according to eternal laws, whenever the conditions under which it can be active are present. But the organization of the whole into parts, as for example, that of the plant into trunk and branches, being wanting, we should hesitate to call the crystal alive. Every one of its qualities is contained in each particle of the mineral, and though there may be many qualities, they are all of them so included in each other, that where one is the other is also. Hence there is no union of many members or organs, each of which, while pervaded by the same life, has a particular

office; but the smallest piece of the mineral is as perfect as the whole. The plant, on the other hand, is a whole, that contains and supports all its parts. These parts are not merely connected as the links of a chain, which cannot support itself, but must be supported by the nail in the wall; they grow forth from and depend on each other, and on the life of the whole. Roots, trunks, branches, twigs, leaves, blossoms and fruits, all differ from each other; each has a peculiar office; each assists and promotes the life of the whole; and while the one depends on the other, all depend on the individual, whose organs they are. The leaf torn from the branch, loses its freshness, its sap, its color, and withers. The branch, hanging only by a few fibres to the trunk, is no longer a part of the tree. One of the characteristics, therefore, of life, is that its parts do not merely cohere externally and mechanically, like those of a machine, but are inseparably connected by concrescence or a common growth, so that they cannot be divided without mutual ruin. The iron, divided into small particles or atoms by the file, still remains iron. The parts of a house, as they are heterogenous and only collected from the different portions of nature, and then put together, so they will remain what they are, stone, timber, mortar, and glass, though they should be taken apart and applied to another building. But the trunk severed from the root, is dead; the hand, lopped from the arm, grows black and decays.

2. The second characteristic of life is the continued process by which, whatever lives, preserves itself. As no living being begins to be by *external* union, i. e. by a mere mechanical composition of its parts, but grows forth from a spontaneous coalescence, so it cannot be supported and upheld by a foreign power, but must preserve itself by its own vitality. The chemist may have all the elements of which a plant consists, and yet it will be wholly out of his power to produce the plant, or that vital tie that keeps the parts together in the form of a plant. The parts of which the machine consists were in existence before the machine was made, but the parts that constitute the plant, as the roots, branches, bark, and sap of the tree, were not before the tree was. Hence the organic or living indivi-

dual produces all its parts by a power within itself, and by this power it also preserves itself. In regard to this self-preservation, however, a great difference appears in the different animated beings. The plant by its roots absorbs those elements which are congenial to its nature; it may therefore be said to eat and drink, to preserve itself. But the activity of the plant is purely external. It does not preserve an organism that may be said to have finished growing, but by assimilation every spring, it produces new limbs, leaves, and blossoms. It grows as long as it lives, and yet every new limb is but a repetition of the original trunk, as are the new leaves of the old. The animal, on the other hand, reaches a point, where all its members are complete and full-grown, and at this stage it preserves its organism by nutriment. In the animal, one limb differs from the other, the nose from the mouth, the eyes from the ear, the legs from the body; but they do not grow in succession, like the branches of the plant, but contemporaneously. Hence it is that the life of the plant is merely external; it presses constantly to the surface, and exhibits itself in color, bark, fragrance, fruit and seed. And as its life, so its self-preservation is external, not felt by it. The life of the animal is more internal, it feels itself, and feels a pleasure in preserving its life.

3. A third characteristic of life is, that form and matter, which constitute a living being, are not brought together externally, so that the matter somewhere exists, and the form is given it by an external power. This is the case in art. The marble exists long before the artist impresses the picture of his imagination upon it. So this picture exists in the mind of the artist before his chisel carves the stone. But it is otherwise in a living being. This grows forth from an invisible power, according to certain, unchangeable laws. This power on the one hand materializes, attracts matter, assumes volume, produces fibres, roots, bark, branches or nerves, muscles, sinews, bones, &c.; on the other it is plastic, giving form to the matter. It is however only *one* power, that acts under two different forms, so that while it assumes volume, it at the same time changes the particles received into that form in which alone its nature can admit them. It is therefore correct

to say, that in a living being the matter does not precede its form. The air we exhale, is no longer what it was when we inhaled it; the light absorbed by the plant is changed into color, and consequently does not exist in it as pure light; and this change begins when the element is received by the plant. The wormwood, the rosebush, the tube-rose, may all of them stand on the same soil, receive the same moisture, the same atmosphere, and the same degree of heat, and consequently live on the same elements; yet the different taste and medical power of their sap, the different color of their leaves, the different fragrance of their flowers, sufficiently show, that while the same elements enter into their nature, they do not remain the same, but are changed and peculiarly modified by the form under which they enter it. Though the elements as such precede the plant, they become elements of the plant only by that plastic power, which in converting them into constituent parts of the plant gives them at the same time form. The light flows into the eye of the mole no less than into that of the eagle, but it exists in the one as it does not in the other; there is a specific difference between the contents of the eye of the eagle and that of the mole.

From these remarks it must be manifest, that the various forms of life do not proceed from dead matter, nor from chance or any blind impulse, but that they are fashioned by a plastic power placed in matter by the divine will, and that this is the power which upholds the species and individuals, and universally produces the same forms according to the same unchangeable laws. This power, then, is the very soul of life, and the question is, *What can we know concerning it?*

---

§ 2. OF THE PLASTIC POWER, OR THE PRINCIPLE OF ALL INDIVIDUAL LIFE.

We daily see thousands of beings begin to be; we see them arise from the ground of the earth, from seeds and sprouts, and eggs in the water and on the continent, on the soil and in the air. Each new being bears the form of the species to which it belongs, and though favorable or unfavorable influences may render this form more or less perfect, no external power can change its specific character. From the seed universally will proceed the form of the plant from which the seed was produced, and leaves and branches, roots and trunk, blossom and fruit, may be anticipated with all certainty. Considering all this, we must admit that there is a type, which precedes the opening and growing being, and which fashions it with so unchangeable a necessity, that the individuals of any species have continued substantially the same in size and form, in nature and qualities, ever since the creation of the world.

This cannot be owing to accidental circumstances; nor can form emerge from chaotic matter, nor life from death, nor light from darkness, nor the organic from the inorganic. The theory of Thales, therefore, who made water the mother of all life, or the Aristotelian hypothesis of a *generatio aequivoca* in opposition to a *generatio sexualis*, could no longer stand, even if Redi's experiments had been less decisive. This hypothesis considered *matter* as possessed of power to produce the various forms of life. We see worms and insects generated in decaying flesh; mushrooms and other plants make their appearance in the different portions of the earth, wherever soil and climate are favorable to them. Certain plants are always found around salt springs and nowhere else; the *pinus pumilis* is met with on the top of the Silesian mountains, and again on the Carpathian; how, it has been asked, could these plants be found so uniformly under the same circumstances, if the same qualities of matter did not always produce the same forms of life? So we discover, in the intestines of animals, worms which differ *specifically* according to the different parts in which they are found, so that they cannot have been generated by such as might have been swallowed in water. Thus the theory. Redi, however, by his simple yet ingenious experiment, completely refuted it. He filled three pots with flesh and exposed them to the sun. One of these pots he sealed up tightly, another he covered merely with paper, and the third he left open. Upon examining all of them, he discovered that the one left open was filled with insects, the second, covered with paper, exhibited but a few, and the third none at all. But suppose insects might originate from matter, could the larger animals, the horse and the stag, the zebra and cameleopard, and above all, man, originate in the same way? And if they could, by what power of matter?

From the time of Redi, the proverb of the celebrated Harvey, that every being originates from seed or eggs, *omne animal ex ovo*, became daily more acceptable: yet ' whether I examine with the microscope the germ in the acorn, or whether I view the oak of a hundred years, I am equally far from its origin.' The seed is already the product of a plastic power, which formed it, as it must produce the form that shall grow forth from the seed. The Greek question—whether the egg was before the hen or the hen before the egg, must likewise present itself. The egg is the chicken in *possibility*, and the chicken is the realized possibility which was contained in the egg.

At length all the different and many hypotheses on the origin of individual life, gave way to that which was called the theory of involution, or *theoria preformationis*. This asserted that all forms exist from the beginning of the world, only infinitely small, all of them preformed, the one included in the other, and many millions of germs in one. Growth is nothing else than evolution or enlargement of these preformed germs. This theory was supported by many strange arguments; but however well supported it might have been, it transferred the difficulty in question only from one place to another. For whether I view the tree in its full size or in its infinitely small preformation, here as well as there I see it already formed, and must ask, whence these forms? When we, however carefully, and by the most accurate instruments, examine the egg of a butterfly, we cannot discover any thing except a white fluid, which is of the same color and substance in all its parts, and fills a small, round, simple cover. Nothing can be seen as yet of the body of the butterfly, nothing of its beautifully colored wings, nothing of its proboscis, which the future fly will thrust into the cups of flowers, nothing of its limbs and many eyes. And yet the possibility of producing all of them, slumbers in the egg, and no sooner is it exposed to the necessary and favorable conditions, than an invisible power will develop member after member in this simple and identical fluid.

The celebrated Blumenbach, who for a long time had taught this theory of involution, was accidentally led to discover its fallacy, and to start one which will be found of much greater importance to our subject than any former one. While spending a part of a vacation in the country, he met with a green armpolypous in a rivulet. He mutilated it repeatedly, and whenever he cut off a part, the whole animal would become thin for a time, and an effort to reproduce the lost part became evident. On the second or third day, tails, arms, and other mutilated parts were fully grown again. Soon after, he had to attend upon a man, from one of whose limbs had to be cut a large portion of flesh; the wound soon healed, and the system directly showed a tendency to cover the cavity. When these phenomena were brought in connection with others,—for example, that the feelers of snails, when cut off, or the limbs of spiders, when lost, are soon restored again,—it could not but strike him, that all living beings carry in themselves a plastic power, from which not only they themselves proceed, but which has a tendency to produce and preserve those forms which are essential to them.

The correctness of this view may be perceived even in the vegetable kingdom; for it is not the germ in the seed, from which the plant originates. This germ is already of a visible and decided form, the result of the flower. In the flower we may discover a whitish, globular fluid, which as the flower unfolds itself, and finally fades away, becomes more solid, and when ripe, is thrown off from the mother-plant as seed. In this seed is contained the germ, the first formation of the future plant, as roots and leaves may be considered the second and third formations. Whence then is the germ? It is the product of a *plastic power*, which is the principle of individual life and its preservation, which forms in the plant the seed, the fibres and the roots, the leaves and the branches; which makes the roots seek for moisture, and the leaves for the air, and the flower for the light of the sun, and which will confine the form of each individual to its species, so that the seed of the palm-tree will never grow up and become an oak-tree, nor the acorn grow up a palm-tree.

This plastic power reigns wherever there is life: whether it be in the depths of the ocean, where it works secretly and unseen, or in the cavities of the earth, where it mysteriously forms the salamander and dragon, or in the bud and blossoms of the plant, which it clothes with beauty, or in the sensations and perceptions of animals, in which the light of intellect seems to dawn. It can no more be seen with the eye, than any other power. But as we conclude from effects as to causes, so we conclude here from the products as to the power that produces them. These products are the *forms* of individual life, and consequently we must admit a plastic power, which produces them. To the thinking and observing man, its existence is no less certain than the sound that falls upon his ear, or the dazzling light that is reflected upon his eyes. The necessity of admitting and knowing this plastic power, will appear more fully when we consider separately the principal phenomena that cannot be explained without it. They are,

First, *a living motion*. When we compare the different possible motions with each other, we cannot but acknowledge a great difference between them as to their cause. The merely mechanical motion, that like the ball rolling from place to place, changes only its locality, is universally caused by a power not contained in the object in motion, but by one that is external to it. The ball on the billiard table, struck by the rod, will roll on until the impulse given it has exhausted itself. The arrow, shot from the bow, is set in motion by a power which does not rest in it, and which gives it the direction it takes. All mechanical motion so wholly depends on an external cause, that where it ceases, it must likewise stop. The cannon ball, discharged into the air, cannot continue to rise, *ad infinitum*, but must sink back upon the earth in a parabolic line. With chemical motion it is somewhat otherwise. Its cause is contained in the peculiar relation or affinity of two bodies to each other· each of which presupposes in the other, what is wanting in itself. Iron filings and vitriolic acid, put together, will affect and set each other into motion, the result of which will be the production of a third body. Mechanical motion leaves a body as it found it, but chemical motion effects an entire change. Again, when we see the seed of a plant, sown in a favorable soil, and exposed to the light, swell and move, the motion, though dependent on proper conditions, is not caused by a power without, but by one within the seed, and the effect is not a new chemical combination, but a living body, growing out from within. We may observe the same, when we compare the motion of an *infusorium* with any other merely mechanical loco-motion. The lowest class of animals, which are so small that five thousand millions may live in one drop of water, and that can only be rendered visible by a microscope, magnifying one hundred times, which indeed have only become known since the invention of Leuwenhoek's microscope and may be produced by pouring water upon decaying substances (*infundere, infusorium*), are called *infusoria*. They are, according to natural historians, mere living points, atoms that eat and drink, but have no organized bodies. And yet these living atoms have a motion of their own. The feather, that floats in the air, the dust that is raised by the attraction of light, the piece of wood that swims down the river, are all carried and moved by the elements, in which they are: but these little, living animals, move with or against the current, and in whatever direction they choose. Their motions, therefore, depend not on any thing external, but on a power within themselves, strong enough to resist the current of the air.

Secondly, *a separation of the living being from the element in which it is born*. The drop of water that flows along in a river, is not separated in any way from the element of which it forms a part. The single grain of sand is separated from all other grains, but it is not separated by its own innate power, for it is not alive. When, on the other hand, in the plant a globular fluid is formed, and when this fluid at length hardens and in the form of seed by its own activity, thrusts itself forth or falls from the mother-plant, we must conclude that there is a simple, secretly-working power, causing the fluid—which originally is a part of the plant, and in as close a contact with it as a drop of water with its volume,—to separate itself and constitute a being of its own. This is the case with the *punctum saliens* in the animal, and with all living beings throughout nature. All commence in such a simple activity, all begin to move, and to grow forth from it and receive members and form by it. Through it, the being that is active, is active in reference to itself. Whatever has an existence of its own must be active, and it must be so either with reference to itself or to something else. An example may illustrate this: when the blacksmith suffers, instead of the iron, merely its shadow to fall upon the anvil, and strikes it with his hammer, the shadow cannot be affected, because it has no existence of its own, its motions, and its whole shadowy, lifeless appearance depending on the iron. But when instead of the shadow, the iron is placed upon the anvil, it will stretch itself out under the heavy strokes of the hammer. It is active, yet not for itself, but only for the hammer. The sun, that shines upon the sand and heats it, is active, yet not for itself, but for something else; the sand, that is heated and perhaps converted into glass, is active likewise, but not for itself either, but for some other purposes. The germ, on the other hand, that under the mild influence of sweet moisture and of a genial warmth, begins to move, to swell, to break the cover and to sprout, is not active for any thing else, but for itself; for the result of its activity is its formation as a plant. As such it preserves itself, breathes, eats and drinks with its roots and leaves. By the simple activity in question, therefore, a living being begins to exist as an *individual;* as such it is related to itself in all its parts; branches and twigs, roots and trunk, are all of them related to each other, and their union is the plant or the individual life, whose organs they are.

Thirdly, *a specific form.* This originally simple power or activity, contains the possibility of producing such forms, as the prototype of a genus necessarily demands. When we observe an egg, from which the future young is to come forth, we are forced to admit this possibility. At first, nothing is visible but the fluid; afterwards a beating point is seen; soon the heart begins to have pulsation; the blood to become red; the head makes its appearance; eyes, mouth, and members shoot forth. Limbs, as yet slender as the threads of a cobweb, wings, toes, and feet become visible. The being in a state of formation, already sleeps and wakes, moves and rests. It seeks light, and without assistance opens the shell. Is here no form-giving power? Must not this power have in itself the type of the formation which it is to produce, and is it not correct therefore to say, that it contains the possibility of producing specific forms? This possibility is not a mere fiction of our fancy, it is a physical possibility, that when all the conditions are present, *must* pass over into reality. As the forms, proceeding from the possibility, cannot be accidental, but must all of them represent their prototype, or the image which seems to slumber in that originally simple activity, this possibility or plastic power has been called *nisus formativus*. By *nisus* is indicated the tendency of a power to effect a certain, definite object. By *formativus* is to be understood the quality of the object, its form and whole organism. There is no such tendency in lines, to form a circle or a triangle, but there is one in the acorn, when sown, to form an oak-tree.

It is the same power too, that forms the being, which preserves it. No sooner is the young born, than all the functions of this power are in operation. The mouth opens itself, the lungs breathe, the stomach digests, and the lips seek their food. Leaves fall every autumn, but every spring adorns the trees with new ones. It is this power that causes a wound to heal, and that in inferior animals, restores lost limbs. Not the individual only, however, is thus preserved by it—for sooner or later it must decay—but after it has fully formed and matured the individual, it takes care by it of the genus, and becomes a tendency of propagation. The period, when it takes this different direction, is indicated externally. The muscles swell rounder and fuller, the face blooms, and vigor and feeling of a youthful freshness is spread through the whole body.

It is remarkable that this plastic power, the principal phenomena of which we have considered, determines also the motions of the organs, and the use to be made of them. It causes the sap to rise and to sink in the plant, the branches to extend themselves towards the light, the roots to move from the centre towards the nourishing moisture, and the leaves to expand and contract in proportion as the cellular textures are filled with juice. So the stamina of many plants move of their own accord, as soon as they are formed; the cups of others close when the sun sets, as those of many tulips; others shut their leaves when a storm threatens, as the Scotch sycamore, and others again sink into the water when the sun sinks, and re-appear when it rises, as the lotos. The light may act here by way of excitement, but cannot act as the sole cause; and as plants have no sensations and perceptions, these motions must be attributed to the plastic power, as the motions in the lips of the new-born child proceed from it.

More instructive, and more to our purpose, however, are some phenomena, which we observe exclusively in the animal world. Here all the productions of the plastic power are more perfect and more regular. They are more perfect; for if we compare the most beautiful flower with the eye the latter will strike us at once as being infinitely more artistical and complete. They are more regular; for the animal has but two lungs, but two eyes, but two ears, while the plant has thousands of leaves, and buds, and flowers. The more nearly animals are allied to the vegetable world, the greater will be the number of their limbs; some reptiles have more than one hundred feet;—yet the number of limbs in any is no longer left indefinite, as in the plant, but determined by the species. The more animals approach man or the sphere of reason, the more perfect their forms, and the less numerous their limbs.

And as this power in animals becomes more perfect and regular, so it assumes a higher character. When we see the vine seek with its tendrils the large tree, and when we see them wind themselves around it, we at once attribute these motions to that power by which the plant grows. But not so when we see that the tortoise, hatched by the sun a mile from the shore, no sooner leaves the shell, than it runs without a guide, in a straight line to the ocean, or when we see ducks hatched by a hen, not listening to her clucking, plunge into the water, and without having learned to swim, enjoy this element with innate skill, or when we see the ox select two hundred and seventy-six herbs for his food, but universally shun two hundred and eighteen, though he never studied botany. The *sphex fabulosa*, before laying her eggs, hollows out a little cell for every one; then fetches half-killed spiders, drags one into each cell, and lays her eggs on them, so that the future young ones may not want for food. The mining spider digs a channel into the earth, about two feet deep, and closes it very artificially by a trap-door. This door is round, formed of different layers of earth, which are held together by threads; its outside is rough, but the inside smooth and lined with a thick texture, from the upper part of which, threads run to the surface of the channel, so that the door hangs on a string, and falls by its own weight into a fold as accurately as if the whole had been effected by mathematical skill. This door the spider has the skill to keep shut by its bodily exertions, when an enemy tries to open it. When we see such phenomena, we must admit a far higher agency than that which works and lives in plants, and this higher agency is *instinct*.

§ 3. INSTINCT.

What comparative anatomy is for the study of the anatomy of man, that, instinct and an investigation of its nature is for the study of Mental Philosophy. Within its sphere we discover phenomena that are full of design and calculation, and analogous to those of reason, and yet reason being wanting, will and self-consciousness being entirely absent, we cannot attribute these designs to animals, but must ascribe them to him who works by eternal laws through their instinct; yet a knowledge of these phenomena will be found extremely useful to the psychologist. The physiologist finds it necessary, in order to understand fully the different organs of man, to compare them with those of animals. He must trace them from their first indications in the lower classes of animals, through all their different gradations up to man. Thus may he discover the importance of each part, by perceiving what degree of sight or hearing those parts of the eye or the ear afford, which are met with in animals that have not those organs perfectly formed. There are animals that consist of a single organ, which, while in its connection with a complicated organism in man, it is subordinate to higher ones, is the only one in them or at least prevails over the few others that they may possess. In viewing such a being, we may see what kind of life a single organ is capable of producing, and what its share must be in the constitution of man. So we know, that in muscles and snails, the liver and heart alone are fully formed; in many insects the wind-pipe; in others the lungs; in the polypous the stomach; in infusoria the gut. Nature contains all the parts of man, but not as man has them. In the lowest animals, single parts are sufficient to form the whole being; more of them become united at the higher stages of animal life, until finally all appear well-proportioned in man, the tree, whose leaves are scattered throughout nature; and as a machine can be known only when its parts are viewed singly, so man can be understood only, when we are acquainted with the inferior tribes in nature, which present to our inspection the different parts composing his system. Thus it is likewise with the psychological life of man. In viewing the nature of instinct we may see what kind of mental life sensation and perception, independent of reason and will, are able to produce, and thus we may learn how to value reason and will as we should. It is not the identity, but the difference, not the sameness but comparison, from which we may learn most, and whenever in a science we have gained a prominent point adapted to exhibit these differences, it will be well for us to pause for a moment over it. Such points are for science, what mountains are for travellers, who desire to observe a country. They will see more, when standing on mountain-tops, than any where else. The nature of plastic power in the vegetable world, and that of instinct in animals, will accordingly teach us more concerning Psychology, than any other portion of human science.

The different general phenomena of instinct have been arranged by the celebrated Reimarus, in no less than *fifty-eight* different classes. It will be sufficient for the present purpose, to mention only a few. Animals, from the time of their birth, move with perfect skill from one place to another, and use all their limbs in a perfectly correct manner, and for the right purpose, without having received instruction. So the squirrel uses its fore-paws at once properly; so the fish swims without teaching. Amphibious animals will move from one element into the other; and birds, insects, fishes, and even quadrupeds will seek, and unerringly find, distant countries, in order to enjoy the degree of heat or cold favorable to their constitutions. Other animals bury themselves when winter approaches. All animals select their food not only skillfully, but also seek it in the proper places, at the proper season, and at the proper time, by day or night; many are extremely cunning in catching their prey, and in laying up provision for inclement seasons; others know how to heal their wounds, how to erect dwellings for themselves, how to defend themselves from their enemies either by houses, as the beaver, or by regular wars, as some species of ants. All these phenomena of instinct, however, may be reduced to *three* great classes, one of which will comprehend all those that have reference to the *nutrition*, another those referring to the *motion*, and the third, those relating to the *propagation* of animals, for the end of all instinct is the preservation of the *individual* and of the *race*.

Instinct pre-supposes, what is not found in the sphere of vegetation, *sensation and perception;* and while the plastic power of the vegetable kingdom extends also to the animal, instinct is confined to such beings as can feel. The plant grows and ripens, but it would be improper to say, except poetically, that it sleeps, or that it is fatigued, hungry and thirsty. It is true, that plants hang their leaves when they suffer from want of moisture; that, like the *lotus ornithopedioides,* which folds its flowers at night and opens them again in the morning, they seem to sleep, yet when all is well investigated, we shall discover that we speak but metaphorically of the sleep of plants. For as they are never awake, so they cannot properly be said to sleep. But hunger and thirst, a tendency for motion and rest, and for the propagation of the race, are the peculiar phenomena of instinct, which we shall now investigate.

It is natural to every living being to sustain itself by food. But neither man nor animals would think of taking nourishment, did not the system and operation of digestion force them to do so. When by exercise or atmospheric influence, digestion is regularly promoted, the stomach will become empty, and the gastric juice will gather. The power of this juice will seek something to act upon, and finding no food, it will attack the coats of the stomach. If no food is administered, the stomach will make an attempt by contractions to remove this juice, and not succeeding in this, *death* is inevitable. It is the nature of instinct,—1st, To feel the pain thus caused by the activity of this gastric juice, and to feel the danger of destruction. This feeling itself is of course painful, and is generally called *hunger*.—2d, Instinct, as hunger, will impel the animal to attack the world around and seek for food. This appears already from the connection of hunger and an irresistible tendency to motion. The horse stamps when hungry, and were it not chained, it would go in search of food. The boa constrictor is constantly active when in want of food, but as soon as its hunger is satisfied, it lies sluggishly down and may be chased by a child.—3d, Instinct will direct the animal to its proper food, and no sooner is this perceived by the particular sense that prevails in the animal and stands in the service of instinct, than a prophetic feeling of pleasure will at once induce the animal to seize upon it. Hence it is, that the sheep, without choice or consideration, will select salt from amongst arsenic, which would be impossible to man. Instinct then is, on the one hand, a feeling of want, and on the other, a feeling of the sympathy existing between this want, and the objects by which it is to be satisfied. This sympathy expresses itself in the animal by an internal urgency to seek, and by the pleasure it feels when guided by its prevailing sense it perceives its proper food, so that no reflection is required to distinguish one herb from another.

If it were necessary to illustrate the nature of instinct, a number of examples might be given. Analogous to it is the attractive power in the magnet, which from among many thousand grains of different substances, attracts none but iron filings. The root absorbs only certain elements of the soil, and excludes others, as appears from the fact that plants set in an unfavourable soil wither. So we see animals of imperfect formations, confined to *one* single food, which they select from among many different materials. The fact, however, that instinct pre-supposes feeling, sensation, and perception, raises it above the power in the magnet, and gives it a higher character than that of the root which also seeks and finds its nourishment. And how can it be supposed that instinct is rather an intelligent power, than that it is a sympathy between the whole nature of the animal and the objects which are congenial to it? Especially when we consider that the ox eats two hundred and seventy-six herbs, but rejects two hundred and eighteen; that the goat finds four hundred and forty-nine palatable, but feels averse to one hundred and twenty-six; the sheep, three hundred and eighty-seven, not touching one hundred and forty-one; the horse, two hundred and sixty-two, leaving two hundred and twelve untasted. When we consider, too, that they not only distinguish different herbs, but that with the same readiness they discover their food, though it should be under ground. The reindeer lays itself down, scrapes away the deep snow with its horn, and its fore-feet, and finds its aliment. Do these animals do so from a knowledge of these herbs, and of the locality favorable to their growth, or from a sympathetic relation between themselves and their food? Animals are certainly not mere machines, as Descartes maintained, but neither are they thinking beings, as many sensualists would like us to believe. Their life is confined to sensation and perception, and all their activity proceeds not from *will*, but from a feeling of pain or pleasure.

§ 4. ON THE INGENUITY OF ANIMALS.

I hope, however, to throw still more light upon this interesting topic, by considering some productions of animals which seem to manifest ingenuity. Of this kind, are all those that on the one hand, answer as *means* for a certain *purpose;* for example, the web, by which the spider catches his prey, flies and insects, as skillfully as the fisher entraps in his net the inhabitants of the rivers. Wherever we perceive an adaptation of means to the end, there we allow ingenuity to be active. On the other hand, they must be something separate from the animal by which they were produced. The shell of the snail, that of the tortoise, and of the armadilla, are very artistlike and beautiful, but they are formed by mere excretion, and by the influence of the atmosphere, and constituting parts of the animals themselves, they do not belong to the class of productions of which we speak. We do not think of ingenuity when we admire the beautifully coloured wings of the butterfly, or when we delight in viewing the regular and beautiful formations of leaves, of buds and flowers, for all of them form parts of the beings in which we discover them, and are the products of the same plastic power which formed the animals or plants themselves; but when we see the cell of the bee, the larva of the caterpillar, or the nest of the tailor bird, we are at once struck with their ingenuity. When we examine the cover in which the chrysalis of a caterpillar awaits its future transformation, we find it full of design. Some of these coverings have a crown on one end, made of erect and stiff threads that form in the inside a smooth and comfortable surface, but offer stiff knots and points on the outside, so that they easily yield to a pressure from within, but make it difficult to be pressed in from without. Here is design, here is preparation for a change which the animal has to undergo but once in its life, and as we cannot feel willing to ascribe these phenomena to the knowledge and will of the animal, we must attribute them to a peculiar modification of instinct. This we feel ourselves the more strongly forced to do, when we ascertain that this tendency for artificial productions is not met with in the more perfect animals which possess all the senses in considerable perfection. The elephant does not show a trace of it; the horse, the reindeer, the ibex, the zebra, are not possessed of it. But the tortoise, a stupid, sluggish, and awkward creature, paddles to the shore, digs with her clumsy feet a hole, and after having deposited her eggs in it, she covers it, levels it with the soil, and creeps several times over it, so that not a trace of the hole can be discovered. From this it will appear, that this modification of instinct is not found every where in the animal world, especially not in that part which by its completeness of the senses approaches most nearly the intellect of man, and the question offers itself,—Where is it met with?

It is not found among such animals as maintain a decided independence of the elements in which they live, such as have five senses, as the buffalo, the bison; nor again, among such as depend almost wholly on the element surrounding them, and are of weak and imperfect organization. It is frequently met with among insects that appear and disappear with certain plants, or live principally on plants; and among birds and fishes that depend on certain seasons, and observe them in their going and coming from one region to another. These facts are of considerable importance to the question under consideration. For who does not at once perceive a connexion between the plastic power which produces the plant and its beautiful formations, and the insect in which this power is continued, and through which it indirectly produces here, the cell of the bee, and there, the pyramid of the ant.

These remarks may aid us in discovering the nature of animal ingenuity. The mere plastic power, as it reigns in the vegetable kingdom, is entirely *external* and objective in its productions; through it the seed germinates, sprouts, and sends forth the root, stem, and leaf, the bud, the flower and the seed; but from the germ to the seed all is external, the plant breathing forth its most internal life into color and fragrance. Instinct, on the other hand, is *internal*, conditioned by *feeling*, by sensation, and perception. The phenomena of the plastic power and those of instinct are the same, the preservation of the individual being, and of the race. The plant needs *nourishment, motion,* and *rest,* and *propagates* itself by seed or sprouts. The animal is subject to the same wants but with this difference: the roots of the plant absorb moisture, its leaves drink the cooling dew and air without becoming in any degree conscious of it; the animal *feels* its wants, and guided by sensation, it seeks and finds the means by which to remove them. The plant, a mere external growth, cannot move from its place; the animal is enabled by feeling itself, to go in search of its food. Instinct, then, raises the animal as much above the plastic power, as reason raises man above instinct. Yet while instinct and the plastic power differ, they are contained in each other; instinct could not exist for a moment without the plastic power and its irresistible tendency to live; it *is* the plastic power, only modified by feeling. Again, the plastic power reigns throughout all nature; it is the soul of all life without exception, while instinct is confined to animal life.

We have now arrived at the point at which animal ingenuity must become clear. It is the *medium* between instinct and plastic power. It is stronger than the latter and weaker than the former. It is external in its productions, like the plant, and at the same time feels its wants, and separates what it produces, from itself by feeling. Its productions are impossible without instinct, and no less so without the plastic power; they are their joint product.

When the bee, without the least knowledge of flower or juice, buries itself in the cup and sucks in the sweet nectar, it is filled with feelings of pleasure; but when it builds the cell, its activity resembles that of the plant, for it is the plastic power that is active in and through it. The cell is external like the flower, but the flower constitutes part of the plant; the cell is separate from the bee, for the bee, feeling itself, will not grow together with such external materials.

The plastic power, as has been before remarked, prevails throughout all nature; compared with instinct it is the *general,* while instinct, belonging only to animals is the *specific*. Now instinct, i. e. feeling, perception, and sensation, may either be so strong that the plastic power of the element in which the animal lives, is not permitted to effect anything in and through it, the nervous strength of the animal resists such a tendency—the plastic power enters into the animal, but does not affect its independence. Or, the instinct, feeling, independence of the animal may be too weak for the plastic power to work through it. Or, finally, the animal is on the one hand susceptible of resisting the *unlimited* influence of the plastic power, and on the other of receiving it into itself, of being penetrated by it, so that when it is active by instinct, this power is permitted to act through it and to give form and shape to its productions. *Animal ingenuity then*, is *the measure of independence given to these little creatures, and of their dependence on those elements in which they principally live.*

Now what can be more comprehensible than animal ingenuity? There are some thoughts that will always require *thinking* to be understood; and as little as one person can digest for another, so little will it be possible, by even the clearest representation, to make such thoughts understood by all. But what can be more easily understood than the skill with which some birds make distant journeys? The element in which the bird lives is the *air*, and it is so entirely pervaded by this element, that the wings and feathers are filled with it, so that even when the windpipe is closed up, the bird will still be able to live if an opening is made in the bone of the wing, and the air thus permitted to communicate itself to the lungs. No doubt the changes of the air must be quickly felt, and the sympathy between the bird and its element must be very strong. When, now the bird, after her young are reared, feels a desire to wander because nutriment has become scarce, the warmth diminished, and the whole state of the atmosphere changed, she will be attracted by the warm south wind, and following it, will find her new home. It is not a previous knowledge then, not a compass, that directs her, but the warm winds alluring to the south, penetrate and bear her onward, as the fish feels itself drawn by the sweet waters of the rivers. The bee lives principally in the vegetable kingdom, in which the plastic power alone reigns. This power enters the bee, and by its laws the cell is formed.

There are two reasons that make us gaze with so much wonder at the productions of animal ingenuity. In the first place we discover in them an adaptation of means to an end, and whenever we perceive this, we presuppose reason and design. And yet there is the same adaptation of the root to the flower in the plant; and in perceiving it, we feel by no means astonished, merely because we consider the one the product of the plastic power, which is wholly external, and the other that of meditation. In the second place, most of us are in the habit of considering nature and its manifold powers as a *mechanical* whole, whose parts have been brought together by some mechanic, and whose powers exist side by side, without having any affinity to, or connexion with each other. But the opposite of all this is the case. Nature is a system, not a conglomeration; alive and active in all its elements and atoms, it is filled with powers, from the mechanical, chemical, magnetic, and galvanic up to the organic, all of which flow invisibly into each other, affect and determine each other. Eternal laws dwell in them, and provide that while these powers receive, and work with and through each other, none interferes with the other, or in any degree changes its nature, but supports and upholds it. Thus we have a constant life, powers flow up and down, to and fro. The drop of water falling from the cloud is shapeless, exposed to the cold, it radiates into a beautiful flake of white snow. Nothing is isolated; nothing disconnected; the air preserves the elasticity of the water no less than moisture a proper temperature of the atmosphere.

It may be instructive to compare these artificial productions of animals with the works of human art. The great contrast between them will show the true nature of the former.

1. Animals are born not only with the capacity, but with the ready skill to produce artificial works. This is manifest from the fact, that these little creatures not only execute these works immediately after their birth, but also in the same way throughout their lives, without in the least

improving them. The spider feels a tendency to weave his web before he has seen the flies, to ensnare which he spins the thread. The ant-eater can scarcely yet move, when his nature already impels him to prepare the funnel, for the purpose of catching ants and other insects. To say that they learned this from seeing their parents do the same, would be contrary to experience. For, as Aristotle remarks, if we have three eggs hatched by artificial heat, one of a bird, one of a duck, and one of a serpent, we shall see the young bird try to fly, before its wings are grown; the duck to swim, and the serpent to creep into the earth, before they have seen any one of their kind do the same. What man does, he must have learned by trial, but the caterpillar has only once in his life to undergo a transformation, and yet he knows how to spin a covering that will suit his future state, of which he cannot have the least idea. The work, to be produced, seems to bear a prophetic character, for while the larva is still of a cylindric form, he weaves a covering fitted to the form of the chrysalis, as if he had his future state before his eyes. Man is not born with any ready skill, like the animal; his arm allows the mere possibility of performing thousands of different operations, but this possibility must be exercised and developed. Exercise demands both time and repetition, and produces experience; but experience is impossible without reason and judgment. All the artificial productions of animals are based on instinct; those of man on reason, will, and consciousness, and hence it is that the former have reference only to physical wants, but the latter to intellectual.

2. Some animals construct their artificial works of materials which they prepare themselves. The paper wasp builds its nest of pasteboard fabricated by its own ingenuity. The celebrated Oken says of it, " This pasteboard not only *resembles* our pasteboard, but it is really the same; equally as close, white, and strong as man is able to make it. Put one of these nests into the hands of a paper maker without telling him anything about it, and he will press, and turn, and tear it, without once imagining that any except one of his own profession could have prepared it." The aquatic spider, that cannot live under water without

air, draws forth from its nipple a moist substance, a kind of varnish, covers itself with it, and bursting this bladder, it forms by degrees a diver's bell of it, as large as half a pigeon's egg; by a few threads it fastens it to some solid object in the water, its opening hanging downward, and then filling it with air, it may sit in it below the water for a long time, and watch its prey. So the bee gains honey and wax by digestion, and forms its cells of them. A little bee, called the paper-hanger (antophora argentato) bores perpendicular holes into the earth, and lines its house with pieces of the soft red leaves of flowers, as handsomely as persons of wealth cover their rooms with carpets. The antophora entuncularis builds its very artificial nest of leaves that are cut perfectly round; it folds them into the form of a thimble, and shoves six or seven into each other. Man and animals may, however, use the same materials, and yet there remains this great difference. The animal uses these substances without knowing their qualities, without having the least idea of the powers that fit them for the uses to which they apply them. They do not use them, therefore, from choice or consideration, but being directed to them by instinct. The swallow builds its nest of the same materials now, which it used in the time of Pliny. Man, on the other hand, knows the powers of different substances, and their fitness for various purposes; he, therefore, selects and judges. Stones may be good for one, wood for another building. He has works written on the different building materials, and architects must be well acquainted with the nature of timber and stone, if they desire their works to be durable.

3. Animals produce all their works by their own limbs, for they have no instruments. "In order to understand the works of animals," says the most celebrated natural historian of our time, the distinguished Oken, "we must know the organs with which they are provided by nature." How artificial seems to us the preparation of wax and honey; how many ingenious instruments would we have to invent, and how much skill would it require to gather pollen, and how easy is all this for the bee. Its whole body, even what is supposed to be its eyes, is so covered

with hair, that viewed with a strong lens it resembles a piece of moss. The hairs are formed for gathering pollen; the head is a flat triangle, running downward to a point; its feelers are extremely flexible. The horny upper jawbones meet in front of the mouth like tongues, they are hollow, and can approach each other like hands; below is the proboscis, bent backward, and well formed, to be thrust into the nectar cups of flowers, and in addition to all, the limbs, that move involuntarily without reflection or will, of which the two behind answer the purpose and bear the name of brushes. These limbs are so shaped, that their natural motions have a tendency to produce the works that seem to us so remarkable. The German rat has a bag below the chin, into which it gathers grain; the mole has protruding fore-feet to dig with; the fish has fins and a broad, upright, standing tail, to swim. But man, according to Franklin, is an animal that can invent machines. The savage, fastening a sharp stone to a club, uses it as an axe; he does not defend himself by his limbs, but by the bow, the arrow, and the tomahawk. Man has invented the saw and the hatchet, the sword and the gun, the furnace and the mill, and is daily increasing the number of machines. There is no animal that ever attempted to fabricate its works by the use of self-invented machines, or by fire. Monkeys, that are generally admitted to be ingenious, never think of keeping up the fire by adding wood, though they evidently delight in its warmth; nor of firing woods, or of destroying the property of those that injure them, or of preparing instruments of iron by the aid of fire.

4. The arts of animals have no history, as have those of man. They have no history in the *objective* sense of the word; they have no gradual development, no cultivation, no improvement; they are stationary, they are the same now that they always were. The arts of animals cannot have a history in the *subjective* sense of the term history, for there can be no historical narration where nothing is to be narrated, and animals cannot be conscious of an improvement, when there is none. But it is the character of history, that on the one hand it develops gradually all the capacities of a nation, or of our race; and on the other, makes us conscious of them by narrating

them; and hence it is, too, that history objectively means the actions related, *res gestae,* and subjectively the relation of them, *historia rerum gestarum.* On the other hand, there was a time when man knew of no arts, not even of such as are now considered indispensable. But animals have always had the same arts in the same degree of perfection, and for the same purposes as at present. Man had to invent his, and he changes and improves them daily. The arts of men differ in different regions, while the same animals will always produce the same works, wherever they are. And so men of different capacities in the same region, will have different success, while animals of the same kind will have the same.

5. Finally, the purpose for which animals produce works of art, is limited to the sustenance of individual life and the preservation of the race. Hence their works are few in number. The spider can only spin a web; the bee can only build a cell. Hence it is too, that the bird does not build its nest before the time of propagation. The purposes, for which man exercises his ingenuity and inclination to art, are manifold. By mechanical art he invents instruments, to serve his desire for knowledge. The press, the paper, the ink, the watch, the electrical machine, the compass, the telescope, give sufficient proof of this; and the yard and the measure, the landmark and the coin, show that his ingenuity is made subservient to his sense of justice. By the fine arts he enters the sphere of beauty and the compositions of Mozart and Beethoven, of Handel and Haydn; the pictures of Raphael and Titian, the poetry of Shakspeare and Homer must serve to satisfy his longing for intellectual entertainment.

From the above remarks it sufficiently appears, that, though the works of animals are full of intellect and design, it is not *their* design, we admire, but that of the Creator, who accomplishes it through the animals.

§ 5. RELATION OF INSTINCT TO MAN.

The plastic power, as it exists and operates in the plant is blind, for it has neither sensation nor perception. The instinct of animals is like the twilight, not clear, but confused in itself, for it can neither comprehend, judge, nor conclude; it distinguishes only by sensations, and such distinctions are faint, unaccompanied by consciousness, and not resulting from comparison, but depending wholly on the strength of the impression made by the different objects on the senses of the animal. The instinct of insects and of those animals that produce artificial works, is interesting, and so regular in its productions, that they seem to be living arithmeticians; yet they thus only appear to us, for in reality these little creatures are not conscious of their powers. Man has the power of thought; here every thing becomes transparent, clear, distinct and manifest; where pure thought prevails, there instinct loses its power. Though the animal is separated from the vegetable kingdom by sensation and perception, the plastic power of plants is continued in it, and the animal is formed by it, grows, matures and decays according to its laws. So man is separated from the animal by reason, but on the one hand, he is formed by the same plastic power, and on the other, instinct still appears in the new-born child, whose lips long instinctively for nourishment, and in many of the actions of savages. The principal manifestations of instinct in man, however, are those of hunger and thirst, of motion and rest, and of care for the race. But, as has been said above, man is separated from the animal by reason; he can think, he can will, and by these powers he reigns over his instinct, and subjects it to his discipline. He must live, in order to think; he must eat and drink, in order to live; but while the animal is wholly under the control of instinct, and while hunger is a tyrant whose dictates must be obeyed, man can not only eat what he pleases, but also wholly abstain from food, and though urged by an excessive appetite he may nevertheless give away his food, or like Atticus starve himself in the midst of plenty. The animal must eat when hungry, and it must eat what its instinct directs it to use. The lion cannot eat hay, the horse will not eat flesh. Nor will the animal eat more than is sufficient to appease its wants, but man may eat and drink much or little, and when he pleases. A glutton is said to have eaten before the Emperor Aurelian a wild hog, a young pig, a whole lamb, one hundred pieces of Roman bread, and to have drank besides, a bucket full of wine.

Such too, is the case with all the other natural powers of man. He may live or commit suicide; the animal *must* live, and though the rein-deer is said to kill itself by dashing its head against the tree, its death is accidental, for it intends only to free itself from pain, caused by the glutton which fastens upon its head. The whole life of the animal is a slavish one. The sight of the hunter puts the stag to flight, and he must bound over hill and valley, over bush and brook. But when the cannon-ball fell into the room of Charles XII, and he remained calmly in his chair, when the Dutch admiral, in the moment he was about to take a pinch of snuff, and lost the extended hand by a shot, took it with the other, and when a British cannonier, whose right hand was torn off by a ball as he was about to discharge his cannon, used the left with the words, " does the enemy think that I have but one hand ?" they showed, that they by their will, were above the necessity of yielding to fear or the influence of pain.

Man possessing reason, has an innate desire for knowledge, which the animal has not. This desire is more than instinct, and not any part of it. This may be easily made clear. The gratification of instinct is pleasure, connected with sensation and perception, with the taste of food, with the motion of muscles or their rest. But the gratification of a desire for knowledge, is pleasure connected with our apperceptions, with our cognitions, with our comprehensions, judgments, and conclusions. In the sphere of instinct all is confined to sense, in the sphere of our intellectual desires, our pleasures, are derived from thought, from a satisfaction of our thirst for knowledge. But while instinct extends not beyond the sphere of sensation, our desire for knowledge includes *instinct*, and it is this which leads many of us to the objects suited to the exercise of our peculiar talents. So Linnaeus, when yet an infant, could be silenced by no other toy so quickly, as by a flower put into his hands. So Mozart, when only six years old, would make distinctions between different notes, which his father, likewise a musician, could not perceive. Instinct mingling with our desire for knowledge, constitutes in union with it, talents and natural capacities.

The life of man and that of the animals, it must be evident, differ widely, not only in degree, but in kind. Where that of man commences, the animal is left behind. A chasm separates the one from the other. The animal may gaze on man, but it cannot understand him, for it is unable to think or to comprehend, and the words spoken to the dog, for example, are not for him what they are for man, sounds full of meaning, they are mere *signs* to him. The life of the animal is like a dream; and even while waking it dreams. But the life of man is fully awake, it is possessed of self-consciousness, and gifted with the capacity to originate constantly new thoughts, and assisted by the powers of nature to realize them.

PART I.
ANTHROPOLOGY.

PART I.

ANTHROPOLOGY.

Mental philosophy has to consider the mind of man, 1. In its connection with the body, in its dependence upon it, and through it upon nature. 2. In its relation to itself.

In the former case its doctrines may be embraced under the general term ANTHROPOLOGY, and in the latter that of PSYCHOLOGY. The object of Anthropology is to examine the external influences to which mind is subject, and its modifications produced by them. The object of Psychology is to investigate the nature of mind, as it is conscious of itself and of the difference between it and nature, and as it has rendered these natural influences more or less subject to its power.

The mind becomes subject to the influences of physical nature only by its connection with the body. Whatever affects the latter permanently, will also influence the former. The qualities of the mind, produced by these influences, are therefore, likewise permanent. The Mongol, the Malay, and the Negro, are the same at present, physically and psychologically, that they were at the time of Herodotus, who describes them as Scythians, Indians, and Black People. The disposition of the Laplander cannot be changed into that of the Frenchman, by emigrating to the South, any more than a transplanted peach-tree can become a palm-tree. This general modification of the mind may, however, be altered by the peculiar capacities of an individual, by temperament, by age, or by exchanging one region for another. Nor is the mind wholly subjected by its connection with the body to these influences of situation and circumstances. Possessed of consciousness and will, it may subject the body and all its peculiarities, and also the solar, lunar, and telluric influences to its control, at least in a great degree.

Anthropology may, therefore, be divided into three parts: or those which treat,

I. Of the *permanent* influences of nature, of race, sex, &c. upon the mind.

II. Of the *transient* influences of age, sleep, dreaming, &c.

III. Of the power of the mind over the body.

CHAPTER I.

MODIFICATIONS OF MIND PRODUCED BY THE PERMANENT INFLUENCE OF NATURE.

§ 1. THE INFLUENCE OF NATURE UPON THE MIND OF MAN.

It cannot escape the observation of any, that every organic form of life is so affected by the quality of the elements surrounding it, that a certain region of the earth, with the plants and animals growing in it, and characterizing it, seems to form one inseparable whole. No sooner does the student of Natural History perceive a salt spring, than he looks for the plants peculiar to springs of this kind. As the osteologist may judge, from a single bone, of the whole animal, so a single plant may indicate to the scientific botanist, the face and soil of the earth, and the elements in which it grew. The same truth is seen throughout all nature. The seed depends for its growth on a favorable soil, no less than on a favorable season. The plant that luxuriates in a mild and rich soil, when transplanted into another, will wither. The elements that called forth its life are required for its support. With animals the same is the fact; some of them, like plants, appear and disappear with certain seasons; others with certain plants. The whole existence of the cherry-worm continues only as long as the cherry; it then buries itself in the earth, re-appears in the following May as a little black fly, lays its egg in the cherry, and dies. The power that renews the life of the cherry-tree, seems also to revive the cherry-worm. No animal but the dog can live except within certain geographical boundaries, so that we may have a geography of plants and animals. The connection of certain animals with plants, and that of plants with some peculiar spot on the face of the earth, is truly striking. The cameleopard, and the cameleopard-plant, are both found in the south of Africa, and nowhere else. The elements too, in which animals principally live, very essentially affect their natures. The fish, living in the water, is mute, cheerless, serious, and phlegmatic. Insects, on the other hand, playing and spending their lives in the light, are agile, beautifully colored, some of them transparent as light, and most of them courageous, choleric, and very destructive. Little insects will destroy whole woods; a little ant in the south frequently ruins the finest furniture. Homer was aware of the boldness of insects. When Achilles protects the body of his friend Patroclus, from the Trojans, Homer compares them to flies, which though constantly chased away by the mother sitting by the cradle of her babe, perseveringly repeat their bold attacks. Again, birds live in the air, and the effects of this element on them is expressed in their cheerfulness, their delight in singing, and their sailing about in the air with intense pleasure.

It cannot be otherwise with man. He too must feel the effect of seasons and times, of heat and cold, and of the elements in general. His body develops itself by the laws which the Creator has given to the earth. The earth supports man by the air he breathes, by the food he eats; it clothes him by furnishing the materials which art prepares; it protects him from storm and rain, from heat and cold, by affording him stone and timber, furs, skins, and his fuel. The earth and its productions arouse his senses, impress his mind, excite his desires, and exercise his activity. The sight of scanty or luxuriant vegetation on the one hand, and the intercourse of man with animals on the other, as that of the Arabians with their horses, of the Laplanders with their rein-deer, of the Greenlanders or Samoiedes, with their seals, or that of the Moors with their camels, must affect variously his disposition. Man, as long as he lives, depends on the earth and its productions; its laws, and characteristic powers must not only influence him, but leave certain traces and permanent impressions on his mind.

The earth, however, became the residence of such a being as man, by the position it occupies in our planetary system. By this position it stands in a relation to the sun, the moon, and to itself. On these relations all life on earth depends.

1. The particular relation of the earth to the sun produces a higher or lower degree of heat and cold. The general consequence in this respect is, that too great heat arrests the development of mind by relaxing the nervous and muscular system, and that too great cold has the same effect by contracting those systems, so that the Pesheraes in the south fully resemble the Esquimaux in the farthest north, both as to size and form of body, and as to intellect. Again, too sudden transitions from one temperature to another, are less favourable to the health of body and mind, than more gradual ones; hence it must follow, that a region, blessed with the regular four seasons, so that spring and autumn are interposed between summer and winter, must be more favorable to the intellectual life of man, than one where either summer or winter continues almost without interruption. The same must be said of the transitions from day to night. Where they are very sudden, a relaxation of the system will take place; where they are more gradual, so that day and night are separated by the twilight of the evening and the dawn of the morning, there the system will feel invigorated by a cool evening after a warm day, and will, by degrees, pass over from the freshness of a balmy morning to the heat of noon. The morning is the threshold of expectation, the day is the season of labor and activity, the evening that of enjoyment and satisfaction, and the night that of rest. The interruption of this natural course, is injurious to body and mind.

The temperate zones for these reasons will always be the seat of intellect and science. Here the mind is energetic: the soft, vernal breezes, the charms of a tender verdure, resting on hills and valleys, which appear gradually, call forth hopes and anticipations and a vigorous activity. As they disappear, a melancholy seriousness and earnestness, a desire for the past, and a consciousness of the vanity of all things will arise in the breast, when forests, and hills, and valleys are gradually stripped of their beauty, when the country sinks into a deep gloom, and the life of animated nature becomes mute and finally dies away. In the temperate zones, however, are differences worthy to be noticed. "In the East," says the distinguished Ritter in his well known Geography, "the sun rises, and describes in its royal course the eradiating arch through the South to the West, and thus, considered with reference to the sun, the fountain of all earthly life, this great cosmical relation indicates from the beginning, the first natural division of the surface of the earth.

There is Asia, the part of the earth, whose essential character is pronounced in the name *Orient;* here is Europe its opposite, the *Occident,* which is characteristically designated in all the parts of its nature and history in every period. Not only their countries and sky but their plants and animals confirm it; the voices of all nations express it, by their songs, by the history of their cultivation, by their religions, philosophies and languages.

Truly, says a highly gifted writer, the Oriental and Occidental nations are turned away from each other, those with their faces towards morning, these towards the sunset or evening; those faithfully preserving the seats of antiquity; these seeking a momentous future in spite of the constant changes of all forms of existence."

The worshippers of the sun are met with in Asia. The brightness of his light is so great, that man, in gazing at it, is lost in admiration and does not notice the things rendered visible by the light, because the glorious light itself too much attracts his eye. He adores, he worships it. In the West the sun sets; his brightness is less brilliant, though frequently sublime and beautiful. Man is not overcome by it, and when the setting-sun sinks behind the mountain before our eye, the idea that he will illuminate other worlds and return, involuntarily offers itself; and if we are reminded of our own departure, our breast will be cheered by the hope, that we likewise shall rise again. Hence it is, that the West is the proper field for science, art and history, for there alone man obtains full possession of himself, and a clear consciousness of the world around him. Says Hegel, "These is an *East* for the history of the world, though East is in itself something *relative.* Asia is the East for history, there the external physical sun rises, and in the West he sets: but here the internal sun of self-consciousness rises, which sheds a higher splendor." It is remarkable, that as the sun rises in the East, so many sciences have originated there, and even religion was there first revealed to man. But nothing gained its full maturity there. The Chinese claim the honor of having discovered gunpowder, but the Jesuits had to furnish them with cannon. They pretend to have invented the printing press, but as yet they have only presses of wood with immoveable letters. What Greece and Rome were in ancient times, Europe and America are in modern.

2. The influence of the moon on the mind of man. Certain as the influence of the moon is upon the earth, it is very limited on man. Some diseases of the mind are undoubtedly modified by the moon, and physicians are of the opinion that bodily diseases are much affected by it. Yet on the whole its influence is not sufficiently ascertained, and we have to confine it here to the effects produced by its light on our imagination. These effects may be seen in the poetry and mythology of nations, and, whenever perceptible, are highly fantastical. The dim light of the moon does not delineate objects accurately, but exhibits them in shadowy and uncertain shapes. The Greenlander imagines the heavenly bodies, sun and moon, pursuing each other in despair of success. "The earth," they say, "rests on immense pillars of ice, that constantly threaten ruin. Demons of darkness desire its destruction, and they are only restrained from dashing the tottering fragment to pieces by the howl of *Angekoks*, which fill the night with their shrieks from dark, icy and barren regions." Such fancies come upon us from the hour of midnight, that begets the fear of spectres, and that in dim moonlight makes us see a ghost in every object.

3. The local influence of the earth upon the mind of man. The influence of the sun depends upon the union of his light with the activity of the earth. The rays, that fall upon morasses, will produce poisonous vapors; those, that in the same region fall upon sand, deadly heat; and those that are absorbed by moist oases, a cheerful vegetation. The nature of the sun blends with that of the earth,

and the earth surrounds man, and possesses him and keeps him, whithersoever he goes, as long as he enjoys the light of the sun. But the surface of the earth is in different regions peculiarly modified by soil, by productions, by scenery, by the serenity and color of the sky, by air and atmosphere. Man must be born on some particular spot, and its whole character will impress itself strongly upon his youthful mind. All his desires, every thought of his soul, every one of his wishes, every hope is more or less interwoven with this impression of his home, and his whole disposition greatly depends upon the region of his birth. So much is this the case, that when man leaves the home of his youth, and when new scenery, new objects, new customs are contrasted with those by which his early desires and habits were modified, and from which they in some measure proceeded, he becomes sick with longing for his home. His feelings and views, desires and habits, that grew up with the objects of his early home, are still the same in his breast, but the visible world around him no longer corresponds with them, and this contradiction induces him constantly to recall the image of his native country. This great influence of locality may further be seen in the modifications which it imparts to the character and disposition of men.

If we compare the Abyssinians and Shangallas, who live in the same zone, we shall be most forcibly struck with the truth of this assertion. The former, seeking the high Alps of north Africa, which are covered with rich prairies, keep large herds of cattle, make use of the horse, of iron, &c. and are a noble race, strong, versatile, acute, active, and possessed of a chivalrous disposition. Living under a serene sky, in a pure atmosphere, and a mild temperature, they are cultivated and humane, and would be much more so, were they not surrounded on all sides by enemies, so that they themselves, according to Ritter, compare their land to the *Donguelat*, a beautiful flower, but like the thistle beset with thorns. The Shangallas on the other hand, dwelling in the morasses and swamps along the river Mahareb, inhaling poisonous vapors, submitting to all kinds of diseases, living on lizards, on the flesh of the ostrich, rhinoceros, elephant, and on fish, never think of improving their homes, or exchanging them for a better region. Thick woods with large trees, that afford an easy protection from the heat of the sun and wooden lances, is all they desire. When the rainy season commences, they, as do the rain-worms when the sun shines, disappear in caves, which they quickly dig in the soft sand-stone along the steep, inaccessible walls of the high rocks. "The negroes along the coasts," says the celebrated Ritter, "differ as widely from those of the mountains, as the inhabitants of cities from those of the country, and so the negroes that live on mountains, differ widely from the negroes of the plain."

The principal differences with regard to the *surface* of the earth, are those of the Highlands, Plains and Coasts:

(1.) *Highlands.* The purity of the air, and the liberty with which the inhabitants roam on their highlands, gives them the spirit of independence, that makes them reluctant to be restrained by laws. They feel depressed when they descend into the valleys; they cannot breathe freely, their eyes cannot pierce the depths of distant horizons; the color of the sky, plants and animals are all so different, that they pine away with home-sickness. Wandering from place to place, free as the birds of the air, they lead a careless and cheerful life. Right and justice rest in the strength of the arm; hospitality and robbery spring up with equal ease, and in the same breast. No tie keeps the Highlanders together, except that of family connection. They split into small clans, and though wars should unite them for a time, they are dispersed in a moment after their battles are fought. They swell like a mountain torrent, and like it disappear. Living in the bosom of nature, however, being strangers to the luxuries of cities, their characters are strong, noble and high-minded. The Foulahs dwelling on the high Alps of Africa, stand as high in this respect above their neighbors living below them, as the natives of Cashmere above the Hindoos.

(2.) *Plains and Valleys*, on the other hand, by the richness of their soil, and numerous streams, invite to a settled life. Agriculture is carried on, and its success being dependent on the regular return of seasons, it leads to order and regularity. The idea of property becomes more developed, for no one would be willing to bestow labor upon the cultivation of land, unless he were sure of the exclusive possession of it, and of a permanent protection of his claims. A regularly established government becomes indispensable. Valleys have at all times been the seats of large empires. Man, by the power of mind subdues the wildness of nature, and by extirpating large forests, in which the cold and snow of winter loves to dwell, he improves the climate, and having once satisfied the necessities of life, he turns his attention to science and art.

(3.) *Coasts* form a strong, bold, independent and kind-hearted people. The ocean was not intended, as Horace sings, to separate nations and sections of the earth. Mountains and not waters, Hegel remarks in his Philosophy of History, are barriers to the intercourse of different people, and Cesar, in crossing the Alps, caused a new epoch in history. Waters between different countries, though vast as the Atlantic, do not keep nations asunder, but as man builds bridges over rivers, so he erects moving bridges, or as Homer says, creates horses of the deep, that will unite one coast with another. Europe and America have more intercourse than Spain and France, though the latter are only separated by the Pyrenees. The mind and disposition of man, living along the coast, near the surface of great waters, is enlarged and ennobled, for while the immensity of the ocean fills the breast with an idea of the infinite, the rising and sinking waves, the constantly changing bosom of the deep, remind him of the uncertainty of all earthly things, of their changeableness, and of the necessity of assisting one another. The watery element invites us, for it offers wealth and a knowledge of distant countries. Its dangers render bold and intrepid, prudent and brave, and give us a feeling of the power of man, who successfully combats the rage of storms and billows, while standing on a mere plank.

Before dismissing this topic we have to add a word on the *elementary* influence of the earth on man. It is well established, that a clear sky, and a pure mountain air invigorate, while a gloomy and moist atmosphere depresses. The sky of Italy and that of England differ no less than the dispositions of their inhabitants. The vapors arising from the soil, are of importance. Pythia, chewing a few leaves and sitting on her tripod, was believed in the superstition of Greece, to become so inspired by the vapors of the grotto, that she could foresee the future.—Next to the atmosphere, the food we take, will influence our disposition. If our digestive power is strengthened by it, our spirits will rise. The black soup of the Spartans, which their youth had to prepare for themselves by mixing bread with water and a few herbs, was simple but strong, as was the character of the Lacedemonians. An Athenian could not relish it; he desired more refined food. When after having been deprived for a considerable time of a favorite dish, we partake again moderately of it, we feel cheered; or when after having endured for hours a burning thirst, we approach a little grove and lay ourselves down by a clear and cool fountain under shady trees, we feel happy and cheerful, and if while thirsty, we would scarcely have listened to the petitions of a beggar, we then feel full of sympathy and kindness. Man may eat whatever nature offers as food; and what animals cannot do, he may overcome the natural aversion that he has to certain kinds of food. The soldiers of Napoleon fed on cats and horse-flesh. The principal food, however, taken by man, is derived from the animal and vegetable kingdoms, and consists of *meat* or *vegetables*, or *flour, milk* and *fruit.* Each of these have different effects upon him. Meat increasing the activity of bile, renders him choleric and passionate. Food prepared of flour, favors a phlegmatic disposition, and is therefore recommended by physicians as a wholesome dish in warm climates, where the digestive activity is much accelerated. Milk, and what is prepared of it, preserves a child-like and harmless disposition, as may be seen from shepherds. The Foulahs on the Alps of Africa, living principally on milk and butter, are said to be a mild and gentle nation; they honor father and mother above all, and their highest title is that of Father and Mother, which they use as we do that of Master, and Old Man, as we that of Lord. Finally vegetables have been commended at all times by persons of sedentary habits. Pythagoras recommended them to his disciples, and Newton abstained from meat when he wished to study deeply, and lived almost entirely on colewort. Some fruits are said to strengthen the memory, and some herbs to excite the organs of speech.

It is admitted by all, that strong drinks, and especially distilled liquors, weaken the memory, deprive of self-possession, undermine health, make men quarrelsome and passionate, and call forth brutal desires in a shocking manner. Some of them paralize the whole power of the soul, take away all remembrance, and while they excite bodily activity and set all the members in motion, they annihilate the capacity of man to control and direct his steps, and as though an evil genius had gained a magic dominion over the motions of the body, the soul sees the dangers, into which the body is driven by an evil demon, and cannot rescue it from them. The effects of gases, when inhaled, of tobacco, &c., are too well known to demand a particular notice here.

As man may eat and drink what he chooses, so he may eat much or little. He may eat more, and bear hunger better than any animal. A dog supported merely by sugar died after a few weeks; geese fed on starch were found dead after twenty-four days. But the Arab, without any injurious effects, lives cheerfully on a little gum for many weeks in his desert; Johanna Naunton supported herself for seventy-eight days by the juice of lemon. Renaud, on the other hand, Archbishop of Bourges, slept only two hours, but had eight meals a day. Among the Kirgises a man of good appetite, eats a whole lamb, the tail of which alone weighs twenty pounds.

Yet we must be careful, lest our wish to acknowledge the dependence of man on these influences, should induce us to over-value them. The mild Ionian sky with its soft and gentle breezes no doubt breathed many an image into the songs of Homer, as the high oaks and vast heaths filled the breast of Ossian with the remembrance of by-gone ages, and with visions of fantastic forms produced by the dim moonlight sleeping on the heaths, or by the moaning winds, as they swept over them; but neither the Ionian sky nor the heaths of Scotland were sufficient to call forth the genius of Homer or of Ossian. The Otomake, bordering the Oronoke, are blessed with a beautiful climate and a rich soil, and yet they prefer living on potter's clay, which they roast, to cultivating the land. On the other hand, we find a noble set of men, of great stature, of high principles of honor, and of a scientific spirit, high in the north, in Scandinavia. The sky is cold, the soil is poor; the winter never recedes from the high rocks; the summer appears only in the valleys, and for a short time calls forth a dark green along the declivities. Yet while an uninterrupted silence reigns over nature, the voice of a lovely, melancholy song greets the ear; science and nobleness of character love to dwell there, and a firm, resolute will knows how to meet the power of an unfriendly climate. The constitution of man fits him to live every where under heaven, and to support his innate dignity. No region is destitute of him; though individuals may suffer from emigration, and find it difficult to become acclimated, the human race is at home every where on the face of the earth. Up to the eightieth degree of North latitude, along the Polar ice, the Greenlander and Esquimaux live; down to the sixtieth degree of South latitude, the Pesheraes exist on the Terra del Fuego. Where mercury becomes malleable, where birds fall down dead from the air, where animals howl from the effects of cold, there man may live; and he can also endure a heat, that is above the warmth of blood.—It cannot be denied, however, that much depends on these influences for the disposition of man, though different people, exposed to the same influences, like plants growing on the same soil, exhibit quite a different aspect. The Foulahs, Gallas, and Abyssinians live on the same high Alps, and yet a considerable difference is perceptible in their cultivation and disposition. The Mandingoes, a numerous nation, of beautiful form, open, frank and cheerful, refined and simple in their manners, have a republican government, and are the merchants of Northern Africa. Close to them live the Negroes, stupid and rude, voluptuous and cowardly, rapacious, and without regard for justice or law.—Considering such facts, we must acknowledge, that it is not the climate alone, nor the soil, nor the food, nor the manner of living, which causes such differences in mankind, but that there must be some cause in man himself, a cause, which will incline him to form certain habits, to seek for a home that will correspond with his feelings and desires. Correct as it is, to consider customs and habits as dependent on the natural influences of a region, it is also certainly true, that a prevailing inclination attracts man to a particular region.

§ 2. THE DIFFERENT RACES OF MANKIND.

Man is every where the same, and there is no *specific* difference in the human race, as there is in animals. All men, wherever they live, to whatever race they belong, have *reason;* they *feel,* they *think,* they *will.* We cannot speak therefore of different kinds of men, as we speak of different *kinds* of animals, because that which constitutes man, is the same in all individuals, and only exists in a modified form. The differences that exist between the *races* of men do not proceed from the *absence or presence of certain faculties or bodily organs, but from their peculiar strength or modification,* which cannot be explained by the influence of climate, but must be ascribed to an innate difference. Such is the *color* of man; cold regions will not bleach the negro, and the southern heat of Africa will not convert the Moor into a black man. *The disposition of the mind, size of the body, formation of the skull, the proportions of the face and language,* exhibit likewise such strongly marked differences, as will enable us to distinguish by them one race from another. These different qualities may be anticipated before the birth of a child, and nothing can extinguish them except amalgamation. Yet while these differences cannot he denied, they are not such as exist between two species of the same kind. Hence it is, that while in the world of animals every *individual,* the *infusoria* excepted, is connected with its *genus* by the *species* to which it belongs, as the single ourang-outang by his species with the monkey-kind, every individual man is in connection with mankind, directly through himself and not by a species. We cannot speak therefore of different species of mankind, but only of various races. By the term *race,* we understand that union of individuals, which is brought about by *mere propagation,* independent of history, or affection, or common interest. The English and Germans are of the same race, but how different their history, their characters, their cultivation and interests. It is certain that these races exist, but it is difficult to say how they all spring from one pair. This difficulty has led many to consider the different races as having sprung from so many different roots, which it would be impossible to reduce to one common origin and which are united only by intellectual and moral elements, by reason and will. There have not been wanting those, however, who with great acuteness have philosophically proved, what we know through revelation concerning the origin of the human race. No less difficult is it to determine the exact number of the human races, because the varieties of tribes, and the transitions from one race to another are so many, that they become easily confounded with each other, when we attempt to classify them. Hence it is, that there are so many different divisions made by the learned; while Linnaeus, and Leibnitz admitted four races, Meiners accepted only two; Pownal, three; Hunter, four; Buffon and Herder, six; Hegel, three; Kant, Blumenbach and Virey, five. The latter is the more commonly adopted view. According to this we have the Caucasian, American, Malay, Mongol and Negro races. A delineation of their bodily forms belongs rather to the science called Natural Description of Man than to Anthropology, as the question concerning the origin of the human race, *where? when? how?* and *by what means* it was called into existence belongs to the Natural History of Man, two sciences that have received the particular attention of the celebrated Blumenbach.

It would be superfluous here to give a characteristic of the disposition, intellect, and moral capacities of the different races, as every good geography, and especially every philosophy of history, furnishes one more complete than our space would permit us to give. All that is required here, is to acknowledge a permanent distinction between the races, which not only affects the body, but also the mind.

National Differences.

1. Cruelty and an absence of love and mercy, and of humane feeling, ignorance and superstition, indolence, arbitrariness, and oppression of the weaker, characterize the the savage. Morality, a sense of obligation and duty, are not acknowledged; and the barbarian, as he does what is pleasing and useful to him, so he prevails by the arm of strength. Nor has he any feeling of personal respect or any regard for truth, beauty, and honor, but destroys whatever will not serve his sensual desires. The first step to civilization is a willingness to submit our individual will to laws and duties, and to seek for liberty no longer in our own arbitrariness. To the savage this step seems to involve the loss of his liberty, for genuine liberty is unknown to him. A limitation of selfish desires and passions, a restraint of arbitrariness and mere good pleasure, is to him a limitation of liberty, and hence he hates laws and duties. Fond of his liberty, he cannot think of relinquishing his stage of cultivation for one, that in his views offers the opposite of what he desires.

The savage is so wholly sunk in the life of nature, that he does not distinguish between its activity and that of mind, but views both as merged into each other. We, accustomed from youth to separate soul and body, mind and nature, find it almost impossible to transfer ourselves into the life of the savage in this respect; and yet this sphere of thinking and feeling in reference to nature, constitutes the most essential portion of the intellectual existence of the savage. From the mountains to the valleys and brooks, all is full of meaning and possessed of will and reason to him. The forms of the mountains, the one being table-formed, another piercing the clouds with its peaks, a third round; all this is not accidental; now clouds gather around them, mist covers them, lightnings flash about them; and now again they lie clear and open in the sun, and their outlines are fully exhibited by the distribution of light and shade. This, in the imagination of the savage, is all dependent on the mountains themselves. So cool brooks, murmuring forth from dark grottoes, refreshing them when thirsty, and dancing over stone and pebble, constantly in motion must be full of life and spirits. The plant, that full of energy and vigor, proceeds from its own seed and luxuriantly spreads and grows as if by its own power, terminating in a beautiful cup, which bursting, unfolds the choicest colors that rest among the dark green leaves of the branches, attracts his attention and admiration. There must be a life like that which animates himself, or even better;—he worships the plant:—But above all he adores the animal; it is silent, it communicates not, and yet it walks about, eats and drinks; it builds its nest artificially on lofty branches, has holes like the fox, houses like the beaver; catches the fly by a web, and leads a life full of mystery to the savage. Some Indian tribe traces its origin to a certain species of the bear, and whenever they kill one, they apologize for doing so by telling him, that they know he loves his grand children and is willing to satisfy their hunger. In this life of the savage, sensual desire rules over him, his attention can be elicited only by objects that may have immediate reference to himself. It is always a single object, *this* or *that* horse, *this* or *that* dog, that interests him. His desire is without measure, it is not satisfied until its object is annihilated; his enemy is not only killed, he must be eaten too. In the strength of this desire, magic has its origin, for it is subjectively the desire to realize what we wish by the mere expression of our will, without any intermediate causes.

3. Savages have no *organized government*. All life is perfect in proportion as it is well organized. The animal life begins with that of the infusorium, but it is highly imperfect in that stage, and equally as imperfectly organized. There is no heart visible, no brain, no liver, there are no functions of different systems, and motion is the only expression of life in these little animals. So it may be said the savage has a government, but it is only the beginning of that of civilization. Whatever is organized has, on the one hand, identity of life or a common soul, a common spirit, and on the other, a variety of members, through which this one life is diffused, and all of which represent it. These members or organs differ from each other, as the branch from the trunk, and yet they have the same life. Each has a peculiar office, and yet all serve but one

purpose. A well organized government has likewise but one soul—morality and liberty. The energy of this soul must show itself by creating a number of distinct institutions and offices, each of which differs from the other by a particular activity allotted to it, while all activities and all offices are united by proceeding from the same common soul, and in being pervaded by it. In such a government all are co-ordinate to each other, and subordinate only to law; in such a government alone, it is possible that occupations and ranks in the greatest variety can co-exist without any interference, and that all the wants of man may be satisfied, for in it each want has its corresponding organ by which it receives its satisfaction. Farmers and merchants, teachers and politicians, mechanics and all other classes of men are so many organs of civil life, all of which, while each has an existence of its own, and seems to be active for itself like the leaves of a large tree sustain and support the whole. Plato illustrates this beautifully by showing the evil consequences that would result to one who while he had capacity and skill for making shoes, would also have to be his own tailor and carpenter and blacksmith. He certainly would do nothing properly. But if he makes shoes for himself and others, and if others, skilled in tailoring, in the business of the carpenter, &c. make his dresses, and build his houses, all will be better off; for each will attend to that for which he has a peculiar talent.

4. Savages have no *history*. History is the intellectual process that begins with the less perfect, and passes over to the more perfect, for it develops what is in man. The plant exists already as a *possible* existence in the germ, but undeveloped. Its development exhibits, by various forms from the root up to the seed, all that is contained in the germ. Though the seed gains nothing by this process, since it terminates merely in a multiplication of seed like itself, we having observed it once, we may know all the possible forms which it has the power of producing. Yet the life of the plant is monotonous, always passing through the same course; and hence it cannot be said to have a history, because it does not improve nor deteriorate, and one plant is as complete and perfect

as any other of the same species. But man can increase in perfection unlimited; the last stage he has attained in the cultivation of his mind becomes always the first of a new development. This may be made clear by an example from nature. For here we see, that the plastic power of the plant first produces a single leaf; but this leaf grows up into a trunk; this again branches out into twigs, and the twigs produce leaves, &c., so that always the last production contains the germ of a new one. Yet in the vegetable kingdom, the last production only repeats the preceding one; the plant is and always will be confined to particular limits. History, on the other hand, has a constant tendency to remove the limits of the present, to go beyond them, to improve and to advance. This progress does not disregard the contents of the past, but it will include them when nations do not become stationary, and fix themselves on the customs and habits of the past as the Chinese. So the trunk does not annihilate the root, though it is a higher development, but it truly preserves it. History includes the past by making us *conscious* of what it was. As long as we live in the spirit of an age, interest in it and predilection for it will not permit us to perceive its real worth, but we generally overvalue it. When from the elements contained in it, the spirit is forced to assume a new form and produce new customs and views; we become conscious both of what was good or objectionable in the old, because then we shall be free and impartial in our judgment. So when a strong inclination, love, for example, holds us chained, we shall not be conscious of its nature while it reigns over us, but no sooner are we freed from it, than it becomes known and manifest to us in all its qualities. From all this it follows, that when the many intellectual capacities slumbering in man are historically developed, he must become conscious of them, and that what before he possessed only by nature, will then come within the sphere of his voluntary action. He thus not only gains, but is essentially changed and enriched, and the once-gained wealth of ideas is never lost, but is constantly pressing onward. Man is born free, but unless he is conscious of his freedom he does not possess it. Again, in nature every thing develops itself peaceably without a struggle; but man, conscious of every change in himself, has to undergo conflicts in making these changes. The idea of development ever pre-supposes some thing to be developed; this must exist previously, and remain the same in the development, only that what there is in it is drawn out. With man, *reason* and *will* are to be unfolded in all their riches. Both, in the savage, are sunk in the life of nature, which by its energy, and by the fullness of its sensual enjoyments, keeps him in bondage. Reason and will ought to break loose from this life, but being satisfied with their state, they would act against themselves in doing so. Hence the savage has no history, for he is what he always has been. Civilization is connected with many struggles, all of which form the theme of history. History is, in what it records, the development of mind; it shows how the savage consciousness became more and more disciplined, its powers drawn out, its mere possibilities realized; and how a rude, passionate, arbitrary will, became refined and subject to the control of higher authority. The history of a nation is its character; if it be humane, the nation will be so; if bloody and rude, like that of Rome, the nation will be cruel; for history only develops what is in man.

Civilized nations differ then from savages by morality in its most extensive sense, by organized governments, and by having a history. Nations differ from each other as races and tribes, but their national differences are *historical* and consequently known to themselves, and thus they lose their strangeness and inimical power of opposition. These differences are expressed in the national manner of thinking and acting, in literature and art, language and style, customs and habits, morals and civil laws, in desires and peculiar inclinations. All of them enter into the habits of man, and whether a person is born of one or another nation, is by no means a matter of indifference. The Roman, even though the doctrine of a metamorphosis were true, could not at once be an Englishman. Anthropology has, therefore, to acknowledge a modification of mind, produced by national difference; and we shall give a short characteristic of the following nations, the French, the Italians, the English, and the Germans.

1. *The French.*

The Frenchman has been distinguished ever since the time of Cæsar for vivacity and excitability. He is full of enthusiasm, and easily roused. His cheerfulness cannot be eradicated even by misfortune, for the quickness and elasticity of his mind makes him seek by every possible means, either to remove the evil, or to render it more light. He deserves particular praise for refinement, socialness, and a great desire to anticipate the wishes of all those with whom he has intercourse. His politeness does not originate in selfish motives, but in a delicate feeling of propriety and decency, and in natural taste. Even when he disagrees with a person, or disapproves of any thing, he tries to express himself politely. With regard to intellect, clearness of understanding prevails in him; he submits every thing in science and poetry to its laws, and is particularly fond of mathematics. Though he is an admirer of poetry, his imagination, subject to the cool deliberation and calculation of his understanding, is not permitted to produce the mystical, nor to be active, by a kind of inspiration, but all its productions are accompanied by reflection, and hence they have more the character of oratory and eloquence, than that of pure poetry. The Frenchman is penetrating, spirited, sprightly, and witty, but he wants soul and solidity, and reverence for existing relations. The Frenchman however is no less proud of his Troubadours than of Lafontaine; of Racine, of Corneille and Moliere; of Descartes and Pascal, of Crebillon, Destouches and Marivau, of Voltaire, Rousseau, Guizot, etc.

The weakness of the Frenchman is his want of deep, decided individuality; his desire to be generally acceptable prevents the formation of a very determined character, for such an one will always stand more or less harshly opposed to society. He wants earnestness, seriousness, and depth of feeling, which the liveliness of his wit, light joviality, that interest only by their constantly changing elements, render impossible. His whole character, as Kant remarks, is expressed in his language, for what language can translate words like these: *frivolité; galantrie: petit-maitre; coquette; bon mot; naiveté?*

2. *The Italians.*

The name of the Italian reminds us at once of the land of beauty, of serene skies, and lovely scenery, of splendid sunsets and sunrises; and as if the genius that has thrown such loveliness over his country, had erected a dwelling in the breast of the Italian, animated his hand, and formed his imagination: we see his public saloons and churches and buildings adorned with the beauties of art. Music and poetry, painting and sculpture, have all met with a friendly reception under that mild sky, and it is in Italy, where even now, we must seek for their finest models. It has justly been remarked, that as the Frenchman is distinguished for good taste in society, and for refined manners, so the Italian is characterized by a most refined taste in art. Imagination is prominent in his intellectual powers; it is nourished by the charms of nature, and easily excited by a hot and fiery temperament. Dante's poem of the Universe; Petrarca's songs of love; Boccaccio's novels; Ariosto's smoothness of style, and flow of images and ideas; Tasso's Jerusalem Delivered; Gozzi's Comedies; Alfieri's Tragedies, and Manzoni's lyric and dramatic poetry, are all of them known to all the world. The Italian is, however, less celebrated for his scientific spirit.

The dark side of the Italian character is his great selfishness, and his unbridled desire for gain. Guided by this desire, he invented banks, lotteries, and checks. He is fond of pomp, of public processions, carnivals, masquerades, public buildings, and is willing to endure poverty if he can only have these pleasures. In general it may be said, that no where do the greatest poverty and riches live in closer connection than in Italy. The Italian is revengeful, and his knife is always ready for use. Banditti may be hired at all times. Cruelty is well marked in his character, and expresses itself even in his physiological experiments. We need only advert to those instituted by Spallanzani.

3. *The English.*

The Englishman possesses a manly, solid, and great disposition. He has spread his political power over a large portion of the earth, and by his commercial life he seems to be destined to cultivate rude nations. This gives him a strong feeling of importance. He is devoted to principles of honor and gentlemanliness, and always supports a lofty character. The greatness of his character expresses itself in all his enterprizes, for they are generally magnificent and on a large scale. A feeling of independence pervades all Englishmen; surrounded by the ocean, England is protected from inimical attacks, while its familiarity with that element enables it to make itself important in the eye of every political power in the world. The Englishman has a deep feeling of personal dignity, and maintains it with strong emphasis. A good, strong, common sense is his inheritance, and he is practical by nature. He comprehends quickly and accurately; perceives at first glance the combination of circumstances, and the most intricate complication of things, and in a moment devises means and ways to remove difficulties, and even to turn them to advantage. His judgment is acute and penetrating, and in whatever direction he desires to extend his business, he has the skill to do so. He is resolute and persevering, always active, and intent on his business. Nor is the Englishman destitute of true and genuine imagination; he has a full share of it. He loves the sublime more than the beautiful, though Shakspeare, the pride of the world, and the greatest poet not only of England, but of all nations, unites the beautiful and sublime. He loves to name Milton, Scott, Fielding and Goldsmith, Moore and Byron, etc., all of whom are poets of great genius. The English poetry is full of seriousness, of melancholy, and again of humor, and the most splendid imagery. Every where do we discover a desire to solve the great enigmas of life, or to meditate on and examine them. In science the Englishman is solid and accurate. He distinguishes well, and investigates accurately, and observes with a great deal of sound judgment. The French are clear and ingenious thinkers, but often superficial; the English are no less clear, but more profound, more solid writers, and stand in point of science and literature, decidedly above their rivals in politics.

The weak side of the English is a certain exclusiveness,

and a national pride, that too often prevents them from acknowledging the good qualities of other nations, merely because they are not their own.

4. *Germans.*

The German is not characterized by traits in disposition or intellect that are very showy or striking, like the Italian or Frenchman, but he unites in himself a number of good qualities, that are met with in other nations, and possesses them in such a harmony, that none prevails decidedly above the other, but all are permitted to be active. Yet there are a few features in his character which distinguish him decidedly. He is devoted to order and regularity, and always anxious to acknowledge the authority of law. He is therefore a good, quiet, and peaceable citizen, opposed to innovation, and full of a pious reverence for antiquity, for the views and customs of his ancestors. With this reverence he connects much prudence and circumspection, a regard for the future, and nothing is more foreign to him than frivolity or levity. Serious and earnest by nature, inclined to deep and solid meditation, and to lasting and warm emotions, he seeks for a worthy and noble aim of his life, and cannot rest satisfied with one that terminates in time, or even in the sphere of his own existence. His genuine disposition it would be difficult to express by English words, for its consists in *treuherzigkeit*, (trueheartedness) *gemuthlichkeit, bedenklichkeit,* (considerateness,) *gruebellust,* and in a *ahnungsvollen, geistrichen Ueberschwinglichkeit und Schwaermerei.* His talents are of a high order, but need long and much polish. Like the diamond, however, they will throw their light in all directions, when once called forth. W. V. Humboldt remarks, that those grapes which are not rapidly, but gradually ripened by a moderate heat, yield the best wine; experience teaches, that the richer a being is, the more it has to develope, the more time it will require to mature. The German certainly becomes by a long training, more conscious of all his mental powers than he would if his intellectual developement were more rapid. He loves truth, and seeks for it, independent of any selfish consideration. He is the *wholesale merchant* in literature, for his language contains the most faithful and perfect translations of *all the most celebrated works* in the world. The English enjoy all the productions of the earth and of every climate, the German appropriates to himself all the products of genius of all nations. As the Englishman is devoted to *gentlemanliness*, so the German reveres *honor*. With him the "word of honor" is equivalent to an oath, and any one that breaks it is considered an outlaw. The Germans were at all times fond of *personal* liberty, and their history cannot be understood without acknowledging this fact. This fondness for liberty was one of the sources of the Reformation, as it also animated the nation in 1813.

The German is proud of the *Niebelaagen lied*, of his Minne Singers, of Lessing and Klopstock, of Wieland and Herder, of Schiller and Goethe and Jean Paul Frederick Richter. He numbers among his philosophers a Leibnitz and Kant, a Fichte, Schelling, and Hegel. He claims a Herschel and Kepler; a John V. Mueller and Schlosser. Luther and Frederic I. are his great representatives. In Painting, Duerer and Cornelius are known to all the world; in Sculpture, Dannecker, Rauch, etc.; in Music, Sebastian, Bach, Haydn, Handel, Mozart, and Beethoven are greatly distinguished. The German style of art, when compared with the Italian may be said to be *significant*, while the Italian is *expressive*.

The weak side of the German is his pedantry in science and art, his too great dependance on external circumstances, which no doubt results from his regard for the customs and views of his ancestors and of all with whom he has any intercourse. The Englishman feels all the importance of his personality, and speaking of himself, says: "*I myself.*" The German is willing to forget himself in the presence of others. It is Shakspeare's delight to represent *persons*; Goethe's great forte is to characterize the objective world around him, and the different *situations*, in which persons might have to live. From his devotion to honor, the German overvalues its external signs, titles, orders, etc., and from his thorough and innate love of liberty, he frequently when passing over from a monarchical to a republican government, becomes rude, and ready to set all authority at defiance.

REMARK.

No two other nations in the world have exercised a more continued influence upon each other, than the Germans and the English. Their characters resemble each other in many respects, in seriousness, in fondness for deep and solid meditations, and in devotion to principles of honor and faithfulness. There were times, when English literature and English institutions were imitated throughout Germany; and there were others, when England drew richly from German works. The German law is still the basis of the English; and Scott and Byron show by their writings, that they were warm admirers of Goethe.

It may be asked: what is the exact difference, where there is so great an affinity? The general answer will be this; "The English are more practical, the Germans more theoretical." This answer is however insulting to both parties at once, and is incorrect. The English have their Cudworth, Locke, Bacon, David Hume, and many others; they have their great Divines and their Poets, all of whom were theoretical. The Germans on the other hand have changed, not by theory, but by their practical exertions the face of politics, by the invention of gun powder; that of practical religion, by the great reformation and that of science and general cultivation by the Printing Art. It is evident that the words *"practical and theoretical,"* are used improperly. They are placed in opposition to each other by the above judgment, while they are intrinsically united. Real practice needs much theory and the better the latter, the more solid will be the former. Genuine theory will always have practice in view as its end and chief object. Practice and theory are related to each other and the question is: what is the difference between them?

1. *Practice* is altogether as impossible without knowledge, as an action without a will. But this knowledge may be called practical, because it has a particular reference to application in life and contains the rules for it. As *knowledge* it must differ from *action*. All action has always a single, particular case in view; knowledge the general, that will apply to many individual cases; the objects of action are peculiarly modified by manifold circumstances, by local and temporary influences; the rules of knowledge are the same and action and knowledge do not entirely cover each other. But with all our actions we have in view *something general* too and thus *action* and *knowledge* are united. We desire either to realize the good, the true, the noble, the beautiful in our lives by action, and in this case we must know what is good and true. This is the fact with practical religion; without a theoretical acquaintance with the Old and New Testaments, or with the nature of God, our practical religion would be idolatry or heathenism, which is practical but has no theory; and it would therefore introduce vice and falsehood rather than the true

and good into our lives. Or we long to become rich; yet riches also are something general, and without an idea of property, of time and its duration, of right and laws, that guarantee an exclusive possession, we could not acquire wealth. But a code of laws, like the English, presupposes much knowledge. Rightly understood then *action* and *knowledge* do not contradict, but presuppose one another and it is only want of a teleological or theoretical judgment, awkwardness in applying it, a want of harmonious cultivation of all the faculties of mind, when the theorist is no more successful in his practice, than the quack.

2. As practice is impossible without knowledge, so theory is worth nothing without practice. The difference between practical and theoretical knowledge is this. The one contains the elements of an immediate application, the other not. The one asks: what *use* can be made of this truth? the other: what *is* this truth? wherein does it consist? The former seeks truth on account of the benefit, to be derived from it, the latter desires it on its *own account*, and not for the sake of something else, which it is to serve as means. In the one case, truth is rendered subservient to selfish interests, in the other it is considered more valuable than any thing else, the supreme good. Practical knowledge, having only usefulness in view, must spread itself over a large field; it thus becomes superficial. But no knowledge is less practical, than that which does not exhaust its subjects. Truly practical knowledge is solid and thorough; but all solid knowledge must be *theoretical*, must be acquired for its own sake, and as it is in itself, since every relation to something else renders it impure. No knowledge is more practical than that of mathematics, and yet it is entirely *theoretical*. So is no language more philosophical and theoretical than the German, and yet it expresses every shade of feeling and is extremely practical. Without examining here the origin of knowledge, we will only exhibit in a few words two kinds of theory. Both are united in having the same principles, but they differ in the manner of representing them. The one begins with single facts, observes and examines them, unites such as exhibit essential affinities under a common head, and as those excluded will show something common with each other, *new* classes will be formed, and a number of classes more allied to each other, than others will again become subordinate to a higher one. Every day adds new facts, and as the whole exists in its parts, this cannot be seen until all the latter have been collected. No one can say when this will be effected. According to this theory all heads and classes, or rather principles seem to have been gained by *observation*, and by uniting those facts, that show similarity. Yet unless man had formed an idea of *union* previous to his making experiments, he would and could not think of investigating single cases, since his investigations could not have any scientific object. This object is the union sought for. The other theory begins therefore with the principle of science, and

experience is to corroborate and prove it. It does not suffer itself to be drowned in the constantly increasing number of facts, nor to become confused by them. The principle is the life of all experiments, and is the same to science, that the centre is to a periphery. All the parts of science are organized by it and filled with it, as every member of the body indicates the presence of the soul. It attracts, what belongs to sciences and arranges it, and excludes what is foreign to it. This principle giving the science a systematical character, throws light upon all its parts by the mutual support, they afford to each other, and which proceeds from their position and relation to each other. This theory, it cannot be denied, has little reference to practice; it will exhaust truth, it will exhibit science as a whole; it does not desire to give rules for action. What then is its value? The former theory is engaged with single actions, for which it gives the rules, the latter examines the general nature of these rules. The former reduces the many single instances of language to general rules, the latter unfolds before us the principles of grammar, gives us the philosophy of it, and shows the necessity and connexion of the many single rules. Both kinds of grammers are necessary. They are related to each other as *history* and *philosophy* of *history*. The latter cannot be written without the former; yet the former is a mere collection of dry bones without the latter. The one demands great discrimination and penetrating acuteness; the other a productive genius. The one makes fine distinctions in given facts; the other derives deep and fruitful ideas from them.

§ 3. QUALITIES OF THE MIND, PRODUCED BY SEXUAL DIFFERENCE.

This difference is one that in the most decisive manner affects both body and mind. It is not transitory, but remains the same throughout life, so that many theologians have been led to ask whether the two sexes—something analogous to which we discover in the Negative and Positive poles, in contraction and expansion, in the relation of the sun to the earth,—will not be continued after death. The sexual difference manifests itself,

1. *Physically.* The whole organization in *all*, and not only in *some* of its parts is different in man and woman. Bones and muscles are stronger and more angular in man, and more tender and round in woman, while some are larger in the latter than in the former. Again, not only

the anatomical and organical systems, but also their functions differ in both. In man the arterial and cerebral systems prevail, and with them irritability; in woman the venous and ganglion systems and with them plasticity and sensibility. So the lungs are stronger, and hence the voice fuller, and respiration more copious in man, while the liver and its activity prevails in woman. Skin and hair are more soft in woman than in man, and it is evident, that the body of the one is better qualified than that of the other to endure labor.

2. *Psychologically*. Man and woman differ both in moral disposition and in mental qualities, as will appear from the following comparison.

WOMAN. As it respects in the first place *moral disposition*, we may say, *chastity* in feeling and imagination, in word and action, is the principal virtue that either of choice or unconsciously reigns in the bosom of woman. It is tender and delicate, like an exotic plant, and cannot endure exposure. Hence woman shrinks from appearing in public, whether in the pulpit or the rostrum, or with the sword in the hand, as the Maid of Orleans. The family is her sphere of action, there she arranges and orders what man gathers, and with propriety and taste embellishes the house, and renders it attractive. She desires whatever increases domestic comfort, as furniture and dress, order and cleanliness, full chests and drawers.—*Love* is the second prevailing virtue, that adorns her character. Without it she is like a closed blossom which exhibits neither its beauty or its fragrance; love reveals her inward mystery. She may love and not be aware of it, and such love is tender and innocent. But when once she loves, she gives her whole heart and person without reserve. She enters into all the wishes and views of him whom she has chosen. Pliny says of his wife, "she loves science, because she loves me. She carries with her my writings, she reads them, she commits them to memory. She sings my verses, she composes her own melodies to them, and needs no other teacher than love."—*Patience* is the third trait in her character and she is perhaps never more beautiful, than when the tear trembles through a smile. Sympathy and compassion, kindness and mildness, cheerfulness and warm-heartedness, are charms thrown around her by nature.

Secondly, as it respects *mental* qualities; here *Feeling* predominates; she receives easily, and appropriates quickly; she forms what she receives and feels herself attracted by all that can touch the heart. Her thinking rests more on feeling than on faith, and is not directed to skeptical investigations. It is not distinguished for productiveness, for if we look at the fine arts, we cannot discover a single woman who has established a new school either in painting, in music, or sculpture. Some women have become celebrated for their skill in imitation, as Angelica Kauffman in painting, or as the nuns of the Netherlands in musical concerts; but imitation as well as learning rests on faithful reception. In architecture no woman ever attempted anything; in music we have no female composer of celebrity; in poetry, the ancients knew one Sappho, but no female Homer or Pindar, and our modern female poets have done little in the highest departments of poetry, the Drama, Epic, Lyric. The sphere of woman being *feeling* and *beauty*, she is not expected to become learned but *cultivated*. Cultivation is no less valuable and difficult of attainment than learning; the former rests on taste, the latter often merely on memory. Yet there have been learned ladies, that had good taste, fine judgment, and quick intuition, as Madame de Stael. Law and juridicial knowledge seems particularly attractive to them, perhaps because they love order. At all events it is remarkable, that it was a woman who presided over right and order among the Greeks, Themis, the mother of the Horae and Parcae. Her servants likewise, were women, the Erinnyae, Dike and Nemesis Adrastea. Demeter gave statutes to cities, and Egeria furnished Numa Pompilius with his laws. Welleda did the same in the north, and the old Germans commenced no war without having consulted their women. Deborah gave judgment during forty years under the palm-trees on Mount Ephraim. And in modern times we see a Mathilda of Tuscany encourage the revival of the Pandects, and give celebrity by them to the University of Bologna. Two daughters of professor Andreas, both of them married to lawyers, lectured to large audiences from the rostrum, when their husbands were absent. So two other Italian ladies were known to appear in disguise on the rostrum, and their lectures on law were well received by numerous students. Many women have obtained the degree of LL. D., and in France many have published large works on Law. In mathematics on the other hand, astronomy, metaphysics, history or medicine, none scarcely have acquired celebrity. And this is not accidental, not because no opportunity has offered itself to their productive genius,—genius will always find its way—but because it is their highest happiness to be *mothers*.

MAN. *Moral disposition.* In man thought and will prevail, and a desire for liberty and honor. He must act and work, toil and labor, and can preserve his dignity and standing in the world only by acting from principles and clear comprehensions. He is to provide for the family, to protect it, procure for it honor and respectability. If patience adorns woman, *courage* belongs to man. In some languages his name is derived from the same root from which the words for *courage and virtue* were taken. Public life is the sphere of man; there he is to labor and to execute his ideas. As he is to drain swamps, to clear woods, to subdue wild nature, to destroy rapacious animals, and render climates mild, and inhospitable regions habitable, so he is to adorn the pulpit and the rostrum, the judge's bench and the art of the physician, and to cultivate music, painting, sculpture, architecture, poetry, and science. As Hercules represents the former, so Apollo the latter employment. If woman is mild and forgiving, man must be *just* in governing himself, his family, and all intrusted to his charge. If woman always observes what is right from a sense of propriety, man must insist on the execution of the laws, when they have been violated. Independence renders man, faithfulness and confidence render woman happy. Man desires what strengthens his feeling of importance. The horse, the sword, the chase and war, riches and titles, honors, influence and power, are welcomed by him. Woman may shed tears without words, man must connect action with them.

Mental qualities. Productiveness, which has no limits in any science or art, as far as they are accessible to the human mind, characterizes the mind of man. Every invention in mechanical art, every style of the fine arts, every advance in science has as yet been effected by man. It is his office to produce and realize ideas in politics, in arts, and science; to know and investigate, understand and represent. Only one government has as yet been found that was entirely managed by women, and this among the negroes in Africa.

When we look on the characters of man and woman, we cannot but perceive that neither is perfect by itself, but that each needs the other for its perfection. Each possesses something which is wanted in the other, and hence only their union forms a complete character. Neither can endure therefore to remain by itself. Strength and courage rest in man, mildness and tenderness in women; united, these qualities form one whole, separated, the former will degenerate into rudeness and ferocity, and the latter into inconsistency and fickleness. Hence the one must be softened by tender emotions, and the other strengthened by firmness.—Again: Cold understanding may easily become too calculating, too arithmetical, too selfish, when not refined by generous emotions of kindness and love. The timidity of woman on the other hand, her fearfulness needs a prop on which to rest.—The union of both in one is externally represented by marriage. Through it the strength of man is rendered mild by the gentleness of woman, his courage is moderated by her softness and timidity, and his understanding receives warmth of feeling. So the qualities of woman receive their finish by their union with those of man, for her feeling obtains proper nourishment through his intercourse with the world, as her timidity relies safely on his strength. Thus both intended for each other are truly what they ought to be when united, and the object of the original difference between man and women, is the richest and closest union of both.

This union, which commences with love, has its pledge and visible appearance in the child; for the mental qualities and moral capacities of both father and mother, continue themselves in their children, and these appear as an individual identity, so that, what before was given to *two*, is now represented by one. This we perceive daily by recognizing in a child some qualities of the father, and others of the mother. The consciousness of this fact constitutes family attachment. It is true, that the sons of celebrated men often appear to be without extraordinary degrees of talent, and again that sons of men, little known, exhibit uncommon capacity. But it must be admitted that in the former case the father may have exhausted the inheritance of his nature, and that the greatness of his name induces us to apply too high a measure, by which to judge of the talents of the son; as was the case with the sons of Goethe and Schiller. In the latter case the natural capacities of the father may not have been developed, or the son inherited his bright genius from the mother. So Goethe says that he inherited his love of poetry from his mother, and many other traits in his character, as, for example, an aversion to all violent impressions, a rich vein of everteeming wit, of humour, &c.; these we recognize in that of his mother. Madame Letitia Bonaparte had four sons, all of whom were energetic and men of talents; her husband is little known, and no doubt the sons inherited what they possessed from her. Hence the great importance of knowing the mother, her disposition, her character and talents, when we desire to judge correctly of distinguished men. We come then, to the natural qualities of the *individual.*

These depend on all the influences we have before represented from that of climate to that of sex, including those of race, nation, occupation, &c. The qualities that exclusively belong to the individual are *temperaments, mental capacities* and *idiosyncracy.*

§ 4. TEMPERAMENTS.

The soul is not only connected with the body, but they are interfused so that the nature of the one must affect that of the other. When all the functions of assimilation are fresh and vigorous, when respiration is easy, when digestion and circulation of blood, excretion and secretion are regular and natural, then the sensations will be full and lively, the whole mind will be youthful, and feel, think and *will* with energy. When, on the other hand, we suffer much from rheumatism, headache, from shortness of breath or dyspepsy, the spirits will be low, the mind feel depressed, and especially the system of sensibility must become weakened. The will and resoluteness of man may, in some degree, overcome such difficulties and sufferings. Tieck is much afflicted with rheumatism, and yet his poetry is cheerful and humorous. Beethoven lost his hearing, and yet he continued to compose the most sublime works. Buttman could not bear the slightest breath of cold air, and nevertheless he was constantly engaged in revising, correcting, and completing his excellent Greek grammar and other works. Such instances are, however, rare, and are exceptions to the general rule.

The body of man consists of *three* principal vital systems. The first of them is that of *sensibility*. By it man feels himself and the world around him. Its principal organ is the brain and nervous system. The second is that of *irritability*. Its tendency is to resist the influences exercised by external objects upon man, and at the same time to bring them into subjection to him. Its organ is the heart and muscular system. The third is that of *reproductiveness*. By it our body preserves itself, and in so doing, seizes on whatever may serve it as food. Its organ is the liver and intestinal system.

Through these systems the body is connected with the soul, and the peculiar manner in which this connection is modified by the prevalence of the one or the other, is called *temperament*. This word is derived from *temperare*, which means to unite or moderate two extremes; and hence the term *temperature* as applied to the atmosphere. Temperament might, therefore, be defined to be the peculiar connection of soul and body in an individual. This connection becomes peculiar by the prevailing fluids of the body, their *lymphatic, sanguine, choleric,* and *bilious* nature ; by the prevailing elements, as *water, air, fire,* or *earth ;* by the nature of the *blood*, which is either *cold* or *warm, light* or *heavy;* by that of the *fibres*, which are either *lax* or *firm, soft* or *hard*. All these must affect our *feeling*, this our *thinking*, and this again our *will*.

It is easy to understand the origin of temperaments. All empirical knowledge and sensual desires are qualified by sensation. Sensation is impossible without the senses, and these are impossible without nerves. All our knowledge is accompanied by feeling, and all the actions of our will pre-suppose both *feeling* and *knowledge*. The more perfect and easy the functions of the nervous system are, the less they are interrupted or interfered with, the greater, stronger and livelier will be the power of feeling, thinking and willing. For the more easy it is to excite our senses, the more clear our sensations must be ; the more clear the sensations, the more definite and accurate our knowledge, and the stronger the feeling connected with it, and the volition proceeding from it. Now if the muscular system prevails, the nervous will be proportionally weak. Hercules, in the Grecian mythology, had strong muscles, but was not distinguished for strength of mind. Apollo, on the other hand, was physically weaker, but prevailed by clearness of thought. If the system of reproductiveness prevails over the others, a tendency to rest or inactivity becomes perceptible. We have *four* different temperaments; the *sanguine* stands connected with the system of sensibility ; the *melancholic* with that of reproductiveness ; while the system of *irritability* by its twofold relation to the arterial and venous blood produces the *choleric* temperament, when the arterial, and the *phlegmatic,* when the venous blood prevails.

The temperaments do not directly originate in the individual, but in circumstances preceding its existence, in climate, locality, in the season of birth, &c. Hence many feel inclined to consider them as accidental. Every man, they say, must have a temperament, but which of the four seems to be wholly accidental. So every man must have eyes, but whether they are blue or black is accidental. Children of the same parents may have very different temperaments, as, for instance, those of Madame Letitia Bonaparte. Though it may be accidental, whether a man is born with the choleric or melancholic temperament, he will retain it through life, and though the phlegmatic may modify his temperament by change of climate, by food, and drink, he cannot change it into the sanguine. Yet while none can change his temperament, he may subdue it, and exercise it as he pleases. With some its power is naturally weak. Leibnitz knew not whether he was choleric, or sanguine, or phlegmatic. Nor does any temperament appear in its perfect purity, but as the prevalence of one system does not exclude the functions of the others, so the phlegmatic does not destroy entirely the symptoms of the melancholic, but frequently they approach so near each other, that it is difficult to distinguish the one from the other. And again, the same temperament will be differently modified in different persons.

The Sanguine Temperament.

This is the temperament of *enjoyment* and *pleasure*. It has great susceptibility to impressions of every kind so that the person is ready and longs to receive them; but many impressions cannot take possession at the same time of the same breast; one extinguishes the other and the last is always the most vigorous. This temperament partakes of the nature of the air, which by its great elasticity yields to every pressure, and directly afterwards regains its former state. Liveliness, cheerfulness, and a never-ceasing desire for enjoyment characterize it, and its mobility is like that of the birds, that constantly live in and are filled with the air. An individual of sanguine temperament finds it difficult to govern his temperament, to conquer its tendency to levity and to trifling employment.—Persons of this temperament incline strongly to Belles-Lettres, but prefer the brilliant, the pleasant, and the copious to the more solid, the truly beautiful and simple. It is the temperament of the French nation; though fond of the fine arts, they have not produced anything very remarkable either in Painting, Sculpture or Music. The system of materialism is principally favored by them in Philosophy. Their courage is full of fire for the moment, but soon passes by; their emotions are quick, but short; they are careless, communicative, benevolent, but feel averse to labor and pain. La Fontaine was sanguine. His poetry bears the stamp of this character.

The Choleric Temperament.

This may be called the temperament of *action*. It resists external impressions, and re-acts on every thing that affects it. Feeling its power, it is courageous, determined, and possesses much energy and perseverance. Its nature resembles that of fire; nothing is more energetic and more active than fire; its activity does not bluster like that of the wind, it does not stagnate like water, but continues without interruption, until the elements of existence are consumed. So, little insects that depend much on the warmth of the sun, are indefatigable in their ruinous activity, and though small, they are very destructive. The choleric temperament is excitable, yet not by little things, as the sanguine; but when excited, it perseveres in the plan which it has chosen. Strong in its inclinations it is faithful, but no less subject to great passions, to ambition, to despotism, to wrath and other vehement impressions. Its activity thus vibrates between life and death, between producing and destroying. It is the temperament of despots, and of such men, as seem to be destined for the chastisement of nations, for, magnanimous and brave, courageous and proud, it is jealous, vindictive and malicious, inclined to violence and obstinacy. Its bent is to practical pursuits; it is quick of understanding, acute in judgment, clear and precise in its expressions, and its productions in the arts are manifold and expressive. This is the temperament of the Spaniards and Italians, and was that of Napoleon. "Every action excited him only to a new one. When at war, he thought of the advantage to be gained from a truce; when he had effected it, he thought of the ways and means to break it. In France he thought of Russia, in Russia of India. Even at St. Helena he was engaged in dictating a history of his own adventures, or in reviewing those of others, as those of Cæsar or Alexander." If the sanguine lives wholly for the *present*, in which alone he can enjoy himself, the choleric is forced to dwell with his plans in the *future*, for all action is preceded by a resolution and separated from it by the lapse of time.

The Melancholic Temperament.

A constant *longing* and *desire*, and inclination to retire or withdraw into itself, are the characteristics of this temperament. All its activity receives its impulse from reflection on the past, on the vanity of all things, and especially of human affairs. The ruins of former days exhibit on the one hand the greatness of man, and thus rejoice the heart, and on the other they indicate the decay of all that is sublunary, and fill the heart with sadness; thus joy and sadness commingle, and give a tendency to seriousness, to meditation, and frequently to speculation. To the melancholy all that is near and clear to others is still at a distance, and as the blue color of the sky, which presents itself to our eye when it gazes into the immense depth above us, or which envelopes distant mountains, awakes a longing for something unknown, so every thing, however well-ascertained, serves only to call up in the breast a desire for something still deeper and higher and purer. It delights to live in the regions of truth, of beauty, of the sublime, and the romantic. It feels indifferent to the sensual world, and the eye, turned inwardly, indicates this by its coldness and want of animation. In science it is deep and inclined to skeptical researches. In art it aims at expression, as in the German school of music.

We find a remarkable instance of this temperament in Chateaubriand. "Brought up in an old castle in Bretagne, his melancholy was nourished, even in his youth. During the revolution he dreams in the woods of America; he sings of the introduction of the christian religion into Gaul; he makes a pilgrimage to the holy sepulchre; examines the haven of old Carthage; reads Milton's Paradise Lost in England; full of romance, he attempts to defend the old stage by writing his Moses, a drama that was never exhibited; he upholds the legitimacy of Henry V., retires from public life, writes the history of France, and in his memoirs complains of ennui, while the world around him is undergoing new developments." Byron is another instance. Nothing could satisfy him except the past, the ancient literature of Greece, &c.

The Phlegmatic Temperament.

In this, *self-possession* prevails, which does not suffer itself to be carried away by external impressions, nor does it permit any of the one-sided characteristics of the previous temperament to reign, but retains its full dominion over all the influences exercised upon it, and over all its re-actions. It has therefore the capacity of entering into every situation and feeling, and is accessible on all sides. It is moderate in all things, in joy and grief, in mirth and sadness, in labor and rest. This perfect equilibrium renders it possible to retain at all times its liberty and personal dignity. The sanguine temperament is dependent on external impressions; the choleric on its internal passionateness, which does not allow cool reflection; the melancholic on its longing, that ever fills all its thoughts and feelings;—but the phlegmatic is independent of all of them. It has its centre and union in itself, and is aware of this fact; it has found *itself*, and while in the other temperaments the consciousness of the world is principally active, in this *self-consciousness* prevails. In proportion as our consciousness is related to something external, we are dependent on it; but in proportion as it is related to itself, and independent of any thing apart from itself, we are free. The phlegmatic temperament has frequently been wronged, and looked on as inferior to the others, because its features are not so striking; and yet it alone renders it easy to man to preserve to himself his liberty, and to move without prejudice and pre-determination, in whatever direction of science or art he chooses. Its seeming indifference and rest is not without activity and deep interest, but like the lake, the waters of which seem motionless on the surface while rivulets and fresh waters are constantly flowing in, and though unseen, keep up a gentle but healthy and lively activity, so this is always devoted to some action, without much display. Its talents are highly respectable, its ideas deep and clear, its style rather dry, but profound and accurate. In art it is faithful, as in the Dutch school with its landscapes and family-pictures.

Its possessor is in danger of becoming indolent, indifferent, and fond of eating and drinking.

Aristotle asserted that the melancholy temperament was most favorable to science and art. He quotes among the rest Socrates, of whom Plato says, that in the midst of the noise of an encampment, he fell into a deep meditation, and stood immovably in one place, from one morning to another, until the rising sun roused him, to offer his prayer. Empedocles, Plato, Homer, Phidias, Dante, Raphael, Handel, and other distinguished scholars had the same temperament. Yet it is the will that reigns in man, and not the temperament; the former, and not the latter, forms the character, nor does talent and genius depend on it. Moses and Paul were choleric. Oberlin was sanguine, and the celebrated Rembrandt phlegmatic. One temperament will make it more easy than another, to lead a life according to determined principles, or to enter on some scientific or practical pursuit. The choleric, for instance, is favorable to practical business, for it is the temperament of action; the sanguine to Belles-Lettres, for it is that of enjoyment; the melancholy to deep speculation, for it is that of desire; and the phlegmatic to thorough and universal learning, for it is that of self-possession and patience. The temperaments will thus connect themselves with mental capacities, and infuse into them liveliness or ease; zeal or indifference; quickness or slowness; cheerfulness or dullness; resoluteness or tardiness.

§ 5. MENTAL CAPACITIES.

Of these a twofold view is to be taken, with regard to the *intensity* of their strength and energy, and with regard to the *objects*, to which they are instinctively directed.

I. In respect to energy, and degree of strength, our mental faculties are to be divided into three classes, that of *docility* or mere *capacity*, of *talents*, and of *genius*.

1. *Docility.*

Every man is born with the possibility to learn, and this possibility has its origin and ground in God, the Creator. Hence Plato, when he was about to die, thanked the gods, that they had created him a man and not an animal. This general possibility may be called the capacity of mind to receive ideas or knowledge, and every one, who is conscious of himself, is endowed with it. It is therefore something *general* and qualifies every one who has it, to become a moral agent, and to feel religious affections. Religion and moral character being the two greatest accomplishments of man in this life, no one has a right to complain that his talents are less distinguished than those of others. Some of us are rich, others poor, but all may live and realize the end of life, if they are diligent and faithful. To *learn* is to be active; but learning, as the act by which we acquire knowledge, is an intellectual activity, that has a certain end in view and is subject to certain rules, excluding the arbitrariness of him who learns. Thus his mind is disciplined. To learn, means therefore in the first place to *receive* what is communicated. But that which is communicated by instruction is not a single thing, nothing sensual, but *a general* idea, a general notion or a general rule. Learning, therefore, demands not only the power of perceiving clearly and distinctly single objects, but of perceiving that which is common to many of them, or it demands the power of comprehending the many in one. The animal may be broken in or taught to perform certain services, but it cannot comprehend principles or general laws. To perceive the general nature of a single object means nothing less than to refer it to its class. I ask, *What is this?* And receive this answer, *A rose.* Thus the single plant is classified, and I henceforth shall know every other flower of the same species. To learn in the second place means to *judge theoretically.* We must distinguish between our perceptions and the objects perceived. There are many objects; all must be classified; every object is related to itself, that is, has parts which are related to each other, and these again must be distinguished. Finally, a distinction must be made between substance and accidents, the essential, and unessential, &c. To notice all these, we must pay close attention. To learn in the third place means to *be attentive.* And in the last it means to *remember* that which has been received.

2. *Talent.*

When the mere *capacity* becomes an *ability*, so that we are not only receiving, but in being taught, teach ourselves and feel an inclination to apply rules and principles and to produce effects we may call it *talent.* The man endowed with talent, has acute perceptions and comprehends quickly, precisely, easily,—hence facility from *facile*—adds nothing and overlooks nothing. He distinguishes accurately not only between the different qualities, but also between the essential and accidental, and he discovers connections and separations, differences and unions, harmonies and contradictions, causes and effects, grounds and consequences, where the man that has mere capacity cannot observe them. His attention is easily attracted and interested in all that presents itself in the sphere of his science; and his memory is not only faithful, but prompt and vivid. To improve a science, demands talent; but mere talent is confined to certain spheres as to the extent of its productiveness; nor is it new and original, but fixes itself always on materials that are historically handed down to it. It transforms, imitates, or leads out. So Virgil imitated Homer; Horace imitated Pindar; Cicero the Greek philosophers.

3. *Genius.*

When any one possesses all the qualities of talent in a still higher degree, he is said to have genius—from *genus.*— Here acuteness of judgment is united with depth, which dives into the nature and being of all things, and is not satisfied with their nearest, but always demands their *last* hidden element or foundation. Acuteness and depth are seldom united, but where we meet both in one person, we see the highest grade of genius. With genius the understanding is flexible and capable of entering with ease into the views, feelings and character of any one, so that a few words spoken by a person will enable it to understand and represent the whole character of that person; or a single outline will cause it to produce the whole picture. Attention is constantly awake and active; and memory, aided by imagination, is not only prompt and vivid, but productive, giving a new, and more attractive form to every thing intrusted to it. Thoughts present themselves without labor; and the progress in art and science demands but little exertion to astonish any one who observes it. Even in times of rest true genius is on the advance. The character of genius is therefore evidently productive and inventive. It is new, and frequently comes in contact with established rules. Yet it is not arbitrary in its productions, but follows a rational necessity, the ground and reason of which it can understand. Nor is it correct to think, that genius needs no study. It is not enough to produce new ideas, we must also know how to express them well. But this demands exercise. Leonardo Da Vinci said, "If your son has genius, put him to a master after he has studied anatomy and perspective." It is for this reason that poverty is more favorable to genius than wealth, for it renders exertion necessary. Goethe rose every morning at an early hour, and studied regularly the whole day. Leibnitz sat for weeks in his chair without taking any exercise. Nothing can be more perverse, than the notion that genius works altogether like instinct. Shakspeare is generally adduced as an example, and though it must be admitted that he had not a complete education, his works show a great amount of knowledge which he must have acquired in some way or other. He lived in an age, which being filled with romantic views, was highly favorable to poetry, and cultivated the genius of the great poet much more than an age like ours, wholly given to practical pursuits could do. In Shakpeare's time, the poet and the public exercised a much greater mutual influence on each other than they now do.

True genius is rare, and hence it is a gift that is desired by many. But as a few only possess it, many may be seen to make pretensions to it, while they have scarcely talent.

II. In respect to the objects to which our mental capacities or talents have a peculiar tendency, we say that a man has the *aptitude*, or *ability*, or *qualification* for the performance of something, or for a study when his talents are perfectly adapted to a certain sphere of activity. Thus far we have only spoken of the energy of mental capacities; here we shall treat of the sphere of action, to which they are directed by nature. At the same time the degree of their energy will exhibit itself in the greater or less ease, with which persons perform the labors for which their talents qualify them. Many may therefore have an inclination to the same art or science or practical pursuit, while their success will be very different, though they should all of them be equally diligent. The objective spheres for the subjective capacities of man may be divided into three general fields: *Science; practical pursuits;* and *the fine arts.* Each of them may be subdivided again, and every subdivision will demand a peculiar qualification.

The qualifications for *science* in general are an innate desire for knowledge, sound judgment, and a good memory. Now it may be that a man has memory as a talent, but judgment merely as capacity, and then he will easily receive and retain knowledge and accumulate a great amount of it, but his knowledge will be only held together by the order of succession externally, as beads are united by the string that passes through them. Here judgment requires much exercise. Or a man possesses judgment as a talent and memory as a mere capacity. Such a man has a limited knowledge, but what he knows, he knows well and according to logical order of cause, and effect, and ground, and consequence. But as all objects of knowledge have a bearing upon each other, memory ought to be exercised. Or finally a man possesses both memory and judgment as talents, and then he will not only learn well and much, but improve science and enrich the store of general knowledge. The study of history requires a strong, prompt and faithful memory, a lively imagination, that can enter into the spirit of past ages, and the characters and situations of historical heroes, impartiality of judgment, and an ardent interest in the human race. And here, again, mere chronology rests more on memory, than on judgment; the representation on the other hand, of the customs, manners, arts, sciences, politics and laws of different nations, their characters, the design of historical actions, their results and historical criticism demand much teleological judgment; and the philosophy of history is impossible without great talent and genius. So the study of metaphysics is founded on a desire for knowledge, that is not satisfied with knowing many things, but seeks for their ground and nature, and desires in all its knowledge such a systematical connection, as will give to every portion its proper place. And the study of Natural sciences; geology, geography, botany, zoology, pre-suppose great powers of observing, skill in arranging our perceptions logically, readiness in naming and describing them well; it requires too, the gift of invention, of making experiments, and of construing, developing and applying them.

The *practical* talent has likewise its different objects, as agriculture, mechanical arts, trade, political, medical, juridical pursuits, &c. The qualifications for them may range from mere capacity to genius. The latter will invent new ways and means, new instruments and machines, new institutions and regulations. Every business demands *tact*, that is the gift to perceive quickly and correctly the point on which all depends; *dexterity* in choosing at once the right means; *resoluteness* to act promptly and without delay or fear; *expeditiousness* in dispatching work cheerfully and energetically, and finally an *enterprising spirit.*

The qualifications for the *fine arts* must always exist either as talents or as genius. We may enjoy the productions of art without having a talent for them, or without being blessed with genius, but the artist cannot produce any thing worth having without a high degree of talent. The object of art is to represent truth in a sensible form. Three things are indispensable for the artist, a strong and productive imagination, the inspiration of a great and noble idea, and skill to realize this idea either in marble or on the canvass. And here again, the different arts pre-suppose different qualifications. Architecture with its labyrinths, obelisks, pyramids, temples and palaces, rests on a sense of regularity, symmetry and harmonious proportions. Sculpture is confined to the white marble, which colorless receives the idea of the master, only by having it fully expressed on its surface. A sense for *form*, and a particular dexterity in wielding the chisel, constitute the particular qualifications for sculpture. Painting adds the eye to its pictures, and thus is able to represent man in all his relations, to represent his feelings, his actions and motives. A sense for colors, for light and shade, indicate talents for it.

Music expresses only sensations and feelings, and its material is *sound*. A fine and delicate ear, an inclination to rhythm, harmony and melody will qualify for it. Poetry, from the epic to the dramatic, demands genius in the highest degree and an unlimited power over language.

Not every artist is capable of moving in every sphere of his art with the same ease. Homer was great in epic, Sophocles in tragic, Pindar in lyric poetry. Petrarch gained immortal glory by his sonnets, and not by those works, from which he expected to enjoy his greatest fame. Shakspeare on the other hand, and Goethe were universal.—Much less still can one artist judge correctly of all the arts or be equally successful in them. Goethe never presumed to judge of music; Michael Angelo's sonnets are forgotten, as are the works of sculpture produced by the hands of Socrates. Roos was an excellent hand in drawing ruminating animals, but he failed when he attempted any thing out of his sphere. There is a relation between the talents of an artist and their proper objects, which makes them completely transparent to the artist, and grants him an insight into their nature, that enables him to transfer himself wholly into their situation. Where this natural relation is wanting, the artist ought to acknowledge the limits of his productive powers.

We have thus seen, that our natural capacities differ not only with regard to their energy, but also to the external sphere of activity for which they qualify man, and the question remains, What is it that causes this difference? As the animal has instinct, so man has an innate *tendency to acquire knowledge*. The greater or less strength and excitability of this natural tendency, will call forth the activity of reason, which is the principle of all talents and genius, in a higher or lower degree, either as a capacity or as a talent. When that tendency is strong enough to remove all difficulties with regard to its object, we possess the activity of mind as a mere capacity. When on the other hand it requires but little excitement from without to act in full energy, we have talent. When finally that natural tendency is not only strong enough to remove all difficulties, but excites to productiveness, and animates, for example, the fingers of the painter, to create forms and proportions, or the imagination of the musician, to compose melodies and harmonies, we have genius.

In the next place it is the same innate tendency, to acquire knowledge, which directs our talents to certain objects. This tendency in its lowest stage includes instinct, which points out to it its proper sphere. The sphere of instinct is sensation, that of the tendency to acquire knowledge, is apperception, consciousness. But all talents presuppose strong and acute senses, and consciousness is impossible without sensation. As instinct directs the animal by one or the other sense to its proper food, so it silently influences the direction, which the desire for knowledge in man takes to certain objects. The painter needs a correct eye, the musician a delicate ear; both are instinctively directed to their arts by their senses. Mozart, when only six years old, on hearing a violin, stated that its sound was one-eighth lower than that of one which he had heard the day before. When both were compared, his remark was found to be correct.

Some talents show themselves earlier in life than others. That for music needs no nourishment from without, but draws all its compositions from its own resources, and hence it early manifests itself. Mozart was but five years old when he entertained large companies with his performances. Beethoven did so in his eighth year, and Hummel in his ninth. As talents depend on the strength and activity of our desire for knowledge, so this must be awakened by our sensations, by the sight of objects, and acquaintance with them, to which they are adapted. Correggio, on seeing a picture of Raphael, exclaimed, "*Anch io sono pittore.*" I too am a painter. Thucydides hears a lecture of Herodotus, his eyes fill with tears, and he becomes conscious of his latent talent. La Fontaine hears, for the first time in his twenty-second year, a few verses of Malherbe's poems, and awakes from a long dream, perceiving at once his innate qualification for poetry. The early or late development may, therefore, frequently depend on circumstances. But a difference in this respect is also produced by the object on which genius is to exercise itself. Ovid, when yet a boy, made verses whenever he wrote. Melancthon received the degree of A. M. in his fourteenth year, and in his eighteenth he was professor of the Greek language in a celebrated university.

§ 6. IDIOSYNCRASY.

By *idiosyncrasy* we understand that *peculiarity* of a constitution, by virtue of which the individual feels either sympathy with a certain object, or antipathy against it, or indifference towards it. *This peculiarity* is based on the correspondence of our nervous system with certain objects or persons. Idiosyncrasy does not belong to the whole race, its character is therefore not generic; as, for example, the aversion of one class of animals to another, or that of man to serpents, but it belongs exclusively to certain individuals, and because of its singularity, it is difficult to account for it. Sometimes a sudden fright of the mother may leave a never-dying impression on the soul of the child, and idiosyncrasy may frequently take its rise in that early state of life, as was the case with James I., who could not endure the sight of a naked sword, or with the Grand Duke of Epernon, who swooned at the sight of a young hare. In all instances it is certain, that the utterance of sympathy or antipathy rest not on judgment, but on mere feeling. In common life the attraction of different persons to each other rests either on an internal equality or resemblance which is recognized in spite of all external difference, or on a common interest which is determined by the capacities of those that feel it. In both cases we are guided by judgment. *Sympathy*, or antipathy, on the other hand, while they likewise found themselves upon such an internal resemblance or inequality of individuals, are the immediate utterance of feeling, and not of a clear judgment. Persons meet for the first time, and feel themselves attracted without knowing each other, or they feel themselves repelled like balls tossed against each other. It is as if this internal equality or inequality were more perceived by a kind of presentiment than any thing else; it resembles the attractive power of magnet and of iron, of the negative and positive pole. In the world of morals, the like loves to associate with like, the good with the good, and the bad with the bad; but sympathy, founded on mere feeling, demands always some polar difference in two persons that otherwise resemble each other in habits and taste. Two persons, perfectly alike, frequently feel an aversion to each other, as two keys, near each other on the piano, harmonize less than two separated by a third. But when there is a polar relation between the two, so that the one possesses positively what the other does negatively, then they will attract each other. This is the case between persons of different sexes. Such a difference is not opposition, but proceeds from an original union. Sympathy then rests on a natural correspondence between the nervous systems of two persons or their disposition. This correspondence is only felt, and not clearly known. Hence it is that frequently a single movement of the lips, or a peculiar glance of the eye may call forth sympathy or antipathy.

An interesting fact is related of two monks, who so sympathised with each other, that when the one was taken sick, the other would feel unwell; and when the former recovered, the latter would be delivered from pain. Petrarch states, that when once Laura suffered much from pain in her eyes, and he felt very much for her, his eyes began to experience the same pain.

Antipathy must be explained on the same principles, and we will therefore only give a few remarkable instances from Schubert in his history of the soul. The celebrated Erasmus became feverish when he smelt fish. The distinguished Scaliger, when near a water-cress, trembled in his whole body. Simon Ponli felt strong palpitation of the heart when fresh apples were brought into his room. A little opium laid in the ear of a patient caused his death, and the sight of white horses acted as a powerful cathartic with another. A man, that had recovered from a long disease, swooned, when he smelt bread, and another felt himself violently purged when he smelt broth. Baco swooned during an eclipse of the moon; and P. Boyle, when he heard the noise, which is caused by water, pouring forth from a spigot. Honey with some persons has the effect of poison; and the aversion felt by many to caterpillars, spiders, mice, and toads, is well known.

It is usual to speak also under the general head of idiosyncrasy of *apathy*. Physically, this is the state of the system when no medicine can reach it. A man much engaged in alchemy could take four ounces of sweetened and sublimated mercury without being purged. Psychologically it is the absence of every kind of interest in many things which attracts others easily.

CHAPTER II.

OF THE TRANSIENT INFLUENCE OF NATURE UPON THE MIND.

All the modifications of mind which we shall have to consider in this chapter, are such, as are not permanently the same, but subject to changes, and periodical. The first are those produced by *age*.

§ 1. AGE.

They are not permanent. The child does not remain a child, but grows and becomes a youth; and the youth developes itself, matures and becomes man or woman. None of these stages is therefore fixed, but the one passes over into the other. Yet with these transitions, changes both of the physical and psychological nature take place, and as may be anticipated, not accidentally, not without some good design. As in the plant, those leaves which appear first and are nearest to the soil, are also least formed, and their substance more rude, so man in his childhood shows physically little expression in his face, and psychologically is confined to mere sensations and perceptions. But as the leaves grow higher from the soil as they are more exposed to the air, and the influence of the light, the juice becomes more refined, the color more fresh and tender and all the forms grow more perfect, until finally on the top of the plant many delicate leaves cluster around one centre and form the bud, from which the flower in all its beauty bursts on us. This is the youth of the plant. When the flower fades, the seed will begin to ripen, and when the seed is matured, the fruit will decay. Here we have the picture of man. His youth is the flowering season of the plant. Sensation and perception have been well exercised and now the powers of imagination, of fancy, of memory, and the capacity to receive and digest new ideas, are to be cultivated, for they are principally active, and indicated in the bloom of the face, in the fire of the eye, and by all the emotions of the heart. When these powers of the mind, have been sufficiently attended to, they fade, and judgment, reflection, thought, and practical activity grow forth from them, until the ripened soul causes the body to decay, as the seed the plant. Should we now venture to pronounce the design of the ages, we should say;—the soul enters the world in a state of involution, and its destiny is to unfold and manifest what it contains. Whenever one great manifestation has been made, it turns to another, leaving the former behind, and this change is indicated by the transition from a lower to a higher age, until when all its developements are effected, it turns from time to eternity, and forsaking its body, which is no longer of use to it, leaves it to decay. For the body, without the soul, can as little support itself, as the rainbow, created by the sun, can continue, after the sun turns away from it to a different part of the globe.

Different periods of this gradual developement have been exhibited by physiologists. Some have admitted ten, each consisting of seven years, thirty one weeks and six days; Shakspeare speaks of seven, but most writers, following the division of the seasons, admit only four. To divide these periods according to years, is a difficult undertaking. Not only, because as the seasons, so our ages differ in the various climates, but they vary with different persons in the same region. That which exists and grows, cannot be fixed in certain stages, but like a stream, that continually flows and cannot be stopped by putting a pole as a landmark into its waters, one stage will flow imperceptibly into the other. Haller collected more than one thousand instances of persons, who lived more than one hundred to one hundred and ten years, and some of such, as died in the one hundred and fiftieth and one hundred and seventieth year; ten periods, each of six years, thirty one weeks and six days would of course not be sufficient in such cases.

We shall in a short characteristic of the ages follow the natural division of the season and the day, the influence of which on all that live is analagous to that of the four ages on our life. These divisions are strongly marked by our mental and physical power, and also by a pre-disposition to certain diseases. In childhood our nature inclines to inflammation of the brain; in youth to disorders of the pectoral system; in manhood to bilious diseases and fevers, and in old age to palsies.

Childhood.

This exhibits three distinct stages, that of the infant, that when the child begins *to walk* and *to speak*, and that when it begins to understand the world around it.

During the *first* of these three periods the child exists more in the form of vegetative life. It sleeps about eighteen hours a day, and like plants, grows rapidly, and is altogether a sleeping monad, for the morning of intellect is not yet dawning on it. It is, however, born a sensitive being, and feels every where on its body, except on the sole of the foot. This experience shows, for when the air streams on its tender body, it moves its limbs and cries; when it is touched, its muscular power attempts to re-act. As the lungs breathe as soon as the air falls upon them, so its lips point themselves and seek for nourishment, when it feels hunger. Drinking and eating are yet united in one act. The pleasure, accompanying the satisfaction of want, runs like an electric spark through all its limbs, and soon not only the lips, but also its little hands seek the favored food. The touch of the hands will attract the eye, which begins to be active four or five days after birth, and thus one sense will awaken and aid the other. Hearing develops itself later, as it is said to continue longest in the dying. It distinguishes first the voice of the mother, for this proceeds from the same breast from which it receives its nourishment.

The *second* period announces itself by the attempts of the child to *walk* and to *speak*. With them it raises itself above the sphere of mere feeling, and enters on that of consciousness. A desire to play indicates a will in its lowest stage. This desire makes the child seize with its little hands, what is offered to them; it grows fond of what it has once seized and pays attention to toys and those, which it sees and handles oftenest, it will soon be able to distinguish from others. This appears from the fact, that it will not suffer one toy to be taken out of its hands and another to be put in its place, but it insists on the one, that was taken from it. Thus it learns to *distinguish* and to *choose*. The interest felt by the child in certain objects will be expressed by its hands, and some inarticulate sounds, until finally, after having heard them named repeatedly, it imitates words. The child indeed had sounds before; it wept, and laughed, and cried; but to form sounds into tones and pronounce them as words demands intellect. Its original sounds were principally vowels; to pronounce consonants teeth are required. Mere sounds the animal has likewise, but its sounds have no variety. The goose hisses, the hen clucks, the sheep bleats. The voice of man is capable of forming all these sounds, as was Madame Catalani to compass three octaves and a half. The child at first indicates by a few words a great many objects; every stranger is an *uncle* or an *aunt*. After some time it forms words of its own, that frequently are full of significance.—With the language the child becomes conscious of the world, and of itself, especially when it ceases to speak of itself in the third person, and begins to name itself by the term I. This conception of itself is like a light in the midst of darkness. Now the child plays with itself, as if it were sufficient to itself. It sleeps less, and is unwilling to be put to bed, &c.

The *third* period is that in which the child desires to become acquainted with the world. The impressions it receives are new and strong, as they are yet few it retains them easily. The fondness for play increases; the boy runs about, wrestles, climbs trees and makes mischief; the girl delights in adorning a doll, and attending to a kitchen apparatus in miniature. Pleasure and displeasure seize the young heart with much vehemence and the will excited by them, attaches the action without deliberation to desires. These change quickly and influence to many actions, that must be imprudent. Not distinguishing between genuine and false pleasures, the child will give the more valuable for a trifle which attracts its attention. The rash and inconsiderate life of the child meets therefore a contradiction in the well regulated and principled life of grown persons, and this contradiction manifests itself as *discipline*. The virtues of *gratitude, obedience,* and *petitioning*, can be cultivated in the earliest childhood by withholding and granting at proper seasons. Cleanliness in dress and moderation in food, are the basis of all education. Exercise of the higher senses, the ear and eye, and limitation of the pleasures of the lower are the best preventives of voluptuousness and sensuality.

Children live wholly in the present; the future does not yet trouble them. One day passes by like the other. As yet boys and girls play with each other; but soon they flee in order to seek each other again. The girl turns in upon herself and grows modest and silent, the boy shunning her seeks the company of boys, and becomes awkward and rude.

Youth.

Sera Venus—inexhausta juventus.—Tacitus.

Now all formations of the body are fully developed; the proportions of all parts to each other, are in their highest perfection; the nerves are vigorous and the muscles swell softly over into each other. The beard and the change of voice in the young man; the delicacy and bloom in the face of the girl indicate this period no less, than a higher respiration and a greater warmth of the whole body. Psychologically this period may be known from a prevalence of the imagination, memory, and judgment, and an irresistible inclination to dive into the future, lay plans, and build castles in the air. The breast is filled with hopes and ideas, with expectations and wishes, with undertakings and plans to reform the world. *Love* and *friendship* are the two principal inclinations of youth; perseverance and courage, firmness and nobleness, magnanimity and self-denial, are in their train. Love ennobles and often forms the transition from a silent and idle life, to a most generous and noble activity. Dante's love to Beatrice ripened into his Divina Commedia; Petrarch's love entered into his sonnets; Goethe's into his Faust. In a moral respect *Honor* becomes the guiding principle.

Manhood.

The growth of the body has ceased, though its intensive strength may still grow higher. The face exhibits impressions of certain fixed inclinations, and passions and expressions of character; the glance of the eye is firm, the support of the body manly and noble, and the walk dignified and serious. The ideals of youth depart, and the reality of life claims the undivided attention of man. In the place of the pictures of fancy, life offers its objects, and mature judgment and knowledge, firmness of will, ripeness of experience, and a resolute but deliberate activity become indispensable. Purposes must be realized; something must be effected to secure to man a position in society. Wife and children must be taken care of, the government and the welfare of the whole human race demand the interest of man. As thinking becomes more logical, the single thoughts clearer, so the emotions of the heart are viewed more correctly, and no longer suffered to exercise an influence on the will proportional to their vehemence. And so all actions are accompanied by circumspection and prudence, and must proceed from a sense of duty, and from a consideration of their consequences in the future. Man must know how to resign and endure, how to persevere and to act.

Old Age.

Jucundissima est aetas devexa jam, non tamen preceps.—Seneca.

The frailty of old age has been the theme of many a poem, and of much complaint. Homer early compared the voice of old men to the chirping of the balm-cricket. And yet old age is not destitute of its high pleasures. Desires and passions, those tyrants of youth no longer rage in it; past experience, and many changes and occurrences, rising and sinking wealth and power, the destructive and reviving facts of history, have taught the aged neither to tremble at dangers nor to overprize things earthly. He can no longer be deluded; his counsel is sought for and valued.

Old age may therefore be called that of peace and serenity; for quick impressions no longer disturb it, unseasonable desires no longer torture it, and its principal attention is generally directed to its eternal home. The more familiar it grows with the home above the stars, the more it becomes estranged to the concerns of life, and this gradual estrangement may be called a gradual dying, and death nothing else than a transition of the soul from time to eternity leaving the body behind. As the soul dives into the other world the colors of this earth grow pale and less interesting.

Yet some old men have preserved in themselves a deep interest in the world, and continued to feel youthful, and labor with energy. Goethe continued his usual activity until a few days before his death; Ruben's Last Judgment, and Raphael's Transfiguration, were the best and last works of those great men.

Many feel neglected in old age, because they have ceased to take any interest in those around them; many lose their memory because they do not exercise it. Robert Constantine had an excellent philological memory in his one hundredth and third year. Many become childish, because they live altogether in the days of their childhood, and pay no attention to the affairs of the day. But when all is as it ought to be, then the old man will rejoice in his age, and as the horizon of his earthly sun grows more narrow, that of his heavenly sun will become more expanded and more brilliant. For the soul that comes from God, having fulfilled its destiny on earth, desires to return.

§ 2. SLEEPING AND WAKING.

Sleeping and waking are the "ebb and flood of mind and of matter on the ocean of our life." They are related to each other as night and day, darkness and light, consciousness and unconsciousness. In proportion as any being may be said to be awake, it will be able to enjoy sleep. We propose to answer the following questions:

1. *What is sleeping, and what is waking?*
2. *Where is sleep met with?*

3. *What is its design?*
4. *What are its conditions?*
5. *What is a regular sleep?*
6. *What is a falling asleep?* and 7. *What is waking?*

1. *What is sleeping, and what is waking?*

Sleep. The words used in different languages to signify the state of life under consideration, express generally a relaxation. *Somnus* in the Latin no doubt is derived from *supinus*, lying on the back, and this from *sopio*, to deprive of feeling or sense, and from which the modern term *sofa* comes; the Greek term ὕπνος is equal to ὕπινος, and this is allied to the Latin supuns, supnius, somnus, and means likewise *lying back;* the English sleep comes from the Saxon slepan, and the German *schlafen*, whose root is *schlaff*, and whose meaning is *lax* or *relaxed*, and which is used of the bow-string when loosened. Sleep in general is, therefore, a state of relaxation. This definition is not, however, sufficient, and we must add that is the negation of consciousness of the world and of ourselves. Yet consciousness is not annihilated, but continued as dreams indicate, and as the possibility of awaking at a certain hour, sufficiently proves. The nervous system, which influences the activity of the soul when directed outward, is asleep, and hence the communications of the soul with the world is interrupted for a time. We must further add, that sleep is the rest of the activity of the organs of sensibility; yet the functions of sensibility, of sensation and perception, are not suppressed, but only limited in their clearness and accuracy; they are veiled and put to rest with regard to external objects. But while at rest in this respect, they reproduce their life, and re-invigorate themselves. Again we must add, that sleep is the prevalence of the functions of bodily re-production, or digestion, respiration, circulation of the blood over those of sensibility. Though breathing, and the pulsation of the blood becomes slower, they are the former more deep, and the latter fuller. Hence it is, that many snore when asleep, for they draw in the air more deeply. Secretion is diminished, but is richer and more energetic, and digestion is more perfect. Persons grow principally during sleep, and wounds heal more at night than during the day. The plant grows quicker than any thing else in nature, and it is therefore considered as the true representative of re-production. A twig broken off and planted, produces a new tree. Now, the life of man during sleep is principally vegetative, as Aristotle remarked, and Leibnitz called man when asleep a vegetable monad. In sleep man is turned in upon himself, and wholly indifferent to the world around him; hence Heraclitus said,—in sleep every man has a world of his own, but when awake all men have one in common with each other. Sleep has been considered by ancient poets as the sister of death; Homer calls death a brazen sleep, ὕπνος χαλκεος; but if sleep is *rest in activity*, and death as it is generally viewed, a cessation from all activity, then sleep and death are not sisters, nor are they in any way related to each other.

Waking. This is the opposite of sleeping, or that state of life in which the system of sensibility reigns over that of re-production, or in which the soul and consciousness prevail over the body. All the functions of sensibility are fully active, as seeing, hearing, smelling, tasting, and feeling; we think, and judge, and will; we distinguish between ourselves and the world, between our perceptions and the things perceived; we remember, direct attention whithersoever we please, and determine the motions of all our muscles.

Sleeping and waking seem to be in opposition, and yet they are not, for the one is founded on the other. While we sleep, something in us is awake, and while we are awake, some powers in us are at rest.

2. *Where is sleep met with?*

As sleeping and watching are closely related to each other, we may at once say, that a being can enjoy sleep only in proportion to the degree in which it may be said to be awake. Beings that are wholly reproductive, that live and grow only externally, and have neither feeling nor sensation, cannot sleep. It cannot be denied, that there are many plants, which under the influence of light and warmth close their cups at night, and open them again in the morning, or protect their flowers by folding their leaves around them, and by forming a bower, or by rolling up their leaves in the form of a cornet;—yet their sleep, if it may be called so, is but distantly analogous to that of man. It is nevertheless remarkable, that some flowers are so regular as to the time of falling asleep, that Linnæus conceived the thought of establishing a Horologium Floræ, that is, a dial of flowers.

Animals, on the other hand, have feeling and sensation; they feel themselves, and they feel and perceive the things around them; they are consequently awake in some degree at least, though their state of waking resembles that of dreaming, and hence Leibnitz called them dreaming monads. Here it will be well to notice, that living and being awake are different states of existence. The plant lives, but is not awake; the animal is awake, but has no clear consciousness. Animals, being awake, they also sleep. The ibex, which climbs from mountain to mountain, when the time of its retirement approaches, seeks for a silent and isolated place to rest and enjoy sleep. The eagle that sailed during the day in the air, and passed over hills and valleys, is satisfied with a small spot when the night breaks in. Some animals sleep not only during night, or for a short part of the day, but through a whole season, or during a smaller or greater portion of it. Some fall asleep when the cold, others when the warm, or others when in some regions the rainy season makes its appearance. The German rat, the marmot, the badger, the hedgehog, the bear, all of which love cold climates, sleep more or less during the whole winter; the hedgehog in Madagascar, and the tanrec in the East Indies, sleep during the greater part of summer; and so does the crocodile, which remains stiff in in the mire, hardened by the sun until a few drops of rain start it, and make it burst the mud and go in search of its prey. Among the birds the swallow, the nest of which is eatable, and some few other kinds are subject to this long sleep, which is also met with among men, but there always as a disease. The question may be asked, whether *all* animals sleep? Some of the lower classes, as infusoria polypi, that have either no nerves at all, or very few only, can of course sleep but little, because they are awake but little, and their existence is more vegetative than animal.

Other animals live constantly in a dull mixture of sleeping and waking, as the amphibious; and some insects sleep so slightly, that their sleep might better be called a kind of drowsiness, for they observe every thing going on around them. Fish have been seen following a ship for seven days, and as yet it is doubted by many, whether the dull life of aquatic animals stands in need of sleep. From these remarks, it may be sufficiently seen, that the sleep of animals differs not only from that of man, but in the different animals according to the degree in which they may be said to be awake.

3. *What is the design of sleep?*

Rest and *activity* are so separated in every being which lives on earth, that the one excludes the other, or no being can be active and rest at the same time. But what cannot take place simultaneously may do so in succession, and as the night follows the day, so rest follows activity, and this again rest. Whenever our activity continues for a long time, it must result in exhaustion, and thus render itself impossible; and when rest is enjoyed beyond a proper measure, disgust and weariness are experienced. The necessity for the alternate transition from waking to sleeping, and from sleeping to waking, lies in the above law, and is contained in the life of man. It is the union of mind and body, and though its activity is originally one, it is organized and utters itself by different systems. These determine and limit each other, so that while each is going on in the same body, neither interferes with the other. Among these systems some serve more the growth and strength of the body, others more directly the activity of the mind. But all of them are equally subject to exhaustion, and stand, therefore, equally in need of rest. They cannot consequently be all of them active in an equal degree at the same time, but they must relieve each other, so that while the one is principally active, the others will be at rest, and for the time being, yield their dominion. Were both kinds of systems equally active at the same time, they would have to fall asleep at the same time, and then nothing would remain active in man to awaken him again; while, on the other hand, a continued activity of the vegetative system of the body would finally stifle the life of the mind, and a continued activity of the mind by the brain, nerves, and muscles would volatilize the body as light volatilizes burning matter. An uninterrupted wakefulness renders the brain soft and watery, and causes insanity, as long sleep suffocates by the growing and accumulating fat. Here, then, we may discover the true reason why plants cannot sleep. They cannot be said to be truly *active*, and hence stand not in need of rest, as the planets and stars, which are ever moving, never experience fatigue. Should we nevertheless call the growth of plants an activity, it would be necessary for us to say, that their activity and rest is so united that the one cannot be distinguished from the other. Without any disturbance, their juices rise and sink; without labor the bud unfolds itself in the light of the sun and scatters its fragrance. But the life of the animal has sensation through it, it is attracted by the objects around or repelled by them and its originally peaceful, and harmonious activity is elicited and spent in all directions, and hence exhaustion follows and rest becomes necessary. And all this takes place in a still higher degree in man. The equilibrium of his mental life is wholly disturbed by the occurrences of the day, by the emotions of fear and hope, of joy and pain, of solitude and anxiety, of love and hatred; by self-interest and interest in others; by desires, inclinations, and passions; by cares and troubles, by the constant exertion of thinking and willing. Thus rest becomes in a high degree necessary, and the design of sleep as regards the *intellect* is,

To grant rest to the mind. For if during the state of waking, the mind may be compared to a living spring, whose reviving waters are constantly gushing forth and flowing into many rivulets; during sleep it gathers and collects itself, draws in its manifold activities; and thus, for a time, it frees itself from the contrast and opposition to itself into which it is brought by the opposite nature of the objects, claiming its power and attention during its waking. The mind returning to itself, delivers itself from the stretch on which it is during the whole day and thus it is at rest.

It not only *rests* in sleep, that is, ceases from labor, but it is positively invigorated and strengthened, and this restoration of mental power is another part of the design of sleep. It descends to the state of its original existence to that of the embryo and like Antæus, who by throwing himself on the earth, gained new strength, so it recovers what it has lost by its activity in the world. It is as if it drew a new supply of strength from the source of its existence, and hence the expressions that one feels like a *new creature* after a healthy sleep or *balmy sleep*, are highly significant.

According to the view here taken of the design of sleep, it would seem that the mind sleeps and not the body alone, or that such is the case of the system of sensibility, and irritability, and this is true. Sleep is not death, nor a separation of the soul from the body; in sleep they remain closely united. The mind sleeps; it is for a time in a state of unconsciousness, while at the same time it has not in the least lost its consciousness, this has only become latent or is for a time veiled. This state of mind has been compared to that of the memory when it possesses all the words of a foreign language, and could call them forth at any time, and yet does not remember one for years because the person whose memory it is no longer speaks that language. This state is similar to another activity of the soul, which in order to reflect on a new idea, dismisses for a time a previous one without loosing or forgetting it. It will be understood that the mind is spoken of here in its connection with the body, and especially with the nerves by which it is principally active. When these become exhausted, the activity of the mind will not cease, but will be greatly diminished and consequently rest. This rest is what we call sleep.

4. *What are the conditions of sleep?*

These are many and various, and that without which all the others would be insufficient, is the law according to which life cannot remain in one and the same state longer than a certain time, and according to which its existence vibrates between activity and rest, sleeping and waking. This is the case, in some degree at least, with the mind.

Here we find, that after serious labors, the mind inclines strongly to something of a lighter nature. Leibnitz, when fatigued with study, delighted in meditating on the improvement of wagons; Kepler turned from his astronomical investigations to music. The more the mind has been productive and self-active in one direction, the more it will desire to be merely receptive in another. After writing much it will be delightful to read for a while. The next condition of sleep is a certain degree of exhaustion caused by activity. He only sleeps well who wakes well. Any thing that weakens the nervous system, great cold or heat, or whatever too greatly raises or depresses the activity of the sensibility, or what even wearies by not affording sufficient excitement, by being too uniform or tedious will make us feel sleepy; while any thing that strongly engages the mind will keep it awake. A certain degree of indifference to the world and to our business is indispensable to sound sleep, and whatever promotes this state of indifference will also promote sleep. Hence the night with its darkness and silence is the time for sleep, for the absence of light suffers the eye, through which the objects of the world receive form and shape and gain our attention, to be at rest. Again, whatever promotes the growth of the body is favorable to sleep. Fat, corpulent and growing persons, especially children, sleep more than old persons. And finally sleep may be caused by strong odors or medicines taken from the vegetable kingdom, as opium, by strong food, which renders a higher degree of digestion necessary, as may be seen from serpents, that after having eaten their prey, fall asleep; by strong drinks, which force the blood inward, while such as tea, that propel it to the surface, keep us awake.

5. *What is a regular sleep?*

That sleep we should not hesitate to call regular and healthy, and refreshing, in which the functions of digestion or of the system of reproduction in general, prevail over that of sensibility, so that we are not disturbed by dreams or by cares. So is waking *regular* and healthy, when we scarcely know that we have a body, when no limb hurts us, and when the process of digestion is not in the least perceived. Sleep is irregular when it is disturbed by unpleasant, feverish, or distressing dreams, and when we often awake during the night. The nature of sleep will differ according to its prevailing causes. Sleep, produced by strong drinks, will be heavy and unhealthy; that produced by cold, will be benumbing; that by too great fatigue, will be deep, &c. Some instances of lethargy remind us of the long sleep of animals. Schubert relates the case of Guiseppe Ciaborri, who was buried during an earthquake by the corpse of his friend, and there lay for fourteen days under the ruins of his native city almost constantly sleeping. A sick person slept for seventeen weeks with but a few interruptions, and after this long sleep recovered from his disease. This shows that such a sleep is sickly. Another slept for seventy days and then recovered from an illness; and Fichet records a case in which a man slept for four years, only waking when he felt hungry. Equally extraordinary are the instances in which persons have fallen asleep while on the rack. The nerves being so weakened that they could no longer re-act, began to die, while the rest of the body seemed yet to live. Sleep and death not unfrequently pass over the one into the other. Poison, introduced into the blood, frequently causes first a deep sleep and then death. As we have many instances of such a heavy, lethargical sleep, so we have some of an uncommon wakefulness. A murderer, according to Schubert, remained awake for fourteen days, and though he took gradually forty grains of opium, his eyelids would not sink and grant him a balmy sleep.

6. *What is Falling Asleep?*

To say all in one word, we may reply: a gradual inactivity of the different senses. First of all the eye ceases to be awake, the eyelid sinks and it closes; then taste and smell become insensible; the ear yet hears, but does not understand; the mouth yawns, the members stretch themselves, the head, as in the embryo, sinks down on the breast, and while for a short time the life of the mind seems to rest under the surface of the body, so that a little excitement will call it forth again, it soon sinks deeper until it wholly disappears. So the English soldiers on the fort of St. Philip heard no longer the thunder of the cannons, but slept standing at their posts. Physically, falling asleep is frequently indicated by a feverish pulsation of the blood, and always by a rest of the muscles, by a decrease of animal warmth, by slower, but deeper breathing. As the thinking power becomes relaxed, and loses accuracy and acuteness as the motion of the muscles grows less energetic, so all activity is turned off from the world and sinks back into the life of the body. The eye of the astronomer, which a moment since enjoyed the millions of golden stars above, and roamed in immeasurable space lets fall the lid —and stars and space are no more seen.

7. *What is Awaking?*

When sufficient strength has been gained, one sense after another becomes active again, and man becomes conscious of himself, and the world around. A feeling of strength and of vigor, of cheerfulness and alacrity, accompanies our awaking, as that of relaxation accompanies our falling asleep. Our connection with the world is renewed, and the last thoughts, before falling asleep again present themselves.—When life is vigorous, the transition from sleeping to waking is short, though generally preceded by a short morning sleep. The dark feeling, in which our intellectual life was resting, becomes gradually more light; figures like thoughts make their appearance, and an electric stream of power passes through limbs and muscles, until we are fully awake. The process of awaking is generally complete, when the eye opens, for through it the objects around us can be distinguished, and hence it elicits our judgment and thinking, and our desire for renewed activity.

§ 3. DREAMING.

The word dream, by a transposition of the letters *o* and *r*, comes from the Latin, Dormio, which word means both to *sleep*, and to *dream*, as the noun somnium, means both *sleep* and *dream*. In connection with sleeping we have to consider that state of the mind, in which it dreams.

Dreaming is generally described as an involuntary action of the soul. By involuntary is meant, that the pictures, images and ideas, running through our sleep, are not subject to our critical judgment, nor to our conscious will, but that they come and go, appear and disappear, as if sent by another power than that of the soul. Yet this definition of dreaming does not exhaust the subject. Dreaming is a state of mind, that is made up of sleeping and waking. The soul, when it dreams, is neither wholly asleep nor wholly awake. We are awake, when we judge, consequently when we distinguish between our soul and body, between our activity and its results, between the world and ourselves and when we know that we make these distinctions. We are asleep, when we are no longer aware of these differences and when we cease to *judge*. Dreaming is the flowing together of ourselves with the objective world; for while in sleep this is wholly merged in a state of unconsciousness, in dreaming it emerges from it; not having however the power of a clear and distinct judgment, we are not able to keep the objective world separated from ourselves, but all our activities flow confusedly together with their results, our perceptions with the things perceived, and our imagination with its own productions. Dreaming then is that state of mind, in which we are not conscious of ourselves or of our personality. We are conscious of ourselves when we clearly distinguish between our soul and body and acknowledge their union. In dreaming this distinction is gone, and hence we are unconscious of our person. This shows itself in all dreams, and more especially in those in which we exchange our personality for that of another. Johnson, in his dreams, frequently disputed with an opponent, and felt chagrined, that he had himself the poorest arguments. An old Professor dreamed, that he was again a student, and when examined could not answer the question to which his classmate, sitting near him, fully and readily replied. In both these instances it is evident, that the dreamers had no self-consciousness. And so it is in all our dreams, for if we were clearly conscious of ourselves, we should not dream, but be awake. Without personality there can be no liberty, no volition, no will. In dreaming then we are incapable of willing decidedly. This it will not be difficult to prove. For when we dream that we are pursued by a mad dog, or any rapacious animal, we cannot, however much we may try to do it, discover the means of escape. Our muscles seem powerless, they will not move from the place, they deny their services. We desire to be delivered from danger, we feel that running could be the only way of safety and yet we cannot take a step. Nor is understanding and judgment active and free in dreaming, but both are merged in mere feeling. Some remarkable instances may seem to lie in the way of this assertion, and yet it is nevertheless true. If by understanding we comprehend the many in one, and if by judgment we distinguish between the different qualities of a thing, and separate one class of beings from another, we cannot exercise either power without self-consciousness, and where this is active, there, as has been stated, we do not dream, but wake. Condillac, we are told frequently finished treatises in his dreams, which while he was awake, offered insurmountable difficulties. Maignan, a mathematician of the seventeeth century, in his dreams, solved problems, which he found correct, when he judged of them after he awaked. Reinhold discovered in a dream the deduction of the logical categories, and so all of us frequently feel, when we awake in the morning, that we have clearer ideas on some subjects than we had, when we retired. Strong as these instances are in favor of a quickened understanding and judgment in dreams, they do not after all prove what they seem to establish. For there is no doubt but the essays of Condillac and the problems of Maignan, and the categories of Reinhold, had not in vain engaged the minds of these men, but they were well matured and ripe, long before they lay down to sleep. It often so happens, that while many impressions, and many activities engage our mind at the time, when we attend to a difficult subject, the results of our meditation and study will not become manifest to ourselves, because some feeling, some impression veils it or does not suffer it to present itself freely, and separate from the other views and ideas, that may occupy our thoughts. After we retire and dismiss the many cares and interests, which divide our mental energies, the *principal* subject of meditation during the day will enter into our dreams and all the other impressions that accompanied it having disappeared, the result of our study will be permitted to show itself disencumbered. So noise around us frequently prevents us from remembering a certain occurrence, which is certainly treasured up in our memory. When the noise ceases, our recollection of it is at hand. The mountains are there, but the mist renders them invisible; as soon as the mist sinks, they rise. We experience the same, when, having been for a long time engaged in some labor unsuccessfully, we return to it, after recreation. Then we are often astonished at the ease with which we finish the work. No new efforts have been made, no new attention has been paid to it, and the greater facility must therefore result from the removal of something, that before obstructed our efforts.

The state of mind, in which it neither comprehends nor judges, nor is conscious of itself, must be that of

Feeling. The mind, as has been shown, retires during sleep from the manifold activities into which it flows forth when awake. Yet its rest is not inactivity, for this is death. Whatever has life must be active, and only what is active is alive. The activity of the mind during sleep is sunk into form of feeling. This, without judgment, is an entire union of subject and object, of the activity which feels, and the thing that is felt; a union, not resulting from the difference of both, but one that knows of no difference whatever. Thus all differences in the activity of the soul are dropped, and the soul places itself wholly and undivided in every feeling and emotion, or in every word and action. When we are awake, we judge of our actions as well as of our words and feelings; our mind, when entering into them, is conscious of their relation to itself, of their consequences and propriety. During sleep no part of the mind is above our feelings or words, but the whole mind rests in an undivided manner in every single emotion, and in every single action. Hence we may explain how words spoken in our dreams are frequently much more beautiful, much more appropriate than those we should have chosen when awake; hence it is too, that our emotions in our dreams are more whole-souled, and consequently more animated; and that our sympathies and antipathies are more vehement than they would be in a state of wakefulness. As the muscular strength of insane persons is very greatly increased, when their whole mind enters into a passion, so are our feelings in sleep, and their utterances in dreams.

Some of the feelings, that we thus have in dreams, will be stronger than others; these stronger feelings will cause a difference in the simple and harmonious activity of the mind, and disturb it. Every difference will lead to variety, and hence the mind will flow forth again with its activity into different channels, as in its state of waking. Yet not conscious that these differences in its activity are its own productions, imagination, the principal power active in dreams, represents them as something strange, as something external, something not proceeding from the activity of the mind, but from some other source. Thus the identity and harmony of the mind is preserved in its dreams, for whatever might interfere with it is thrust out under the form of a strange being or power. On the one hand the mind seems to distinguish, while on the other it remains still under the influence of mere *feeling*. But the activity of the mind which thus unites *thinking* and *feeling* is

Imagination. This mental power does not demonstrate nor produce pure thoughts, and make us conscious of them, but it gives all ideas in a sensual form, in a sensible image. While we are awake, its operations are accompanied by critical judgment; we reflect on the images and their appropriateness to render a thought visible. In our dreams this critical judgment is absent, and though we may compose poems while dreaming, their value can be judged of by us only when we are awake; and frequently what may please us in our dreams, will be found wholly incapable of satisfying our waking judgment. Imagination is therefore active, without our being conscious of it; this is sometimes the case with poets, who write without cool reflection, but then they write by inspiration, and may be compared to a burning torch which illuminates all around, but does not see itself, nor understand its own nature. As it is the province of the imagination to express a general thought or truth, or that which is common to many things of the same kind by a single concrete and individual image or symbol, so in our dreams it produces images, concrete signs or symbols by which it speaks or acts. The course of an unfortunate life, for example, it will describe by a high mountain which we have to ascend. Agreeable or disagreeable feelings which connect themselves with the labor we have in climbing up the mountain, will call forth the images of beautiful flowers or disgusting animals. Hence it is, that we cannot only speak in verses while we are dreaming—because imagination is principally active, and the soul is wholly thrown into it—but that the language of dreams in general is replete with poetical beauty, with energy, and appropriateness. Instead of words, we have a fine imagery; thus, pearls indicate tears. The wife of Henry IV. of France dreamed a few days before the murder of her husband, that two splendid diamonds had been changed into pearls. So Goethe, shortly before he visited Italy, had a dream of a symbolical character. He dreamed that he landed from a large boat on an island, fertile and richly covered with vegetation, where he knew the most beautiful pheasants were offered for sale. He directly traded with the inhabitants for these beautiful creatures, which they brought killed, and in large quantities. They were genuine pheasants, but as dreams usually transform every thing, they had long, colored-eyed tails like those of peacocks or birds of paradise. They were brought by scores into the vessel, their heads turned inward and arranged so ornamentally, that the long, variegated tails hanging outwards, formed in the sunshine the most brilliant arches imaginable; and so richly indeed, that room was scarcely left in the front and rear for the oarsmen and helmsman. Thus they cut the peaceful waves, and Goethe named to himself the friends to whom he intended to present these gay treasures. Though Goethe neither sent nor brought pheasants from Italy to his friends, he sent many a letter, filled with the riches of his poetical genius, which received new impulses and new materials from the world of art surrounding him.—Knowing the power of imagination, we cannot feel astonished at the choice which it makes in our dreams of images, by which to convey its dark notions. A man, suffering from cramps in his breast, saw himself attacked and wounded by cats whenever his disease was about to return. Nor shall we consider it strange that it frequently makes use of images, which are directly opposite of what they are to indicate. Weeping in dreams is said to announce great joyousness; cheerfulness in dreams foretells mourning. To eat earth means to gather riches; beautiful lilies apprize us of scorn which we shall have to endure from the world. Marriage-feasts in dreams are the messengers of misfortune, as funeral processions those of joyful occurrences. Romeo in a dream sees himself elevated to the dignity and splendor of an emperor, shortly before he hears of the death of his Juliet. In these images of our dreams a certain law prevails, when we think them to be arbitrary. This law is, *that extremes elicit each other.* Cheerfulness and mournfulness, marriage and death, the sounds of joy and those of grief, are found more closely together in nature, than we are inclined to admit.

Nearly allied to imagination is the activity of memory. This likewise is often active in our dreams, and when not divided, and when it is animated by the whole activity of the mind it will of course be more lively, more vivid, and perhaps more faithful in the detail of occurrences. Thus a gentleman dreamed that a person appeared before his bed, offering to reveal to him either his future or past life. He agreed on having his past life represented to him. The person then gave him a review of all that had occurred to him, the greater part of which he would not have been able to recall when awake. To explain this dream, we must remember a remark made above, that memory as well as every other power is subject to dissipation, and that it may treasure up occurrences, which the manifold employments of the day prevent it from bringing to our recollection, while dreaming, its whole activity dwells on one point only. It therefore represents past actions more in the detail, and not merely recollects them, but gives them all the novelty of recent occurrences. Dead persons die again before us; we, in old age, go again to school with our books under our arms. Yet memory in our dreams is mechanical; not subject to our will, so that we might demand certain things intrusted to it. It gives them according to the association of ideas, or in some external connection, or in one borrowed from the memory in its state of waking. Consciousness does not accompany its operations. When awake, we classify the contents of memory, and call upon it to give them according to general heads and classes; this tendency to generalize, renders the memory less inclined to depict and delineate. In our dreams memory dwells more on the individual nature of occurrences, it loves the concrete, and hence its greater vividness and detail. There are some dreams that continue successively for a number of nights, to complete a long story. Here it must be remembered that similar feelings and circumstances will produce a type of a dream, which will continue as long as its causes and conditions are the same, until its subject is exhausted.

1. *The Form of Dreams.*

One delights in the illusions of dreaming, because originating in ourselves, they must have some analogy with the rest of our life and our fate.—Goethe.

Dreams being destitute of a clear self-possessed consciousness, they of course can have no logical connection. This has been already shown from the entire neglect of the laws of space and of time. In space one place cannot be where another is, for different places occupy different positions; and so whatever exists in a bodily form, while it must be somewhere, cannot be every where. Dreams know nothing of these laws, but the persons and beings in them have a kind of *ubiquity*. In the twinkling of an eye we now are in Asia, and now in Africa. Our imagination may likewise travel fast when awake, but then the critical consciousness is closely following it. And so in dreams the laws of time are wholly neglected, such as those of succession of the past present and future. This succession enters into our thoughts and actions. Before we act we resolve; our resolution, as something present, is referred to its execution as something future. In our dreams, resolution and action coincide in one moment; the future is present. Thus all logical and all voluntary connection is destroyed. To have clearness and distinctness in our knowledge, we must arrange it according to the laws of space and time; we must, for instance, cause our memory to give up its contents in the regular order in which they occurred. And not only so, we must perceive the relations of cause and effect, ground and consequence. Where the things contained in dreams have nevertheless a strictly logical connection, it is not produced by our dreaming imagination or memory, but merely repeated by an involuntary association of ideas, or by our mechanical memory. In this limited sense it may well be said, as it has been asserted, that there is both an objective and a subjective connection in our dreams. Dreams arising in ourselves must have a *subjective* connection, an analogy with our disposition, knowledge, talents, and skill. There must be too an *objective* connection, for our dreaming imagination must have materials for its activity; these must be given to it, and their original connection may preserve itself in our dreams. Such a connection, however, is mechanical; it is like the connection of leaves, that shaken off by the wind, attach themselves to each other on the ground, or like leaves that flow down the same rivulet, and are united not by their nature, but by the water that carries them. The *subjective* connection of our dreams demands, however, our particular attention, for these very frequently betray our true disposition and moral character. If during the time of busy activity our conscience is not permitted to speak, it will frequently burst its chains in our dreams and announce loudly to all that hear it, and especially to ourselves, what is in us. Shakspeare represents the dreams of conscience very beautifully in Lady Macbeth. A celebrated professor, who for some time had omitted offering his morning and evening worship, prayed in his dreams a number of nights in succession, and repeated all the bible prayers which he had learned by heart in his youth. The dream may be an illusion, but the disposition from which it arises will be true. It was on this principle, that a **Greek** emperor had a person executed, merely because he dreamed of having killed him.

2. *Causes of Dreams.*

These are manifold, and it would be difficult to enumerate all of them and arrange them in classes. We shall therefore point out only a few, and among the most fertile ones are,

1. Impressions on our senses. Thus we feel cold, and our imagination leads us into ice-fields; light falls upon our eyes, and we exclaim *Fire!* A philosopher dreamed that thieves were about to kill him, and to render his death more cruel, they introduced a large pole between his toes, and tried to break them out. He awoke and found a straw in the place of the pole. Sometimes a disordered system, any thing lying undigested in the stomach will cause dreams.

2. Whatever has much engaged us during the day, whether it has been agreeable or disagreeable, will become a source of dreams during the night. Perhaps a strong emotion, suppressed by our will, while we were awake, disturbs our sleep; or a strong wish, the fulfillment of which we would not for a moment consider possible when waking, presents itself as realized. Persons desirous to be rich, dream that they are so. Talents, that are not permitted to exhibit themselves, because our daily employment is hostile to them, will seek for an opportunity in our dreams of exercising themselves. And so whatever impedes any activity, whatever disturbs body or mind, will cause our dreams and enter into them. The nightmare is a remarkable instance of the kind. A thick and impure air renders breathing difficult, and our imagination, which views every thing under the aspect of a concrete form and being, perceives a bear or a cat lying on our mouths. Carus, Junior, relates a case from Sedillot's Journal de Medicine, which is to the point here. Laurent, the physician of the first battalion of the regiment, Tour d'Augergne, was lodged during a night in a deserted monastery at Palmi, in Calabria, when suddenly some persons, lying togeth-

er in narrow rooms on straw, which was spread on the floor, came running in much frightened, all saying that they had seen a ghost-like, long-haired black dog, and had distinctly felt him running over their breasts. During the next night Laurent with some other officers, remained watching, after the soldiers had been persuaded to retire, and without their seeing any thing suspicious, the soldiers were frightened by the same dream, and could not be induced again to return to their lodging place.

3. When our intellectual activity has been exercised but little or at least less than its power would demand to become relaxed, when consequently it stands in no need of recreation and sleep, then dreams will follow one after another, in case we retire to rest. Our senses close, but our mind feels reluctant to sleep. As a general rule it may be stated, that we never dream more, and sleep worse, than when we wake little.

4. The nervous state of the system when weakened, may produce many dreams. Persons in fever, in delirium will imagine they see all kinds of images and so the dreams of nervous persons are full of them. If in this state of health we have no clear and distinct dreams, we toss about, groan and sigh, and it frequently takes us a long time to awake.

Dreams, springing from the same causes, may be much modified by the disposition and character of the dreamer. The natural difference of the imagination, its degree of liveliness and strength, and its cultivation, will considerably affect its images and productions. The imagination of the painter, and that of the musician, of the poet, and that of the sculptor will certainly preserve their peculiar characteristics in their dreams. If the imagination is naturally productive and plastic, the materials furnished it in the dream, will be connected in new ways, and as the judgment is absent, these combinations will frequently be of strange character. The most opposite things will be united, caricatures will be formed, animals speak, serious persons will appear in ludicrous situations and countries will present the most beautiful combinations of water and mountain scenery, and of landscapes of all kind. From these few remarks, it must be evident, that the dreams of children, and those of old persons, must differ widely not only in their substance, but also in reference to their form, liveliness and distinctness; and so again the dreams of savages and those of cultivated persons. The former will consider them too as being sent by a higher power and regard them as possessed of divine authority. Animals too dream; but their dreams stand in the same relation to those of man, in which their instinct stands to the clear thinking of man. They may dream of pursuing a hare or chasing a stag, but their dreams cannot go beyond the sphere of sensation; they cannot produce new images, &c.

§ 4. PROPHETIC DREAMS, PRESENTIMENT, VISION, AND DEUTEROSCOPY, OR SECOND SIGHT.

Somnia sunt alia physica, alia divina, alia diabolica.—Melancthon.

We propose to consider these different states of mind together, for they are to be explained on the same general principle. When speaking of sleep, we found it useful to glance at the phenomena of waking, and so here prophetic dreams which we have when asleep, and presentiments which are the dreams of our waking mind will mutually explain and interpret each other. What we mean by prophetic dreams, will be easily seen from one or two examples. And here we cannot help thinking of one, handed down by Cicero, who, as is well known, was by no means credulous. Two Arcadians came to Megara and took different lodging-places. The one of them appeared twice to the other in a dream, first seeking aid and then murdered, and stating that his corpse would be taken early in the morning on a covered wagon passing through a certain gate out of the city. This dream agitated the other, and going at the appointed time towards the gate, he met the murderer with the wagon and handed him over to the police. A lady of the writer's acquaintance, was from home, when a little brother of hers was killed by an ox. The night after this occurrence she dreamed that an ox-cart was sent for her, in which she was expected to return. This dream affected her spirits so much, that she expressed her apprehensions to her friends in the morning. When informed of the misfortune she directly understood her dream. The dream of Mr. Williams of Scorrierhouse, near Redruth, in Cornwall, is fully related in the London Times of the 16th of August, 1829. He saw the Chancellor killed in the vestibule of the House of Commons, and having had the same dream thrice in one night, he communicated it to many of his acquaintances all of whom were living when the Times gave the account. Afterwards it was ascertained, that on the evening of the same day Mr. Percival was assassinated by a certain Bellingham. This dream resembles the second sight of Mr. Lodin, who in the hour of death saw the murderer of James V.

From these few examples it will appear, that prophetic dreams are such as give us information concerning things which would seem to be inaccessible to our common senses at the time. It cannot be denied, that it is difficult to point out the possibility of such dreams, yet it must be admitted, that there have been dreams of the kind. To refuse belief in them altogether, would not annihilate them, but merely remove them from our consideration. It is more easy to disbelieve a thing that is difficult to explain, than to attempt to understand it. No doubt many dreams have been exaggerated, and to receive all without a critical judgment, would indicate great credulity. We shall therefore divide prophetic dreams into two classes; the one embraces those dreams, the subject of which is the dreamer himself, his health, his state of mind, his conscience; the other comprises all such as foretell something foreign to the dreamer, but always something that will stand in a necessary relation to the present, so that if nothing occurs to prevent it, it must develop itself from it. Dreams of the *first* class have never been much doubted, for physicians have too many opportunities of testifying to their truth. Persons while yet well receive by a dream an impression of a future disease. A woman, about to be taken sick with an inflammation of the brain, dreamed that her heart was changed into a serpent which rose with awful hissing up to her head. Her imagination represented her disease symbolically. Diseases do not all at once and suddenly seize our system. They have their beginning and course, and frequently develop themselves very gradually. Yet however small the beginning of a disease, it is the disease begun. If a strong nervous and muscular constitution may not perceive it until it has grown considerably, there is no reason to doubt the possibility, that a person whose nervous system is out of tune and highly sensitive when asleep, and when his whole mind is sunk into the state of a general feeling and raises and animates this, should perceive a future disease even in its very infancy. This will become more credible, when we consider that our body is a system, which consists not of parts as the machine, but of organs, each of which while it has a peculiar office represents our whole life. The drop of blood, that now runs through the veins of the eye, will soon pass through every vein in the body. In the state of health, when all the organs are active in perfect harmony, no difference is felt; but when one of them is about to separate its life from that of the others, a difference between itself and these must be exhibited, and this will be noticed. Our explanation of prophetic dreams, it will easily be perceived, strips them entirely of the power of prophecy, for they do not foretell that which is not yet, but that which is, and which in our common state of mind would be imperceptible, because it could not sufficiently affect our *strong* nerves.

The dreams of the *second* class, on the other hand, that seem to foretell future occurrences or to have a sensation of things going on at the time, but at a great distance, like the dream of Mr. Williams, are founded either on *sympathy*, as we shall see when we speak of presentiment, or on our knowledge of a necessary connection existing between the foundation and that which rests upon it. So Franklin often perceived in his dreams the results of the labor to which he had attended during the day. These results were owing to the faithfulness with which he executed his business. The plant lies likewise in the seed as to possibility, and any one who sees the seed may prophecy what the plant will be that shall grow forth from it. Only those occurrences may, therefore, be foretold by our dreams, the premises of which are known to us, but it would be mere superstition to believe that we could anticipate in dreams the actions of a free-will.

The whole subject before us will become more plain by considering the nature of presentiment, vision, and second sight. We shall also here preface each of these states of mind by giving one or two examples:

Jung Stilling, in his Almanac of 1808, relates a remarkable presentiment of a minister, who was taking a walk with the intention of visiting a rocky mountain near his house, and of enjoying the beautiful view from it. While approaching the summit of the mountain he felt restless and uneasy; unable to explain this feeling, he asked himself, whether it was right for him to spend his time thus idly, and busied in such thoughts, he stepped aside for a moment to seek a cool place under a wall formed by the rock. He had scarcely left the narrow path leading to the top of the mountain, when a large stone, breaking loose from the rest of the rock, with great vehemence struck the spot, where one moment before he was standing. The Reverend John Dodd, one evening, when already undressed, felt a great agitation in his mind which was wholly unaccountable to him. It seemed to him, that he ought to go and visit a friend, who lived a mile or two off from him. His family tried to dissuade him from going that night, but their efforts were in vain. Mr. Dodd went, dark as it was, and on arriving at the house of his friend, he found him ready to commit suicide. His unexpected visit and counsel prevented the deed forever, and his friend became converted by divine grace. Schiller, the great poet, was in the habit of walking with his steward; at one time, when passing on a rugged path through a pine wood and between high rocks, he was seized by a feeling that some person must be buried there. Some time after he was informed of the murder of a wagoner committed at the place, on which he had the presentiment.

Presentiment—if now we should define it—is the dark foreboding of something taking place either in ourselves or around us. This foreboding is a dark feeling not understood by us; a general feeling of restlessness, strange and altogether uncommon. Its possibility must not be considered as a privilege of the mind, to dive into futurity or distance, but as a disease and weakness, by which it sinks from its state of clear waking into that of dreaming and drowsiness, or from its state of human life into that of animal existence. For animals, whose life is more or less plunged into the general life of nature, and penetrated by it, and whose feeling is that of sympathy with the elements in which they live, have a high degree of presentiment. They seek, like the fish, distant waters, or like the bird, countries afar off; they announce, while the sky is yet serene and clear the approach of a shower, and when the inhabitants around Vesuvius feel secure, the nightingale prophecies a near eruption, and flutters about, sending forth heart-rending notes. The less a being is independent of the element in which it lives, the more quickly it will perceive the changes going on in it, and again the less it can counteract an impression, the more vehemently it will be affected by it. If in a state of health we handle metals as we please, and perceive no effect from them, the mere touch of a ruby on the hand will cause to some diseased persons pain in the arm, or a feeling of coldness and heaviness in the tongue.

It is certainly an erroneous idea to think, that we can perceive by our common senses all the powers of nature. Many of them have only lately become known to us. The celebrated Brown divided substances into parts so infinitely small, that they were smaller than the four-thousandth part of an inch; he then scattered them into the air, while not a breath was stirring, and observed them moving about. As the motion could not be their own, he concluded that there was a power which communicated it to them. This power is now ascertained to be in constant motion, and to pervade us, but we have in a healthy state of our nervous system no sense by which we may perceive it. This magnetic stream is nevertheless equally as certain, as the electric influences upon us, though we cannot discover by our senses the polar relations in many chemical affinities. These activities, however, exist, and may become known to us in two different ways, either by a change taking place in them, or by one in ourselves. That only is perceptible to us, which can affect our senses, because it is strong enough to resist their activity. If the senses are excitable, the impression needs not be strong to be perceived; if they are healthy, it must be energetic. We are penetrated by electric powers, without our feeling them. The eye, when it is pressed against any thing flashes forth electrical sparks, and the skin of the cat, when rubbed, emits them. As soon as this electric power approaches us with sufficient energy, we perceive it. So when we touch an electrical fish or eel. From this it follows, that when the external state of a natural power is changed, we may receive impressions from such as left us perfectly free before. And so it is when our own nervous system becomes more excitable; then natural agencies will be perceived, though their energy should remain the same. The distance from which these agencies reach us, cannot form any objection, or even cause any difficulty in understanding this theory. For if the eye, by the medium of light, may be set in connection, for example, with the Sirius, which is so many thousand miles distant from us; if the ear, so small an organ, hears the sound that originated twenty or thirty miles from us, and if we cannot conceive the possibility of all this, what right have we to refuse belief in the possibility that magnetic and electric powers, may impress us from a greater or shorter distance? If these remarks are correct, it cannot escape us, that the more we are merged in the general life of nature, the more we shall sympathize with all its changes, and the more distant activities with which its agencies are connected, will become perceptible to those whose nervous system is capable of receiving impressions from them. On a similar ground we must explain presentiment concerning friends; they rest on deep sympathy with them, on a kind of polar relation. Should a presentiment become more clear, and assume the form of prediction, it must be remembered, that the future has its origin in the present, and that it must spring up from this source, as does the tree from the seed.

Presentiments may become *visions* when our imagination gives them form and shape. They then will appear to us from without as images, which to the visionary seem to have reality. The images will not be produced arbitrarily by our imagination, but they will emerge from our feelings and be calculated to represent their general nature, which is either *agreeable* or *disagreeable*. When they proceed from the feelings, that accompany the activity of conscience, then they will often assume the forms of good or evil spirits, because they will symbolically represent feelings, flowing forth from a quiet or disturbed conscience. Yet before we define *vision*, it may not be disagreeable to give a general notion of it by a few instances:

Petrarch, when at Vaucluse, saw Laura approach him at three different times during one night; fear seized his limbs, and the blood returned to his heart. Trembling he left the house, to breathe more freely. He climbed a rock, he walked through the woods and looked around on all sides to see whether Laura was following him. "No one will believe me, but it is true; I saw her in remote places, where I thought to be alone; from the trunk of a tree, from the basin of a fountain, from the cave of a rock, from clouds, &c. Fear made me immovable, I knew not what would become of me, and whither I should go!" Torquato Tasso during the last years of his life, was firmly convinced that a friendly ghost was in the habit of appearing to him. His friend, the knight Manso, expressed his unbelief to him, and was requested to convince himself by being personally present at one of his conversations with the apparition. Manso agreed to it, but while Tasso conversed with his spectre, he could see nothing at all. One of the finest visions ever seen by any man, is no doubt that of Benvenuto Cellini, which we shall give here in a free extract from Goethe's works. Cellini, the Italian artist, during his last imprisonment frequently prayed to God, that he would show him in a dream once more the disk of the sun. One morning he arose early and prayed fervently that God, by divine inspiration, would communicate the cause to him, why he was not worthy of seeing the sun even in a dream. While praying, and lost in the wish of seeing the sun, the Lord seized him in the manner of a wind, and led him into a large room, where he appeared to him in the form of a beautiful youth. He then saw a great number of persons, through the midst of which he had to force his way. At length he arrived at a narrow door, by which he entered a small street. Raising his eyes he perceived the sun, shining upon a high wall. The Lord then told him to walk up to a high edifice by a few steps, where he saw the sun in its full glory. After a while the rays of light inclined to the left of the sun, and the disk became pure and clear, and appeared like a bath of purest gold. Soon after this, the middle of the golden circle expanded and became elevated, when all at once Christ on the cross became visible, of the same pure gold, of which the sun was, and so beautiful and so benign, that no human mind could have imagined the thousandth part of such beauty. Then Christ moved to the left, and the centre of the circle again expanded and showed the beautiful figure of the holy virgin. She sat elevated, her son in her arms, and a smile on her face. On both sides two angels stood of great beauty. "All this I saw clearly and really, and thanked God constantly with a loud voice."

The images of vision originate in the same way, as those of our dreams. Here also it is a strong feeling, by which our whole mind is absorbed, by which its volition and clear consciousness are held down. The mind resting wholly in this feeling—as for instance that of Petrarch in the feeling of love—will animate and raise it. Thus this feeling will re-act in uncommon strength, or render every other emotion subject to it, and as the mind is lost in it, imagination, which is nearest allied to feeling, will represent it in a concrete form, under an individual image, and place it without us. This is indeed the case with every artist, with the painter, the sculptor, the poet. Their imagination transfers a thought or feeling into an image, which of course they must see as clearly before them, as if it existed in reality. Yet there is this difference between the images of the artist and the visionary. The artist controls his imagination by a conscious judgment; he distinguishes between it and its productions, and comprehends the latter as his own. The visionary looks upon them as possessed of reality; he views them not as proceeding from him, but as approaching him from without. And here it must be remarked, that the feeling, which gives rise to such a vision, may again be represented as being itself caused by the vision. So a woman entertained, for a considerable time, the idea of committing suicide; but the voice of her conscience unnerved her arm. One morning however she plunged herself into a deep well, and while standing up to the chin in the water, she suddenly perceived a guardian spirit, that extended his hand to assist her in getting out of the well again. This friendly apparition no doubt was the voice of her conscience, whose words were put into the mouth of an image, which her own imagination had produced. So it is known that the celebrated Blake, the English painter, frequently saw before him the forms of Dante, Milton, Virgil and Pindar, as if they were his contemporaries. Once Milton communicated to him a poem, that had not been published before in his collected works. The poem was by Blake, but his vision made it appear to come from Milton.

Visions, though their name is derived from *visus*, sight, are not confined to the eye only, but all the senses may share them. Suso, for instance, ate strawberries that were offered him in neat baskets. Nicolai felt all the pain, caused by a bristly serpent, winding itself around his body. Jacob Boehme, in the hour of death, heard beautiful music, which was inaudible to every one of the bystanders. Yet the eye is most favourable to visions. It easily produces phantoms. Irregular points, indistinct outlines, confused spots will induce it, especially during moonlight, to draw them out into regular forms. If our imagination be strong, and our judgment weak, and our conscience not perfectly at peace with us, we shall see spectres and ghosts of all kinds, and thus tremble at the creations of our own mind. The eye is the sense too, that more readily obeys the internal urgency of imagination, and will more easily see those images, which imagination necessitates it to form.

Second sight is the last of the phenomena of mind under consideration. It differs from presentiment and vision, and again contains both united. Vision has but rarely any thing to do with predictions and future events; it considers its images to be present and not future. Presentiment, on the other hand, is a dark foreboding of something distant, either in space or time. Second sight while it differs from both, has much in common with each. It unites in itself the forebodings of presentiment, and the clearness and distinctness of vision. Or it is a presentiment, that exhibits its foreboding in such an image, as its substance demands. Hence it is a vision, that without much imagination, indicates exactly what it represents. A lady, whose husband was from home, saw him return on the public road, when all at once he disappeared before her eyes. Afterwards she received information of his death, while travelling homeward. The explanation of second sight seems at first to be extremely difficult; but if the theory of presentiments and visions has been understood, that of second sight cannot remain concealed from us, for it is nothing else than the union of both. Here as well as in presentiments, nothing can be foretold that has not its foundation in the elements surrounding us, or in the intimate and close sympathy which we feel with near acquaintances, friends, and relatives. There have been little islands on which the second sight was extremely common. Thus Faro Island, the islands around Scotland, and some valleys in other parts of Europe, the Steinthal, &c. have been long known for their number of seers. The inhabitants of these islands and valleys are much separated from the rest of the world; the silence and retirement of their residences makes them meditate much on themselves, and live more in each other; their cultivation is not that of the mind in general, not that of judgment and reflection, but more that of feeling; hence their relation to each other is based on the heart more than on the calculations of the understanding. Circumstances well known to the seer, impress his mind, and as this is merged greatly in feeling, affect deeply the latter; this affection of the feeling, instead of reflecting on it and expressing its substance clearly, will be pronounced darkly, and in the form of presentiment by the seer, whose imagination will see the future in the present, and the effect in the cause, and represent it as vision does. Or the probability of an occurrence is to be ascertained by judgment; but the seer, not exercising it, perceives it by mere feeling, and his fears or hopes set his imagination into operation, and he sees as real and present what his fears and hopes anticipated.

This explanation will be found correct, at least with regard to one kind of second sights, when we consider that the seers in Scotland have been generally of very low rank and almost without any cultivation, wholly living in the state of nature; and when we add, that those clans which had seers were frequently isolated, living entirely within the sphere of their own families. In such a life every feeling and motion of one member would easily communicate itself to all. As the cultivation of the mind becomes more refined, and the intercourse with the world greater, second sight becomes less frequent. When *we* have often a presentiment that some friend or other will pay us a visit, the seer adds the image and such other circumstances as may render themselves probable to his feeling. The more retired we live, the more important the visit from a friend would be, and the more it will engage our imagination. If our presentiment is called forth by circumstances that render such a visit probable, for instance by fine weather, or by the idea of leisure, or any thing known to be favorable, the seer does not leave it with this dark impression, but perceives the ship at great distance and the persons in it, and even the dress they wear. Thus the seer perceives at a distance what in reality he only sees in himself. Second sight, no doubt, in many instances is produced by magnetic or other natural influences, which will even affect animals, as for example, horses; but there is certainly nothing miraculous about it. Another remark may not be out of place here. Thousands of impressions, ideas, notions, pass through our mind, and are no longer remembered; they seem to be gone, without having left a trace. And yet while every sensation appears and disappears, none is lost, but each affects the mind, and exercises an influence upon its character. This influence will be felt long after the individual impression is forgotten. Though never remembered again as single impressions, they may nevertheless breathe life into our words, and a peculiar power into the productions of our minds. The elements lie in the soul, unknown to him, whose soul it is; how much might be explained concerning visions and second sight, if these dark elements were always known to us.

Second sight is not any thing arbitrary. Some seers it is true, received payment for second sights, but their visions were frequently full of deception. Seers cannot call them forth when they desire to have them, nor keep them off when they approach them. A seer who was warned by his minister, and admonished not to indulge second sights, saw during *a sermon* the corpse of a person then alive on the same place where that person afterwards was buried.

Second sight is principally met with among the uncultivated, as Johnson has remarked, and as will appear from the history of idolatry,—the Shaman are a remarkable instance—Swedenborg, however, though a learned and cultivated man, imagined himself to have travelled into other worlds, and thus mistook the productions of his own mind for genuine realities. So it was with the pious Oberlin, who was in possession of a map, on which he was in the habit of showing to the family that had lost one of its members, where the soul of their departed friend was to dwell. Savages, like Swedenborg, say that their souls are traveling when they dream. The idea that the soul can leave the body and wander into distant places has been favored by many cultivated persons, yet always by such as were a little diseased in their minds.

The fear of ghosts and spectres, so common among all nations, and especially in their infancy, originates in a manner similar to visions. The spectres are but the productions of the imagination, sometimes called forth by an external impression on the senses. The state of the conscience will render them more or less terrible, so that in proportion as we fear these ghosts, we in reality fear ourselves. If our hearts are pure, and we are heavenly minded, the fear of ghosts will vanish, as legends give us to understand, when they require nothing more than a prayer to disperse spectres. When our conscience is troubled we shall feel alarmed, especially at night, by the supernatural world and its inhabitants. As we see ourselves in part when we see spectres, so we may see ourselves wholly, and such a sight of ourselves generally is thought by the credulous to indicate death. Goethe saw himself on the public road near Strasburg, in a gray suit on horseback, as he really eight years afterwards rode on the same spot, but continued to live a long time afterwards.

§ 5. MAGNETIC SLEEP.

There is scarcely a subject of Psychology more contested, than the one which we now approach. While some reject it, without having cooly examined it, others superstitiously and without any discrimination receive every fact related, if it is only uncommon and miraculous. It may be well to glance at both parties.

The one of them rejects animal magnetism, because its phenomena are extraordinary or out of the common experience. They do not faithfully investigate and then judge, but determined to admit to be true only what can be handled, and what will easily be explained on common principles, they are ready to condemn whatever is not analogous to their own experience. They wholly forget, that nothing is true, because we experience it; but that we experience it, because it is true or because it has reality. Experience does, therefore, not affect the truth of any thing, but only corroborates or confirms it. If Whately, in imitation of Thomas Campanella, who died in 1639, and who attempted to prove that Charles the Great never lived, wrote an essay, the object of which was to show how, by historical scepticism, the life of Napoleon might be considered a fiction, he could expect to succeed only on the principle of Sallust, according to which men are willing to admit what is common, but always inclined to respect what in the least extends beyond their own capacities. These persons who prove everything by facts, and consider facts the basis of all knowledge, will reject them as soon as they do not correspond with other facts known to them. Satisfied with the use of the world, they never dream of any thing besides that which is visible, and yet every production of nature rests on an invisible power, everything that is perceptible on something that is concealed.

The other party is always looking out for facts of magnetic sleep, that will astonish the world. If these phenomena could be *explained*, their interest in animal magnetism would be gone. They are, therefore, as anxious to receive all facts without reflecting on them, as the others are to denounce them. The former party *thinks*, but thinking makes it an *unbeliever;* the latter *believes,* but fears to think, and thus want of thought makes it *superstitious.* To it the facts are too high and too strong; it cannot grasp them, but must admit them and hence feels an unbounded respect for them, almost considering them of divine origin and as divine communications.

Both parties, it may be easily seen, render it difficult to themselves to get a correct idea of magnetic sleep. If the thinker could once convince himself of magnetic phenomena in sleep, he could certainly no longer continue his opposition; if the superstitious believer could understand their laws, he would cease to gaze with reverence upon them. But how can the one become convinced of facts, and the other of their laws, if both either do not investigate the subject or examine it with preconceived notions? When persons, prejudiced against the idea of magnetic sleep, offer themselves to the magnetizer, and then find that manipulation will effect nothing with them, they will at once have done with the matter. And yet they forget, that the relation between the magnetizer and the magnetized is a polar one, that on the part of the magnetized it is a disease, both bodily and mentally, that it demands confidence and faith, without which persons, subject to animal magnetism will feel an antipathy and yet be thrown into convulsions if an attempt is made to put them asleep. A sympathy between the magnetized and magnetizer is indispensable, and such a relation between both, that the nervous system of the latter is neither too strong nor too weak, but of the exact energy required to excite that of the former. If too strong, it produces cramps and pain; if too weak, it cannot cause any effect. When, on the other hand, the believer is constantly prepared to receive stories of all kinds of visions, of apparitions, of departed spirits, and even of journeys into other worlds, to what else can this predilection, which fears critical judgment, lead than to superstition? Neither of these two parties take a correct position in reference to animal magnetism, and we shall have to deviate from both. On the one hand it will become candid examiners to exercise their full power of judgment, as one of the parties does, and on the other, to admit all well-authenticated facts, as the other does, with this difference, that we distinguish between well authenticated facts, and those relations that are the fictions of an imagination which delights in the supernatural and mystical.

We do not propose to give a full theory here—this would be presumptuous and out of place. Nor is it our design, to include at present the artificially produced magnetic sleep or Mesmerism. We shall therefore confine ourselves to the natural magnetic sleep, which was in existence long before Mesmer discovered it, and which, if somnambulism is taken in its widest sense, may be called *Idio* or *Autosomnambulism*. Much that has been said on presentiments and visions, must necessarily apply to magnetic sleep, for what presentiments are in our state of waking, the phenomena of magnetic sleep are in our state of sleeping. These phenomena are in general the following; Persons speak, act, and walk about in their sleep; they see themselves, their viscera, anticipate diseases, have presentiments of things future or at a distance, and frequently have apparitions. Their moral disposition seems to be raised, they speak a purer language and are in general elevated above their common character. The phenomena of the artificial and natural magnetism are nearly the same, for the so-called *clairvoyance* is peculiar to both; but there are a few that belong exclusively to the former.—Such are the effects of manipulation, when the eyes close, the pupil turns upward, pain is assuaged, breathing becomes more easy, the face brightens up, and all heaviness departs from the limbs. Again: the dependence of the magnetized upon the magnetizer is so great, that it has been compared to that of the embryo upon the mother, and the feelings and ideas of the magnetizer are said to communicate themselves to the magnetized, who if the magnetizer is a physician, will prescribe medicines for themselves according to his system, or if he is a poet, write in his style. These phenomena will take place in natural somnambulism, in which persons likewise prescribe for themselves, and foresee the course their disease is likely to take.

A few instances of magnetic sleep or somnambulism may throw light upon its nature: When the archbishop of Bordeaux was in the Seminary, he knew a young minister who was a somnambulist. In order to become acquainted with this singular disease, he went every night into his room as soon as the minister was asleep, and observed among the rest the following facts.—The young man arose, took paper and ink and wrote sermons. Whenever he had finished a page, he read it over from the top down to the bottom with a loud voice, and without making use of his eyes. When a passage did not please him, he would erase it and write the correction with much accuracy above it. The beginning of a sermon pleased the bishop much. It was elaborate and well-written. In order to ascertain whether he had made use of his eyes or not, a piece of pasteboard was placed under his chin, so that he could not see the paper on which he wrote. He continued, however, to write without noticing anything that the bishop did. Again, in order to ascertain how the somnambulist could perceive the presence of objects, his paper was exchanged for another of a different size. He directly discovered it, while a paper of the same size laid in the place of his own, did not in the least disturb him. This case is related in the French Encyclopedia. From another remarkable case it appears, that somnambulism is not confined to the night, but may take place during the light of the day. A girl of fourteen years of age was seized by somnambulism while attending divine service. She rose and went home with her eyes closed; afterwards she was found half undressed, sitting on her bed. All attempts to awaken her were in vain; after some time she went to a table, took a hymn book, sought and found the hymn which had been sung in the church, and with closed eyes she continued to sing where she had stopped when at the service. The same girl was sent by a minister, in whose service she was, to a Doctor Mueller, who lived at a distance of about three miles. She went while under the influence of somnambulism. The Doctor, aware of her disease, ordered something for her and sent her to his apothecary. There she waited for the medicine. Having received it, she went homeward while still asleep. Doctor Mueller followed her for more than a mile and a half, to observe her. She noticed every impediment in the path, and carefully avoided wagons and persons. When she awoke and noticed the Doctor, she was frightened, and knew not how she had come there. See Carus Junior, in his Psychology, and Nasse's Archives. This last mentioned case proves that it is not the influence of the moon which gives somnambulists so much safety in climbing roofs of houses, and passing through dangerous places. The feeling of perfect safety, to anticipate this remark, is derived from their ignorance of the danger in which they are. A foot requires but a little small spot to stand on with perfect safety; whether this spot be given on the roof of a house or on the solid ground, is a matter of little consequence to somnambulists, who do not judge while they are asleep. As soon as they perceive the danger, when suddenly awakened, they fall down or injure themselves.

The above examples might be sufficient, were we not anxious to exhibit the strength of sympathy and antipathy in the state of somnambulism, and the great excitability of the nervous system. And here we shall allude to a woman of Prevorst in Wurtemberg, whose case has lately caused much sensation in Germany. Minerals when touched by somnambulists, will frequently produce the most astonishing effects in different parts of the body. It is remarkable, that these effects not only differ widely from each other according to the different minerals, but also according to the different parts of the body with which they are brought in connection. They will produce convulsions, cramps, lameness, they will exhilarate or make desponding. With the woman of Prevorst, salt put into her hands immediately caused salivation; copper, colic and nausea. Without taking it into her mouth, she felt the acid taste of spar. Crystal laid upon her, awoke her when asleep, but when placed upon her heart, it made her whole body stiff. Other metals made her laugh, and others again cry. It is certainly worthy of our notice and may aid us in some considerations hereafter, that she seemed to feel the *nature* of these metals, as she could enter into the views and feelings of persons. Very hard metals, universally caused her muscles to grow stiff and hard; soft spar produced the contrary effect.

Somnambulists, as has been seen, speak, act and walk, while the four senses of the head are asleep. How then is it possible, that they can walk or write or act? How is it possible, that a somnambulist, with closed eyes, can run faster through a large dark cellar, than other persons, with a light in their hands, can follow her? The following theory, accepted by many, is offered to the consideration of the reader:

Here we must remember what has been said on the nature of sleep and dreaming in general, that the life of the soul is merged in that of the body, and rests principally in in the ganglion nervous system. This now is so much excited in its activity, that to some degree it may be substituted for the upper senses. The sense of feeling as spread over the whole skin, is the source of the four senses of the head, as may easily be seen from comparative anatomy. With the crab for instance, the ear is nothing else than a skin, softer than the rest, below which lies a bag filled with moisture and nerves. The eye of flies consists only of a thin skin, to which runs a filament of a nerve. Oken, in his Natural History says: "at the sides of the head are two eyes, composed of many single ones, which have a great many surfaces—the eyes of the butterfly have seventeen thousand. These eyes are only the arched and thin skin, to which extend nerves, that lead out single filaments to each surface." With snails no organ of sight can be observed, and yet according to Oken they distinguish, like some maggots, between darkness and light. Flies have undoubtedly a good scent, and yet they have no nose. Some have therefore thought that they smell with their windpipes, others with a soft place behind their lips, and others with their feelers. These remarks fully establish the truth, that our common way of perceiving things is not the only one, and therefore what is not analogous to it, deserves not to be rejected for that reason merely. In somnambulism, feeling, as spread over the whole body, is heightened and changed into a capacity of *perceiving*. The mere feeling of any thing within or without becomes a sensation or perception; hence somnambulists see their own viscera, and especially those which are much excited during the state of somnambulism. The power of perceiving thus produced will be strongest, wherever many nerves are concentrated, as on the cavity of the heart and other parts of the body. The nature of this sensation is, however, indistinct and confused, since it is only by the division of the sensitive power into five distinct senses, that we can obtain clear and transparent ideas of things around us. Salt, for example, is white to the eye, sharp to the taste, and angular to the touch; we observe these different qualities, by bringing one after the other in contact with our different senses. When all the senses are merged in one, that is, when the divided activity of sensation, is reduced and without order to one simple activity, the impressions received from objects can be nothing else than dark and confused. It would therefore be wrong to say of somnambulists that they see and hear, taste and smell, but like snails they have only a dim impression of light and darkness, and like animals that have no regularly formed ears, they have but a dull, dreamlike sensation of sound. With this view of the sensual life of the somnambulists, it may safely be said that the general sense, which develops itself from feeling, takes the place of the others, as does feeling in some degree that of sight with the blind. The blind, though by mere feeling he may distinguish between black and red, can get no idea of color by it. So the somnambulist can get no clear idea of objects, but only perceives their presence and general difference. When Spallanzini cut out the eyes of bats, and then set them free, he observed with astonishment, that they avoided every obstacle in their way. How could they do this? Certainly only by the development of a *general* sense.

We ought not to object to such a *general* sense, because we cannot conceive of its nature and activity;—though both may be understood from the general nature of sleep. Such an objection would be in no wise better, than if the blind should object to a sense like that of sight, merely because all our explanations will not give him an adequate idea of it, he having nothing analogous to it in his experience.

The strength of sympathy and antipathy may now be easily explained. When we have the full use of all our senses, we can govern the impressions made upon us, at least to a certain extent. We may exclude the light from the eye, the noise from the ear. But when the life of the soul is sunk into that of the body, and has resigned its dominion for a time, when the distinctness of sensation is gone, and when instead of many senses, but a general sense is active, then we are more receptive, more passive, more under the dominion of an impression, and as it affects us pleasantly, we either sympathize with the object from which it comes, or feel an antipathy to it. The nature of feeling always expresses itself directly, without reflection. The fact, that somnambulists frequently prescribe correct medicines for themselves rests on the feeling of disease, which makes them seek for relief, and though man is not under the dominion of instinct in somnambulism, something analogous to it makes its appearance. Their sympathy with vegetables known to them, will guide them. The dog when sick finds an herb to cure him. The disease in him impels, by a feeling of want and pain, to seek for something, and finding the herb, he will be made certain by the impression he receives from it through scent, that it will afford what his diseased system demands. As the magnet attracts the iron, as the negative pole attracts the positive, so a relation between the disease and the natural remedy will force the dog to seize the latter.

With regard to perceptions of distant objects and to presentiments, we refer back to these subjects as above. With a few modifications all will pertain to the present case. We only add an extract from Goldsmith's history, which may give us a case analogous to the perception of distant objects in animals. Speaking of the pigeon, he says: "the letter is tied under the bird's wing, and it is then let loose to return. It is seen on such occasions, flying directly into the clouds to amazing height, and then with the greatest certainty and exactness directing itself by some surprising instinct towards home, which lies sometimes at many miles distance, bringing its message to those to whom it is directed. By what marks it discovers the place, by what chart it is guided in the right way, is to us utterly unknown." The carrier pigeon cannot possibly see the place whither it is to go, and yet it is certain of it, though we cannot comprehend *how* it became so, because the sense by which it is made certain of it is wanting to us. So it is as to somnambulists.

§ 6. THE HEALTH AND THE DISEASES OF MIND.

Our body as has been already remarked is not a machine, but an organism. A machine is externally composed; its parts are joined in each other by a power not resting in it; the idea of the mind producing it, is not contained in it but in the mechanic, and precedes it as all its parts exist, before it is finished as a whole. This external composition, in which one part is connected with the other, not by its internal nature or by *one life* pervading all the parts, but by mechanical cohesion renders it possible, that when one part of the machine gets out of order, it may be mended or another substituted for it. With the body this is different. Its members are not merely parts, but *organs*, for they are alive, and their life is that of the body, as the life of the body exists only in them. All the organs together constitute the organism; the former do not precede the latter, but all grow forth simultaneously from one point that contains them, as the seed the plant. In such an organism each organ has a peculiar position and importance or design; both position and design are given it by the general life of the organism, so that the root as of the plant cannot be where the stem is, nor the stem where the flower, and so that the stem has a design different from that of the root. But it is one life that unfolds itself in the root, stem, and flower which connects them, and which is the same in every one of them. This life they have to manifest, and while each organ is active for itself, it is so only in reference to the whole, from which it derives existence and activity. Thus it is with our body. Each nerve is connected with all the nerves. The body may be said to be *well*, only when all its organs are harmoniously active. By the term *harmoniously* we understand that there are *different* organs, but that they all of them are united and serve one common end. In health, therefore, no organ obtains an ascendancy over all the others, or isolates its activity, or absorbs that of the rest; when, however, any organ does become active without reference to the whole— by what cause is here entirely indifferent—then the body is diseased, the organism is deranged: this is indicated by pain, for pain is the feeling of a conflict or separation between parts belonging together.

The definition of bodily disease will render that of mental derangement easily understood. The mind is pure activity, and as such a perfect union. But this activity takes different directions and unfolds itself in different ways, and thus it may be said to be the union of manifold activities, all of which are internally united, each being what the other is, and all serving the same whole, yet each in a specific manner. When these activities harmonize, that is, when each in its place fulfils its design, and no one interferes with the other, so that while many and different, they still are one and united in their tendency to serve the whole to which they are subordinate, the life of the mind may be said to be healthy. Or in other words the activities of the mind are many, but when they are co-ordinate to each other and subordinate to the mind as their whole, so that all are equally penetrated and governed by the whole mind, then the latter is well. But when this co-ordination is interrupted, when one of the mental activities succeeds in gaining the exclusive interest of the mind, and thus by an increased strength absorbs all the others or suppresses them, the mind is out of order. There is none of the *activities* wanting, but the *order* in which each ought to be active in its sphere without interfering with the other, and in which all should aid and support each other is deranged. When, for instance, the imagination is active without or independent of judgment, it will produce phantoms and fantastical notions. With the poet, imagination is likewise principally active, but it is at the same time aided by the fancy, by the memory, and by the judgment. The latter pervades it, for a poet must know what beauty is, and to know this he must judge much and constantly, compare his productions with the laws of beauty known to him, and control his imagination.

Division of the diseases of the mind.—Some have thought proper, to divide them according to the three principal activities that may be diseased, and thus have considered *melancholy* as a disease of feeling, *insanity* as a disease of the understanding, and *mania* as a disease of the will. Yet the activities of mind so relate to each other, that the disease of one will affect all the others. The maniac is not only diseased in his will, but also in his imagination and judgment, for how can any one will any thing without a knowledge of it? And how can he know it without judgment? Another principle of division has therefore been proposed, one derived from the relation of the mentally diseased to the objective world around him. This principle must be correct, if it is right to say that derangement in general is that state of mind, in which our mental activities being out of order, we live only in our own ideas and notions, in the fictions of our brain, and substitute them for the realities and relations of real life; in which consequently the mind by supposing its fictions to be true, comes into contradiction with the world. The position which the derangement of mind assumes, may be a threefold one:

1. *Melancholy.* Here the deranged on the one hand is fully convinced, that his notions and wishes ought to be realized, but on the other he darkly feels the impossibility of effecting their realization. He therefore makes no effort to render possible the impossible; yet he cannot resign the ideal, which he bears in his bosom; he loves his fictions or the objects of his wishes so much that he cannot part with them. Thus he consumes his existence in a monotonous grief; he cannot take interest in any thing, except the object of his sadness. A young girl of cultivated mind was known to stand the whole day mute and immovable, with her head bent down. After long and repeated attempts nothing was drawn from her except a nod or a shake of the head. When she was asked if any person had injured her, she shook her head. When asked if she had injured others, she nodded. But how? no one could learn from her. One Monday the unfortunate girl at length determined to repeat the Lord's prayer. When she came to the petition; "Lead us not into temptation, but deliver us from evil;" she raised her voice with the strongest emphasis, and some time afterwards she cried out most piteously: "Alas! the sin against the Holy Ghost." Here the idea, that she had committed the sin against the Holy Ghost, was viewed by the girl as real, while at the same time she desired it to be otherwise, and feeling the impossibility of

undoing what she supposed she had done, it threw her into the state in which we find her.

2. *Insanity.* In this state the deranged has lost every idea of the world as it is and of its relation to him; he feels convinced that all his imaginations are real, and exist in full truth. He is therefore satisfied and cheerful, and very ingeniously assimilates the whole world around him to that of his dreams. He is no longer sensible of any contradiction of his phantoms to the world. If he fancies himself a king, he will act as a king with the most logical consequence. So the Jesuit, Father Sgambari imagined that he had been created a Cardinal. To convince him, that his flattering fancy was an error, Father Provinzial, in the hope of curing him, made a friendly representation to him. He answered in this dilemma: "You either consider me insane or not. In the latter case you do me great injustice, in speaking to me in such a manner. In the former I consider you with your permission, a greater lunatic than myself, because you think you can by mere persuasion bring me to my senses." Aside from this fancy, his understanding was sound, and disposed to scientific investigations. Whenever students addressed him with "Your Eminence," he was social and communicative. As the body is often partially diseased, but otherwise well, so may the mind be partially deranged. Sometimes persons have become estranged to themselves. A soldier looked on his body as a miserable machine, made to replace his former real body, that had been destroyed by a cannon ball. Or persons, whose judgment is diseased, and whose imagination is active without restraint, produce all kinds of images, when they feel pain, and consider them as the cause of the pain. Animals bite them or sting them. Tissot relates the case, of a man, that became deranged from constant study. He was convinced, that seven horsemen were constantly fighting in his stomach.

3. *Mania.* This state of derangement unites in some degree the two former. The *melancholy* man conscious of the impossibility of realizing his wishes, dwells with his whole mind constantly on the object of his exclusive interest, and compares it with the reality of the world, and discovering the permanent contradiction, he has an ever-

teeming source of sadness in the results of this comparison. The *insane*, on the other hand is determined no longer to acknowledge the world around him, as it is, but to re-model it so as to bring it in harmony with that of his imagination. The *maniac*, like the melancholy man, feels that what he takes to be real, is not so, but that the opposite of it, is; at the same time he has the tendency of the insane, to realize his fictions, for he considers them to be true and correct. This realization cannot be easily effected as with the insane, for the maniac feels the contradiction of his fictions with the world; he therefore, finding the world in his way, turns against it with the hope that by its destruction he may realize the purposes of his diseased will. He rages because he cannot effect what he designs, nor can he resign his will. He is like the passionate man, that kills in his fury whoever opposes him. His whole mind will have fixed itself in one idea, and cannot retire from it, because he has given it dominion over himself. Hence the immense muscular power in the fits of mania.

All the diseases of the mind have their longer or shorter intermissions. This shows, that the reason exists, and is only deranged. Many insane persons are so merely with regard to a single subject, but on every other they are perfectly sane. Others are insane only during a certain period of the year. A celebrated physician of Venice imagined during the dog-days, that he was an earthen jar, and locked himself up for a whole month. After the four weeks were past, he came down again, and went as usual to his employment. Every kind of derangement, according to the statements of many physicians, abates in old age, and the deranged state of mind is therefore one that will pass away sooner or later.

The above division of mental diseases is, of course, susceptible of many subdivisions. *Insanity*, for instance, includes *imbecility* of mind, weakness of the understanding and will in which man cannot take care of himself; *incapacity* of connecting ideas, or of seizing a thought and fixing the mind on a single idea; *idiocy*, when a person is active without having any particular object in view; *lunacy*, when the insane considers himself perfectly rational. *Melancholy* comprises *hypochondria*, which tortures man by making him constantly brood over future or present, real or imaginary evils. *Mania* applies to those that find pleasure in abusing others, in ridiculing them, or who desire to destroy others, and cunningly watch for a proper opportunity. Our division will be found to comprise all the possible relations which the subjective mind may, in its state of derangement, assume to the objective world around. At the same time it agrees with the division founded by others on the principal activities of mind, for melancholy seems to rest on deep feeling and emotions; insanity on the thinking activity in man, and mania on the will.

One question is left which seems to be of great importance. How is it possible that the mind, a purely intellectual activity of divine origin, can become diseased? It would seem to have the power to keep itself free from every thing that might entangle it. But here we must remark in the first place, that the soul is already diseased in its state of nature; for turned away from its proper objects, truth, and holiness, and the love of God, it is sunk in sinfulness and vice, and instead of deriving its food and nourishment from a study of the good and noble, it seeks for it in the sensual and transitory. But that which nourishes a power communicates also its nature to it, as may be observed in every thing living, in every plant, which, in absorbing the light, becomes colored, and in receiving the air, receives fragrance. As little as the magnet could be said to be in its vigor, if instead of pointing towards the north, it should suffer itself to be attracted in other directions, so little is the mind healthy, when it once has lost its only proper direction, but it must be said to be in error and in a dangerous deviation from the right path. To express these remarks more fully, we will consider, for a moment, the nature of will. The *will*, one of the activities of mind, is healthy, when by its own power it freely directs itself in accordance with the divine will, so that it agrees with it both externally, as to the action, and internally as to the disposition. When on the other hand it does not so, but directs itself either by desires or passions, then it is not free, but under the dominion of something different from itself, which is the ground of its determination. The divine law is the divine will. It is the only source of freedom, and it alone is free; the human will directing itself by it or by the divine law, returns to the source from whence it came, becomes filled with its nature, and consequently free. To enter on this subject fully here, would lead to discussions that would take up too much room. One idea it may however be useful to mention here, an idea, according to which it is supposed that our will is free, when it *can choose* between the evil and the good. This idea is wholly erroneous, and instead of calling such a will free, it would be better to call it arbitrary. For if freedom, like every thing else in creation, has its own nature, and if without it nothing can be said to be free, then freedom includes the *necessity* of acting in accordance with its own nature, or else it destroys itself. This nature is contained and expressed in the divine law, which, like the divine will, cannot be influenced by any thing except itself, because whatever is, is created by it and dependent upon it. The human will can be free, therefore, only when it receives the divine will as its soul. But if a will should rather choose evil and sin, it would miss what it seeks for, *liberty*,* and become the slave of sin; for sin is so wholly opposed to *purity* of will, that it destroys its freedom. As long, therefore, as a will is capable of choosing between the good and evil, between heaven and hell, between the source of its life and that of its death, so long this will is not free. It would no doubt at once be considered erroneous, if any one should assert that fire, in order to be fire, might choose between burning or not burning, or that water might be water, whether it would moisten or not; or that light might be light, though it should be able to choose between itself and darkness. Every one will admit, that in the moment light chose to turn into darkness, it would lose itself and cease to be the free light. So it is with liberty. It must, in order to remain what it is, always preserve its own nature, and this nature

---

* It will be easily seen that it is by no means the author's desire to discuss the nature of will in this place, that it is rather introduced for the sake of comparison, than for its own; he hopes therefore that the mere incidental allusion will not be made the basis of either friendly or unfriendly criticism. He here speaks of the *contents* and not of the *form* of will, and again of pure and *genuine*, and not of common liberty.

is, to determine itself freely by its own activity, and not by any thing different from itself. Liberty is therefore a free activity that is not arbitrary, but includes necessity. But the human will, in its state of nature, is averse to necessity, and instead of perceiving in it the protector of its liberty, it views it as its enemy. It has therefore lost its liberty, and may, in this respect, be compared to a planet that has no light in itself, but must receive it from the sun, around which it revolves. If the planet remains in its path, and preserves its relation to the sun, it has light, and whatever grows on it is filled with light, and grows and blooms in the most beautiful colors. But if the planet at any time should choose between its regular course and another, and really pursue one leading off from the sun, darkness and death would reign on it and destroy all life. The sun of the will is that of righteousness or the divine will; it alone can make us free. Rejecting it, we reject the only source of freedom, and become mentally diseased. The eye of man has a latent light in itself, but this light is darkness, and will remain such unless it be excited by the light of the sun. Suppose the sight to be the freedom of the eye, the eye can be said to be free only when turning towards the light, but not when diving into darkness. So the will is free, only when living in its proper elements, in the good and true, in the beautiful and divine, and when it does not suffer any attraction or power to separate it from the divine law.

From these remarks it will sufficiently appear, that the will in its state of nature is diseased. It is not directed towards its proper object; nor does it receive its proper nourishment; nor is it pure, but much more determined by sensual appetite and desires, by inclinations and passions. Every passion is a transient derangement, and the only difference between it and a real derangement is this. The man in passion may be so overpowered, that he, as for instance in anger, can no longer control himself; yet he enters into this passion arbitrarily, and might if he chose avoid it. The maniac, on the other hand, comes under the influence of his passions, independent of his will. Some maniacs frequently foresee their fits, and beg that they may be chained lest they should hurt some person. With this view history agrees. For a spirit of revenge and wrath infuriated those heroes, whose insanity is mentioned among the first that have become known historically for their derangement, *Hercules* and *Ajax*. Some have therefore thought that a mental derangement was merely psychological, and always caused by sinfulness. This idea, no doubt is correct, if it means to assert, that the body itself became subject to diseases only by the fall of man. Certain it is, however, that by the close connection of the body with the soul, the former has frequently been the cause of the diseases of the latter.

Passion, as haughtiness, revenge, wrath; *deep emotions*, as terror and fright; *inclinations*, as unfortunate love, may become the causes of derangement, and the works of Shakspeare exhibit the most interesting examples of this kind. If the will of man were pure, these powers of sin could not affect it. If man had faith in God, and loved him supremely, if he confided in his providence, then he would not become the prey of every passion, nor would loss and misfortune harm him. But placing his sinful affections wholly on earthly things, he must despair when they are taken from him, or when he cannot attain to the objects of his highest wishes. He lives in the sphere of delusion; how easy then must it be for the demons of pride and wounded ambition, of unsatisfied vanity and sore jealousy to derange a mind that has no hold in any thing which is permanent and solid. If that on which we stand constantly turns around with us, we must become giddy. Again, the constant use of one and the same mental activity may so awaken all others, that a derangement will be the consequence. This is the case with such as have become insane from the study of mystical books. Or the whole mind of a person is so constantly devoted to one single object, it becomes absorbed by it and so fixed upon it, that it cannot keep off its image. So Orestes constantly saw the blood gushing from the wound inflicted on his mother by his own hand. So when Spinello had painted Satan in the most hideous colors, his imagination was filled with the picture, until at length he saw Satan constantly at his side, reproaching him for having painted him so ugly. And what else than the silent beginning of derangement was it, when a painter, who had killed a person, afterwards drew a picture that was beautiful in every respect, but over which such a gloom was spread, that no person could look upon it without feeling an awe for which nothing could account, except the diseased imagination of the painter.

As derangement is caused by the activity of the mind itself, so again the activity of the body may operate on it and derange it. And here any thing that destroys the health of the body, will more or less affect the mind. Intoxication is in itself a transient derangement, for it causes such an excitement of the nerves, that they with their whole activity, especially that which principally depends upon them, as the imagination, withdraw themselves more or less, from the dominion of the mind, and act independent of control until exhaustion and sleep follows. A drunken person walked at night through a street, beautifully illuminated by the moon; and thinking it was a river, undressed himself to bathe, and could only be convinced of his mistake by the hardness of the stones. Another in falling down a flight of stairs, rose calmly and asked a friend that happened to be with him with much concern, "whether he had hurt himself in falling down so many steps?" He could not be persuaded that it was himself that had met with the accident, but insisted on his friend's having fallen. The delirium tremens, or mania potu are too well known to be mentioned here. In America and Europe more than one third of all the deranged persons become so from the use of liquors; in China, on the other hand, from that of opium. Poisonous food may likewise cause delirium. Two monks ate water hemlock. Both immediately felt much thirst; both plunged into water, the one thinking that he was a goose, and the other that he was a duck, and both declaring that they could live no where else except in the water. Tissot knew a child four years old that raved several times a day. He ascribed it to the food which it had received from its nurse. Want of sleep may derange the activity of the mind as well as too long a deprivation of food. Ugolino ate in his delirium his own child. The idiocy of children is frequently the consequence of the sinful life of parents.

It may be easily understood how bodily sickness may

produce mental derangement. Our ideas, our whole thinking depends in some degree on our nervous system. Where nerves are, there is feeling; and where feeling is, there is either instinct, or in its place *consciousness.* Man becomes conscious of every feeling produced by impressions on the nerves, and when the nerves are diseased, the feelings must be so; and if they are unsound, the ideas called forth by them must become unfavorably affected. With every feeling is connected pleasure or pain, and with the latter a tendency either to indulge the pleasant, or to remove the unpleasant feeling by action and activity. Want is a state of necessity, in which some organ of our body finds itself; when this state of the organ enters the nervous system attached to it, it is felt; of this feeling we become conscious, and produce in accordance with it certain notions and ideas. While we therefore must agree with those physicians, that derive many mental diseases from organic derangement, we must at the same time deprecate the idea that the body is the sole source of mental sickness. We would rather repeat it as our conviction, that the mind, if it were directed to its proper object, to God and a Savior, could rule over its body as well as over its passions, for it would then possess purity and a power over all things which are merely earthly. If it would keep itself aloof from them, and be ready to lay down the life for Christ's sake, it could not be absorbed by the care for health or bodily defects. Some may perhaps feel inclined to reply, that mental derangement arises frequently from too deep a *religious* solicitude. This may be true, and yet it will not affect our theory. Good wine will become spoiled in an impure vessel. When a man will not surrender his life, and yet longs for the privileges of religion, when he will not give up his sin, and yet cannot resign the possession of divine favor, and when he then feels the contradiction between his state of sinfulness and that of desired sanctification,—he may easily become deranged, not through religion, but by his relation to it.

CHAPTER III.

THE POWER OF THE MIND OVER THE BODY.

We have seen that the mind depends greatly on external influences and on the body of man, and yet it exercises by its energy a control and dominion over the elements around it and also over the body. It affects the form, the health and vigor of the latter, and leaves on it an impression of its strength of character and disposition. To direct the attention to this power of the mind over the body, is the object of the present chapter.

1. The mind has an influence on *the form* of the body. This assertion may be easily established, for it is too well known how a fright of the mother during pregnancy, or the sight of any disagreeable or deformed person affects the form of the embryo. The deformity of many children, the deficiency of some members, the weakness even of some senses, as for instance of the eye, in Albinos must be traced to the influence of which we speak. Howshipp, an English physician, relates a remarkable case of this kind. A woman in the state of pregnancy was frightened in crossing a frozen river; the ice burst and cracked, she was terrified, and when delivered of a child, its skin was rent and gaped considerably in many places, but had begun to heal up. The Lacedemonians were familiar with this powerful influence, for they placed the beautiful statutes of Apollo, Hyacinth, and Narcissus in the rooms of their wives when pregnant. The sight of an epileptic has frequently transferred the disease to the embryo. The mind of the mother has its influence not only on the body, but also on the disposition of the child, as we have seen in another place. The Jesuits, well versed in the subject of educa-

tion, showed therefore much sound wisdom in always ascertaining the character of the mother when they received a new pupil. The reason of this influence is obvious. The life of the mother and that of the embryo-child is one. One blood circulates in both, the same nourishment sustains both, and the feelings of the mother are, at least in some degree, also those of the embryo. The body of the child being in a state of developement, is of course more subject to the reception of so powerful impressions, and of the changes produced by them, than that of the mother which is already formed. And yet we may see similar effects of the power of the mind on the body of adult persons. Vice and crimes seem to have been the causes of great deformities of the heart. Testa found the heart of a great criminal, hard, hairy, and skinny; and Riolan found that of a very vicious man gristly. The same observation has often been repeated.

2. The mind exercises a power over *the health* of the body. It would be superfluous, to repeat here, that certain diseases of the body are accompanied by weakening emotions of the mind, as anxiety, despondency, melancholy, fear, a tendency to commit suicide, &c. Such diseases are those of the liver, obdurations of the intestines. And yet other diseases have a cheering effect upon the mind, as for instance consumption, diseases of the lungs, &c. So the mind in its turn exercises the most powerful influence upon the health of the body. Fear relaxes the muscles and strips the whole system of energy, and exposes it to the attacks of a fatal miasma; on the other hand, a strong will and courage keep off the enemy. We will here allude to a few instances. When in the orphan house of Harlem, a boy was seized with epilepsy, all those in whose sight this occurred, were so terrified that the disease soon spread through the whole asylum. The celebrated Boerhave knowing the cause of their disease, after having used all other means in vain, had instruments brought, such as pincers, hooks, hammers, &c., had them placed in the fire, and then threatened that the first child that became epileptic should be pinched and tortured with these hot instruments. The children fearing this, were all of them delivered from this dreadful evil. This statement agrees

with another recorded in Schubert's History of the Soul. In the year 1800 the fever raged awfully in the city of Cadiz. Two hundred dead persons were daily carried out of the city, and all the streets were filled with the smell of death. All ties of friendship and sympathy were torn asunder, when all at once the powerful fleet of the English appeared before the city. The citizens forgot the pestilence, and instead of despairing and committing suicide, they collected and fought for their liberty. From that moment the fever disappeared. A student of Boerhave always felt the symptoms of every disease, on which this great physician lectured. Tissot relates two cases, in which one was freed by violent anger from the gout, and another who had been mute for four years received his speech again. So a son of Croesus, who was mute from his youth, when he saw a soldier threatening to kill his father, was enabled by the powerful emotions of anger with a loud voice to speak the words, "Do not kill Croesus!" The celebrated Stahl became acquainted with a similar fact during his practice. Lameness has frequently been healed by fright, caused by fire or other dangers. Hydrophobia is said to have sometimes originated in groundless fear. The power which the mind frequently exercises during times of revivals, is known from the history of one which took place a few years ago in the west of our country. Persons walking to church were seized on their way by strange feelings and fell down. Similar phenomena were perceived at Redruth, in the church of the Methodists; the upper members of the body trembled and were convulsed, and the muscles of the face were distorted. See Schubert's History of the Soul, p. 834—852. These examples will sufficiently show the power of the mind over the body. The question yet left is, How is it possible that the mind can exercise such a power on the body? To understand this possibility we must consider, that all the emotions of the mind have each its peculiar nerve on which they act. This nerve, becoming thus affected, will in its turn affect all those immediately connected with it. If the emotion is invigorating, as that of courage, hilarity, &c., the life of the nervous system will be elevated and strengthened; if the emotion is of a weakening character, as fear, sadness, &c., the nervous system will become depressed. The nerves pass over the whole body, and every organ is surrounded by them; hence it is, that as they are affected, so the pulsation of the heart, the circulation of the blood, breathing, digestion, and even the voice will be either impeded or promoted by emotions.

An example or two will serve to make this more clear. When we are under the influence of the emotion of *joy*, we feel our pulse beat higher, our cheeks redden, breathing becomes easy, and the muscles elastic. A fresh and vigorous life is spread through all the nerves; the eye sparkles, and digestion is accelerated. And all these changes in our system proceed from the nerve, upon which joy principally acts. Joy is the pleasant feeling that connects itself with the realization of a hoped-for good or pleasure. This feeling has not therefore a physical origin, but its ground is *the idea* of good, which we anticipate. When this anticipated good presents itself to us, the feeling of pleasure excites first our cerebral system, and thence it sends its rays of life into all parts of the body.

So again *anger* has the most powerful effect on the body, healing diseases, as we have seen, by rousing violently the slumbering life, or more frequently producing diseases. Anger is an emotion, in which a strong feeling of displeasure arouses the desire and an expectation of destroying the cause of this displeasure, or of causing a similar unpleasant feeling in him who is the offender. This is at once perceptible in the external appearance. For all the muscles, subject to the will, are in motion. The eye rolls about; the face is distorted; the teeth are grated; the voice roars or trembles; the fist is clenched. Our organism forms a whole, and every local excitement, if strong enough, will communicate itself to all parts of the body. The agitation of the muscles and nerves, immediately subservient to will, will be propagated upon the ganglion nerves, and from them upon those that entwine themselves around the viscera. Hence the secretion of bile will become more copious; the circulation of the blood will be more rapid, and warmth will be quickly developed. And here we may remark, that the secretions do not only become more copious, but are essentially changed in their quality. The saliva, for instance, becomes poisonous in a high degree, the milk of nurses causes cramps, convulsions, and colic in children nourished by it. A person, biting in his wrath another, may cause his death by the introduction of the venomous saliva into his blood. This also may be easily explained. For the saliva, according to Oken, has the office to kill the life of all the substances we eat and assimilate; strictly speaking, all saliva is poisonous, and even that of birds has been fatal to persons. When now the hostile nature of anger communicates itself to the whole body, and consequently also to the saliva of the glands of the mouth, it will not only excite to a higher degree its poisonous nature, but positively impregnate it with its own fury. In the same manner the foam of a mad dog becomes poisonous, and also the saliva of many furious animals.

It would be easy to show the effects of other emotions upon the body, as for instance, of fright, which sometimes deprives us of our senses, causes us to swoon, makes the voice tremble, and takes away all self-possession. But the above examples will suffice. One remark, however, we will here add lest we should be misunderstood.—On the one hand, one and the same organ may be affected by different emotions, as for example, the liver by fear, fright, discontentment; and on the other, the same emotions do not always produce the same effects, for while the feeling of shame makes some blush, it will cause the faces of others to grow pale; and while wrath affects the liver of one, it will derange the digestion of another, and promote the appetite of a third. Therefore the idea of Plato, which was before entertained by Homer, that each emotion and passion had a particular organ as its seat, as courage the breast and lungs, (thus in Homer a strong and loud voice is a sign of strength) wrath the liver, must be accepted with much caution. This much however may be seen from the above remarks, that a general excitement of the blood and nerves may become beneficial to an existing disease, as well as dangerous to an otherwise healthy system.

3. The power of the mind over the body may be seen from the *formation of habits*. Habit is the regular return of actions that, by frequent repetition, have lost all feeling of strangeness. Nerves and muscles have their natural po-

sition, and the feeling connected with it is simple. When a new action demands a change of this position, a new feeling will connect itself with it, and this new feeling will interfere with the former simple feeling, until a frequent repetition of the same action makes the blood, nerves, and muscles, run repeatedly through the same position, and thus makes them familiar with it. Then the feeling of strangeness will also disappear, and what before attracted our attention by its novelty, will be no longer noticed. Though the action to which we have thus accustomed ourselves, by frequent repetitions, has lost the feeling of strangeness, it is still felt, but we no longer distinguish between the feeling connected with it and that of our existence. Thus we may accustom ourselves to the influence of the weather, to storm and rain, to cold and heat; and even to the endurance of misery, diseases, and misfortunes. An unfortunate occurrence, when visiting us for the first time, may appear extremely hard, and almost threaten to destroy our life; if the same occurrence should take place the second time, its novel impression would be weakened, and so on, until its effects on us would be trifling. The fable of the hare, that was much frightened at the first sight of the lion, but gradually grew so familiar with him as to accost him, contains therefore a full and important truth.

Habit leads to skill, and skill renders the most difficult labor easy. The arm which constantly hammers on the anvil, will no longer feel the fatigue which at first was caused by a few strokes. The fingers of a performer on the piano become so familiar with every key, that they miss none, though the performer has his eyes constantly directed to the notes and not to the keys. It is, to speak with Leibnitz, as if the monads of the fingers were set free, and no longer subordinate to the monad of the soul; they act for themselves. Yet the mind of the performer has, nevertheless, to watch them, for as soon as he thinks of something else, the fingers will miss the keys. Skill renders work easy by reducing the effort at first required to a very small amount.

Habits may be formed by design or involuntarily. Examples, education, inclination and passion, lead to involuntary customs, while those willed by us are acquired by our own determination, and because we find them useful and good. When a habit is once formed, we become attached to it, for it becomes natural to us, and *will* and *nature* are united in it. Hence it is that habits become periodical, and when the hour of a certain action arrives, an excitement is felt in the muscles and nerves, which can only be allayed by the performance of the action. The power of habit is therefore great; it frequently keeps us bound as its slaves, and prevents us from receiving what is better, merely because it is strange and new to us. The question may therefore be asked, whether we ought to submit to this power? Custom, in general, is beneficial to man, provided it is morally correct and good. For, being itself good, and reigning with regularity over the life of man, it will pervade and ennoble it; it will rescue it from the sphere of mere arbitrariness, where every new desire invites to a new action; if habits, which are good in themselves, extend over whole nations, they will unite individuals, break the strength of selfishness, lead them to submit to higher authority, and render them social and communicative. If habits are not good, or morally correct, our moral feeling ought to exclude them from us, and if we have formed them, our will ought to remove them again. However great may be the power of habit, that of our will is still greater, and to exercise the latter, it would be well, from time to time, to free ourselves from certain indifferent habits, merely to prove to ourselves that we can do a thing if we are resolute and determined.

4. The power of mind over the body is perceived in *the art of representing the emotions and thoughts of the mind by the motions of the body.* This power exhibits itself in the control man has over his voice. He can modulate it according to any feeling or ideas contained in words or works. The character of a piece will determine the key of voice, so that every tone and semi-tone will be guided by it. Every emotion of the heart has a tone to express it; in fear, the voice is trembling and low; in joy, clear and full; in anger, loud and roaring. Each kind of poetry has its tone, the lyric, dramatic, and epic; each is to be declaimed in a different key of voice. The oratory of the bar or pulpit demands each a different tone. So again the *arsis* and *thesis*, or raising and sinking of the voice, and

the accent and emphasis are all wholly under the control of the mind; and he who thinks well, will generally speak well, as he who understands well, will generally read well, for what is felt and understood will enter into the voice.

Gesticulation aids very essentially the understanding of words, and frequently where words would not be sufficient fully to express a feeling, a single glance or a single gesture will be sufficient. So Octavio, at the close of Schiller's Wallenstein, says more by a glance towards heaven, than a whole speech would have communicated. The expressions of certain feelings by gestures are at first involuntary. The hair rises when we are frightened; the face grows pale, when we fear. This natural expression becomes artificial when it is produced by our will, and from a consciousness of its appropriateness to convey an idea of our feelings and emotions. To know this appropriateness, we must know the reason why certain motions of the body are expressive of certain emotions of the mind: hence this art has its science, and has been treated by several writers.

It subjects the whole body to its designs. The walk, and the motion of the hands, the posture and keeping of the whole frame are all used. But especially the face, the head, and the hands.

The face has to serve it by its expression; by the curling of the lips, by the rolling or fixing of the eye, by the drawing in of the nose, by the wrinkling of the forehead, &c.

The head affirms by nodding, and denies by shaking; in the former case it moves towards the object, in the latter, away from it. Bending gently down, it may indicate humility, as in prayer, or shame and confusion, or modesty. Looking up towards heaven, it may acknowledge our dependence on a higher Being, and ask for its blessing or its curse.

The hand, when clenched, threatens; when stretched forth and open, it salutes; when one of its fingers is directed toward something, it points out or commands; when folded, it indicates that, as the hands are clasped together, and turned inwardly, and for a time give up their accustomed activity, so the mind is collecting itself to direct its devotion to heaven, abstaining from earthly thoughts. The hand, moving away from the body, gives a sign not to approach; moving toward the body, it invites to come. The hands clasped in marriage, unites two persons into one; striking hands confirms a bargain. "With the Hebrews, kissing the hand, the knee, or the foot, indicated submission; with us, kissing the lips, friendship."—*From De Wette's Commentary on the Psalms, page* 88.

Other parts of the body may serve, in a similar way, to express the feelings or thoughts of the mind, as for instance, shrugging the shoulders, and the like.

When one part of the body is not sufficient, several are used at one time. Shaking the head may be united with a repellent motion of the hand. The hand will here principally assist the head, especially when signs for intellectual emotions are to be given. The hand covering the eyes, closes up the fountain of observation, and shows that we either meditate on some subject, or are given to spiritual devotion. Laying a finger on the nose invites attention, for as the nose is thus divided, so the judgment is accurately to divide, but the judgment cannot be without attention. Rubbing behind the ear has reference to the understanding, for the ear is the most theoretical sense. Putting the hand upon the heart confirms what we have said.

It will easily be seen, that the meaning of these signs or gestures, does not depend merely on the motions of the hand, but on the parts of the body touched by them. The nearer they are connected with the intellectual activity of the mind, the more noble will be the signification of the gestures; the more these parts are connected with the system of re-production, the less noble the meaning of the gestures concerning them.

In conclusion the whole body may be used by the mind, as bowing to express its respect, kneeling its entire homage, a straight and unbending posture its haughtiness.

5. The power of the mind over the body *leaves its traces and impressions on the face, on the forms of its single parts*, as nose, lips, eye, forehead. A well-formed head indicates strength and fullness of understanding; a head thick and fleshy, stupidity; a head small and thin, weakness of mind. If the face is too long or too round, it betrays a low disposition. Thus in Shakspeare's **Cleopatra**.

Cleopatra. Bear'st thou her face in mind? Is it long or round?
Messenger. Round even to faultiness.
Cleopatra. For the most part too they are foolish that are so.

The chin and the lower jaw have reference to the sensual disposition of man. The upper lips, together with the nose and eyebrows, and including the eye and the ear, refer to feeling and humor, and to theoretical knowledge; the rest of the face up to the hair, to mind in general. " The forehead is the portal of understanding, the seat of thought; raised eyebrows indicate wrath, eyebrows hanging down, dark and cheerless emotions. The eye is the mirror of the soul." To judge of the disposition of a person, the proportions of the three regions into which face is divided, must be carefully examined, while every organ, as the nose, the eye, the mouth, forms also a whole by itself. The roughness or smoothness of the hair, its color, and that of the eye and of the skin, declare to the physiognomist the temperament of a person.

There is certainly much truth in physiognomy, if confined within its proper limits, but if it aspires to the character of a science, or if it assumes a judgment over the *moral* character of man, it becomes insipid. " When Zopyrus perceived in the face of Socrates that he was naturally inclined to voluptuousness, why did he not read in the same face, that he had a power too, which was strong enough to correct this natural tendency? If this tendency deserved to appear in the head of a Faun, that power was worthy of being honored with the head of a Jupiter." When Porta in his attempts at physiognomy went so far as to compare the faces of animals with those of man, he made two mistakes. He supposed that animals had really a physiognomy; but if we call physiognomy the external expression of the internal and invisible mind or disposition, then animals having no mind, cannot be said to have a physiognomy. And if they had, their faces are grown over with hair, and thus their expression is concealed from the observing eye. We cannot speak of a physiognomy of animals because all animals of the same species have the same expression if they have any, and whoever has seen one lion, has seen all, and in describing the face of one, he describes the faces of all. So it must be admitted too, that children, when born, have no expression in their faces, as persons when they die, generally lose those they had in their lifetime. Savages have a physiognomy but little variegated, while physiognomy will vary in proportion as nations become cultivated. This shows that the expression of the face depends on the moral character of man, and not the latter on the former. Who can say by what a wrinkle on the forehead is caused, whether by care or dissipation? Many a one may have had the nose of Shakspeare, without having had his humor, and no doubt the whole face of Shakspeare has had in some age or other its like, while in no climate and in no age has Shakspeare yet been equalled. The same causes do not produce the same effects, because man does not suffer causes to act as such, but controls them. " Green wood, when placed near the fire gets warped, dry wood only brown." Two men of equal strength and age, may spend the whole night in dissipation, and after all not have the same appearance in the morning. How much more must this be the case in the sphere of liberty, where we by our mere will may bid defiance to every line in our face. In London, Macklin, the actor, of whose face Quin said: " If this man is not a rascal, God does not write a legible hand," received in the year 1775 public praise on account of his honesty and nobleness. One and the same organ—and this may be said with regard to phrenology no less than with regard to physiognomy—may serve two very different purposes. The nose for instance is the organ of smell and for conducting off the mucus; the tongue of taste and of language.

6. The power of the mind over the body is indicated too by *the formation of the skull*, which must bear witness of the life of the mind. The observation of this fact has likewise given rise to the idea of forming a science called Phrenology. The manner of reasoning is this:—Every activity of the mind seems to demand a particular organ. It is not the eye that sees, nor the ear that hears, but mind sees and hears by the eye and ear. But the mind could not see without the eye, nor hear without the ear. The eye is the organ of sight, as is the ear that of hearing. It is reasonable to expect that this should be so with every

other activity of the mind. Again, it is not the organ, but the nerves in it, that are active, and to know the amount of activity, of which the organ is susceptible, we must observe the nerves embodied in it. Yet they cannot be laid bare during the life of man, and all we can do is to judge of their volume and strength by the elevations or indentations of the skull, and their proportions to each other. For all the nerves, in whatever direction they may run over the body, will finally concentrate in the brain, and as the skull surrounds it, and conceals it from our sight, the skull only, its formation, its depressions or elevations, are left for our examination.

It has been fashionable of late, either to decry phrenology or to raise it above all other sciences. We, on our part, have to acknowledge that talents and capacities will, to a certain degree, be indicated by the formation of the skull. Character, on the other hand, is the effect of will, and not of the nervous muscles. Nor can phrenology much aid our science, for to understand any elevation on the skull, we must know the psychological activity symbolically indicated by it. The want of a good psychology in Gall and Spurzheim misled them, and their errors are exposed in a masterly manner with all due acknowledgment of their merits by Professor C. Hartman, in his Geist des Menschen, from page 255 to 291. Carus, in the second part of his Psychology, and Hegel in his Phenomenology have likewise spoken against the extravagancies of phrenology.

The internal and invisible mind, expressing itself physiognomically and on the skull of man, will be the subject of our investigations hereafter. We shall view it not as a compound of many mental activities that exist by the side of each other in one common receptacle, and that are externally united, we cannot say *how?* but as a whole of many branches, all of which proceed from one identical life, and are held together by it.

PART II.
PSYCHOLOGY.

PART II.

PSYCHOLOGY.

INTRODUCTION.

§ 1. SELF-CONSCIOUSNESS.

In every science we may discover one point which is the centre of the whole, and which, well understood, will shed light upon every portion of its whole extent. In the system of divinity, it is the idea of *revelation;* in moral philosophy, it is that of law in connection with that of conscience; and in mental philosophy it is that of self-consciousness. Without self-consciousness we can know nothing clearly, either within ourselves or in nature. It is the light, by which alone we can see in the sphere of knowledge; before it is fully developed in the child, all his ideas must be confused, and nothing can be known in relation to other things, nothing be classified or arranged, but every object will appear to him without distinction in itself, and without a generic difference from that which is not itself. When, in an adult, self-consciousness disappears for a moment, all consciousness of the things around us and of our personal qualities sinks into transient oblivion, and we no longer notice what is going on around us, though we continue to hear and to feel. Self-consciousness then, is the root of all our knowledge: it must accompany our mental activities, and without it it would be in vain to investigate the nature of the soul. For this reason it ought to be examined, before we approach the activity and nature of the soul, and for this reason also it deserves a full share of our attention.

What then are we to understand by self-consciousness? It is not a thing that is ready wrought in us, and the qualities of which, like those of minerals, chemical substances, one has only to analyze in order to know; *but it is an activity that constantly produces itself.* The activities of mind, however, are manifold, and it will here be necessary and instructive to distinguish it from them. The first of all the activities of the mind is *feeling*. It is the most subjective, the most internal and inexpressible in man. Yet difficult as it may be, to convey a clear idea of it, we cannot pass it over in silence. " *Feeling, in general, is passion called forth by its own activity.*" This definition demands some explanation. The passion spoken of here, is one conditioned by its own activity. Hence it follows as a first rule, that *that which cannot affect itself, cannot feel*. The ball on the billiard table, for example, is set in motion by the billiard-stick; it is active, but not of its own accord. Touching another ball, it communicates its motion to it, and is put at rest by the resistance it meets with, and consequently is affected; but this affection or passion is not produced by its activity, but by the resistance of another ball. Every metal expands by heat, and contracts by cold; but this activity in the metal is elicited by an activity without; the metal is affected, but not by itself. Hence though warmed by the heat, it neither feels warmth nor cold.

A second rule is, that *nothing can feel which affects itself or acts upon itself, but not for itself*. A machine acts upon and affects itself, but not for itself. The plant, on the other hand, that stands in the sun moves its twigs and leaves; its juices rise and sink, it is active, and both affects itself and acts for itself. This appears clearly from the fact that after a hot noon, it re-creates itself in the dew of the evening; and that from the germ to the blossom and seed, it grows only for itself and not for any thing else, for it will grow whether an animal is near to eat it or not. But this activity of the plant is wholly called forth and conditioned by something different from itself, by heat, rain, atmosphere, &c. We therefore add a third rule:

When an activity which conditions itself as passive, is not conditioned by a third and foreign activity, as that of the nerve, then we have *feeling*. Feeling is an activity that affects itself; *affecting* itself, it is active; *being affected*, it is passive; *activity and passion in one is feeling*. Such an activity may be called a "*trembling in itself.*" This motion is not like that of the planet turning on its axis; nor like that of the plant turning spirally, nor like that of the string, which touched moves away from itself, but it is an inward motion, one *in* itself. Such is the motion of the nerve when touched; the life of the nerve seems by its own energy to touch itself, the parts of the nerve to tremble in themselves.

Feeling pre-supposes one who feels and something which is felt. Is the thing felt, different from him that feels; then the feeling is called a *sensation*. The light of the sun is felt by the eye, the acid of the grape by the tongue, both feelings are sensations. But when feeling does not depend on the senses, when the object felt is also the subject that feels, then we have what may be called *self-feeling*.

This self-feeling, like a feeling in general, is enjoyed by the animal, but consciousness is not. It may, therefore, be proper to point out the difference between them. By self-feeling every individual is related to itself, and through it is certain of its existence. The plant cannot feel itself, and consequently could not support itself, had it not struck its roots into the soil. But the animal, feeling itself, feels its wants and satisfies them, and can move from place to place. It feels itself in its members and feels them as its own. It feels itself when it stretches them in the warm light of the sun, or in its dreams. By self-feeling, therefore, the animal is an individual; not only externally, that is, not merely like the plant, *externally* separated from other things, but *internally* by feeling itself and taking interest in itself. A plant when torn into pieces offers no resistance, but an animal about to be slain, either rages or looks piteously at him who destroys it. And so again feeling itself it cannot exchange its existence for that of another. The "elephant which was intended to frighten Fabius," and that, which is exhibited in a menagerie, take each such an interest in itself that it would be impossible for them to be other than itself. In proportion as the animal takes an interest in itself, it opposes every other animal of which it receives a feeling by sensation. The stronger the self-feeling, the greater will be the opposition, the more determined the separation from all other animals, and consequently the more complete the isolation. Rapacious animals love to be alone in their caves, on high rocks or in ambush. They live together, the old with the young only during certain seasons, and separate again as soon as the instinctive care for the race becomes unnecessary. It is true there are animals that seem to be social; the sheep, the goose, the ant, the bee; but all of them are held together by instinct, by the pasture on which they graze, by the hive or cell which they build in common. And even then they take little notice of each other, it is only in times of danger that the voice, or some other sign, which is the same in all the individuals of the same class, calls them together for mutual defence. When the danger is past each lives again by itself.

However much self-feeling may seem to resemble self-consciousness, it differs from it in the following points:

1. Self-feeling does not enable the animal to distinguish between the subject that feels and the object that is felt. The difference exists but is not known to mere feeling. The animal feeling itself, does not judge that it feels, and again, that it is itself the object of its feeling.

2. The animal having self-feeling does not distinguish between itself and its members; it feels its members, but cannot make a distinction between itself as the whole, and them as its parts or organs. Just as little can it distinguish between a sensation and its organ, the object of the sensation and itself which has the organ, and through it the sensation. The difference is there; but it is not distinct and clear, it is only *felt*, not *known*.

3. The animal having self-feeling, does not distinguish between itself and its race, so that it would refer itself to its class, but it isolates itself by its self-feeling. Every animal capable of feeling itself belongs to a class of animals; the pigeon, the hare, the dog and the lion; all are individuals of a certain kind, and the instinct of each class directs all its individuals to the same modes of life, &c.

Self-feeling gives them the same degree of energy, the same kind of sensations, so that for example all moles differ from all eagles in the same way as regards sight. But while the kind is distinctly expressed in all its individuals, no one of them refers itself to its class, but they are all of them, even when gregarious, only single among many. Self-feeling chains a being to itself, makes it not only a *self* but *selfish*. However different the degrees of energy may be in the self-feeling of the different classes of animals, each animal is by it a single isolated being; selfish even when it exhibits a tendency to association, for no sooner do we offer food to sheep, for instance, than one runs to outdo the other and all fight, each to get what it desires. Want, necessity, instinct may hold them together, but they are not conscious of these facts. To define then self-consciousness it is,

First. That activity of mind, by which man distinguishes between his body and soul, and while thus distinguishing between them, refers the one to the other, and again comprehends both united in one. It is consequently an act of judgment, a power that perceives distinctions as they are and makes them, and yet judgment does not precede it, but is a part of it, and self-consciousness only expresses itself by it. In a machine all the parts are likewise distinct, they are related to and connected with each other, but by a power not in the machine. The parts of the plant are distinguished, the roots from the trunk, the twigs from the leaves; they are related to each other, and systematically connected. The power that produces these distinctions, that which in developing itself, causes part to shoot forth from part, and as their common soul keeps them united, is contained *in* the plant, it is the plastic power, but it neither feels itself, nor is aware of its productions. The animal feels its different parts, its liver and stomach—its senses, and feeling *them* it feels *itself* in every one of them; but it has no consciousness of them nor of itself, it does not *perceive* its members as its own, for it neither distinguishes between itself and other objects, nor between its organs and itself. Self-consciousness makes us clearly aware of these distinctions and their union.

Secondly. Self-consciousness is the activity of mind, that distinguishes between man and his senses, and by which man has it in his power to use them for whatever purpose he chooses, for making observations, experiments, &c. And as it distinguishes between the senses and their possessor, so it distinguishes between the sensations and the senses, between the objects and the sensations produced by them.

Thirdly. It not only observes things in nature, but recognizes their relation to each other. But the principal relation is that of the individual to its genius.—It recognizes the genus in every individual, and thus suffers nothing to enter it as an isolated being. When I ask, What is this? I desire to know its general nature. If am told that it is *a sheep*, I feel satisfied, for the name sheep is not a proper but a general name, expressing a certain and definite *class* of animals, consequently the general nature as it exists in the individuals belonging to that class. Self-consciousness comprehends therefore the general in the individual, and the individual in the general. Nothing in nature is wholly isolated, but every thing is connected one with another, this with a third and all with the whole.

This relation self-consciousness perceives and acknowledges.

§ 2. MUTUAL RELATION OF BODY AND SOUL.

Before speaking of Personality, we shall attempt to gain some idea of the connection between the soul and body, as it will aid us much in forming a correct notion of what we are to understand by the term person.

The views entertained concerning the relation of the soul to the body, are quite various, but may be divided into two classes, the one comprising those who admit of two different substances, the other those that either consider the soul as the efflorescence and result of the body, or the body as *built* by the soul. The former keeps soul and body so separate, that it is difficult to say how they can act in unison. According to it the body has a life of its own, and the soul likewise; both are, however, intended for each other, and the former receives the latter, as the engine the steam. Or to express this difference still more strongly, the soul and body are connected, as Plato represents it, like two horses yoked together, one born of earth, and sensual in its nature, the other of heavenly origin and spirit:—one prone to the earth, the other rising towards heaven, and their owner, incapable of controling them, hanging between heaven and earth, unable to reach the one, and unwilling to descend to the other. A dualism that admits of two principles for *one* being, offers many difficulties, and the greatest is, that it cannot tell how the principles can be united in a third. A river may originate in two fountains, but a science cannot, and much less individual life.

The latter class of theories represents the soul as the final result and efflorescence of a continually refined life of the nerves, so that reason and will are nothing but the organic life of matter, which, by a refined process, attains the power of thinking and willing,—here a soul becomes superfluous, and Materialism, in its rudest form, prevails,—or it takes the soul for the original activity, and considers the body as *built* by it. This is the theory of Stahl, Treviranus, and others. As the caterpillar spins and weaves a texture fitted for its future metamorphosis, so the soul, like a mason, builds its own tabernacle. The first of these opinions is too gross, and the last spiritualizes the whole existence of man too much. We cannot, however, enter into a scientific refutation of the theories alluded to, and must be satisfied with advancing one that seems to be nearer to truth. Yet we would not assert that it is not open to objections.

Before it is possible to come to any conclusion on this difficult and yet exceedingly interesting subject, we must clearly define what we understand by *body*. For as the English language not only calls our organism a body, but speaks also of the sun, moon, and stars, as heavenly bodies, it is evident that the term in question is not used in the same unchangeable sense. Other languages, as the Greek and German, make a careful distinction between dead and living bodies; the German calling the former Koerper, *corpora* and the latter Leib, from Leben, life.

The general idea connected with the term *body*, is that of an external frame animated by life. According to this view, the body and soul are wholly different, and as opposite to each other as life and death. Yet this view must be erroneous, as it not only brings the soul and body in opposition, but also the bodily life and the external frame. The body, as an external frame, has been ascertained by chemists to consist of nine different substances, gases, earths, metals, and salt. It is therefore dust, and must return to dust. No man would be willing to assert, that man consists of a soul, bodily life, and nine different kinds of earthly substances; but all would be ready to acknowledge that earth is by no means an essential part of man. This must appear the more true, when we consider that this external frame of man " never ceases to perish," but is constantly undergoing changes; that it is in an unceasing flow. It is like a foaming place in a smoothly flowing river; one viewing it from a distance might suppose the foam to be unchangeably the same; but, on examining more closely, he will discover that the water thus foaming, is in an uninterrupted flow, changing its drops so constantly, that they are not the same for a moment, and that only the rock which breaks the water, remains the same. Thus it is with the body. The gases constantly escape, and all the particles undergo incessant changes. Hence the necessity of renovating our bodies. This renovation demands new elements, which originally foreign to the body, must be *assimilated* and rendered subservient to its organism. If then the particles of the external frame are incessantly changing, they cannot be the body itself, since new elements are every moment received and old ones excluded, and all of them are but dust. The true and genuine body must be that which retains and preserves its *organical* identity in all these changes which remains the same in the never-ceasing stream of matter. But what is this organical identity? The life or power which connects the gases, earths, metals, and salt, into one whole, which penetrating them, keeps them together, or dismisses some and attracts others. No sooner does this penetrating power retire, than the body becomes a corpse, and the elements fall asunder. This power is the true body; it is invisible, but connecting the elements according to an eternal and divine law, it becomes manifest by its productions.

We seem to have gained, then, this one idea, that the external frame is not the body, and that it is not to be opposed to the soul, but that the life and power which connects the elements is the body. Again, that it is the connection of the elements that is *human*, and not the substances themselves, and finally, that these substances and elements do not remain the same, but are constantly passing away, while new ones are taking their place. That which is permanent in these changes, and combines the elements in this manner, is *life*. The idea of life is therefore to be next considered. Though we gave its characteristics in the Introduction, and must refer to them, it may not be superfluous to view it here under a different aspect. All life wherever it exists is formed and organized. Form is not and cannot be the result of matter, which itself is chaotic and shapeless.

Form, in man, and throughout the Universe, is the result of thought. Hence life, being formed, does not proceed from matter; but is a thought of God, accompanied by the divine will, to be realized in nature, and to appear externally by an organized body. As the thought gives the form, so the divine will, resting in the thought and inseparably united with it, works as power and law in all nature. Is there not every where reason and wisdom, and an eternal and unchangeable law manifested in all the productions we see? The plant before me, is it not the product of an intelligence; or does it not represent a thought, that by the divine will became not only external and corporealized, but received also the power to propagate itself? The animal with its members and senses,—what else can it be but a divine thought exhibited in an external form? All nature is full of divine wisdom and reason, but it does not *possess* reason, for it is neither conscious of itself nor of any thing else. Hence we should hesitate to speak of a soul in animals, for as gravity is not a mere quality of matter, but as matter would be wholly annihilated without it, so the soul has thinking not merely as one of its qualities, but cannot be conceived of without it. The soul of man and the life of the animal are therefore wholly different. In applying this to man, to the union of soul and body, we may say—The soul of man is likewise a divine thought, a creation of God, filled with power to live an existence of its own. But it is *soul*, for it comprehends itself and all that is; and not only does it comprehend itself, but it is also able to produce new thoughts in accordance with its laws of thinking. Again, it develops itself like all other life in nature; and develops itself in a twofold direction; outwardly and inwardly. There can be nothing *merely* internal, but it must be so only in reference to itself as external. The flesh of the apple is internal only in reference to its skin, which is external. The internal or thinking life of the soul has its external, and this the sensitive life of the body, by which the soul is connected with the world. The life of the soul and the body is therefore *one* in its origin; a twofold expression of the same energy. The particles of the body on the other hand, are not at all a part of man; they are dust, and only their *connection* and the *life* connecting them, is truly human. Flesh, in so far as it is merely earth, cannot feel; but in so far as this earth is connected by life, it is life in this *peculiar connection* that feels in a peculiar manner. In order to render this somewhat difficult and abstruse idea more clear and distinct to all classes of readers, we will make use of some illustrations. "The rainbow is a phenomenon well known to all; how is it formed? When the sun sends his rays in a particular angle upon a watery cloud, the beautiful colors and form of the great arch, will be directly seen. Let us examine of what this rainbow consists. Does it consist of drops of water on the one hand, and of light on the other? By no means. The drops of water are to the rainbow, what the body as a mere corpse is to man. The drops constantly fall, and only serve to represent or reflect the different colors of the light. It is the sun that produces on the sheet of rain both color and shape. When the sun disappears, the rainbow with its colors is gone, but the gray rain-drops are still left. Yet as necessary as the sheet of rain is for the rainbow, so necessary is the body for the soul." Or let us take another example. When the artist first conceives the idea, either of a musical composition or of any noble work in literature or art, it will be yet rude and unorganized. Carrying it in his mind for a long time, this idea will become more clear, one part shooting forth from the other until the whole is matured. To see this idea clearly, he feels impelled to give it an external form, as on the marble, if the artist be a sculptor. The marble receives the image of the idea, and if fully and well expressed by a skillful chisel, the image will call forth the same idea in the bosom of every one who examines it with judgment. It would, however, certainly be wrong to say that this image of the artist consists on the one hand of marble, whiteness, smoothness, and on the other, of the internal idea, for the marble only represents the image, but it is not in any way the image. So it would be wrong to say, that man consists of two essentially different substances; of earth and the soul; but he is *soul only*, and cannot be any thing else. This soul, however, unfolds itself externally in the *life* of the body, and internally in the life of mind. Twofold in its development, it is one in its origin, and the centre of this union is our personality. Several remarks naturally flow from the above view:

First. As the plant can never pass beyond itself and become an animal, so the animal cannot by a continued development reach the nature and life of man, but it remains an animal for ever. For so much only can be developed, as exists according to possibility in the germ of a being; what is therefore not contained in this possibility, or germ, or origin, cannot proceed from it. Thinking, judgment and reason, or soul in general, not being originally in the idea realized in the animal,—the animal of course differs from man by not having a soul. Though it has sensation and perception, these again must differ from those of man, as they do not include the power to judge. The life of man, as it is the union of physical and psychical, is not to be considered as a higher development of animal life, differing only in degree, but it is wholly and essentially different even in its principle. It is therefore not a transition from that which is not human to the human; from the unconscious to the conscious. It is not the same animal activity, only clearer, more distinct, and more refined, so that the whole difference is one of *quantity* and not of *quality*. Feeling, however, elevated and refined, still remains feeling.

Secondly. We admit, therefore, of a difference between soul and body, but one that proceeds from, and terminates in a union. As the common principle of both differs from every other in nature, so the bodily life of man differs from that of the animal. It is from its beginning and in its principle different, and does not merely become so at a certain stage.

Thirdly. This theory upholds the idea of a creation and not of emanation. God remains what he is, the unchangeable Jehovah after the universe is created. So the mind of man is not diminished, however great the number of thoughts which it produces. On the other hand, neither the body nor the soul is the ground of their existence, but God himself.

§ 3. PERSONALITY.

Deus nos personat.

The term person comes from the Latin *personare*, the original meaning of which is to *sound through*. It was used of one, who was not, like a slave, a mere thing saleable and transferable, but who had a right to speak and defend himself in courts of justice. In this respect the German word for person fully agrees with the Latin and English, for *laut*, plural *leute*, has exactly the same meaning. From this it must appear that those who consider the external, visible body as that which is named by person, are mistaken. It is true that *persona* signified a mask, but in distinction from *larva*, one that by an instrument rendered the voice of the actor more audible. The term person has, therefore, a direct bearing upon the intelligence of man, since only an intelligent being can comprehend rights and duties, and consequently defend them, and since only such a one can *speak*. The animal has a body, and in the more perfect animals we discover all the organs of the human frame, yet should we hesitate to speak of animal personality. The animal is an individual, that feels itself, but cannot be a person, because it is not conscious of itself.

Before giving a definition of personality, it will be well to define the term *individuality*. We have it in common with the animal, while we share personality with the Deity. Individuality is the *centre* or *union* of many organical functions, that proceed from it and return to it. It is the power that produces all of them, and keeps them related to each other, and to their whole. It is, therefore, that by which a being is concentrated upon itself—the centre of all organic activities. It renders a living organism indivisible, hence it is called individuality. The stone remains what it is, though it be broken into small particles, but an animal is destroyed when its members are torn asunder. That which is wanting to individuality, in order to make it personality, is a soul capable of thinking and willing.

Personality is likewise a centre and union of the manifold, but one that is awake in itself, that has found and laid hold of itself, and having once found cannot again lose itself, but will enjoy itself for ever. It is the centre of all our bodily and mental activities; emancipated from all that is not itself, it reigns over all the powers of body and soul, for it is that which must take care of both. It is the person within us, which determines itself to be this or that; to open itself to any influence, or exclude it; to follow one or the other direction; to enter a sphere of activity, or withdraw from all, and retire within itself. *Person* is the union of reason and will, for *I* know, and *I* will; it is the identity of self-consciousness and self-love, and whatever takes place in either must centre in it, and only thus can it be identified with the being that knows and loves itself. It remains the same, whether it is active practically or theoretically, or whether abstracted from all without, it confines itself wholly to itself. Neither character nor age, neither knowledge nor temperament can affect it. The expression for our personality is the little pronoun *I*. A short explanation of it will render clear what we are to understand by person and personal identity

Every word contains a thought, and every thought contains truth, if its contents correspond entirely with those of its object. Is the object a physical or historical one? then its contents, and those of the thought of it, are not exactly the same. I have, for example, as correct an idea of the sun, as the present state of astronomy makes it possible for me to form; but the contents of the sun are light, and other qualities, while those of the ideas which I have formed of it, are but the sensations and perceptions of these qualities, but not light itself. Of all the thoughts we have, there is none that in this respect is equal to that which we express by the pronoun *I*. Every thought, as we have seen, pre-supposes a subject that thinks, and an object thought of. In the thought contained in the word *I*, subject and object are perfectly the same, for it is *I* that thinks, and *I* that is thought of. There *I* am active, because *I* think; here *I* am passive, because *I* am the subject of thought. There is a difference, consequently, but one, that when rightly considered, is really none. For the identity between the thought and its subject, expressed by *I*, is such that the being of the one is that of the other also; that the one cannot be separated from the other, for the one is the other. This it is that we call *personal identity*. Our consciousness may be enriched with knowledge, and again forget all it has learned, and yet our *I* will remain the same. I can possess nothing else in the same way that I possess *myself*; for no where else can subject and object be united as they are in the word *I*. The same that I express by this term in my youth, I express by it at the most advanced age; and even in the hour of death neither form nor contents being in the least changed. This personal identity remains so much the same in spite of all changes, both in body and mind, that though two children resemble each other much more in their natures, than the same person resembles himself as regards bodily vigor in his youth and old age—yet will the personal identity be the same with him in all periods of life, while the two children, resembling each other in other respects, widely differ in their persons.

It is this *I*, this personal identity, which, as the conscious centre of body and soul, attributes both to itself in saying, I must take care of *my* body and of *my* soul. Without it, there could be no *mine* and *thine*. It is invisible, can neither be seen nor felt; is neither bone nor muscle, neither nerve nor sinew; and is only accessible to thought. If I say, I have wounded myself, I speak inaccurately, for I ought to say I have hurt my *limb*, my *body*. This invisible *I* is that general activity, which accompanies all our actions and knowledge. It is I that feels and perceives; that comprehends and recollects; that judges and concludes; that resolves and wills and acts. I am active in all these different ways, and yet remain the same in every single activity. I may enter upon any activity or exclude all.

The idea of personality, as may be easily seen, includes that of independence of every thing that is not itself. It rests upon itself, and as it is the centre of all in man, so it is the centre of nature around, for it is not only conscious of itself, but conscious of all other things. If by self-consciousness it inclines to itself, taking an inward direction, by consciousness of other things, it takes an outward direction, one away from itself. And in this light we have yet to view personality.

The *person* is not only the centre of *man*, whose radii and periphery are all the activities of body and soul, and by which all of them are *pronounced*, that is through which they sound, *personat*, but it is also,

1. The centre of nature, the echo of the universe. What nature contains scattered and in fragments, is united in the person of man. Every isolated feeling, every solitary sound in nature is to *pass through* man's personality, and to centre in it. His personality is the great, beautiful, and complete *bell*, that announces every thing, while nature contains only parts of it, the sounds of which are dark and dull. This by no means teaches any form of Pantheism; all it says is this, What would be the most glorious sunset if man should not perceive and enjoy it? What would be the order of the universe if man were not conscious of it? What the laws of Astronomy if a Newton and Kepler had not discovered them? They might exist, but as without an eye there would be eternal darkness, without an ear uninterrupted silence, so there could be no order or regularity without an understanding capable of perceiving it. The songs of birds, if not heard by man, would neither

be plaintive nor joyful. It is he alone that perceives the nature of things, and their systematical connection with each other. But again, the personality of man is the centre of nature in another respect; as we have seen that there are animals which having but one of the many physical organs of man, constitute nevertheless a full and complete being, so the moral qualities are distributed, and a single one frequently makes up the whole character of a certain species of animals. The serpent is sly, the tiger treacherous, the fox cunning; and so each animal has a prevailing quality which determines its whole nature; but man unites *all* in himself. Like the fox he is cunning, and like the serpent he is sly; hence he can sympathise with every being in nature, and may in this respect be called the centre of nature. Nature is external, knows nothing of itself, mind alone can seek and find itself and all other things.

"*Was will die Nadel nach Norden gekehrt?*
Sich selber zu finden es ist ihr verwehrt."

2. Our personality is the centre of the whole human race, for it contains the generality and individuality united in one. It expresses a single and individual being, separating it from all others; and again it is most general, since every one is an I like myself. This *I* is, therefore, not like a proper name, but it is a word that conveys a most general idea. Thus in our personality, the general and individual are so united, that the one is contained in the other. This will appear from the following remarks:—We speak of a national spirit, of national honor, of national art and literature; these do not and cannot exist in the abstract, their existence must be concrete. It becomes concrete when the general and individual grow together, *concresco*, or are united, when, therefore, the general becomes conscious of itself in the individual. Greece, as such, could not become conscious of its honor or literature, but when this general national spirit becomes individualized in a Plato or Sophocles, it becomes conscious of itself. Hence it is their personality, in which the Greek spirit must centre, and through which as its organ, it expresses itself by works of literature and art. True genius, must therefore always bear the character of a national generality,—genius comes from

genus—and the less individuality appears it its productions, the more valuable it is. The history of a nation, and its institutions will all express the national spirit, as the actions and feeling show the character of a person; but without individuals a nation could have no history. According to this,

3. Our personality is complete only when we are conscious of God and our relation to him, and when we suffer God to speak to it and through it. It is not nature nor matter that produces personality, but God, who is the *ground* of all personality. We can know a thing thoroughly only when we are acquainted with its ground—so man must know God before he can become truly acquainted with himself. In saying that God is the ground of all personality, we mean, that he freely created man; that there was no *emanation*, by virtue of which the Deity flowed forth into man, and could not return to himself again. If that were the case our highest wisdom would become an Egology, and the Bible and Theology would become superfluous. So the personality of God differs widely from that of man. Its elements are omniscience and omnipotence, and all the other infinite attributes. Those of human personality are a limited reason and will, attached to nerves and muscles.

This personality of man is not, however, active immediately after birth. The child feels as soon as it enters the world, but it is only with difficulty that it becomes conscious of itself. It may soon notice its single members, the hand, the foot, the lips, but to enable it to comprehend the body and soul as a whole, whose centre it is itself, requires much time and labor on the part of its instructors. Hence, long after the child speaks, it names itself, not by the term *I,* but by its proper name, speaking of itself in the third person, as "William wants this or that." It is with the personality of the child as with the life of a plant, which needs the aid of many physical influences. Or like a torch that must be lighted before it can illuminate. Hence it is that children exposed in their infancy and grown up in the woods, can neither speak, nor think, nor remember. A boy found in the Hanoverian woods, about eleven years old, ran on his hands and feet, climbed trees with great skill, and was perfectly wild. When caught and properly attended to, he could remember nothing beyond the time when he was placed under the influence of man. And so it was in many other instances of the same kind, eight of which have been noticed by Linnæus under the head *Homo sapiens ferus,* or the wise wild man.

This awaking of the child in itself is like the rising of a light in the midst of darkness. The state of existence, preceding that in which the child *finds* itself, is dark, and we are not conscious of it. So man is like a night-plant, whose top only is penetrated by the light, while many powers and qualities are left in the dark soil below, which will never wholly rise into the sphere of light. As regards even our person, therefore, we are surrounded by darkness in the midst of light.

§ 4. DIVISION.

Until recently, mental philosophers have been in the habit of representing mind as a compound of many faculties, as a whole made up of parts. This view of the soul is a mechanical one, and does not regard the character of life in general. It is scarcely necessary now to refute an idea so spiritless, for who can believe that the faculties of mind are as separate and distinct as drawers in a chest, each answering a certain purpose and occupying a place, from which all the others must be excluded. According to this view the faculties do not proceed from one general principle, for the power of perception and that of memory, differ as widely as the various parts of a machine. These faculties are united, but only as the different cells of wasps are held together by the sheet of comb on which they are built. As to the rest, the wasp occupying one cell, does not and cannot know much of its neighbor residing in a different one. The question has, therefore, justly been asked—How, if the mind consists of so many faculties, each of which is separate from the other, can they be united in *one* consciousness? If fancy, in its cell, re-produces an image, how can consciousness, a power different from fancy, take cognizance of it? To say that each faculty has a consciousness of its own, would be highly absurd, since we should then be forced to admit a plurality of consciousness. How this plurality of consciousness could be internally united into one, it would be hard to understand. This whole view has been, therefore, more or less relinquished, and one directly opposed to it has been received. There is but *one* thinking power in man. It is the same when it judges as when it observes, comprehends, thinks, or wills. The apparent difference is produced either by the object to which it is directed,—as for instance it is designated as *memory* when directed to the past, *imagination* when turned to the future;—or, by the greater or less degree, in which it exerts itself. For whether I have a sensation of a thing, or a comprehension, it is nearly the same, only that the latter is a higher stage of thinking. By sensation I comprise many qualities and pronounce their union a *thing* or individual; by comprehension I unite many individuals, and call this union a *class*. It is the same activity only raised in the latter instance.

But the mind is neither a multitude of faculties, nor is it a simple, identical activity, but it is a *union* that not only comprises the manifold, but produces it by unfolding its life organically. There are many kinds of union: a mechanical one, as that of a machine; and an organic one, as that of a living plant. The latter will serve to explain the union here spoken of. When we, for the first time, watch an apple tree from its earliest growth till it blossoms and yields fruit, we are at once ready to say that the first leaves of the young tree which sprouts from the soil differ as widely from those which afterwards appear on the trunk and branches, as these from the blossoms and the blossoms from the fruit. We are, therefore, inclined to view this tree as made up of so many different organs, as the old psychology considers the soul as consisting of so many faculties. But then again, if some one should direct our attention to the fact that each succeeding formation is but a repetition of a former one, that the first leaves, for instance, which sprout forth near the ground, thick, colorless, and full of unrefined rude sap, are repeated by, or transformed into leaves of the trunk, that, being raised above the ground and more exposed to the sun and purer atmosphere, they become more refined, more vigorous and more beautifully formed,—we should willingly acknowledge that the plant could not be made up of parts independent of each other, but that the whole was produced by the plastic power contained in the seed. And we should do so the more readily, if we should discover that as the tree spreads into twigs and leaves, the succeeding leaves still become more refined, more perfect in shape and color, until many cluster together and form a bud, which opening, shows itself clad in red and white, surrounded by the tender green of the leaves nearest to it. This is not all. The fruit itself, consists but of a cluster of leaves, which, absorbing the finest juice of the tree, and constantly nourished by the rays of the sun and the warmth of the atmosphere, are peculiarly organized to filtrate all the nourishment they thus receive. These compact leaves at first taste like other leaves and are of their color; but they expand, and finally appear as a fruit, wholly different from any other part of the tree. The fruit, be it an apple or a grape, is only the capsule of the seed, and as the latter ripens, this decays. In this respect the pod of the bean has the same design with the finest pear. In proof of our assertion, it may be remarked, that the pod of the bean is merely a leaf bent together. The same is true of the pods of radishes, peas, &c. In the apple then, we eat nothing but the refined and filtrated moisture of the earth, the light of the sun, and the balm of the atmosphere, as it lives and works in the other leaves.

It is remarkable, that in proportion as we nourish a plant with rude and heavy manure, it produces dark, strong and large leaves, thus retarding its state of bloom. This shows that these stronger leaves filtrate and prepare the juices for the higher and more delicate leaves, and that these again are the same leaves at a higher stage, that we before noticed at a lower one. It is therefore certain, that it is the same organ which first appears at the root, then higher up, and finally as blossom and fruit. Considering this we might be induced to suppose the plant or the tree, as simple an activity, as some have represented mind. Yet in examining a plant or tree a little more closely, we must perceive that while all the different parts constantly repeat but one organ and proceed from one common power, they nevertheless differ, each having a peculiar office to perform for the development and preservation of their general life. This view, the only correct one, unites the two former. For according to it we perceive on the one hand a union, an identity, and on the other a variety; but the variety and difference proceeds from the union, which appears in every single organ, and only unfolds itself by all of them. This leads us once more to the idea of development. Whatever develops itself, changes, yet it does not become any thing else than it was when undeveloped. For while it takes different forms, it remains the same in all of them; while it exhibits itself under different aspects, it does not pass over into any thing that is not itself, nor does it receive any of its various forms from without, but all develop themselves from within. It becomes and exists otherwise when developed, than when undeveloped, but it has not become any thing else. Developing itself, it becomes *in reality*, what before it was according to *possibility and energy*. So the bulb of a hyacinth may be said to be and not to be the hyacinth. It is the hyacinth according to energy, and nothing can grow forth from it, that is not in it; and again it is not yet the hyacinth, for it has not yet grown forth. The growing forth is the development of the energy slumbering in the bulb. The idea of development contains, therefore, the idea of a transition from the invisible to the visible, from the dark and unknown to the manifest and revealed. Thus the soul contains in its simple identical activity, all that afterwards appears in succession, under the form of faculties. They are but the development of the energy of the soul, but its representation and its organs. Hence the soul is an energy, that in developing itself, remains the same that it was, and yet becomes different. It remains the same, for nothing is added from without, all comes from within; it is different, for it exists in its developed state. The first developments of the plant are, as we have seen, the roots and rude leaves, which become more refined as they grow higher on the stock; the first development of the soul, the leaves near the roots of its existence is sensation, which is followed by attention. Higher than these are conception, fancy, imagination and memory, which may be considered the blossoms on the tree of knowledge, while pure thinking, under the form of the understanding, judgment, reason and will, are the ripe fruits. And here we may remark, that there could be no blossoms, were there no leaves near the root; but as the juice in them rises higher, it becomes more refined, until it appears pure and clear in blossom and fruit. So sensation is the beginning and root of all knowledge, and nothing can enter the understanding that has not first been received by sensation. As it passes from the lower to the higher activities of mind, it becomes more and better known, and like the fruit, more refined. Again, as the blossom of a plant may be retarded, or wholly prevented by rude nourishment, so sensual persons may always move in the sphere of sensuality, and satisfied with it, never look for any thing beyond.

Before closing this paragraph, however, it may not be superfluous to add a remark. I have spoken of higher and lower stages of the development of mind, and some might feel inclined to consider sensation, for example, a lower faculty than conception. This would be wrong. The mind, as has been repeatedly stated, is a *whole;* a whole cannot exist without its parts, as these cannot be without the whole. Were a single one of these parts wanting, the idea of the whole would be destroyed; but the mind is a *living* whole, and hence its parts are *organs,* that is, filled with the life of the whole, of which they are parts. If one of these organs were wanting, the mind, as a whole, would be ruined, could not operate, would be insane or deranged, etc. Hence one part is as necessary as the other, and it would be wrong to speak of *higher* and *lower* faculties, as if the one were *better* than the other. Who would say, that the root of the tree, because it is in the soil, is less valuable than the branch, because it grows in the air? The one is as valuable as the other. Sensation, it is true, when compared with thinking, stands lower than fancy or imagination, and yet, in as far as it belongs to man, it is *intellectual* and pervaded by reflection from the beginning. The sensation of the animal is without reflection; it always remains, therefore, below thinking; but the sensation of man contains, from its motions, the possibility of *reflection*. If, however, with reference to the *development* of mind, we should nevertheless speak of its *lower* and *higher* stages, we must remember that while one and the same life developes itself, each faculty is not merely a *higher* stage of that life, (in that case it would only be *stronger* and *fuller* than the one preceding,) but is also a qualitatively *different* one. Thus the objects and contents of sensation and imagination are wholly different; those of sensation are given from without, those of imagination produced from within. The difficulty here is to distinguish between *sameness* and *identity*. The latter includes difference, and is as impossible without it as harmony; the former excludes all variety. An identity of the powers of mind, therefore, does not exclude their qualitative different and distinct operations, but pre-supposes them. Thus *sensation* is originally the same, whether it be that of *hearing*, *seeing*, or *smelling;* yet by reflection upon it, the greatest variety is observed, not only in its *contents*, but also in sensation as such. With regard to their contents, it is easily acknowledged that the sensations of red and white in color, and of sharp and flat in music, differ widely; and so likewise with regard to the sensations themselves; for those of sight and hearing are certainly as different as they can be.

Psychology will be divided into two sections; the former treating of Reason in general, the latter of the Will.

SECTION I.

ON REASON.

REASON.

The section on Reason will be divided into *three chapters*. The

I. Treating on Sensation, or the *receptive* powers of Reason.
II. On conception in general, or the form-giving nature of Reason.
III. On pure Thinking.

This division is not made *arbitrarily*, but is derived from the nature of reason itself. It is reason that is to be developed before us, and its development consists really in nothing else than its becoming conscious of itself, and of all that it contains. But reason, as such, is abstract; we must see it in its concrete form and state. As such it appears in man, and here in the form of *self*-consciousness. The development of reason and self-consciousness is therefore the same. Now sensation is the indispensable and first condition of all intellectual developments, and of that of self-consciousness likewise; for, by feeling the objects of our sensations, we darkly feel ourselves, and in proportion as we become conscious of them, we must become conscious of ourselves. But as we become conscious of ourselves, reason awakes in itself, and this is its first stage of development.

The second chapter, on the other hand, treats on that portion of reason which works in itself, as fancy, that forms new images. If it receives all its excitement from the outward world before, it now delights in its inward operations, as appears from the life of the artist, the poet, etc. It gives form to all that it receives from sensation, and by doing so, becomes conscious of its power. The consciousness of the world, under the form of sensation, may rouse self-consciousness to a considerable degree, even in children; but man must awake *in himself*, and become conscious of himself by looking into his own bosom. All the mental operations mentioned in this chapter, as conception, fancy, memory, are therefore termed inward; thus differing, not in the degree of development only, but in quality also, from the mental activities of the first chapter. Reason thus becomes conscious of itself, and of its contents, by its operations within itself.

The third chapter finally leads us to reason freed from every thing not properly belonging to it, and standing pure on its own fully developed ground. Here nothing prevails but *pure* thought. Images, symbols, signs, are all of them sensual in their nature; for the eye or the ear, they *represent* thoughts, but are not the thoughts themselves. Now it is entirely *accidental* what image, or symbol, or comparison, I use to signify a thought. If I lead the life of a shepherd, my imagery will be taken from the scenery, circumstances, nature, and incidents of that life. So we find it in Gessner's poems. If I am a seaman, the ocean will furnish me with images.

So again my choice of images among those at my *command* is *arbitrary*. The sceptre or crown—both are symbols of dominion. But when I express a pure thought, reason, no longer satisfied with *accidental* and *arbitrary* representations, and fully conscious of itself, will appear in its own form, which is that of *generality* and *necessity*, that is, every thought, if it is to contain truth, must, by these two qualities, show itself independent of all *objective* and *subjective*, of all external and internal authority, must be, as truth really is, its own authority, and the authority for every thing else. Self-consciousness must not be absorbed by pure thinking, but it must fully awake in it, and thus raise itself into a higher sphere of life, where neither nature nor our egoity reign, but pure thought alone. When I, for example, say, God is the highest *Being*, I express by the term *Being*, a thought which cannot be made plain by any image or symbol; I must, in order to understand it, re-produce it in my own mind. So it is *general* in its nature, for it demands the same thought every where, in·all countries, and in all individuals; it is *necessary*, for it cannot be otherwise than it is. The term *highest* is not a *pure* thought, it has reference to the lower, and is only the *highest* when compared with all running on the same scale with itself. It has neither *generality* nor *necessity* for what I consider high may be low to another.

CHAPTER I.

§ 1. SENSATION AND THE SENSES.*

Nihil est in intellectu, quod non antea fuerit in sensu.

Sensation has several times been the subject of our consideration; it is the soil from which all knowledge arises; the chaos from which mind creates its intellectual world. With it the development of mind commences, and in it mind has all the materials with which to establish its sciences. Sensation is, therefore, the first stage, in which the general possibility, from which all the developments of mind proceed, realizes itself. For feeling an object, we we must feel it in ourselves. In having a sensation, we therefore feel ourselves, and something different from ourselves, and thus we are roused to self-consciousness by the object felt. Hence, sensation may be considered as the indispensable condition of self-consciousness. Sensation, as we have seen, differs from feeling, and yet has many things in common with it. Like it, it pre-supposes nothing but life for its existence; as we do not need to learn how to feel, so we have sensations without instruction, all they require being life itself. To learn how to judge, time is necessary, but feeling and sensations are inseparably connected with the activity of animal life. On the other hand, feeling and sensation differ as before seen, for the former is not circumscribed in its form, nor are its contents clear and distinct; the latter is a limitation of the feeling activity,

* For *sensation* some writers here would use the term *perception* as referring to the notice which the percipient mind takes of external objects. The author, however, prefers the term *sensation*, since his principal object here is to speak of the *affection* of the senses as called forth by external impressions on them, and he trusts that he will be pardoned this somewhat unusual application of the word, and that candid readers in forming their judgment of his views will bear in mind the above explanation.

an affection of one of the senses. Not every limitation of an activity, therefore, is *sensation*,—the light, for instance, is an activity ; falling upon a smooth, well polished surface, it is reflected, consequently its flow is limited, but no sensation is produced. Sensation is the limitation of an activity, which is felt by the activity. Hence, every sensation pre-supposes the limitation of an activity, and a feeling of this limitation :—This limitation is only *felt ;* feeling is *dark and indistinct ;* hence it is, that mere sensation does not distinguish between itself and its contents, and that no being can, by sensation alone, distinguish between the sensations of the different senses. We have sensations of the eye, and the ear, of taste and feeling ; they differ essentially, and have different contents ; but sensation does not distinguish between them and their contents. Again, the sensations of the *same* senses differ in themselves not only with regard to the objects by which they are affected, as the fragrance of the syringa differs from that of the hyacinth, but also as regards the subject affected ; here the contents of the same sense differ strictly in themselves, and almost enter into an opposition, for those of sight are either dark or light, those of the ear either flat or sharp, those of the nose fragrance or stench, those of the tongue sweetness or sourness, those of feeling roughness or smoothness, softness or hardness. But as long as sensation *merely* prevails, all is confusedly mixed together, and it is only by attention and judgment that distinction and order are produced.

Again, the contents of our sensations and the objects which produce them are not the same. The bird, for instance, that flies through the air, is not contained in my eye, but in the air ; its image, however, its plumage and motions are contained in my sensation. To enable us to separate the contents of our sensations from their external objects, judgment is necessary. This sufficiently appears from a remarkable case that came under the observation of Dr. Cheselden, in the year 1727. He succeeded in giving sight to a youth of twenty years, who was born blind. When the bandage was removed, the lad supposed that whatever he saw, was not without but within his eyes. After some time he perceived that the things seen by him were not in his eye, but now he saw all of them on *one* surface before him. It was only by using his hands that he obtained an idea of distance and separation. This was quite natural, for that which we feel, is not the object; this is without us. We feel only an impression, and this is an affection of our senses. We feel, therefore, strictly speaking, only ourselves or the affection of our senses, and hence it is, that the child does not distinguish between sensations and their contents, nor between these and their objects. Distinction and order are, therefore, not by sensation as such, but by thought and judgment. Another example may serve to make this still more clear. When we first cast our eye over a scarcely legible page, all seems confusion; but as soon as we examine the writing more closely, as soon as we can discern the letters, and connect them into syllables and words, the confusion disappears. This connection is, however, not the act of sensation, but of attention and judgment. Nor can we by sensation discover any thing that is general in its nature. The eye cannot see to what species or genus a thing belongs, this can be perceived only by the judgment. Life, for instance, is something general; but it cannot be perceived by the senses; no one has yet seen life as such with his eyes, or heard it with his ears. From its productions, we may *conclude* upon life as the power that calls them forth; but when we draw *conclusions*, we *think*. So we may feel the smooth bark of a plant, see the pure white of the lily, or the tender red of a rose; but the *life* of the lily we cannot see. We may taste the juice of the grape, but its life we can neither taste, nor discover by tasting the grape. Lifeless elementary nature alone is subject to our sensations; life, as such, is not, though its productions may be seen, or tasted, or felt.

If sensation is a medium between man and natural objects; if by it only, man can become conscious of the external world, the senses which render sensation possible, next demand our attention. It is by them that the universe is opened to us, and we may become conscious of all its beauties and laws, its powers and their productions, and thus enrich ourselves with knowledge. Their physiology is here to be left out of view, and their psychological importance can only be touched on, nor is it necessary to do more, since so many works give a full exhibition of the manner in which the notions of time and space, of substance and accidents, &c., are formed by the aid of the senses.

That which is to be felt, must have power to affect the senses. Whatever is too weak to do this, cannot impress them, and consequently cannot be perceived by them. We must not, therefore, imagine that all the activities of nature are perceptible to our senses; there are doubtless many of which we are at present entirely ignorant. The following are the principal objects of sensation:

1. Matter in general, its gravity, its mechanical cohesion, the structure of bodies, their smoothness, roughness, sharpness, softness and hardness; the temperature and its changes. The sensation is that of feeling, and in man the organ is the skin. The skin is sensitive in proportion as it is tight. The lips, the arms and hands, feel very quickly. The structure of a body may be felt by the hand. Forming a semi-circle, it can easily adapt itself to almost any form; both hands joined form a sphere, the prototype of all other forms. In the lower classes of animals, the nerves are hard, and possess but little flexibility. The higher classes are generally covered with fur, feathers, or scales, and feeling is therefore not very fine. Some have feelers and proboscis, others a tender skin, as snails and serpents; but none have arms and hands, carried by the body and perfectly free for the purpose of feeling.

2. Its chemical qualities. Matter has internal qualities that can only be perceived in a state of solution, and this state is either that of an inelastic or that of an elastic fluid. Under the first form, it is liquid in general, the sensation is taste, and the organ is the tongue. Nothing can be tasted before it is dissolved. The medium of taste is water. Tasting is a complete chemical process. The thing to be tasted is separated by the teeth, tongue and saliva, and its qualities are caused to penetrate each other. The sense of taste discovers more chemical qualities than any chemical analysis. Hence the term taste is ever applied to the investigation of beauty in the sphere of art. Finally, the tongue stands in a close relation to the stomach, it is indeed

a mere continuation of it. Tasting is the beginning of digestion. The tongue proves the food for the stomach. It is remarkable that while animals surpass man in other senses, the tongue is not found fully among them. Zoophytes, worms, and the lower classes of fish, have no tongue; insects have frequently only a wart; and the tongue of other animals is often covered with scales.

Under the second form it is the elastic fluid, the sensation is that of smell, the organ the nose, the medium the air. Every thing smelled is assimilated; it enters through the nose, the cerebral system and lungs. Hence there is a close connection between the lungs and the nose, the latter proving the air for the former, and warning it not to inhale it, when corrupt. Strong vapors and exhalations frequently cause swooning, nausea, cramps, &c.

3. Light and Sound. *Light.* That which is seen is not pure light, nor space, nor matter, but light as rendered visible by matter. The sensation is that of sight, the organ is the eye; the mediums of sight are the fluids, solids and gaseous elements. The sense of sight having reference to judgment, we must *learn* to see.—*Sound* is produced by the elastic vibrations of bodies; the sensation is that of hearing, the ear is the organ, and ether the medium. As optics and accoustics treat very fully on these two senses, they are only mentioned here for the sake of completeness.

General Remarks on the Senses.

General feeling is the root from which all the senses grow forth. It has no external organ and is not related to external objects, but has only reference to the living and feeling being, informing it of the state of its organism. By it we may form an idea of what will benefit or injure our bodily system, so that we may govern our appetites and regulate our diet. Its organ is not properly speaking, a sense, not a cluster of nerves, but all the nerves as a whole. It is called *general* feeling, because it indicates the general state of the system, general debility or vigor, general warmth or chilliness, general pain or pleasure:—and again, hunger or thirst, refreshment or satisfaction. The objects of this feeling are, therefore, the changeable states of the functions and organs of the body, which could not be perceived by the *single* senses. As all the senses have their root in this *common* or *general* feeling, so it is again affected by all the impressions made upon them. Hence every sensation we have is the feeling of a change in our general feeling, and as our disposition and humor depend greatly on the state of our general feeling, it will on the one hand modify the influence of these impressions upon us, as on the other it will be influenced by them. The former appears from the fact, that the same temperature affects persons so differently, that each if asked would give a different degree of heat or cold. The latter is substantiated by the effects which impressions, made upon the senses, have in cheering or depressing the spirits.

A sense, affected by an external object in harmony with its own nature, feels pleasure, but if affected too strongly, or against its nature, pain—this feeling, whether of pain or pleasure, will be communicated to the whole system, and to what has been called *general feeling* by the connection of the principal nerve of the sense affected, with all the nerves of the body. Hence cold and heat, a clear or cloudy sky have such an influence upon us; a good dinner renders us comfortable and satisfied; delicate odors enliven the imagination and spread pleasure over all our feelings. The opposite of these will, of course, have an opposite effect.

On these usual effects of impressions from the senses on our *general feeling*, depends the symbolization of colors and music, which of course will vary according to different climates, like language, art, &c. According to Goethe, " every color leaves a peculiar impression on man and thus reveals its nature both to his eye and his mind; men in general delight in color, the eye stands in need of it as of the light, etc. The colors which we see in bodies are not something entirely strange to the eye, by which it is *forced* to that sensation; this organ is always disposed to produce colors of itself, and enjoys an agreeable sensation when something corresponding to its own nature is offered from without. Hence it is that the single impressions of colors will work specifically and produce a decided specific state in the living organ—so in the mind also, experience teaches that particular colors produce particular dispositions. It is for this reason that colors may be applied to sensual, moral, and aesthetical purposes, and that they are used allegorically, symbolically and mystically. To give a few examples, black is the color of mourning, because it extinguishes all other colors; white is the color of innocence, because it is the general ground for all colors. Black and white mixed, form *gray*, the color of resignation, fear, uneasiness and twilight. Hence nearly all nations represent good beings in white, evil spirits in black, and ghosts in gray. Blue, the color of the atmosphere we inhale, and which quickens us, attracts, hence it is the color of desire, longing, faithfulness, for faithfulness belongs not to itself, but to another. Pure yellow, the color of gold, attracts us strongly and is the color of cheerfulness. Red, the color of fire, like it pierces the eye, and is the symbol of power. Popes, cardinals, and kings are therefore clad in the different shades of red, some of which express violence, as orange, others a concealed tendency to power, as the crimson of cardinals.

The same may be observed with regard to sounds. Some of them, as that of cutting glass, grate on the ear; others soften or rejoice the heart, and excite the activity of the limbs. And how various are the emotions called forth by the rustling of branches, the murmuring of a brook, the sighing of the wind; by the war-like sound of a trumpet, or the soft tones of a distant flute? The power of music may likewise be seen from the great influence it has on animals. Mice are known to have been killed by it; horses are animated by the sound of the trumpet.

The degree of a nation's cultivation may easily be recognized by their fondness for penetrating or lively colors, and their copious mixture on a small surface; or by the more refined taste that prefers delicate colors, their regular distribution, and harmonious connection. Music is likewise a criterion of the cultivation of a nation. Delight in simple melodies, or in a grand composition, in a single instrument, or in the concert of many, will indicate the state of civilization and refinement. Smell and taste have also their fashions, by which the civilized differ from the uncivilized.

The noblest senses of man are the eye and the ear. For, while the others have reference either to matter or its chemical qualities, they refer the one to the judgment, the other to understanding. If we compare them with each other, we find that both are senses for form; and therefore the mediums of art and literature. Painting, sculpture, and architecture, depend on sight, as music, poetry, and science, on hearing. While the eye opens the universe with its thousands of objects, the ear is their common echo, and communicates to us their internal being. The eye is cold, dwelling only on the surface of things, while the ear listens to every sound of nature, and makes us feel with all that lives; for, whatever can emit sound, from the gushing water, and the singing bird, to man, expresses by it the degree of its vigor, the manner of its life. The ear excites, therefore, more deep sympathy than the eye. The statue of Laocoon leaves us more cold than the description of his sufferings in Virgil. Music breathes more life into us than a picture. If in this respect the ear has an advantage over the eye, the eye being more removed from feeling, is nearer to thought. We compare truth with light; a prophet is a *seer*. Truth illuminates. Again, thunder can be heard at no greater distance than twenty or thirty miles, while lightning may be seen at the distance of from one hundred and twenty to two hundred and fifty miles; but what the eye seems to gain in this respect, it loses in another, for it cannot see in the dark, while the ear hears as well in the night as at any other time. We know, too, that instruction must be addressed to the ear, and that a single word from a commanding officer will animate his soldiers far more than a mere signal. Hearing makes social intercourse and the cultivation of mind possible; for, as we have said, it has a direct bearing on the understanding; as what we hear, we naturally desire to understand. Sight has more reference to the imagination, to hope, and other emotions, hence the eye so easily betrays these emotions. The eye was the sense appealed to by the pictures and statues of Polytheism; in Monotheism, it is the ear; lawgivers, prophets, and the Saviour addressed themselves to it.

The erroneous idea that the senses differ from each other only in *quantity*, that, for example, sight is only a *more re-*

fined sense than feeling, taste more refined than smell, led to the notion of the substitution of one sense for another. The eye of blind persons, it is asserted, is altogether reduced to mere feeling; with some animals taste is wholly absent, and scent is their only pleasure in eating. The degree of acuteness of the nerves, their greater or less development, and the external elements affecting them, produce the different sensations. In accordance with this view it is said, that one sense may take the place of another. When I speak of sounds that are *dark* or *clear*, or of a *sweet* scent, I ascribe the attributes of one sense to another, as if no qualitative difference existed between them: and who has not noticed that the scent of many an animal or fruit exactly resembles the taste of something with which we are familiar? And yet, notwithstanding all this, it would be highly incorrect to deny a total difference between the different senses and sensations. However fine and sensitive the *feeling* of the blind may become, if he was born blind, he cannot form a conception of color, though he may be able, by touch, to distinguish between the surfaces of colors. But such a distinction resembles that which the ear of the animal perceives in the sounds of the human voice: it hears them, but not the words formed by them.

The forms in which alone we can perceive objects of sense, are those of space and time. The former being extensive, is external, the latter protensive, is internal. Things in space exist contemporaneously as the numerous stars of the firmament; things in time succeed each other, and time is itself its own succession. Whatever is in space must assume in its form the dimensions of space. These are the *point*, the *line*, the *sphere*. Infusoria are globular points; worms and serpents are long; fish and beetles are broad or flat; and all the mammalia are voluminous. Time is divided into the past, the present, and the future. Whatever is in it must belong to one of these divisions. Now we say, all that is in time and space may be perceived by one or another sense, but space and time themselves are inaccessible to the senses; the past, for instance, is one of the divisions of time, but neither the eye nor the ear can perceive that which no longer exists. The future, as yet, is not, and consequently cannot impress the senses. So it is with the geometrical line—it is not tangible like a ribbon or string, but can only be seen by the eye of the mind, as the geometrical point cannot be felt by the finger like the point of a needle.

Oken, the renowned Natural Philosopher, has very ingeniously spoken of an *external* and *internal* sense, by which to perceive the dimensions of *Space* and *Time*. As the five senses stand related to *sensation*, so this external and internal sense is related to what we may anticipate here, *Intellectual Perception*, or that power of mind which perceives objects in space and time. Space and Time are the subjective forms of all our perceptions, and we can perceive nothing except in them. We can by continued abstraction empty space and time of their contents, but no imagination can remove space and time themselves. But they are not only, as Kant maintained, the *subjective* forms of our perceptions, they have an *objective* existence; they are independent of our perceptions. Now all that fills space, for example, may be felt and perceived by our senses, as they are the conditions of our sensations; but space itself, in which all material objects are, cannot be felt, cannot become the object of a sensation. But it may become the object of our external sense, which stands, as was said above, related to our intellectual perception. Space, when regarded by itself, in abstraction from all it contains, is nothing else than extension, (the " *out of each other*," according to Kant;) it has three dimensions, which, to follow Hegel's views, are the *point*, the *line*, and the *sphere*. Neither of them is *material*, neither accessible to the touch, the eye, or the palm. The point of a needle may be very fine, but it is still a *material* point, one that may be felt; the point in space is without any dimension, cannot be felt at all, it must be *perceived* by intellect, and hence it is that the external sense, which perceives it, is related to our *intellectual perception*, and intermediates it as the senses do sensation. The power to perceive these dimensions of space is called sense, because it has reference to the five senses. So the point in space is a mere *negation*, nothing *positive*; yet we may point to it, and if we do so it is with the point of a finger. The line is likewise wholly inaccessible to our sensations; for though we may stretch a cord in a straight line, and handle it, it is not the *line* which we touch, but the material of which the cord consists, which may be silk, or flax, or hemp; yet here also our intellectual perception of the line is aided by the feeling or touch resting in the point of the finger. And with the *sphere* it is not otherwise. The eye, which is the sense for it, cannot be affected by it, as it is affected by the stars of heaven, or by any material object, it cannot have a sensation of it. The sphere is only the object of intellectual perception, and the *eye* is the sense that aids this perception. Its own form is spherical, and as the feelers of snails and other insects seem to be living lines, so the eye is a living sphere. Yet to see a sphere, we must think; for a *sphere* is, where from a common centre, (*the point*,) all the radii, (the lines,) stream forth and form a periphery, so that neither a point nor a line either recedes, or projects beyond the others. Light forms the most perfect sphere, for all its rays flow from one common centre, and exhibit a perfect periphery.

The internal sense has reference to *time*, and as the senses of *feeling* and of *sight* aid our intellectual perception of the dimensions of space, so those of smelling, tasting, and hearing, aid our intellectual perception of the dimensions of time. For though the future, for example, is wholly inaccessible to our sensations, yet is there some distant relation between it and scent. Dogs, for example, discover by their smell the distant both in space and time; the *scent* of food causes a perception of the *taste*, which is as yet a *future sensation.*—The sense of hearing is related to our perception of the *past*. This can no longer be felt, we can no longer have a *sensation* of it, but we may have a *perception* of it, and this perception will be intermediated by hearing.—The third dimension of time is the *present*, and our perception of it is aided by the sense of taste. While *eating* and *drinking* we forget past cares, and feel unconcerned about the future. We indulge ourselves, and think not of the evil consequences which may result from the brief pleasure.

With reference to time itself we may say the same as of space; it is wholly impossible for us to abstract from it, though we may abstract from all contained in it. In that case time only is left, and in this emptiness it is nothing else than protension, or its own succession, the dimensions of which we have considered above. We become conscious of time and its nature by the changes that take place in it, and which we partly observe in nature, and partly in ourselves. But our consciousness of time and space in the abstract is gained by reflection on the external and internal sense. Both are active; the former flowing forth *outwardly*, as sight, the organ of which is convex and projecting; the latter *inwardly*, as hearing, the organ of which is concave, immitting, not emitting. When we now reflect on the activity that flows outwardly, constantly expanding or extending, this activity will assume the character of rest, and present itself to us as space. And so it is likewise with the activity of our internal sense. Its *protensive* activity, when it becomes objective to us, assumes the character of time.

Now the external sense might be called too the *natural sense*, or the sense for nature; for all that is in nature, is either by the side of each other, or in each other, or out of each other, and this is the *nature* of *space*. And so the internal sense may be called the *historical sense*, or the sense for history; for all that is historical is after each other, in a constant flow or succession. Nature is the sphere of reality; history that of ideality. By reality we understand the existence of an object for another, whether the object be conscious of this fact or not; as for example, the fountain of water has reality for the thirsty that drink from it. Nature, in which all exists, the one by the side of the other, is therefore the sphere of reality, and has a hold upon man and his scientific investigations that is strong and lasting. By ideality we understand on the other hand the existence of a being *for itself*, its perceiving, understanding, knowing itself. Here all is contained in the sphere of thought, for without thinking no one can be for himself. I may exist as I for another who is like myself an I; but not for any being below me, not for the animal for instance, that is not an I.—Now realism and idealism belong together, as nature and history, as the *external* and *internal* sense. But as the one or the other prevails in a person, we see him incline to the study of natural sciences, and feel averse to history; or incline to the latter, and disrelish the former. And so he will be either a *realist* or an *idealist* in principle. But keeping himself within the sphere of nature or history, and not admitting a world above sense and touch, he cannot remove the contradiction between realism and idealism, nor move freely in a science of pure truth, holiness, beauty, etc., for that demands more than a mere intellectual perception, it demands pure thinking.

---

§ 2. OF ATTENTION.

We have seen that feelings and sensations are in themselves indistinct and confused, and that though they are the beginning of all knowledge, yet knowledge cannot be produced by them alone. This is manifest from the fact, that while animals feel and have sensations like ourselves, they have no knowledge or science. That by which distinction and clearness is produced in the feelings is attention. It is the basis of all knowledge, and even of self-consciousness. Without it, we could neither perceive accurately, nor remember well, nor take cognizance of our own perceptions. So when we are deeply engaged in meditation, we may meet an intimate acquaintance, look in his face, and yet pass him by without being conscious of knowing him. Persons employed in iron works, take no notice of the noise around them, but converse as if all were silent; and in the field of battle, amidst the thunder of cannon, generals will listen to the report of an officer as if not a breeze of the air were stirring. This they can do, as all will say, because they pay no attention to the noise around them. Hence it is correct to say, that without attention, nothing exists for the mind of man. Without attention we may think and have no thoughts, for our thinking will be only a kind of dreaming or reverie: without attention we may travel for years, yet gain no wisdom; we may be surrounded by the choicest productions of art and discover no beauty. Attention therefore deserves our notice, and we shall inquire: *What activity of mind is called attention?*

To understand *Attention* fully, we must consider it first, as it is *voluntary* and as we are conscious of it, and secondly, as it is neither voluntary nor conscious, but as it precedes all the other mental faculties, and is active in the child, which is as yet neither conscious of the world nor of itself:

1. Attention in general, and as it exists in mature persons, is that activity by which the mind decides to turn for a time, from every thing else, and direct itself to a particular object. It differs from observation, for this has an external object, and its aim is, to ascertain the nature of this object and its relation to others. Observation pre-supposes and requires attention. Again, attention differs from judging, or thinking, for judgment likewise has objects, which it compares with each other. Attention is only the activity of mind, by which it resolves to fix itself upon a single object; it is therefore impossible without will—yet it may be drawn forth in various ways. The novelty or contrast of things, the pleasant or unpleasant manner in which they affect us, or the interest which from any cause we take in them, may serve to excite it. So one sense will elicit the attention of another—as, when we feel something crawling under our fingers, our eyes involuntarily turn towards it, to see what it is: or if we hear a gun discharged behind us, we turn to see whence the report came. The eye also directs the ear. An officer in glittering uniform, riding up and down before his soldiers, who change in their position at every word he speaks, attracts the attention of the ear. Or a preacher of dignified exterior, appears for the first time before us in the pulpit; the eyes of all watch his motions, and the ear is ready to catch his words. Interest in a thing will call forth the attention—the musician will easily be attracted by any thing concerning the life of a Mozart or Beethoven, a Weber or Bellini; or by any of their compositions. The psychologist discovers beauties in Shakspeare, that many readers pass without perceiving. Manifold indeed are the sources of attention, and it would lead us far to mention all of them. Yet we must add one more, and this is the *will* or resolution; it is easy to pay

attention, where interest or inclination urge us to do so; but such attention has no moral value, nor is it sufficient for the study of a science. Every science has branches, that at first excite no interest in us; we must therefore determine by our will to attend to them. This attention alone is a moral one, and deserves regard. Not that which we do from natural impulse, deserves credit, but that which receives attention by virtue of our will, even though it be against our inclinations. This is the case, when accustomed to lighter reading, we for the first time take a scientific book into our hands; we read a few pages and lay it aside —neither interest nor inclination is attracted, and we pay no farther attention to it. It is here that a resolute will is necessary to urge us to give attention, even against inclination.

The objects of our attention may be various at the same time. The captain of a ship in a storm has to direct his attention to many things. The rope-dancer, who while he walks the rope, moves a cane on a pivot, must attend both to the cane and his feet. Cæsar dictated seven letters at a time. But however different the objects to which it may be directed, attention is always and universally the same identical activity of the mind—as the nature of sight or hearing is never changed by the objects from which they receive their impressions, but remain the same whensoever the impression may come.

2. It is more difficult to comprehend attention in its origin, as it exists in the child, before it has become conscious of itself, and consequently before it can will. Attention as a state of mind, is always voluntary; but attention as it must necessarily precede *will* and every other activity of mind, cannot be voluntary. This has been felt by all psychologists, and some have, therefore, tried to explain its origin by saying that it is caused by a heightened excitement of one of our sensations or senses. But in this case it would be difficult to say why animals, especially the higher kinds, cannot pay attention as well as man; yet it is well known that they cannot do this. If the view alluded to were correct, our attention would necessarily be proportional in its strength to our impressions; yet we know that very strong impressions sometimes draw forth very little

attention, while slight ones attract much. It is true, that sensations attract attention in a greater or less degree, but attention does not originate in them. What then is the origin of attention?

This question does not propose to ascertain how attention is drawn forth after we are conscious of it, after we by our will may charge ourselves to be attentive;—its aim is to examine attention as that activity of the mind, which brings order and distinctness into our chaotic feelings, and renders consciousness and judgment, and all the other activities of mind possible. As such it is a *spontaneous*, but not a *voluntary* activity, and precedes the whole development of mind, as the plastic power precedes the growth of the plant.

In its origin, and as the common basis of all the other activities of mind, attention is the power by which mind gives itself a direction, when as yet it has none, and is yet unconscious of itself. The mind at this stage exists as *feeling*, which includes all the succeeding stages of development, as the germ of the seed includes those of the whole growing process. *Feeling*, however, as we have seen repeatedly, is without an object and without a direction, the mere chaos, from which mind as the demiurge, is to build its own world. If feeling had an object, it would be sensation and as such have a most determined direction. The sensation of sight is directed outwardly to objects in space, that of hearing inwardly to objects in time. But mere feeling in general, however rich in contents, from the deepest pain to the hightest pleasure, has no *object* and no *direction*, and the mind in its first stage of existence is nothing but *feeling*. Now the question presents itself: How does this feeling assume a direction, and mind become conscious of itself and of the world around it? This cannot be effected by the will of mind; for it is as yet undeveloped; nor by a conscious or arbitrary activity, for in that case we should move in a circle and pre-suppose what we wish to explain. We are therefore forced to admit *an activity in feeling*, as the first stage of mind, which, neither willed nor conscious of itself, but in distinction from both, is *spontaneous*. This spontaneous activity slumbers in feeling and needs an external excitement, the influence of a developed and matured mind upon it. But this excitement is only its *condition* and not its *cause.*

Another question with regard to this activity presses itself upon us, and it is this: What is its character? It must be in the first place, without any direction to an *external* object, for in that case it would be the same as perception, or *developed* attention, which may be demanded and willed, as has been shown above. The activity before us, as spontaneous attention, is the *first and original direction*, which the mind takes. This direction it takes not to any thing different from itself, but to itself. The direction takes place in itself as feeling, where all is yet chaotic, without distinction, without separation, without order. The direction is constantly repeated, and is the same, no matter what may be its contents. It being the first direction which mind gives itself, and being the direction, which mind gives itself to itself, we may say with truth, that without it, mind could never develop itself, and that only with it mind begins to exist for itself, as every thing else of which the mind becomes conscious comes to its knowledge only through it. With this direction itself the whole development of mind commences, for once conscious of itself, it will not rest until all within it is drawn out. It is only after the mind has taken this direction to itself, made itself the object of its own reflection, that it may take a direction away from itself to any thing else. As little as the eye that is without light in itself can see, so little can mind without distinctness in itself, distinguish between the external and the internal. When we look into the eye of a child during the first weeks of its existence, we see that it is active, constantly moving, but we see also that its activity has no direction. The light falls upon it, images of surrounding objects are reflected on its retina, but it does not yet see them, because its eye is not directed to them. Thus it is with the feelings, before we are conscious of them, they are of course active; they possess pain and pleasure, as they, for example, precede hunger and accompany its gratification: but they are not directed to any *particular object*, and are therefore without a conscious direction. The same is the case with the whole mind. It is for a long time in a state of unconsciousness, and while in this state, has no direction. For when it is conscious of an object, it must be directed to it; as long as it is not conscious of any thing, it cannot have a direction, since no direction which the mind takes can be entirely without consciousness. The developed mind is then a self-conscious activity. Attention in its beginning, is spontaneous activity of the mind that is not voluntary; but by which only choice becomes possible; it is that activity by which mind, which as yet has no direction, gives itself one, yet not to an *external* object, but to itself in its first stage of existence, that is, to feeling. Reflecting on feeling, it afterwards reflects on the causes of feeling. By this direction of the mind to itself, *distinction* is produced; one feeling is separated from another, sensation from sensation, and subject from object. Were it not for this activity—the name given it is of little consequence, we should be incapable of giving conscious and voluntary attention to any thing; the animal has not the former and consequently not the latter. It may point the ear when an unusual sound excites its nerves and irritates the muscles, and correctly speaking, it cannot avoid doing so, but *must* follow the direction from which a strong impression reaches it: but it has no *mind* to direct to these sounds.

The difference between attention, perception and observation, may be shown in the following manner. Attention is the *psychological* ground of observation, and sensation must furnish it with the particular object to be examined. Our sensations and observations are limited to the sphere of visible objects; we cannot observe things to which the senses have no access: but attention has no such limits. The last star that can be seen by the eye, does not arrest and limit attention; it may direct itself farther, for its activity is infinite. Sensation and observation therefore are limited, attention unlimited. Again, sensation is always of necessity. We cannot see without light, and cannot avoid seeing when light is present. So we cannot hear without sound and must hear when surrounded by noise. But attention is a free activity—by it I examine what I please; analyse and re-unite parts, compare them with each other, and determine myself to turn from one to another. The condition of all thinking and willing, is attention, as that direction which is not *determined*, but which mind determines itself to take. Finally, sensation contains objects and contents all united; attention, as preceding other mental activities, separates and distinguishes them from each other; it is in this respect an act of disruption, by which—and this deserves notice—the objects of our sensations are placed without us, in space and time; by which their contents are separated from our sensations, and our sensations from ourselves. It is judgment in its lowest stage, and judgment is attention in its most refined form. As long as we have merely a sensation of light, light and sight are yet undivided: but *attention* will enable us to perceive that the one may be where the other is not. The power perceiving this is higher than that of sensation; it is *conception*. Thus the transition from sensation to conception is formed by attention.

CHAPTER II.

CONCEPTION.

In commencing this chapter, I cannot avoid quoting the words of Stewart: "In a study such as this, so far removed from the common purposes of speech, some latitude may perhaps be allowed in the use of words, provided only we define accurately those we employ, and adhere to our own definitions."

We have seen that attention in its commencement is an activity that separates the objects of sensations from their contents, and from the sensations themselves.

---

§ 1. INTELLECTUAL PERCEPTION.

We feel a smooth surface, or touch something rough. Smoothness or roughness are produced in our feelings by the greater or less affection of the senses; they are therefore felt as being in ourselves. By attention, however, we transfer them into the object, and pronounce them its qualities. As such they exist no longer in ourselves, in our senses, but in the object that is in space and time. Seeing things as contained in space and time, we do not merely see them with the eye of sense, but with the eye of the mind; our seeing them is accompanied by consciousness; it is an intellectual, not a merely sensual sight by the senses. To distinguish this seeing as accompanied by consciousness, from the mere sensation, we may call it an *intellectual perception*. It is the same with sensation, and differs from it only by seeing its objects in space and time, and by being conscious of them. To understand this fully, we must remember that originally, and before *attention* has made the distinction, the objects of sensation do not exist as yet at all for us, that they consequently are not at all distinguished from their contents in our sensations, nor *referred* to each other. If the objects may be called *external*, the contents are *internal;* now during that original state, the external object and the internal contents are merged in each other; there is, as yet, no *external* or *internal*, and the *object* becomes object to man only by attention, which separates the contents from our sensations, and uniting them places them in space and time. The sensation thus deprived of its contents, ceases to be what it was, and becomes an *intellectual perception* or *intuition.*

We must here guard against the idea, that the objects of our sensations not only *preceded* but *produced* them. The tree, it is true, may stand many a decennium and never be noticed; but if it is to become an object for me, it can become so only through that activity which separates the contents from my sensations, and transfers them into space and time. That activity does not, of course, place the contents in my sensations, but finds them there, and all it does is to unite them, and pronounce them, when *united*, the *thing* or *object*, and when considered *by themselves*, the *qualities* of the object. The contents of my sensations are for example, *sharpness* to my tongue, whiteness to my sight, and hardness to my feeling. I transfer these contents, which severally fill and burden one of my senses, into space, unite them, and there *see* or rather *perceive* salt. Before this act of separation, the object does not exist at all for the mind, and hence we may see once more the importance of knowing something about attention, not as it exists ripe and mature, but as it is the activity, that precedes every other mental exercise, and through which not only every thing else, but mind begins to have an existence for itself. The example of the blind man, to whom Cheselden gave sight, may be remembered here, but another instance may serve to make the above still more clear. The child, before it is attentive, undoubtedly has sensations; it sees, hears, feels, and smells. But it does not yet distinguish the objects and contents of its sensations from the sensations themselves: it does not separate them from each other. It sees, for instance, the table in the room, but runs against it and hurts itself; it sees the precipice, and does not shun it; it sees the moon, and stretches its little hands to seize it. Why does it so? Because all it sees rests yet undivided on the retina of its eye; but no sooner does its mind reflect on its feelings, than it will be induced by them to reflect on the objects which called them forth, and thus learn to distinguish. This is not yet an act of judgment; children, in their infancy, especially before they have become conscious of themselves, do not judge. When the child, therefore, no longer runs against objects, but shuns them; when it no longer sees things only with its bodily eye, but perceives them as they co-exist in space, or as they succeed each other in time; when it sees them with its mind—then the child unconsciously, and yet freely, has made distinctions by virtue of that abstract attention which is represented above as the origin of all attention. When I approach a large city for the first time, and view it from a neighboring eminence, it appears like a confused mass of houses: if, after examining it, I see the houses and streets in their regular arrangement my sight of it is no longer merely bodily, but mental. Or if we hear music below our windows while asleep, we do not hear the melody or harmony, but only sounds. We awake, and a feeling is excited. We reflect upon it, that is, our mind is directed to it, and tries to discover what is going on in it, and thus by it is led to attend to the sounds, and to discover the melody in the sounds as they fall upon the ear. This whole process, from feeling to perception, may be very rapid, and in most cases may not be at all noticed by us. Yet though its single stages may melt into each other, they must always be passed through. These few examples, it is hoped, will sufficiently show that there is a difference between seeing a thing only with the bodily eye, and seeing it as contained in space and time.

§ 2. OF CONCEPTION.

We have seen the origin and nature of intellectual perception. It has no contents in itself, for it perceives every thing out of itself. Yet the contents of sensations continue as objects in space and time, as does also the person who once had these sensations; by the intellectual perception a connection is kept up between these objects and the person. The objects were once present to his sensations, yet not as objects, but merely as contents of the different senses, confused and without order; as *objects* they are not contained in the senses, but in space and time, and are *external*. They are, however, to become *internal*, and the power that renders them so is *conception*. It transfers the objects of space and time into ourselves, and gives them an internal existence. Yet not the objects, as they would burden the senses, but only their images are received.

The contents of conception are those of our former sensations; they were, as we have seen transferred into space and time, and now they are received back into the mind, not as they really exist, but by their images. By these images, which are wholly ideal, a relation is brought about between ourselves and the things of which they are the images, for while the objects exist without us, or in space and time, their images are within us. What then are we *to understand* by *an image?*

1. There are many images which are no conceptions; as when the infant is held before a looking-glass, its image is reflected, but it does not notice it. Here is an image in the mirror, but not in the mind of the infant. This image may be perceived by other persons, and they may form a conception of it; but it will be in the mirror whether seen or not. So when a tree stands near clear and transparent waters, its image will be reflected by them; this image rests on the surface of the water, but it is not a conception, until our eye has seen, and our mind perceived it. The image of our mind must be gradually formed; the object of which it is the image, must have been felt, it must have been separated from our senses by that act of disruption before mentioned, and transferred from our senses into space and time, must have been formed, and there received back by us. Without sensation then we could form no image of an external object, and those who are of opinion that Homer, whose works are replete with imagery

was blind, must have a film over their own eyes. Milton and Ossian were blind, but had sight in their youth.

2. The image is therefore the same as the thing which it represents, and yet there is a difference between them. The thing is not the image, for it exists in space or time. Thus the zebra is the object of which I have an image; it is made up of life, feelings, sensations, blood, nerves, limbs. All of them have reality, they exist in the animal, as they do not in the image we have have formed of it. On the other hand again, the image is the same as the object, for it cannot be without it, and unless it include what the object includes, it is not its true image. We see here two views of the same subject that are in direct opposition to each other. Neither of them is wholly correct: the image is, and is not the object. It is not the object, for the object has reality, independent of the image and of man;— it would exist, whether we perceive it or not. So its contents are all of them real qualities that exist independent of our conceptions. Again, it is the object, for it could not be found without it; but it is the object, not as it exists in space and time, as it is *real*—it is the *ideal* object. The image has therefore the *same contents* as the object, with this difference, the one has them as they exist in the mind *ideally*, the other as they are in the material thing, *really*. We would say, therefore: by the power of conceiving, the contents of an object, and the object itself become contents of our conceptions or images.

3. Though the image is the ideal object, and fully represents the latter, yet it is less complete than the object represented by it. When we first see and examine a thing, all its parts, whether essential or not, impress themselves upon us; but these unessential parts would burden without benefiting us. Conception, therefore, refines these contents, and thrusts out what is not necessary to give a faithful image of the nature of the thing. In examining a beautiful statue, I observe every little thing about it, and even such marks as do not form a necessary part of it. When I leave the statue, I take its image with me, but the accidental circumstances under which I saw it, and all that does not strictly pertain to it, I suffer to be left out of the image. The image of a beautiful person has impressed

itself deeply upon my mind; but the unpleasant voice or the large foot are no longer included in it. And as the image in the course of time grows less complete, so it becomes more *general*. Every image is that of a *single object*, and is consequently itself single; but the person that has the image, as he sees *one* object, sees many others of the same kind, and thus of the whole forms a *general* image. I have the image of a certain rose, which I saw in the hand of a friend; this rose has faded—but I have seen many other roses like it, and the image of the former rose, however well defined and accurate it may have been, will at length become so *general*, that it would represent all roses as well as it represents this one.

Though sensations are the general source of all images, so that a poet who had never seen a sunset would be unable to depict it, yet it is not necessary that all the images in our minds should have originated in our *own* sensations. The descriptions of travelers are a rich source of images; yet unless we have seen something similar to what is described to us, we cannot form a conception of it. A nation that lives at a distance from the ocean, will find it difficult to form an idea of a storm at sea.

Of these images the mind is full, and as one after another enters the mind, many must be rendered dim and indistinct by those which are newer and more vivid, and sink as others rise to consciousness. Thus they would be lost to us, like jewels dropped into the ocean, if the mind had not the power to recall and revive them. It is the mind, and not a lifeless receptacle in which these images sink; the self-conscious mind, therefore, retains them as it formed them, and though they are not present to consciousness, they are not lost. If they have ever existed in the mind with clearness and vividness, with order and accuracy, they will never be forgotten, though their colors may fade. As the vase filled with perfume will retain it as long as it exists, so the mind will be affected by all its past images, and must be able to summon them to re-appear, and this its capacity is called, **Fancy**.

§ 3. FANCY.

Fancy is a higher stage of conception. Its images are those of the latter, perfectly free from all accidental additions, from every appearance of impressions by sense. This will appear from the following—an image may exist in the mind independent of the perception of the object; the image and perception may, therefore, be separated, for though the image may disappear from the sphere of consciousness, the mind has the power to recall it, and has this power without being reminded of the image by the sight of the object. The image is, therefore, freed from all dependence on the natural object, or the perception of it. It is a true conception by which the mind can represent a thing or object to itself, whenever or wherever it chooses, and however distant in space or time may be the object to be represented. Again, the recognition of the image in the object, or of the object in the image, is an act of *subsumption*. For, when after we have a conception of a thing, we recognize it as soon as it presents itself again, we refer the image to our perception of the thing, and thus recognize the one in the other. By this recognition the image in our mind may be corrected, no less than our perception of the thing may be guided by the image previously formed of it. For example, the image of a beautiful landscape remains in my mind; traveling the night, I approach the same scenery without knowing where I am—on awaking I at once feel as if the scenery were known to me; I observe more closely, recognize in the scenery the image I had before formed of it, and thus confirm my image no less by my perception than this by my image. Or, a beautiful melody slumbers in my mind; I have neither heard nor thought of it for years; when, unexpectedly, it is played in my hearing; I do not at first recognize it, though it sounds familiar to me. I listen with the ear of the mind, and joyfully salute in the melody an old acquaintance. Let us now inquire, first, How this re-production of past images is possible? And, secondly, What are its laws?

1. All images, as we have before said, remain in the mind; they are numerous, and of very opposite natures.

Yet they are not isolated; but all are connected by a common tie; this tie is our personal consciousness. A thread may connect the most beautiful pearls; but each pearl is unconscious of the others, and the thread knows nothing of the treasures it serves to unite. But the *I* which connects these images, knows of all of them, predicates them as its contents, and thus unites them with each other and with itself. Though many of these images disappear from *present* consciousness, the *I* which keeps all in a relation to each other, and holds them as its treasures, can at any time dive into its own depths, and raise the seemingly lost image to light. And this re-production is not connected with much labour, but the images appear spontaneously like the tables of Hephaistos, that spread themselves whenever the gods wished to feast; or, like Solomon's ring, which presented a new assemblage of spirits with every turn.

It is then our personal consciousness that includes and governs the images of the mind. Yet there are some that seem to force themselves upon us against our will, and how much soever we may desire to repel them. Shakspeare has illustrated this very forcibly in his Macbeth, and Goethe in his Iphigenia, when Orestes is haunted by unpleasant images.

2. The images in the mind are related to each other by the *I*, which formed them from the materials furnished by the sensations, and which possesses and keeps them all connected. Hence, as a general rule, it may be stated, that as different images are subjectively united in the mind, so they will present themselves in this relation to each other when one of them is re-produced. This is the principal basis of the *association of ideas*, and on it rest all its laws. These we will consider in a few words:

And first, When different images have been produced by different senses at the same time, the one will be recalled to the mind when the other makes its appearance. We have spent a pleasant hour in agreeable company; the room was filled with delicate perfumes, and we were delighted by the fragrance. Whenever we recall the fragrance, the images of the persons we then saw, the order in which they stood or sat, and even the conversation that took place, will be vividly recollected.

Secondly. The images in the mind have their objects in space. They exist together—none is isolated, but the beautiful cathedral is surrounded by houses, streets and open squares. When the image of the cathedral rises, our fancy, if it be energetic and vivid, will reproduce the images of all the objects surrounding the cathedral. Any one who has seen the City Hall of New-York, and preserved an image of it, will also have transferred to his mind the surrounding space as the common platform of many other objects; when at a distance from New-York he recalls the image of the Hall, the image of the space around, with all its objects, will present themselves—the park, with its iron railings, the broad streets encompassing the park, and the fine buildings lining the streets, &c.

Thirdly. Space remains always the same, though what is in it may change. Time is but change and succession. The place where old Athens stood, still remains; the time when it first stood there is gone for ever. Yet we rarely remember a place without remembering the particular time when we saw it. The images, the objects of which are in time, must, like the latter, succeed each other, so that the image of one thing is followed and preceded by other images. In this connection images likewise exist in our mind, and one revives all of them. We recall the image of a dying friend, and all connected with it rise to view: we see his suffering face, the positions in which he lay—and then his funeral procession. Persons of lively but uncultivated fancy, will so fill their narrations of past events with accidental circumstances, that it is often difficult to keep the train of their ideas. On the whole, images, the objects of which were in time, present themselves more easily than those, the objects of which are in space. It is likewise more difficult to represent the latter to others than the former. This Homer knew, when, instead of describing the shield of Achilles, he leads us to the place where it is manufactured, and shows us part after part as it is fabricated. Thus he communicates, in succession, what he would otherwise have had to depict simultaneously. Hence, too, poetry is more generally attractive than painting.

Fourthly, Images elicit each other by *contrast* or *resemblance*. An Otaheitan youth called the falling flakes of snow, white rain. A chief of the Otaheitans called a repeating watch, a little sun. In both instances, two images presented themselves together, while they had only a single mark in common with each other. The image of a fine commodious rail-road car may readily call up that of an old uncomfortable rattling stage-coach. Images that contrast, at the same time complete, and thus render each other more vivid.

Fifthly, The law of *cause* and *effect* brings images in connection. Whoever thinks of a Gothic building, will involuntarily perceive in his mind the taste of the age when Gothic architecture prevailed, the manners, laws, habits, religion, all of which harmonized, and were active in producing this noble style of architecture.

Sixthly, Many concrete images are brought in connection by a *general* one, which comprises them as the whole does its parts. Every image is at first as concrete as the thing of which it is the image; it is therefore single, occupying a certain place, and in a certain time. But when once we have conceived it, and then perceive it in ourselves we gradually free it, as we have stated, of its individual peculiarities, and thus abstracting from them, we form an image that is more *general*. I have, for instance, the image of a mocking-bird; as such it is a single image, in which plumage, bill, eyes, and wings, are vividly represented. So of the Baltimore Oriole; its colors, and lively motions. But abstracting from colors, motions, bill, &c. I retain an image, which is that of *birds* in general, and not of a single individual, so that when it presents itself, the images of many species, as eagles, ravens, doves, &c. will be suggested, and in number proportioned to my knowledge of ornithology. So every one has a general image of all butterflies, which he has gained from individual ones. Having it once, he is by it reminded of the different classes of butterflies. The image of a general character, loses more or less its reference to the single object of which it is the image, and gains a more direct relation to the species, yet these *general* images are not the same as the classes or species into which judgment divides nature; they are *collective* but not *generic*, they express what is common to many, but not the soul that unites them internally. The image by its general character, however, becomes thus still more free, and refined, and the activity of mind we have called conception and fancy, are elevated and become,

---

§ 4. IMAGINATION.

We must ever keep in view, that mind is an identical life, but at the same time existing in different organs, which have been called faculties. The comparison of the life of mind with that of a tree, may be once more noticed. The contents of sensations are those of conception, and they are also those of imagination. As contained in imagination, however, they are less sensuous and more general in their character, and are, therefore, less limited in extent, and leave us more free in their application. Imagination is consequently a freer activity than conception. The latter takes originally all its images as they *peel* off from their objects; fancy calls them forth from the depths of the mind in certain connections and combinations; imagination *unites them freely, independent of the laws of association.* There is another difference between imagination and conception, which deserves mention here. The image of conception, as has been stated, is not exactly the same as its object; for the object has reality independent of the image. The images of imagination on the other hand, are the free productions of imagination, and have no existence in *reality,* as for example, the image of the centaur: these images of imagination are therefore truly the objects themselves. This independence of the mind, in uniting the most different conceptions, and produce new ones, begins to exhibit itself at least in some degree in fancy. 'Every conception may become the centre, from which I may summon many others to appear. What is there to prevent me, when I think of the cathedral at Strasburg, from directing my attention to Erwin of Steinbach, its celebrated architect, or to Goethe's treatise on it, or to the misconception of Gothic architecture which so long prevailed. So I may turn to the guild of architects of the middle ages, to masonry or mysteries in general. Or I may direct my thoughts to the stone of which the cathedral is built; to its pictures, its bells; the French Revolution that once threatened its destruction, or Alsace of which it is the ornament.' Now if law is the power which is the union of the manifold, their common soul and which unites the individuals and brings them in relation to each other, upholding order and regularity, *what is the law* in the above transitions? Fancy is undoubtedly more free in associating conceptions or ideas, than those who place so great a stress upon the laws of association, or suggestion as some prefer, would be willing to admit. Not ten nor twenty laws would fully show the nature of association, for as the fancy of a person is more or less vivid and distinct, more or less active or inert,—so it will combine more or less freely. Why may not the idea of substance call forth that of accidence? or that of phenomena the idea of cause? or that of end the idea of means? It is certain therefore, that fancy is free in its combinations, and more so when it associates different ideas by its own power. In the latter respect it rises towards imagination, yet it is not the same, for fancy is only *reproductive*, while imagination more free is *productive*. The richer the former, the richer the latter. To define imagination, we would say,

1. It is the activity of mind which with ease and freedom unites different images or creates new ones, having been furnished with the materials for them, by sensation and conception. Such images of imagination are those of Amazons, Cyclops, Syrens, fairies, elves, giants, and dwarfs, &c. These images cannot be seen in nature, they are therefore in one respect *new*, and yet the parts of which they consist, are furnished by sensation or perception, and consequently met with out of us.

2. Imagination is the power to call forth images for the purpose of clothing an idea or thought which arises in the mind. The images thus called forth may be variously modified to render them appropriate vehicles of thought. This no one will dispute who is aware that as the mind constantly grows in cultivation, its conceptions must likewise become more correct, so that as often as they are re-

produced, they will bear the impress of the mind's improvement. *Imagination then, is the power which modifies the images once received, creates new ones of them, and gives them contents which do not originally belong to them.*

Some examples will show this more satisfactorily: I think of strength; my imagination being lively, seeks for an image by which to express it; it takes the image of the lion, places its thought in it, and thus the lion becomes the symbol of strength. Again, the idea that man if left to himself, is without any knowledge of heavenly things, and cannot speak concerning them, is a thought produced by reflection. This thought imagination desires to *represent* in an external form. It therefore creates an image to which it gives it as its contents. The Egyptian statue of Memnon was the symbol thus created. It was made of marble, its face turned towards the rising sun, and it gave forth lovely sounds when the first rays fell upon it. So man is mute and dead till heavenly light awakens him. Guido represents a pious and beautiful virgin, sitting alone at her needle; two angels attend her. What does this mean? Innocence and diligence are honored by heavenly spirits.

The contents placed in an image, may be a number or *cluster* of thoughts, and then instead of one we must have many images. When connected it is called an allegory. The thought that man consists of soul and body, is connected with the idea, that whatever he is in regard to intellect, he is by having freed himself from his animal passions. The Egyptian sphinx is an allegorical representation of this; in it the head of a woman grows forth, and rests on a body composed of parts of different animals, mingled with each other. This means, that humanity,— here represented by a woman—must by its own power emerge from the dominion of animal desires. Or Eros, *love*, sitting upon a lion, *strength*, and guiding him with a silken cord, *moderation*, shows that love softens the strongest. Cerberus with three heads, and Argus with a hundred eyes, express the ideas that watchfulness must look in every direction. The centaur is the symbol of prudence, swiftness, and considerateness.

Imagination, as it may place its contents in the works of

painting and sculpture, may also express them by *sounds*, that is, music, and words, which is poetry. A person of imagination, not only feels anxious to express his thoughts and ideas in a sensible form, but his feelings and emotions likewise. Joy and grief, pain or pleasure, fear and hope, anxiety and expectation, gayety and melancholy, fill the breast of man, and go and come with never-ceasing changes. The greater part of our inmost feelings and most tender emotions, do not become entirely objective to ourselves, but are *grown together* with the heart their common seat, mysterious and not understood. Images have their objects existing in reality; the images of imagination, though they are not real, may be made to assume an external form, and thus become objective to us by the chisel or the brush; but it is utterly impossible to represent our *feelings* in an external form, or to convey them by language. For the latter is also intended for general conceptions only. The medium by which alone we can make a representation of our feelings to ourselves and others, is that of *musical sound*. But sounds are not all musical; the murmuring of brooks, the roaring of forests, the humming of bees, the whistling of the wind, and the song of birds, are not in themselves *musical;* they also become so in relation to us, after we place feelings with which they harmonize in them, and hear the feelings expressed by them. What is it—if this slight digression may be permitted,—that interests us in the mournful sounds of the nightingale, when concealed in the thicket, she sends forth her plaintive notes, that sweetly swelling fill the valley and touch every heart? Is it not that we imagine the nightingale giving utterance to her grief, as we would to ours, in song? Does not the Greek *mythos* inform us that she is grieved, and that she breathes forth her grief in melodious notes? Suppose some one should accurately imitate her, should we after discovering it, consider this imitation attractive, or the sounds musical? Every bird that sings, expresses the peculiar feeling of its own existence, by its peculiar note, and how different is the note with which the mother mourns, when a mischievous boy has stolen her young, from those with which she *calls* them, and those which she has in her common state of existence! Sounds become musical also by their richness, clearness, fullness, purity, and by the relation of the different sounds to each other, by rhythm, time, harmony, and melody, by their connections, transitions, and various modifications.

What is it now, that makes musical sounds susceptible of representing our emotions and feelings? Sounds like feelings cannot assume a shape or form in space; they float only in time. So our feelings have an existence in time only, not in space, since they are without external form and visible expression. They change and pass away like sounds; sounds, therefore, closely resemble feelings in this respect, and are the very element in which they may live and move. Hence the movements of music easily enter the seat of feeling, the heart and its emotions, and as while we listen, consciousness has nothing external to engage its attention, as the music draws its attention to the feelings of the heart, it becomes merged in them, and is borne along on the stream of expressive harmonies and lovely melodies. Thus we see that music is an excellent medium by which to express and call forth the feelings. Again, as harmonies and melodies affect our feelings and not our judgment like paintings, statues, &c., so it is *time* that renders sounds in their connection *musical*, and that affects us pleasantly. For we are in time, and time is in us; and so sound again rests only in time. Thus we and sounds have a common element, and when sounds are well measured and follow each other in order, they enter into our feelings, and produce the same rhythmical motions in us. Now it will be understood why all sounds are not musical, for time is the first element of music; yet no animal can keep time, neither in its walk nor in any thing it does; neither do birds keep time in their songs. The art of keeping time belongs to man, and is not met with in all nature, even in the motion of the heavenly bodies, which accelerate and retard their course; the music of the spheres must therefore differ from ours in this respect.

We see, then, that music has all its elements in *common* with ourselves. In it we do not hear any thing different from ourselves, but the heart hears itself, as if the light in its purity could see itself. Time is common to our feelings and to sound; sounds in themselves, by their purity or clearness, softness and richness, accord with particular feelings, like interjections and exclamations; while harmonies and melodies unfold our joy and grief in all their depth and fullness.

But imagination does not only place our *emotions* and *feelings* in music, but also thoughts and conceptions. In this case we are in the habit of saying, music accompanies songs, while songs are themselves already music. Music, by itself, and music as an accompaniment, differ only in their contents; the former has *feelings* for its contents, the latter *conceptions*. Here again we must distinguish. For the musician places either the feeling which has been produced in him by reading a poem, in his music, or his desire is to represent by music conceptions themselves. In the former case, the composer studies a poem until he enters fully into its spirit, and receives an impression which will resemble the feeling under the influence of which the poet composed the piece. He then will, by his imagination, place this impression or feeling in sounds. The character of the poem will be that of the melody, and this will call forth sympathy in the hearts of the hearers. This is the case with Zelter's beautiful and classical compositions to Goethe's and Schiller's poems. Zelter says himself, that he learned those pieces by heart, studied their character, *gave himself up wholly* to the impression received from them, and sung the melody in his mind.

Haydn's Creation, on the other hand, Handel's Messiah, Bethoven's Oratorios, Mozart's Operas, have, as their contents, conceptions and ideas placed in them by imagination. These composers did not wish to throw their private feelings into these compositions, but to represent ideas themselves. Yet even here these ideas are not represented by music to the *judgment* or *understanding*, but to the *heart*, and the feelings called forth, for example, by light, by the seasons, by the crucifixion, are intended to be awakened in us by sounds. We shall feel the emotions produced by these phenomena; we shall merge ourselves in them and experience them fully. It is scarcely necessary to say, that nothing arouses us more quickly than music. The Marseilles Hymn of the French revolution, the classical church music of the middle ages, the operas of Mozart, the lovely melodies in *Freischutz*, how they excite and animate! The Requiem of Mozart, his master-piece, how it makes us feel the melancholy of the composer, which remains so fully in it!

After this rather long digression on music, in which we have indulged, because music generally receives less attention than the other arts, it only remains for me to say, that the poet also, by imagination, places his thoughts in his poetry. To do this he makes use of language. The sound as the articulate word is no longer desired on its own account, but as means; and words become the mere vehicle of thoughts. Thus Homer embodied his reflections on wrath, haughtiness, and voluptuousness, in the characters of Achilles, Agamemnon, and Paris, his reflections on connubial fidelity in Penelope, on prudence in Ulysses, on life in general, in his Iliad and Odyssey. Goethe, in his Iphigenia, represents the thought, that truth and humanity in the beautiful genius of a mild and tender girl, will conquer even the rudeness of a barbarian. Sophocles exhibits the power of a sister's love, by bringing its divine power in contact with the human statute of Creon, and by exhibiting the victory of the former over the latter, in the bosom of the tender Antigone. And what is the case in epic and dramatic, is, of course, so too in lyric poetry. Does not Pindar's grave imagination place all its high and noble thoughts in the stories it relates? Does it not use these fables as if they were invented for these contents, which Pindar is desirous of representing in a sensible form?

From the above it must sufficiently appear, that imagination as the basis of arts creates an unreal but powerful and beautiful world. By it all objects and images receive ideal substance, and there is nothing too good to become the receptacle in which imagination may place the contents of the mind. While the man of business sees nothing in spring but flowers and hills, the eye of imagination perceives in the flowers and ornamented hills the connubial garlands of spring; when the former hears nothing but the noise of a running brook, imagination hears the murmuring waters express their joy, that they are no longer chained by the ice, but have been freed by spring to which they sing their song.

Characteristics of Imagination.

In continuing the subject of imagination, it must be understood that its character is also that of art, that in describing it, we in truth represent the nature of the latter. With this view we suffer ourselves to indulge this interesting topic somewhat beyond the symmetrical proportion which the different parts of a book ought to exhibit in their relation to each other.

And first, Imagination is originally *imitative*. This assertion, however, has been disputed, for it seems at first sight to make nature the teacher of man—to indicate that he learned from the fish to swim, from the beaver to build houses, from the spider to weave the net with which he can catch the fish in the water, and the bird in the air. This is repulsive to the laws of nature; all offence, however, will be done away as soon as we ascertain the true meaning of *imitation*. It means nothing else than " to reproduce the exact measure of such phenomena as we perceive in nature or in the lives of other beings." This capacity is by no means to be despised, for here also man shows himself to be the lord of nature, since there is nothing in it which he cannot unite with himself and make subservient to his purposes. All the lower classes of animals, some of which are docile in a high *degree, feel* no inclination whatever to imitate, and only birds are attracted by sounds, and monkeys by the motions of man to attempt it. But this imitation of animals rests on an instinctive, dark and confused sympathy, while that of man is voluntary and designed for certain purposes. These are at first the removal of wants and necessity; but soon man delights in the *skill* he has acquired in imitating nature, and cultivates art for its sake. This skill manifests to him his power; especially when, as was the case with several distinguished painters in ancient times and in the Dutch schools, the resemblance deceives the eye. Who is not here reminded of the grapes of Zeuxis at which birds pecked; of the painted insects, torn to pieces by a monkey, anxious to take hold of them; of the horse on canvass, neighed at by that of Alexander; and of the painted linen cloth that even deceived a master in the art of painting? Yet imagination cannot for a long time delight itself in this mere skill and dependence on nature. The productions of nature have, on the one hand, a decided superiority over those of imagination, for the flower in my garden blooms, breathes and exhales, while that on paper is but *imitation* and has no life. It is for this reason no doubt that the Mohammedans object to art; for they say that all these works of art resembling so much the works of nature, will rise in the day of judgment and demand a soul of the artist. On the other hand, if mere skill is that which delights, *beauty* cannot be the object but only *correctness*, and in this case it could not matter whether the object imitated is a blade of grass or a beautiful bird, if the resemblance is only effected.

Imagination is not satisfied with such imitation; freeing itself from it, it will at first indulge fancies and images that cannot be met with in nature. Elves peeping forth from the cups of flowers, or fairies slipping into them when the sun rises; clouds surrounding a picture, that exhibit angels when closely examined, and garlands of flowers, in the cups of which we discover beautiful faces;—such pictures are the products of an imagination freeing itself from nature. When the desire to be perfectly free, is indulged to excess, we get caricatures, witches, and faces that have no truly intellectual character whatever.

By imitating all that nature contains, man becomes acquainted not only with its usefulness, but also with its general nature. In it he soon recognizes something divine; for while all the individual beings are constantly going and coming, appearing and disappearing, it remains permanently the same, unchangeable and the prototype of all the individual forms of a species. Having compared image with image, the eye of genius sees what is no where realized in one *individual; it sees the prototype of all*, which the individual is wholly incapable of expressing in a faultless manner. The idea of perfect beauty has arisen in the mind of the artist. He seeks for it in reality but cannot find it. A hair, a mole, a large foot, will render the otherwise perfect beauty of a lady imperfect. So it is with every thing in history and elsewhere. Our purposes may be noble, but external circumstances attach themselves to their execution, and they are not what they were designed to be. Historical actions may have been well and fully designed, but only a part of the design has been carried out, the rest of the actions were accidental. The imagination of the artist having conceived the ideal of beauty, and having sought in vain for it in reality, sketches it on canvass, represents it in the statue, or breathes it into language. This idea of beauty is infinite and invisible, and placing it in a sensible form, the artist unites the infinite and finite, the invisible and visible, and as by a magic mirror he renders the one visible in the other. This union of the invisible and visible, of thought and sensible form, is *beauty*. To see it, there is more than an accurate bodily eye required; and he who has not the soul of beauty in his own mind, will never discover it out of himself. Compositions like those of Mozart; cathedrals like those at Cologne and Strasburg; landscapes like those of Claude Lorraine, are not met with in nature. And here it may be well to introduce the views of some celebrated artists on this point. Raphael and Guido confess, the former, that he could not find any model for his female beauty, his Galatea; the latter, that he sought in vain for a model for his archangel. Raphael adds in his letter, in which he states the above: "Because I cannot find the ideal of my Galatea in reality, I make use of a certain *idea*." [This word used in the sense of Plato.] When Zeuxis, requested by a city to paint Helena, asked for five of the most beautiful girls as models, did he not say, that there was no single virgin equal to his *ideal* of beauty? Hence Winkelmann is correct in saying: Nature may exhibit single parts of as great beauty, as art ever produced; but beauty as a whole, nature must yield to art. Goethe said once to Eckermann; the heads of two horses of ancient date and lately found are of such beauty, that the English, the best horsemen in the world, are constrained to acknowledge that they never saw such horses in reality. And again: when once asked respecting a picture of Rubens', he said: such scenery has never been seen in nature; this we owe to the poetical genius of Rubens.

A good imagination, however, is not *unnatural*; it makes use of the objects of nature, and puts the riches of its own soul into them. So Goethe says of Claude Lorraine; he knew the world, and used it as a means by which to express his rich soul.

Though we fear to swell this portion too much, we cannot deny ourselves the pleasure of adding two questions more with regard to art; *What is its truth? What is its aim?*

With regard to the *former* question a host of views ought to be met if space would allow it. " Poetical truth is fictitious, and hence having no reality, is of no value." This is the creed of many persons. With them all truth consists in the mere real *existence* of a thing, and yet so much every falsehood, every theft, every crime claims for itself, for all of them have at least an existence. Real truth, however, is not the mere external existence of a thing, but its *rational* and *general* nature. If I say: "*this plant blooms,*" and a few days after any one goes to see whether it is so, it may have shed its flowers, and consequently what I said is no longer true. But if I name the species of the plant, its kind, describe its form and manner of life, as this belongs not only to it as an individual, but to its species, I have given truth; and whether any one sees the plant that I see, or another of the same kind, he will know what I know. Or the truth is a historical one. Here the opinion is that the correctness of the *fact* is the truth of history. If so, the French would be right in asserting that we have no history, but only the notions of historians. For all history is related by language; language, however, is so *general* in its expressions that it is wholly impossible for it to express any thing entirely individual. If I say: he *squints,* I can convey only something general; many squint, but each one in a peculiar manner, and this peculiarity cannot be represented by the word *squint.* It can only be pointed out to the eye with the finger. Every historical action is to be performed by individuals; their feelings enter into it as elements; it pre-supposes a certain place, a certain hour, all which affect the feelings of the individuals;— but who would or who could by the strongest imagination discover all the particulars of such an action? Hence it follows that what might be called the *real* existence of an action cannot be conveyed by language which is so general that it cannot utter our feelings at all except by interjections. And again: the action as it occurred, existed differently from what it does in our conceptions. There is its reality, here its ideality. Now all of us know how differently actions are described by different spectators, though they are most impartial. And yet we speak of *historical truth!* The truth of history consists in the spirit that produces the action, in the development of national intellect, prosperity, intercourse, &c., so that one action is interwoven with another by one and the same national spirit. This *spirit*, this national exertion to preserve, to improve, to advance itself, is the truth of history. I may know, for instance, the hour and place, when and where a battle was fought, the individual persons who fell, and those who escaped; and yet I may have no historical truth. But when the design for which the battle was fought becomes known to me, and its effects upon nations and the succeeding history, then only I have truth.

From this it must appear that truth does not consist merely in its having an existence in *reality;* but that it is the rational generality, the general spirit which appears in and through a thing. The thing is perishable, the spirit eternal. Now in this respect the truth of art agrees fully with truth in general. The artist's eye perceives the truth resting in the objects or historical occurrences; he perceives that it is clouded there by many circumstances, and loving the truth he feels an irresistible desire to represent it as he sees and loves it; free from every thing not pertaining to it, pure and transparent. This of course can only be said of true and genuine art, and not of its inferior branches; of Shakspeare, and not of Bulwer; of the better parts of Byron, but not of his poetry in general.

Thus then we have answered the first question, and with it also the second. For if the truth of art is what we have seen it to be, the *representation* of this truth is its aim. Artists do not merely desire to imitate, for then their labors would be vanity; nor merely to entertain, for then they would stand on the same scale with jugglers, ventriloquists, &c. Their aim is to represent the invisible in the visible, the infinite in the finite, eternal truth in its purity, by rendering it manifest in a sensible form and shape. By this its aim, art differs from all sciences, all of which make constant efforts to generalize single objects, and classify them, and therefore, proceed in a manner directly opposite to that of art. Yet art and science serve each other, for the latter gives the rule for the former, and the former furnishes materials for the latter, and painting, for example, may aid by its pictures the study of natural history, &c.

Secondly. Our imagination is either *rich* or poor, that is, it produces *many* or few new images, or it is strong or weak, fiery in its productions, vivid and distinct, or cool and indifferent. Here, according to the law, that a power spread over a large surface, will be less strong than when apart in smaller circumference—the rich imagination may be less accurate and precise than a strong one, for the former will produce more new images than the latter. An imagination that has but a few objects attractive to itself, cannot, of course, have many materials for the formation of its productions. It shows both strength and riches, when it knows how to use the few materials it has, with the most various and always new modifications. Such an imagination produces from the object the greatest variety of the most beautiful imagery, as for instance, that of Ossian. It differs likewise in quality. The imagination of the gardener, the geometer, the man of business, and the architect, easily perceives regularity and order, symmetry and harmony. The imagination of the painter and sculptor is aided by the eye, and form, colors, light, and shade, flow easily from the chisel and brush—the ideas of the artist's animating hand and fingers. Imagination, aided by the ear, fits for music and language.

Thirdly. Imagination differs also with regard to its *form.* This is either *symbolical, classical,* or *romantic.*

The form of imagination is *symbolical* when it places its contents in an object, which is more or less capable of indicating them. Truth, for example, is the same in the sphere of science, that light is in the sphere of nature. Thus far both are homogeneous. But truth is spiritual, and cannot be felt by a sense, nor perceived by the mere bodily eye, while the rays of light may be felt. When now truth, as an invisible power, is represented by the orb of the sun, we have a symbol. The symbol is something external—a form perceptible by sense, which by its peculiar position convinces us that it contains a hidden meaning. This meaning is invisible and internal. In symbolical imagination, therefore, we must distinguish the external form from the internal signification. The owl at the feet of Athena, for instance, held by a chain, is the symbol of darkness, for it cannot see by day; the chain in the hand of the goddess of wisdom is the symbol of the powers of light over darkness. We can only see the owl and the chain, but being connected with Athena, we must believe that the artist had some design in placing it there, and that the owl is but the receptacle of some of his thoughts, which we must discover by reflection.

Imagination is *classical*, when form and contents so fully receive each other, that the former is transparent and seems only to exist in order to represent the latter, and when the latter fully expresses itself so that the artist not only shows the best form, but also knows how to communicate by it every particle of its contents, leaving nothing unexpressed, retaining nothing in his bosom. This entire *intus-susception* of form and contents is the only classical form of imagination, and we meet with it in Greece alone. If, in the symbolical form, contents and form are only brought together externally; if we must reflect in order to discover the one in the other, the contents in the form, if consequently we may make a mistake; with the classical form all is otherwise, for all is clear, transparent, and perfectly beautiful. Who that looks at the statue of Apollo, will not at once recognize an ever-blooming youth, that, free from care and trouble, rejoices in the feeling of existence.

The form of imagination may be *romantic*. As such it was not known to the ancients; for it has become possible only since the introduction of Christianity, which opened to the mind of man the world of infinite spirit; this world, filling the breast of artists, imagination seeks in vain for conceptions and images in which to place, and by which to express it. Nothing in the world can represent, in an adequate form, that God whom Christ has revealed. The spirit is only accessible to the spirit; we cannot convey it by any image. The symbol, it is true, may represent the Infinite by the finite; but what a defective representation!

And yet, however defective, it satisfied the ancients, for they had no clear idea of the Invisible and Infinite; they felt it darkly, but knew it not. Now the Infinite is clearly revealed; hence it is that no representation given it by imagination will suffice, for our consciousness of the Infinite will flow beyond every visible, finite form, and leave it far behind. The poet is overpowered by the riches of his theme, and yet he cannot dismiss it. He feels that he cannot fully express what agitates his breast, and yet he is irresistibly urged to give vent to his deep and lasting emotions. The elements of the romantic imagination are, the love of Christ, the vanity of all things, a desire for an eternal home, the transitoriness of this, and the immortality of a future life. Its elements are, on the one hand, the spirit and the world, for which it is destined, and on the other hand, this world of sense in which it lives, and which cannot satisfy its spiritual longing, nor represent its ideas. This romantic character is indicated by the steeples which are peculiar to Christian churches; they rise high into the clouds, and point to world above.

If we compare these three forms with each other, we shall find the symbolical to be *sublime*, the classical to be *beautiful*, and the romantic to be *sentimental* and *mystical*.

Fourthly. The power of imagination is susceptible of cultivation. At first, it is rude, colossal, and without measure. So, for instance, the mythus of Uma and Siva, or of Sagaras and Vishnu in India; of Faust in Germany. It becomes cultivated when it produces according to *laws*. It will become piquant, paradoxical, *barroqué*, full of caricatures, when it is arbitrary. The statues of an Italian count, made of the finest stone, are examples of arbitrary imagination. He had the head of a goose put upon the body of a lady; or the neck of a goose with the head of an eagle on the body of a lion.

Fifthly. Imagination and cool reflection seem to be antipodes; the youthful fire, and warmth, and freshness of the former, are extinguished by the considerateness and logical calculation of the latter. Yet imagination needs the *measure* which thought only can give it. In proportion, however, as pure thinking prevails, the imagery of imagination becomes superfluous, and imagination itself is made subservient to reflection. As man lives in the sphere of theoretical truth, so he moves in that of practical life, in which the naked reality only avails, and images and beautiful pictures are of no value. Yet, as was remarked above, the man of business, and our practical life also, need the aid of imagination. The yard, the scales in the hand of justice, are the symbols in which imagination places the practical idea of *right*. It was imagination that taught savages to lick property when transferred from one to another, for the tongue is the organ of assimilation; or to break a straw—*stipula*, hence stipulation—for as a straw exactly divided, so each receives full value. Here the productions of imagination are no longer beautiful, but *useful*. In the progress of time, these symbolical actions become superfluous; a word becomes sufficient, and where it is not, a legal instrument of writing, *or the word written*, is necessary. Thus the will of man becomes independent of external things. Imagination, in this *practical* respect, takes the following course: it is, at first, *symbolical*, then it becomes *emblematic*, and finally *semeiotical*. It is symbolical, when the object by which it represents a thought, and the thought itself are *homogeneous*. Darkness *cannot be* the symbol of light; but "when a genius with an inverted torch is placed as a monument upon a grave, it is symbolical. For there a life has been extinguished, a light, an eye, beneath that monument the dead lies without life, without light—the light of the torch and the light of life are homogeneous." On the other hand, the productions of imagination are *emblematical*, when the form and contents become inadequate to each other, or are heterogeneous. The feeling of thirst, and a glass of beer on a tavern-sign, have nothing *homogeneous*; the sign is, therefore, not the *symbol* of thirst, but its *emblem*. Yet there is still a relation between them; if a relation no longer exists, the imagination works *semeiotically*. Here the form intended to represent certain contents, does not in the least resemble them; it therefore represents something entirely different from *itself;* the imagination determines that a thing independent of its fitness shall signify or indicate a certain thing, though it bears not the slightest relation to the thing signified. Two triangles, for instance, put into each other, are, in many countries, used as signs before beer-houses; there is certainly no relation between two triangles and beer. If the things used as symbols and emblems continue to have an existence, whether we place contents in them or not, the sign loses all importance when the thought signified is drawn from it, or when it is no longer used significantly. Many signs, which we daily make, can be understood by no one except ourselves; the boy, for instance, breaks down a few branches near where he has discovered a bird's nest; this is to him an indicative sign, but not to us; hence we can attach no importance to these broken branches.

We have yet to consider imagination, as producing *signs*, and as such it may be called,

Semeiotic Imagination.

The term *semeiotic* is not found in the English language. It is of Greek origin from the word σημεια, sign. With this explanation we may be permitted to use it here. Every thing in nature, upon which man may impress his will, must suffer itself to be used by him as a sign. Even rivers may become the signs of boundaries. Yet the more susceptible a thing is of receiving a mark from the hands of man, the better it is qualified for a sign. Thus, the staff in the hand of Agamemnon, "which sent forth no leaves, and retained no life, after the knife cut it from its trunk and peeled and smoothed it," is the sign of power; so the hickory pole with its flags is a sign, intelligible to all the citizens of the Union. The signs of semeiotic imagination are contained either in space or time, either in rest or in motion, and may be thus classified: Signs in *space* have different forms, yet they are not to be valued by their forms, but by what they indicate. The cockade, the flag, which indicates a nation's ideas of its liberty, and which though at rest themselves may cause the greatest commotions, as the flag when unfurled and waving in the air; are of more importance than the most showy sign before a tavern. The signs that are only in space are innumerable; those that I make in a book while reading it, in my walks, and those made by private individuals in their gardens or houses, used by companies on their seals, by nations in the uniform of their soldiers,

&c. At first these signs had a meaning in themselves, but this meaning was gradually lost, and semeiotic imagination used them for whatever purpose it pleased.

When, on the other hand, the sign is something which exists only in *time,* it must be always in motion. The numerous signs that belong to the art of expressing thoughts by the motions of the body, have been already alluded to in Part I, Chapter III., to which the reader is referred. Other signs are; rockets discharged in the air; the waving of a handkerchief; the hoisting of a flag, &c. These are all of them for the eye, and must be noticed at the very moment, when they are in motion. Imagination is more rich, however, in the signs it produces for the ear. Sounds become signals. Clapping the hands may indicate applause; hissing, disapprobation. The same sounds may affect us in the most different ways, and these different effects depend wholly on the meaning we attach to them. In Germany, where in former times every occurrence of the day was brought into connection with religion, it was announced by the same bell that summoned worshippers to the house of God on Sabbaths and holy days. The bell accompanied the life of an individual from his cradle to his grave; and it was also the tongue to announce the grand divisions of the day. All these things the bell proclaimed by the same sound, and yet how different are the feelings excited in us when its rich sounds fell upon the ear at Easter, from those called forth by the same bell on Good Friday, on the Sabbath, or early in the morning when it announced the rising of the sun! Again, the chimes of a bell that reach us from the summit of a hill covered with forests, where silence reigns and nothing is to be seen but a solitary chapel—how sweetly are we affected by them! Poets like Uhland, Schiller and others, have made these chimes the themes of some of their finest poems.

Next in rank are organical sounds, or such as are produced by the organs of man; hence sounds of instruments, the trumpet, flute, &c. The sounds of the trumpet govern the motions of a body of cavalry, those of the flute are fitted for the expression of love. Whistling is likewise a signal, but a signal of uncertain character. The watchman in pursuit of a thief makes use of it, and so does the thief.

Finally, articulate sounds must serve as signs. But what sounds are *articulate?* Those produced by *articulos*, by the tongue, teeth and lips; those therefore that are formed by all of them. The sounds of animals differ from those of instruments; the latter are based in the vibrations of bodies, the former rest in the voice. The superiority of the latter may be seen even in the external form. Musical instruments are either long, as the flute, the horn, the clarinet, or voluminous as the drum, &c.; but the throat of the animal producing the voice, unites both length and depth. Yet while the voice of the animal is superior to the sounds of instruments, the voice of man is superior to that of animals; for it is capable of producing the *word*. The Latins have one root for voice and word, *vox—vocabulum*. The word contains more than a mere sign—a sign for light indicates only light as visible to the eye. The word *light* contains all that natural philosophers know about it. Hence with articulate sounds as words, we approach a higher sphere of the mind, and as conceptions are connected with each other by the power of our self-consciousness, so are words as the signs of thought, and in this union they form *language*.

---

§ 5. LANGUAGE.

All our conceptions depend upon our sensations, and are impossible without them. Our sensations depend on our individuality, and are impossible without it; for that, which has no individual life, cannot feel. Conceptions without words are, therefore, confined to the individual, transient as itself, and limited to its peculiar existence. But when a conception is expressed by a word, it receives an existence independent of that of the individual, and is rescued from the danger of being lost with it. Through the word a conception becomes permanent; without it, it would disappear with the person that formed it, as the gilded cloud vanishes with the setting sun. The conception is *internal*, as we have before seen; the word is so likewise, for it has no *existence in space*, no external form; yet it is for the ear and consequently audible. Thus while the conception originally is not for the senses, it receives by the word an external utterance for the ear. *Language, then, is the external expression for our internal conceptions.* This, however, must not be misunderstood, for though the word is external as *sound*, it must become *internal* by hearing. This shows itself, when uncultivated persons read; here the word has its corresponding signs in space, but such persons nevertheless either read *aloud*, or imitate the sound with their lips.

Language is either that of *signs* or that of *words*. The former we have spoken of in the division on semeiotic imagination. It is not so much the product of mind, as of the necessities and wants of our nature. It is limited in its extent, and can only cause others to feel as we do, or to understand our sensations. I am hungry, another has food; I make a sign, chew, or point to his food and thus make him understand my appetite. It would be difficult to express thoughts or ideas by such signs, had they not been conveyed by words before, and had they only been placed in these signs. Something similar to a language of signs we undoubtedly meet with in nature. The ants that touch each other, when danger threatens; the bird that on the watch, gives a sign to warn; the hen that calls its young —have all of them a language of signs; yet we must not say that they *understand* each other, for they live in the sphere of mere sensation and perception. These signs only serve to call forth the same dark sensations, the possibility of which is easily comprehended, when we consider that one hen clucks like another, and that animals of the same species have the same self-feeling, and that this will express itself by the same peculiar voice and note in all the individuals.

The language of *words*, on the other hand, has a different origin, and one that is more disputed. And indeed we must confess that it is difficult to be ascertained. For the more carefully we examine the subject, the more we are led by the consideration of the different elements of language to different views. There are two hypotheses on the origin of language, which are in direct opposition, and whose elements it may here be proper to point out.

I. It is admitted by all, that where there is design and an adaptation of means to an end, there must be a cultivated intellect, there must be *knowledge* of the design. Without language, however, there can be no knowledge, since a conception will be without clearness and distinctness, until it is expressed by a word. This shows itself in children, who as long as they do not speak have no clear conceptions; but when they learn to speak, they learn to understand. Language here seems indispensable for the development of mind. But any one who has paid a little attention to speech, must observe from the etymological part of grammar to the highest syntactical rules, the laws of reason; so that it may be said with truth that language is embodied reason, or reason which has become objective to itself. If reason is undeveloped before there is a language, and again, if language is developed reason is an external form, or as it has uttered itself, how can the undeveloped reason be said to have invented language? Especially when it is considered, that the languages of the most remote times, have those words by which the relation of the finite to the infinite may be expressed with the greatest accuracy—such, for instance, as life, sight, being, truth, spirit, good, right, holy, justice, salvation, &c. Again, to say that man has *invented* language, would be no better than to assert that he has invented *law*. To make laws, there must be a law obligating all to keep them; to agree or make a compact, to observe certain institutes, there must be already a government protecting this compact. To invent language, *pre-supposes language* already, for how could men agree to name different objects, without communicating by words their designs? From all this it must follow, that man did not *invent*, but received his language from God.

Thus far it seems all correct, but this view is nevertheless one-sided, and does not notice one fact of great importance. Reason and language, as the Greek word *logos* indicates, are identical. The conception I have is a word unuttered; the word I pronounce is a conception sounded with the lips. If I have to produce by my mental activity the conception, I must undoubtedly create the word for it, since the former is wholly impossible without the latter. The conception could no more be received by the mere word or its sound, than a word could be understood without the conception which it invests; and if God had taught man language, he must either have given him the conceptions, together with their comprehending words, and then it would be incomprehensible how man could receive either without his own spontaneous activity, or he must have given merely the words as *shells*, in which to place his thoughts. If the former were the case, man would become a mere machine, through which another thinks and speaks; in the latter it would be impossible to see how man could be taught mere words without having already an idea of language. Hence, this view was abandoned, and one directly opposite embraced—"Man has *invented* language by his own ingenuity."

II. If God taught Adam language, he of course taught him but one; but we know, so the hypothesis asserted, that every savage tribe has its own tongue, and that the less cultivated nations and savages are, the more various their languages will be. Not less than three thousand and sixty-four languages have been already discovered. Klaproth, on his journey through a small part of Asia, met with no less than thirty-six; among our Indians every tribe has a language unintelligible to all the others. There must have been more than one language from the beginning of the world, as mankind spread and existed in different races, its languages became multiplied, so that to understand the language of one tribe, an individual belonging to another, must acquire it with hard labor. Again, we see that birds sing, that quadrupeds express their wants by their voice, the lion roars when hungry,—should not man, gifted with reason and excellent organs to articulate sounds, be able to express his wants and necessities by sounds framed in words? A close examination of many words will lead us to believe, that man imitated nature. This imitation could not be difficult, since his organs of speech will enable him to form every sound that nature can produce. Words of this kind are, for instance, *rustling, murmuring, whistling, rolling, lisping, roaring.* And again, we find many words, the sounds of which are the same in different languages: thus, Sanskrit, *pita ;* Lat., *pater ;* Gr., πατηρ ; Eng., *father ;* Ger., *Vater ;* &c. Sanskr., *mata ;* Lat., *mater ;* Gr., μητηρ ; Eng., *mother ;* Ger., *mutter.* Sanskr., *rohitah ;* Lat., *rufus ;* Eng., *red ;* Ger., *roth ;* Italian, *rosso ;* Fr., *rouge ;* Dutch, *rood ;* Danish, *rod.* Sanskr., *padas ;* Gr., πούς ; Lat., *pes ;* Eng., *foot ;* Goth., *fothus ;* Ger., *fuss ;* Frank, *vuoz.* Sanskr., *tan ;* Gr., τεινειν ; Lat., *tendere ;* Eng., *extend ;* Ger., *dehnen ;* Goth., *thanjan ;* Frank, *denen,* &c. These parallels might be much multiplied, but the above examples are sufficient to make us ask: Whence come these words into the different languages?—Man will not only notice, but by his attention distinguish sounds in the most precise manner; he will then imitate them, desirous of communicating some things to his fellow-men by their sounds or form. Thus by an innate desire to imitate, man was induced to form some words, and finally the entire language. It was not necessary for him, to be in the full possession of the reason, for how many even now speak without being aware, that there are rules, or grammars, exhibiting them.

This also appears to be a very mistaken view. It severs what God has joined together, reason and language, conception and word. It admits that the conception could exist long before the word, and that man might seek for the latter after he has the former. This idea is not much better than to say, that man invented sleep; for the act of thinking and that of speaking is so much the same, that no person can think without speaking, if not loud, at least to himself, though he should not notice it. Feelings and sensations may do without words, but conceptions need words, and thinking is but an internal speaking, as speaking is an external thinking. Another mistake is this. The question before us, has no reference at all to will; it must be left out of view; yet both of the views exhibited refer more or less to it. But the exercise of will pre-supposes the existence of language.

I shall attempt to answer the question above in the following manner:—Reason is the source of all our conceptions and thoughts; thoughts are the same internally that words are externally. As reason produces our conceptions, so it produces inseparably with them also their corresponding words. As the plastic power produces at the same time *sap* and *bark*, *form* and *contents*, so reason produces *thought* and *language*. But reason has not its origin in itself; its author is God, whose will lives in it as its law. The author of language is, therefore, not *man*, but *God*. Yet we must not understand this as if God had taught man language as a teacher makes a scholar learn; but God gave man a power, that in developing itself, would necessarily with itself develope language. God did not give language as something ready formed, as we give our scholars the elements of the Greek tongue in dictionaries and grammars, but—and this God alone, and no other being could do—gave him a *power* by which to name all things, and made the animals pass before Adam, to see what he would name them, and the names he would give them should be their names. This view comprises what is true in the two former, and avoids their errors. Or, in other words: God gave man in his reason the *possibility* of *thinking* and *speaking*, as he placed in the germ the possibility of growing and developing a specific form. The process by which to realize this possibility was left to man, without will or design spontaneously language proceeds from the development of reason.

A few remarks will corroborate this idea. Reason, the possibility of thinking and speaking, is essentially the same in all individuals; its laws are the same, and its functions. So nature surrounding us,—however modified its phenomena may be,—is essentially the same in all its laws and activities, and these are the same as those of reason, given by the same Divine Being.

As by reason we think and reflect, so we receive all the impressions of the senses, from which we form our conceptions, from nature. On account of this identity of reason and nature, we are able to know the latter, otherwise no communication would take place between it and ourselves. In so far as all persons have the same laws of reason, and are impressed by nature according to the same laws, so far it is one and the same substance or being that lives in all and connects all, so that every thought proceeding from this reason, must be the same in whatever individual it may originate, and so that one can lead out a thought and render it complete, though it took rise in another.

But if reason is every where the same, whence the difference of languages? Why have we not *one* language only, as we have *one* reason? We answer: Reason, though essentially one in its laws and nature, is, nevertheless, modified by its connection with the body, the constitution, and through it with climate, as has been seen in Anthropology. All the modifications caused by the influences of nature, race, nation, occupation, &c. must here be recalled, and must be admitted to have a considerable influence on our attention, conception, fancy, and imagination, memory and thinking. Reason is thus the same, and again differs in the various regions of the earth. So the flame remains, though spread from one to a thousand torches; but the torches kindled, may produce a slight difference, if one is of hickory, another of pine. As now thinking is the same on the one hand, but modified on the other, so language is, in accordance with it every where *language*, and yet at the same time it has its peculiar differences, not only in different nations, but even in its dialects in the same nation. An example will illustrate this. The Greeks, living in a mild climate, under serene skies, surrounded by a beautiful country, and gifted by the Deity with a vivid and strong imagination, had their thoughts every where bent upon the discovery and production of beauty. They would, therefore, notice, in all they observed, the *beautiful*; this would strike them, and from this quality they would name the thing in which they discovered it. The Romans, on the other hand, of an entirely different cast of mind, looked every where for the *useful*, and waved all considerations of beauty in its favor. The Germans, finally, are peculiarly inclined to speculation, and seek for the *foundation* of all things. This difference will exhibit itself no less in these respective languages, than in literature and art. The Greek, noticing the beautiful motions of lightning, calls it $\alpha\sigma\tau\rho\alpha\pi\eta$; the Roman, attracted by the splendid light, and its destructiveness, names it *fulgur*;

the German perceives the difference of this motion from all others, and signifies it by the term *Blitz*. Leibnitz conceived the idea of inventing one language for all nations. Nothing could be more unfortunate than the complete success of such an undertaking, if by it—what Leibnitz did not intend—all the other languages would become superfluous. For, as each language views the same things differently, the human mind is left free to express every shade of difference in its thought. This liberty we desire in the same language, where the best writers have their individual style, so that while they use the general language, they make it assume a peculiar form, and with it a peculiar freshness. Every writer must, of course, observe the general rules of his language, or his works would be unintelligible. But the general nature of the language will become tinged with that of the individual; it will yield to it the more, the more flexible it is; and while in the latter respect it may demand a hermeneutical explanation, its general nature, which is modified by the style of the writer, will make such an explanation *possible*.

We frequently hear it asserted, that man was urged, by necessity, to form language, and that this necessity was that of communication. Though it is true that man could not, without language, be what he is, and what he ought to be, yet many persons have been found wild who lived without language. The use of language rests, therefore, not on a *physical* necessity, so that man could not live without it, as he could not exist without breathing, or without food. The spider is driven by an irresistible tendency to spin his web; so man to eat; but he may live without thoughts or words. While at the same time, however, that when all the necessary conditions are present,—conditions which we have before considered,—his reason will *think* and *speak*, it is not only *impelled* to do so from necessity, from a mere desire to communicate, but it *delights* in giving form to its thoughts. Man desires every where to recognize his own activity in that which surrounds him; in this desire art has, in part, its origin, and fashion, and ornaments. The joint desire to communicate our thoughts to others, and to form them, originate the effort of reason to think and to speak. The desire to form our conceptions produces *single words;* the desire to communicate them to others forms *language as such, or as speech.* And this again must not be understood mechanically, as if words were first formed and embodied in memory, as in a dictionary for future use; but words are formed for the sake of communication, so that a word is no sooner formed, than it enters into a relation with others, and thus a word, according to W. Von Humboldt, originates as much in connection with others, as a connection arises out of single words. Hence language is not merely a compound of words, but a system of kindred conceptions, all of which are brought in connection by the forms of words, by prefixes, affixes, by compositions, &c. The pleasure we take in giving form to all surrounding us, in impressing the traces of our mind upon all it touches, is the *self-activity* which causes the child to speak; while with reference to the particular language, it is dependent on the nation in which it is born, and consequently *receptive* instead of *spontaneous.* In this dependence an individual can only have such thoughts as are already expressed in his language. Yet, if this is youthful, and has the root of its life in itself, so that new sprouts may come forth from it, *new* thoughts will clothe themselves in new words. The language of a nation will, therefore, exercise a considerable influence on the thoughts of those who use it. As language is the medium by which mind manifests itself to mind, by which the barriers of an isolated existence are torn down, and man is drawn to man, it will justify us in making once more a slight digression before approaching the elements of language.

Language as we have said, is the objective existence of a national spirit. Studying a foreign language we study the spirit of the nation whose language it is, and thus our mind is united with that of the nation. Now we may study a language merely on account of the thoughts it embodies, and thus enrich our own mind; for every thought, received by it in ourselves, is like a spark, that kindles a new light. But it may be studied to exercise our thinking, as there is no other science that will teach us better, to think correctly and logically. For in the first place, grammar contains the categories of thinking, it is full of rules and laws, all of which are those of reason. Studying grammar we study the logic of understanding in its simplest form. We learn here to reduce the most various phenomena to one head or union, which combines all of them; and if learning does not consist in merely *receiving*, but in *understanding and reproducing* what is given to us,—the exercise by which we are made to apply rules in different ways, especially in writing, compositions and the like, will make us wholly master of them. Thus we learn to think logically.

Learning a language for the purpose of obtaining access to the riches placed in it by a nation, or for the purpose of speaking it, however, differs widely from making language as such the object of our investigation. When we do this, we study the philosophy of language, and this cannot be done without the study of the human mind. Here rules as such are not the object, but their *reason* and *ground*, and necessity. We know the rules, but we desire to know more. Such study exercises pure thinking. We want to ascertain the *nature* of a word *not words*, its connection with others, the *nature* and *law* of sentences, periods, speeches, style. But words, sentences, and periods, cannot be perceived by the senses; here we must *think*, if we would understand them. When I say a *pronoun* or a *verb*, or a *noun*, I pronounce words, but at the same time in their qualifying *distinctions;* these distinctions cannot be heard; that by which a pronoun differs from a verb, rests not in the sound, but only in the thought. Hence the philosophical grammar must be studied, that which is not satisfied with adding rule to rule, with placing them only externally under a common head, as apples, pears, potatoes may be put in one bag; but which exhibits the nature of all rules, and unites them as it finds them already united by their nature. Again, every word includes a thought; the nature of a word may be fully ascertained by etymology, its contents not. Reflecting on the *word* in this respect, is reflecting on the *thought;* thinking reflects on itself as resting in a word. This thought, however, not being *my* thought, nor reflecting on it on account of the thing of which it is the thought, I can take interest in it, only for its own sake, and thus impartial and abstracting both from myself and the thing expressed, or abstracting from all subjectiveness and objectiveness I discover the true nature of *thought.* It is language then, that renders reason more manifest than any other science, for all the conceptions and thoughts, contained in *all* the sciences of the human race, are embodied in it. Natural sciences show likewise reason, history and philosophy; but language is the external reason, as reason is the internal language. If I wish to know a nation, I must know its language. Again, we acknowledge by these views, that nothing can cultivate the mind more than the study of languages, and especially that of ancient languages, the perfections of which in every respect are unrivalled, and whose antiquity makes them more attentive to the imagination. It will be necessary to speak a word on the elements of language; they are,

The Etymological Elements.

It has been a favourite idea, ever since grammar has been treated philosophically, that there exists in the sound of letters and words some fitness to express the conceptions placed in them.

This idea founds itself philosophically upon the fact that the sounds of all things rest on their internal vibrations or trembling motions, which following certain decided polar directions, announce the *true nature* of every thing; for nothing can vibrate against its susceptibility of doing so. Water, fire, wood and metal, all vibrate differently. The nature of water for example, is not to *hold* together in itself but to *be held* together, hence it *falls in drops.* Its sound is therefore hollow, murmuring as it passes over the pebbles in its bed. The air on the other hand is not held together externally, but holds itself together and though fluid it does not fall in drops but is elastic, yet its sounds wants clearness and purity, it whistles, blusters, moans. But the sound of bodies is different. They are not held together externally like the water, nor elastically like the air, but *cohere intensively* in themselves. The Greeks called this properly τεινειν, wherefrom τονος, tone. Such is the property of a well stretched string, and how clear it sounds. The clearest of all sounds is that of the voice. It is not the product of a mere vibration, into which a body has been put by an external impulse but the free product of a living organism, which by it renders its whole peculiarity manifest. Chladni's discovery, that every vibrating motion which reaches the ear in the form of sound, has its corresponding geometrical figure in space confirms the above idea. This may be seen, when sand is scattered upon a pane of glass, or water poured into a cup and when we then draw the bow of a violin across the glass, every new stroke will call forth new figures, and yet each particular note will repeat the one corresponding to it. These *spectres of sound* indicate the nature of the internal vibrations; hence it is that sounds may be said, to convey to us an idea of the nature of every thing, and of what the hand of the Lord has written upon all the bodies, that he has created. The idea alluded to above, must be explained by this fact. Words are either more or less correct, more or less happy imitations of the sounds that are peculiar to the phenomena indicated by them, and as every thing expresses its nature by single sounds, according to which man names it, man in his language expresses the true Being of all that exists. The single sound is enough for the animal; man stands in need of a language that will contain all the sounds of nature. We must remark here that the same desire which appears in language as such, to give form and to communicate, strikes us again in the constituent parts of every word. For the *vowels* open and sonorous, are communicative, while the *consonants* surrounding the vowels, and mute without them, give form. Vowels then are the product of the desire of communication, consonants that of our pleasure in *forming* whatever comes in contact with us. Articulation and formation of sound is the same.— The opinion now is, that both vowels and consonants had originally some significance, some natural fitness to be the signs of the ideas or impressions, to be represented by them; that for instance, what is *lovely, light, mild*, would be impressed by similar sounds, as what is rude, rough, harsh, by others. This fitness shows itself,

First in the *vowels.*—*U* and *I*, for instance, are indicative of deep emotions and clear and lively colors, thus; huhu! hihi! roth! ἐροθρος! *rufus. A signifies pleasure*, in general something handsome or great; for example, *brahma*.

This significance of *vowels* is beautifully exhibited in the Persian imitation of the nightingale: "Dani tscheh guest mara an bulbul sehheri—Iu ehud tscheh ademi kes i' sehk bichaberi."

Secondly, in the *consonants*.—These are

1. Altogether *imitative*. Though produced by articulation, they imitate inarticulate sounds. They *paint* for the ear, they represent things by closely imitating their sounds. Of this description are all such as express emotions, joy or pleasures, disgust or mourning, love or hatred. Pshaw! sh! tsch! dsch! These sounds, however, grow less in number in proportion as nations become civilized and languages cultivated.

2. *Symbolical.*—Sounds here are not immediately imitative; but they attempt only to produce the impressions upon the ear, resembling that which the object produces upon the soul. The sound S, for example, is used in words that express something *strong, solid, fast*, hence: *sto; stand; stehen; ἴστημι; schtha*, in Sanskrit; *stout; sturdy; stick; stiff; stop; stone; stubborn; steel; stuff; sturgeon*. The Sanskrit sound *li*, indicates that *which* is *melting, flowing asunder*, the *fluid* in general, the little, the *similar*. From it we have λειπω; λιπαζω; λιπαινω; λιθαζω; λιπαρος; &c.; *light; licht; leuchten; laut; laugh; smile*. The sound W, indicates whatever is *wavering, restless*, confused in its motion, as *wind; wave; wish; swim; swing; swift; whirlpool;* to *wind; wenden; wirren.* The letter *R* signifies the *crooked*, the *rough*, the *rude*, the *irregular, separation;* as *tremble; shritjali* in Sanskr.; *schreiten; ruehren; trappeln; tremo; zittern; rennen; run; rent; rid.* The letters *b, p*, and *f*, as they require full lips to be pronounced, so they are expressive of fullness, as: *bloom; blossom; flower; breast; brust; briost; broad; spront; spriessen; flow; blow; blast; bundle; glow.* Plato in his Cratylus made some attempts to discover the origin of letters and words, yet he did it more in play, than in earnest, while what he says on the origin of language belongs even now to the best, that ever has been said on this subject.

The Grammatical and Syntactical Elements.

As it is reason that produces language, and as this reason is in all nations the same, only modified by external circumstances and descent, we must discover in all languages the same logical elements, and thus only it is possible for us to learn foreign tongues. These logical elements are, first, the verb; secondly, the noun; thirdly, the adjective; fourthly, the preposition, &c. The *nature* of sentences, periods, and speech, is likewise the same in all languages; for example, each subject and predicate must be connected by a copula, for thus only can their union be asserted. So is this union in all languages a grammatical judgment. When sentences are connected, we obtain periods, &c.— One thing we will yet state here. Words, as we have shown above, do not originate singly and disconnected, so that we carried single words in our memory, and then united them like cents to make a dollar. But words originate in connection with each other, in sentences. As one thing in nature is related to the other, so man perceives nothing entirely by itself. This relation of things to each other, will determine the word used by man to express a thing. If I consider, for instance, a portion of land between two hills, and direct my attention principally to its meandering course, and the rivulet passing through it, bordered with flowers, I call it a *dale:* if, on the other hand, I direct my attention principally to its usefulness to man, I call it a *valley.* There is the same difference between *chalice* and *cup.* Hence the difference between prosaical and poetical expressions; the former originates in our desire to express the simple relation of things to each other, the latter to convey their relation to beauty.

Written Language.

If language as such is the memory of our conceptions, writing is the memory of language. By writing, language receives an existence in space, consequently greater permanency. The external signs for mere sounds are *notes;* those for words may be hieroglyphics, pictures, images.

These images may be *symbolical*. "A lion, a sword, a man, if used as pictures, indicate what they stand for; or *metaphorical*—for instance, the image of a handle signifies authority; or *semeiotical*—as, for instance, a man below a line, indicates that he is dead; or *allegorical*—fire and a circle mean to roast,—or it has *characters*." Yet here every change of ideas makes a change of character necessary, and hence their use is still imperfect and inconvenient. The Chinese character for *old*, for instance, according to Medhurst, expresses, when turned a little to the right instead of the left, *to examine*. The only way of representing words in space, is to represent the elements of which they consist, letters and syllables. Hieroglyphics cannot express the abstract, they cannot convey by signs or symbols an idea of *greatness* as such, of *goodness*, of beginning and end, cause and effect, &c. They render abstract thinking wholly impossible. This difficulty is removed by the use of the alphabet.

Language gives to all our conceptions, and through them to all things, a higher, a more noble and more permanent existence. Children that have yet no names for the things, of which they have sensations and perceptions, do not know them, and as long as they do not know them, so long all is chaotic for them. They see, for instance, the flamingo, its bright color, its partly black bill, the size of its neck, the length of its slender legs,—the flamingo exists for them, but only for their senses. Black and scarlet are different colors, and the sensations from them are different, yet they are not separate and distinct to children. There is no mark, no particular quality in the feeling the child has of red, or white, or blue, by which to distinguish one from the other. Thus flamingos exist, yet merely in nature. Children form a conception of them; this conception at first is that of a single bird, and has all contents of sensation, including the particular red, the particular size of the bird seen, and all its peculiarities. As yet children need no name, for their fancy is sufficient to call up the single image. But the conception becomes more general, the particular contents of sensation are dropped, and children seek for *names*. The child has, for instance, a conception of bread; this conception at first includes the taste, for it comes fresh from sensation; the bread is of wheat, baked in a particular way; as this particular bread it could not be named. Now the *single* conception of this particular bread becomes a general one, and thus it not only can be named, but the name is the only medium by which it can be communicated. Bread is a general name, whether baked of wheat, or rye, or oats, or barley, makes no difference. So it is with the term apple, it stands for every species of apples. Hence it is correct to say, that language gives a higher and more noble existence to all that it names. As much as *thinking* is superior to mere feeling, to sensations or perceptions, so much is the existence of a thing in language superior to that in mere nature. It is by language, that whatever is in nature is classified, and all confusion is removed from it. As long as the thing exists merely in nature, as long as we have merely a sensation of it, so long we have no name for it, and need none because by our single image of it, we can recall it. But when we have a *general* conception, a single image is no longer able to recall it, we must have a *name*.

Again, to have the thing as it is in nature, I must go and see, and feel, or hear it. The roaring of Niagara, the dashing foam, the silvery spray, exist for my ear and my eye; and to have it exist thus, I must be near it. But after I have formed a conception of it, and have a name for it, it does not matter where I am, whether in Europe or in Asia, in the name *Niagara* I have the thing itself. We easily perceive, that here the same relation exists between the thing and its name, that was observed between the image and its object. In the name I have the thing, but not as it exists in nature—for there it would be only for my senses—but as it exists in my conceptions. To illustrate this I need only say, that my senses may perceive a *tree*, but not the *species* or *genus* as such; this species or genus is *the tree* contained in my general conception of it. A tree existing in nature is for my senses, but it exists in my general conception as it does not in nature. Thinking of this general tree, or tree as a *genus*, I need not have an image of a tree at all, of its roots, trunk, branches, but my conception is altogether general. This general conception is not one of a tree that blooms and grows—such a conception would be a single one, that of a tree before my house. Of a kind no sensation or perception is possible; we can only have a conception of it. Hence, every name is the thing, in so far as it exists in our conceptions. So far all seems correct. But as there is a difference between an object and its image, so there is one between our general conceptions and their names. The former are wholly internal; names as words written or spoken are *external*. And again, our conceptions of a thing, of an individual, species or genus, cannot be manifold, but to be correct, each genus can have but one *corresponding* conception. But as regards the names for these conceptions they may be various. So what we call *food* may also be called *nourishment* or *sustenance;* the idea of diminution may be expressed by the words *small, little, petty, short, low,* or *mean.* It is true all synonymous words have slight shades of meaning by which they differ, yet it is certain too that one and the same conception may have different names without losing or gaining any thing by it, as for example, the same animal may be called giraffe or cameleopard. If now we say the name is the thing as it exists in the sphere of conception, and again if we are constrained to admit that our conceptions can choose any name, that they are internal, but names external; that names are but the signs for our conceptions,—we must admit the existence of a contradiction. For what the one judgment asserts the other denies. This contradiction must be removed, and the power to remove it is memory. It is the power which always unites the external sign with the conception for which it stands; it unites the word and its meaning so inseparably, that when the former is pronounced, the latter is understood. This inseparable connection of word and thought produces their real identity, so that I need not go and see the thing in order to show it to another, but naming it is sufficient; for memory produces a complete identity of thing and name. Thus the dispute of Nominalists and Realists is removed by that power, which we have to consider—by memory.

§ 6. MEMORY.

It may be easily seen, that this power differs from reproductive fancy, and that in this difference it has reference to conceptions and things, as contained in names, while reproductive fancy recalls the image or conceptions of single things. It is an act of reproductive fancy, when I recall the image of a friend, or of a beautiful landscape, or that of a sick-bed;—or in other words, places, times, single things, and persons, are the objects of reproductive fancy, while the names and the general conceptions expressed by them, are the objects of memory. *Memory is that activity, which finds for every general conception or thought the appropriate word, and recognizes in every word the conception it contains.* To speak well demands a good memory; to know the thing, but not its name, immediately causes confusion. Yet we know that all psychologists speak of a memory of things as well as of words, of locality as well as of time, of numbers, persons, and language. But the fact is that they commingle two distinct activities of the mind, fancy and memory. These pre-suppose each other, they belong together, as the basis and that which is founded upon it; as the root and the trunk; yet ought they to be kept distinct, for the objects of the one are not exactly the same with those of the other; they exist in a more refined manner in memory. But even if they were one and the same, we ought not to speak of different kinds of memory, because memory guided by the interests which different persons take in different objects, retains conceptions of one class more easily than those of another. It would excite a laugh, if it should be said that we had different kinds of eyes, because the painter's eye finds it easy to distinguish the slightest shades of colors; and that of the architect more readily perceives symmetry, regularity, and harmony. It is his great interest—on whatever that may be based,—which constitutes the eye of the painter different from that of the sculptor. So it is with memory; whatever interests a man he will remember with ease. The interests of some men will spread over a great many objects. Leibnitz took not only a great interest in philosophy, but also in history, languages, &c. A long life enables such men to acquire an immense knowledge. Memory retains either without will or by virtue of it; if the former, it is *reproductive,* if the latter, it is *mechanical.*

1. *When memory is productive,* it is a *general* conception that unites all the particular ones belonging to it, and whenever it is recalled, these are included. The term *theology* expresses such a general conception; it includes the particular conceptions of exegesis, hermeneutics, critique, dogmatics, christian ethics, pastoral theology, homiletics, &c. The recalling of these parts of theology is not an act of *fancy,* for all these conceptions are without images,—they are the names of thought, and memory, the power that retains them, keeps off all such names as do not belong strictly under the general head. It will not suffer, for instance, that the name civil law be connected with theology, but will point out a place for it in jurisprudence. Fancy gives the images as it received them, memory exercises judgment concerning the association of its conceptions.

2. *Mechanical memory.* In the above, *words* are held together by their common affinity, internally. The same is the case, when noun and adjective are joined by a copula, when words are brought together by the sense, to be expressed by them, by metre, alphabet, by grammatical and lexicographical connections. But when there is no objective connection whatever between the different words, and when we nevertheless desire to *hold* them together, then it is our will that must determine us to do so, and determine their connection, while our intellect is the power that enables us to *retain* them. The connection of the words here is an entirely mechanical one, wholly external, wholly brought about by the will of man, and preserved by his intellect. This demands *little or no thinking,* for the meaning of the words is not observed here. I send a boy to a store to fetch salt, sugar, snuff, and also a piece of linen, a quire of paper, a pound of nails, and other things. There is certainly nothing that sugar and nails, or linen and paper have in common, and which would bind the one to the other; it is, therefore, the power of intellect that keeps

them together, not by reflection on them, but by will and the simple power of the mind, as it does not think at all. Hence it is that young persons who think less, commit with the greatest ease to memory, and hence too, that the false prejudice is so current, that men of very acute judgment have generally a weak memory, and yet judgment, in order to be acute must have materials to judge of, and how can it get them without memory? The strongest judgment, if memory is weak, will constantly make mistakes, never find the right word, the right comparison, the right fact, and it will constantly have to correct itself even in its common language, for it will always seek for the right word, and yet miss it.

The spirit of ages, that makes things fashionable, or not, has exercised its irresistible power even on the faculties of the mind. There was a time when memory was neglected, when especially in schools children were taught to reason only, and when the mechanical memory was despised. The disciples of Pythagoras had to be silent for four years, and only to receive and listen. Pythagoras thought, no doubt, that to speak rationally and intelligently on a subject, a student ought first to have made himself acquainted with it; and to do so he ought to have learned to abandon all preconceived and immature ideas, and to listen with obedience to those of his teacher. This is right. The mind must learn obedience as well as the will, or else it will have no doctrine pure, but always commingle its own notions with it. *Discipline* of mind is the true basis of study. The mechanical memory ought, therefore, to be much exercised; for by it the judgment will gain materials for its *reasoning*.

Memory seems, however, to be too much valued at present. Historical learning, the union of all past experience in our memory, is the most valued science, and this rests principally on memory. Yet this view mistakes the term *science*. Not he who has collected a great number of facts, and knows their elements of usefulness, and how to apply them, is the scientific man. For every man has some such knowledge, and yet we would not say that all men are men of science. Such a definition of science renders the term science relative, like that of riches. According to it all men of a country are scientific; they form a pyramid, and while the most scientific becomes its head, those that are least so have to form the base, and all the rest come to stand between according to their greater or less amount of knowledge. Yet the accumulation of facts is not *science*, it is merely *learning*. Learning may place value upon facts, and their correctness; science requires the form and spirit of these facts; learning is satisfied with the facts, and their external mechanical connection, science demands their leading principle, their internal union, and hence it is that we may speak of a scientific spirit, but not of a learned spirit. Science has, therefore, two sides; it has an internal one, a soul, a union, a penetrating principle, on which all the facts belonging to it must rest; and again, it has an external one, which spreads itself over a large surface, and daily increases, for experience is added to experience. If it demands *memory* to acquire the external materials of a science in our power, *judgment* is required, and a *noble* spirit, to enter into the life of a science, and to perceive how it pervades and animates all. Judgment and memory, the spontaneous and receptive activities ought therefore to be exercised in an equal degree; and neither at the expense of the other.—In conclusion, we must speak a word with regard to Mnemonics, or the art of exercising the memory.

No doubt the memory may be *strengthened*: this, however, is not so much the aim of Mnemonics, as by certain means to facilitate the recollection of a particular name. I desire, for instance, a person who knows mythology, but not geography, to remember the name Athens, and tell him to recall the names of the Greek goddesses, and Athena will certainly remind him of Athens. Yet we easily see that as I must *retain* in my memory the means by which to remember something else, I only double my labor, for I may as well remember the thing at once, as the means which recalls it.

Memory may, however, be truly strengthened by continued exercise. How this is possible, and how it is to be understood, has been beautifully illustrated by the nature of the magnet. This activity in the first place slumbers in all kinds of iron, and may be called forth by an appropriate external influence on it. The light of the sun may awaken it, the rays of electricity, the stroke of the hammer, but especially an already magnetized iron, when drawn across in certain directions. We then see that it is the realized magnetic activity in the one iron, which elicits the possible magnetic activity of the other. The thus awakened activity of the magnet is strengthened by exercise, and disappears again when it is not used. To strengthen it we must bring it in contact with other iron, and lay it for this purpose in iron filings. Now the question is: *How* can it thus be strengthened? As the magnetic activity, when once awakened, has the power to awaken that which still slumbers, so this, when once active will have the same power: it must, therefore, react upon the magnetic power, by which it was elicited and strengthen it, in the same degree that it was itself acted upon and strengthened. It will excite as it has been excited; it will strengthen as it has been strengthened; for it is one and the same activity that awakens, and that has been awakened.

If we apply this to memory we may say, that all the conceptions which we receive by memory, are the productions of our thinking power; but as they are the contents of words we must reproduce them, in order to have them as conceptions. Or these conceptions rest in names; but language does neither speak, nor understand itself; they are therefore like the slumbering magnet in the unmagnetized iron. Our mind approaches them, and receives them by breathing the breath of life into them: being thus received, and as our mind acted upon them, so their life will act upon our mind and strengthen it, as the magnetized iron strengthens that by which its latent power has been roused. It is the same mental activity that produces the conceptions, and places them in names, and which again receives them by recalling them. The former might be called the *productive*, the latter the *reproductive* memory. From all this it must follow, that as the body is strengthened by appropriate food, so is the memory: that the many conceptions and ideas are all of them filled with the nature of our own intellect, and that as intellect is power, they will strengthen memory in proportion as many or few are received by it. It must be evident, however, that an acute perception, a faithful reproductive fancy, and continued interest, will render memory very tenacious.

We may remark yet, that however different and manifold may be the objects committed to memory, its union will remain the same. As the globule of quick silver, to which is added many other globules, increases in size and bulk, and remains a perfect sphere, so it is with memory. Memory in this respect may be compared to a monad which constantly attracts other monads, and thus becoming conscious of all of them, strengthens itself and reigns over them according to its own pleasure.

In conclusion, it may be stated that memory holds the same relation to pure thought, that fancy holds to imagination. Imagination is the union of thought and sensuality; it represents a thought in a single image, and this image is either created by it, or borrowed from fancy. Memory gives the thought in a mere sign, or word, without any image, and attaches thought and word so to each other, that they become **inseparable.**

CHAPTER III.

ON PURE THINKING.

The chapter now before us is one of the most difficult in Mental Philosophy. Its object is to ascertain the *nature of pure thinking*, as such; it must therefore abstract from thinking, as it is subjective, my or your thinking, and it must look away from the objects of our thoughts, whether physical, as the sun and moon; or historical, as the actions of heroes, or the import of moral notions: we must, in a word, direct our attention merely to *thinking*, as such.

This is extremely difficult, and cannot be effected without much effort. Most persons employ their *external* senses more than their internal thinking power, and in proportion as one mental activity is exclusively exercised, it will become more acute; but the others will grow weak. The feeling of ability and skill is pleasant, and man delights, therefore, more in the investigation of objects in which he can enjoy the feeling of power, than in such as demand effort, and remind him that he has yet something to learn. Add to this the aversion felt by all to well disciplined thinking—for all of us like to have our own thoughts and opinions on subjects—and also, that we sooner have sensations and conceptions than pure thoughts, that we must consequently with considerable labor raise ourselves into the region of pure thought; that language too, is better calculated to express general conceptions than pure thoughts; and especially that it must borrow the words by which to convey the highest thoughts from fancy and imagination, and that therefore the same word may serve the lowest and highest—and we shall find it natural that so few only should take delight in a question like the one before us. And yet we cannot dismiss it, but must request our readers to follow us with patience. The question, What is *pure thinking?* must be solved. Thinking is the true basis of all our knowledge, for until we have penetrated our conceptions by thought, until we know their nature, their ground, their connection with each other, we have no *science*. One may have collected a great deal of knowledge, but if it has no connection, it is not *solid*, not *scientific*, and though it have full *certainty* for the possessor, the truth it contains is not drawn out. The knowledge that in the year 480 B. C., the battle of Salamis was fought, is disconnected, as it stands here, neither solid, nor valuable; every boy may learn thus much; he may know the year, the name of the place where the battle was fought, and who gained the victory; but it requires thinking to discover the secret causes that led to it, and perceive the influence which it had upon the national cultivation of Greece, and yet it is only when we see historical facts strictly connected, when we see their necessity and their influence upon each other, that we have historical truth. The boy may know the facts chronologically as well as his teacher, but the latter must know more than the mere facts, or he is not fit to teach history. The additional knowledge is only accessible to pure thought, which needs neither images nor sensations nor perceptions. The same is the case in other spheres. I may have, for example, a conception of *blue*, but unless I can show its origin and nature, I have no knowledge of it. So, pointing to the blue in the sky, and defining it to be "darkness seen through light," are very different. Again, as thinking must penetrate all our conceptions, and the contents of our sensations and perceptions, so it must show their relations to each other. Every object has a number of distinctions in itself; these enter into our conceptions; but these distinctions, as contained in our conceptions, stand beside each other, and are not known in their common origin: thus the *thing* is *one*, and yet it is *many*. This is a contradiction which our conception does not notice, or if noticed, it does not remove it. Thinking perceives the one in the manifold, and again the manifold as one. God is *just*, and is *merciful;* these are two qualities, which when penetrated by thought, have *one and the same nature,* so that justice is mercy, and mercy, justice. And finally, thinking must show the necessity of things, or show that a thing must be as it is. This it can do only by exhibiting its ground and general reason.

From all this it will follow, that though we should at first feel indifferent to the present question, we shall take an interest in it, as soon as we desire to treat a science logically, or to solve difficult questions, or to remove doubts and scruples, ignorance and error. To free ourselves from them, neither the decisions of an infallible church, nor the majority of votes taken on such subjects, nor any external object, as the magnet that may guide the sailor, or a polar star, will suffice. Thinking alone will avail. But if I do not know the medium by which to remove an evil, or by which to acquire a good, how can I make a proper use of it? And again, if I desire to know myself, but do not know my highest power, how can I pretend to be acquainted with my mind? Men like Plato and Aristotle; Cudworth and Locke; Leibnitz, Kant, and Hegel; Spinoza and Des Cartes, have, therefore, not hesitated to bestow much time and labor on the subject of our present chapter, and what man ought not to be willing to bestow at least some attention on that noblest of all powers within him which he daily uses? We shall, therefore,

1. Inquire, How *thinking* differs from the other faculties of the mind?

If we compare thinking with sensation and perception, we shall find that both are *activities,* and that in this respect they are the same. But sensation is an activity, whose nature is *receptive;* it receives impressions, and receives them as they are made upon our organs. The activity, as sensation or perception, is therefore wholly determined by the object felt; it *must* feel the object as it presents itself, and must receive an impression as it flows forth from it. It is consequently an activity that is not in the least *free.* Conception is also an activity, but one that differs from sensation or perception, for it is not merely *receptive,* but freeing sensation more or less from its immediate contents, transferring them into space and time, and producing the images of their objects, it is a *form-giving* and *productive activity*. In my conceptions I am therefore more free, than in my sensations, more self-active, more independent of the objects the images of which I conceive. Thinking, however, differs both from sensation and conception. Like them it is an activity, but an activity having both for its medium, and impossible without them. Feeling is possible without thinking, and so are sensations: thinking demands feeling, sensation, and conceptions, as the fruit demands the preceding stages of growth. What kind of an activity then is *thinking?* *That* activity which *generalizes*. By generality is however not to be understood a mere collective union, which may have been gained by *abstraction* or *negation*, or by observing what is *common* to many; nor is it that which is often expressed by the term *universality*. The term, many, includes only single ones—the one stands by the side of the other; many stars, many grains of sand, are all of them each by itself, whatever they may have in common with each other. If the many are reduced to a *collective* whole, we may use the term *all*. But whether *many* or *all*, they are accessible to my senses; as I see one star, so I may see many, and if my eye could reach the infinite, I might see all. The *generality* which is here spoken of, is not gained by *abstraction*, but by *position;* it is not the product of *man*, nor that of any *object*, it is neither subjective nor objective, but above both; its origin is pure reason, as such. It exists not merely in our thoughts, but equally as much in nature; it is in the sphere of nature the *genus;* in the sphere of mind the *identity*, and in that of science the *generality*. As such it would remain *abstract*, did it not become concrete by its own innate power, which entering into a difference becomes through it concrete in the individual. Hence the genus in nature divides itself, and enters the species, and through it realizes itself in the *individual*. This is the case already in the planetary system. The sun is the *general;* the planets are the species, and each planet, by its peculiarities, is individual. Thus with every class of animals. The genus contains the possibility of the species, and this possibility is realized through the species in the individuals. And with every science it is the same. What the genus is in nature, the generality is here; the species is the particularity, and the individual is the singularity. The *single* specimen of a mineral has only value by representing its species and kind.—Now, it will be admitted, that the eye cannot see a genus or a species, or the sense of touch or of hearing, perceive any thing like it; yet it must be also admitted that the genera and species *are*, that nature has them, that a Linnæus, Haller, Cuvier, and Oken, do not classify nature, nature has classified itself, its genera have specified themselves; we only discover its classification, and correct our discoveries daily by new observations. And yet the genera of nature may be experienced, may become accessible to our sensations, for they exist not in the abstract, but in the concrete, and every individual of a species represents them. Thus they become objects of our sensations, and the objects of our sensations become the objects of our thoughts: as the latter, however, they exist in an entirely *different form*. To make the above more clear we ask, What is the object, and what are the contents of pure *thinking?*

By comparing them with those of the preceding activities of the mind, we may here also render our subject more generally intelligible. The *objects* of our sensations or perceptions are always something *single*, contained in a certain place, and existing in a certain time. Beyond this singleness the objects of sensation cannot extend. I see a single sheep, or many at a time; but, however many they are, they are only present to my eye each as a single one. Conception receives its objects from sensation; it forms the contents of sensation, and noticing that which many objects have in common with each other, it forms a more or less general image, one that needs no longer a sensual existence, though it was gained from it. The object of pure thinking is nothing *single;* not an *image;* not any thing visible to the eye or to any one of the senses. Its object is *thought*, as such. Of it no image can be formed; it is shapeless and colorless; it has no existence in space and time, like a tree or a cloud, that passes by. Hence, it is without interest to the sensualist, for he wills only what is *agreeable*, what touches his senses; or to the mere man of business, for he desires by his understanding only what is *useful*. Yet it *is*, for who would say, that the *thoughts* of justice, of truth, of right, had no being, no objects? And what are their objects? Any thing different from themselves? The object I have for my conception of the sun, differs from my conception; the sun is in the firmament, my conception in me; my conception and its object are separate, the one is where the other is not; but my thought of justice, and justice are not separate; they are *identical*. Take away all mind, and justice is taken away; take away all possible conceptions, the sun still remains. And what are the *contents* of pure thinking? *Pure Being*. Not external existence, as that of the sun, or of any object of conception. The contents of a conception is the image of its object; those of the object are qualities which become sensations in us;—but justice or right have no material qualities; all that can be said of them is that they are. It happens here most fortunately, that these ideas may be rescued from the charge of being abstract or abstruse or mystical, by one of the noblest sciences, by mathematics. These are the product of pure thinking; nature knows nothing of *figures*, nor of *Geometry*; it has neither triangles nor circles. What then are the objects of mathematical thoughts? These very thoughts themselves. Are they now imaginary? or arbitrary? By no means, the relation of the sides of a triangle remain eternally the same, though our senses cannot *see*, and nature cannot *show* them.—But thoughts without a material existence, what are they worth? Nothing for him, that wants only to eat and drink. Such a question ought not to be answered, it is beneath science. Yet it is by thoughts, that stir the inward soul of man, that something great may be effected, not by fine images, by conceptions and fanciful representations. The Reformation could not have been effected by smooth poetical phrases; it could only be brought about by a mind like Luther's. What science effects even now greater things than Mathematics?

A few examples will illustrate the above: man as an *individual* may be the immediate object of my sensation; I see him, I feel him, I hear his voice. The same man may be the object of my conception, yet not the latter without having been present to my senses. As an object of my conception he may exist in it merely as an individual;

as he lives, and moves about, as he eats and drinks. But I may have formed a conception of him as belonging to a *certain* nation. As the object of this conception he is no longer merely a single one, but of a more general character, he is an American, because both the external features, common to all Americans, and the spirit and manner of thinking are represented by him. Thus he is the object of my conception, as he cannot be the object of my sensation. As the object of my thinking he is neither a mere individual, nor belonging to a particular nation, but he is *man*. This is his true being; as such he can neither be the object of sensation, nor of conception, it is only pure thought, that can conceive the idea of *humanity*. For humanity is that *generality* that pervades all nations, and all individuals, that will survive all the nations of the present time, and continue to live in all the following generations. Or to give another example,—nature produces by crystalization the icicle and the diamond; by organization the moss and the beautiful calla; by animalization the toad, and the proud deer of the forest. These productions of nature are and may be perceived by our senses. But as far as they are accessible to our senses they will pass away. The calla, of which I had once a sensation, may exist in my conception, in my reproductive fancy. But when I place it under its species, and this under its kind, I *think* and *judge*, and the object of my thinking is no longer the single calla, as it exists for my sensation, nor the image of that calla as it was conceived by me,—it is the *species*, the *kind*, that do not exist in nature in a particular form or shape, having a peculiar color, or size; but become manifest only in individual beings. The *kind*, or genus is the true *generality and necessity* of all the individuals belonging to it, and while the individuals may be the objects of sensations and conceptions, *kind*, as such, can only be the *object of thought*. Or, finally, I have a conception of a *knife*, an *axe*, of *scissors*, *saw*, and other instruments; as such, my conceptions have their corresponding objects in space or time. But now I place all of them under the general term, *instrument*, by which to sever, to dissect, &c.; and this idea I again place under that of *means and end*, and thus all the single conceptions and their corresponding objects are gone, and that which is left is their general character, or that which makes each one of them an instrument. The thought of instrument is identical with *the instrument;* for this has no existence whatever independent of the thought, and yet it *is*, it has an energy, for by it as the general idea all instruments are produced.

Now, it is easy to understand that the objects of sensations and conceptions are also those of thinking; but while those of sensation exist wholly in nature, and while those of conception, though more general, are still only *collective*, those of thinking are *wholly general*, and as such have no existence independent of thinking. Yet they truly *exist;* they are not a mere *abstraction;* they are the pure being and nature of individual things, their soul, and life. The abstract is *lifeless;* it has no being; the *general*, the *genus*, the *species*, on the other hand, *is*. Morality, as something abstract, exists only in my head, and no where else: but morality, as that which is *the general* in all moral actions, *is* and is their general nature. To make this clear we would state it thus:—*Morality* in its *generality* is the agreement of human will with the divine law. This human will does not exist in the abstract, but it particularizes itself and becomes *national* will, and thus morality in particular is the agreement of the national will, as expressed by its history, laws, literature, &c., with the divine will. But the national will cannot act as such, it must have its organs, and these are the single citizens of a nation, and hence morality is individualized, expresses itself by the single actions of single persons, and may be said to be the agreement of our *personal* will, with the divine, so that we observe *all* duties towards ourselves, our fellow-men, and God, because they are the expressions of the divine will. Thus the general morality is realized in that of the individual, and while otherwise it would be merely abstract, it thus becomes concrete. Or I say, that one of the qualities of the divine law is its *generality*. How is this to be understood? Is this generality merely *abstract?* The generality of the *law* is that power which alone constitutes every other commandment a law, and without which there could be none. This *general* law lives, therefore, in all individual laws, and becomes manifest by them. No one feels himself morally obligated to fulfil the mere arbitrary will of a despot: it has not *the* law as its soul, and hence cannot bind us to obey it by external force.

Thinking, then, being the same as generalizing, seeks every where for the *true* nature of things, for their generality and necessity, for their real and genuine truth. This does not consist in the perishable part, which may be seen with the senses; but in that which, while the individual dies, continues to live. It is the Dryad of the Romans, for instance, which as the soul of the tree passes into another, animating it, when the one in which it lived is hewn down. The object of thought, therefore, is not a single thing, not this, or that; nor is it a collection of things, or something they have in common with each other, but it is the general nature of all those individuals through which that nature flows, and that are internally united by it.

If we consider that all nature is full of reason, that every being is the expression of it, then we must acknowledge, that what we thus perceive by thinking, is reason itself, or flesh of our flesh, and bone of our bone. The laws of reason and nature are the expressions of the same divine will, and they differ only by their objects, and by the fact that in nature they work unconsciously, but in man with his consciousness. The law of gravity which attracts all particles to a common centre, and the law according to which in times of danger, all citizens incline to one great individual, as for instance, to Washington, is the same.

Unwilling to leave the present subject in the least dark, we will add yet a few words.—The objects of sensation or perception are something *material;* the contents of conception are *images*, however they may be generalized; language and memory can do in part without these images. But the objects and contents of thought are wholly without *imagery*. The *living tree* may be seen and conceived as an image; but *life*, as such, has no image. So it is with the thoughts of *justice, holiness, virtue, truth;* with the thoughts of *cause* and *effect, ground* and *consequence*. They do not exist as such in space, and yet no one would deny their existence. Here it is, where Nominalists and Realists must cease their opposition, and discovering each their one-sidedness, they must unite; for when I say *holiness*, this thought has in its generality, of course, no *corresponding external object*, and yet it cannot be without an object, or it would be an *empty* thought. What then is its object? *The thought of holiness itself.* This then is the last and principal difference between feeling, sensation, conception, and thinking—that feeling cannot become objective to itself, nor sensation, nor conception, or with other words, feeling cannot feel itself, nor can sensation, or conception perceive themselves: but thinking has this power of doubling itself, it may become objective to itself, perceive itself, think of and reflect on itself. As thinking has the power to render itself objective to itself, so it is the power that can reflect on every thing else, on the lowest and the highest, on the rudest and the most refined.

2. The contents of our sensation are dark, and little understood, before our thinking penetrates them; and so the contents of our conceptions are not perfectly transparent. But those of thinking are *clear* and *lucid*. "Thinking is a *simple, undisturbed, quiet* activity; 'cogitatio est actio sibi perspicua, et in se continua.' It flows without interruption, and is every where perfectly clear to itself. Feeling is a *trembling* motion in itself; sensation is a dark and confused *weaving* of the mind; the act by which we become conscious of the world and of ourselves may be called an awakening. But thinking is a flowing activity, perspicuous to itself, and conscious of itself, and known to itself in every one of its pulsations. Its symbol in nature is the *ether*. Ether fills all space, and yet it is transparent: it is constantly in motion, and yet this motion is not perceptible to the eye, for it is always *equal, quiet,* and *undisturbed*. The air is thick, not clear, nor transparent: it is cloudy, and blue or gray of color. But the ether is clear, colorless, and pure; of unfathomable depth, open to the eye, but mysterious to the understanding. In the air it storms; its motions are not quiet and flowing, but crossing each other. Again; ether is contained in all that has existence, whether animate, or inanimate, elementary, or concrete. Art may, therefore, extract ether from every thing. So it is with thinking. That which truly *is* in nature, are the divine thoughts, the divine laws, and all the rest is but matter; that which truly is in history, are likewise the thoughts and

will of nations, that have realized themselves in actions, customs, institutions, art, &c. By thinking we may extract those thoughts in nature and history, as by art we may gain the ether contained in all things." We need not carry *our* thoughts into nature and loan them to it; they are there, and all we have to do is to open our eyes and perceive them. Reason, like ether, is every where, but we can only discover it by thinking, as a Sir Isaac Newton, a Kepler, a Cuvier.

Thinking, as this uninterrupted flow, as this generalizing activity, is as yet without *distinctions*; it is not without contents, for being perspicuous to itself, it has itself for its contents, it is the light that sees itself. But thinking is an activity, that according to the divine laws contained in it, produces distinctions, and these are,

First, *Comprehension or Apprehension.* Thinking in this form unites the manifold in one, but according to its internal nature. And this nature consists in this—every single individual belongs to a species, and through it to its kind. The kind is the generality, the species the particularity, and the individual the singularity. The general nature specifies and individualizes itself *by its own power*. The comprehension consists in this trichotomy. It comprehends the individual in the species, the species in the genus, and the genus in the individual. There is nothing arbitrary in this activity, nothing depending on our will or pleasure; it is thinking in the form of comprehension or understanding, that by its own laws is necessarily thus active, and that discovers the same laws in the activity of nature.

Secondly, *Judgment.* By judgment thinking renders the contents of comprehension more distinct, by separating them, on the one hand, and on the other, keeping them united by a copula. The term *lion*, is a comprehension, when I perceive the genus in the individual lion. When I say, "this is a lion," I have in the term *this*, a single lion in view, a lion that is perhaps before me in a menagerie, but in the term *lion* the whole class or genus of lions, and thus separating the individual from the genus, I nevertheless keep them connected by the copula *is*, and thus show their identity. Judging, I do not comprehend the one in the other, or the manifold in one, but subordinate the one to the other, or *analyze.* Both are, and remain distinct; the subject being the single individual, the predicate the genus, as when I say, "*the rose is a flower,*" yet in this distinction they are related to each other. Thinking, in this form, is judgment, and as such, it is the power that every where produces light and order. Yet we must have comprehended, before we can judge, for every judgment consists of two *comprehensions* or *apperceptions;* mere *sensations* and *perceptions* may form *sentences,* but cannot form a *judgment.* When I say, for example, "it is cold to-day," I connect a perception (to-day) with a sensation, (cold,) by thinking, or the copula, is. Yet I have merely a grammatical sentence, not a judgment. But when I say: "the rose is a plant," I have united the *general* with the *specific,* and thus have *judged.*

Thirdly, *Syllogism* or *Conclusion,* is the activity by which thinking removes all difference, and effects a permanent identity. In every syllogism we have *three* thoughts; each is distinct, and differs from the other, but one of them is capable of removing the difference, and of uniting the others in itself. Hence, this process is called *Conclusion* or *Syllogism.* This activity of thinking is *reason,* the fruit on the tree of knowledge. In considering the nature of the syllogism, it is easy to discover its infinite power to move in endless circles within itself. Every syllogism contains three judgments; each is finite, the mere product of understanding. Yet none is independent of the other, none is of any value detached from the others. The syllogism unites all, and is infinite in itself. This will appear thus. Two of the judgments in every syllogism, as (the proposition major and b.) the proposition minor make, the former an infinite *regress,* and the latter an infinite *progress* possible. Every propositio major of a syllogism may become the conclusion of a second; the propositio major of this second, the conclusion of a third; the propositio major of this the conclusion of a fourth, and so on ad infinitum. This may be called the *infinite regress.* Again, every conclusion may in the same way, only in the opposite direction, become the propositio major of another;

the conclusion of this the propositio major of a third, and so on without end.

So again; every syllogism contains three apperceptions; each finite, but in the syllogism, in relation to each other. They are the terminus major, the terminus minor, and the terminus medius. One of them unites the two others, because it contains them according their nature and being. In the syllogism each may come to stand in the place of the other, for none stands independent of the other; the *minor* may become *medius*, the medius, *major;* and the major again minor, and so on. This gives the syllogism an infinite, internal motion. The syllogism is the only true form of thought, and from its nature, that of pure thinking may be seen. Single thoughts the insane man may have; they may flash forth from his deranged mind like lightning from dark clouds. The prudent man, that is wholly indifferent to truth, may have closely connected thoughts, but the connection is brought about by *him*, by his purposes, not by the nature of the thoughts themselves. But pure thinking demands of us, first of all, to resign our views and pre-formed notions, and yield to thinking, as as such, and its results. Pure thinking, like the syllogism, is not intermediated, but intermediates itself. All finite knowledge is intermediated by other knowledge. That of Napoleon's exploits by that of the French nation; that of the sun, by that of the moon. But pure thinking flows incessantly in itself; it is infinite already in its motions, from the general to the particular, from the particular to the singular; then in its passing over to judgment, where by the greatest variety of judgments, all of which have their strict necessity, it passes over to the syllogism. The connection of thoughts is not an external one; it is one brought about by the energy and nature of thought itself. So one *doctrine* of the Bible contains all the others, and if well developed, it contains the whole system of divinity. Such thinking is not *determined* by any thing else, as it is not intermediated by any thing else; now, if we say, that the identity of thinking with itself is *truth*, and that not to be determined by any thing foreign is *liberty*, we must say, that the form of pure thinking is the syllogism, and its contents are *truth* and *liberty*. By truth is to be understood *the truth,* not physical, historical, or any isolated single truth. Pure thinking, or reason and truth and liberty are inseparable.

But few only are permitted, however, to enter the sphere of such pure thinking. The demands of life, their calling, the whole direction of their minds, are averse to it, and they have neither time nor wish to cultivate it. Yet there are many who might, if they would, give attention to pure thinking; they live in the sphere of science; it is their duty to do so. Some of them make unsuccessful efforts, and abandon the undertaking, embittered against all *school logic,* as they say. The question might, therefore, be asked,

Who is qualified for pure thinking?

1. Not he who is satisfied with knowing much, but does not desire to see all his knowledge internally and systematically connected; who desires to know every thing clearly and distinctly, but is indifferent about its ground and origin. Where, on the other hand, the qualification or talent exists, there will be discovered an irresistible, instinctive urgency of reason to penetrate every thing with thought, to unfold its origin, its nature, its connection with the whole to which it belongs, to break down the limits of matter and sense, and press forward to the infinite, which alone is of value, and which is the only proper object of all scientific investigation.

2. Not he, who considers nature as a mere mechanism, stripped of thought and reason, and into which his wisdom has first to place thoughts, in order to find them there. Nature does not think, is not conscious of itself, *has* not reason, as man has it; but its productions are full of reason and thoughts that are corporealized; the mechanical systems of the starry heavens; the productions of the earth, the minerals and their qualities, the vegetables in their more or less regular formations; the animals with their more or less perfect organizations; all give witness of reason, and show the union of *thought* and of *being,* even in nature. He who is qualified for pure thinking, seeks every where for pure thought, and seeks for it in nature also. The object

of all his investigations in nature, history, and elsewhere, is thought or reason.

3. Not he that interests himself in science, not on account of *truth*, but for his own sake. Unless we take an interest in our studies we can make no progress; but this interest may be taken, because we desire to make a living, and consider the science we study as the best means. To live then we must study it. Here our desire for knowledge has fallen back into a mere desire to eat and drink, and support life. *Thinking* is here of no account, if we only have bread. Or our interest bases itself upon vanity and self-love. We wish to distinguish ourselves, to effect something great, and force ourselves to take an interest in whatever we consider the best means to lead us to this end. The less pure thinking there is required, the more all is made dependent on our own fancies and imaginations, giving us the appearance of originality, the better. Or, finally, our interest in science is based on our love of truth, as such. Truth cannot be reached without pure thought, and he whose interest in study rests on this love, is qualified to move in the sphere of pure thinking.

4. He is not qualified for this sphere who opposes experience and pure thinking to each other. True experience must be *rational*, and true thinking must be *experimental*. When experience constantly opposes philosophy, as if pure reason had nothing to do with it, the qualifications we speak of are wanting; but when the scientific man takes a deep interest in the facts of learning and experience, because they all of them contain thought, if sought for, the qualifications are there.

We commenced the section on Reason with Feeling, and gradually developed from it pure thinking. *Feeling* and *Pure Thinking* are the two most simple activities of the mind, yet the latter is intermediated by a number of different activities, preceding it, while the former presupposes nothing, except life. We commence with Feeling, because it is on the one hand the first motion of life, one that needs no exercise, and which co-exists with life itself; and because it is thinking according to its possibility. The term possibility must here be properly understood. The *Real* is that which has an existence for something else. The sun exists for the earth, the earth for the plants, the plants for animals. The *Possible* is that which on the one hand is, and on the other, is not. *It is* according to its energy, its power of developing itself in case all the conditions are favorable; it *is not* as long as these conditions are not at hand. When the conditions unite with the energy or power of development, the contradiction is removed, and the mere possibility becomes reality. *Now, feeling, is thinking according to possibility: it becomes real thinking by development, which is called forth by external excitement.* The development accomplishes itself in three stages. Commencing with Feeling, it becomes *Sensation* and *Attention*. *Sensation* is already another activity than *Feeling;* with *Sensation*, the *possibility* contained in Feeling, begins to *realize* itself. Yet sensation is wholly determined, wholly receptive; this *receptiveness* is of course, self-activity at the same time, yet so that the form of the senses and the self-feeling of the being whose senses they are, determine the sensations. The next stage is that of Conception, or as I may be permitted to call it, *representative* Thinking. If sensation is determined, and if it is a feeling of something objective, conception, as a form-giving power, is more subjective, determining, more than determined. Thus the possible thinking has developed itself to a still higher degree. Conception, from intellectual perception, fancy, imagination, language to memory, is the constant effort of mind to realize itself, until intermediated by all these stages it comes forth as pure thinking. As such it is as simple an activity as feeling, but feeling is without distinctness, a *dark weaving* in itself, while thinking is clear and lucid as light; again, man *must* feel, but nothing can force him to think; thinking is a perfectly free activity. Man is born with feeling, but not with thoughts. The way from feeling to pure thinking is long and laborious. It is delightful to observe the gradual and methodically *intermediated* becoming of pure thinking.

One remark flows naturally from the above considerations, which is this. We must not think that feeling is the *origin* of thinking. Thinking cannot originate in any thing else than in itself. Thinking may be said to *begin* as feeling, but not to *originate* in it, as if feeling were the mother of thinking. The fountain, from which cool water gushes, is not the *origin* of the water. So buds might be said to be the origin of fruit, because without buds there can be no fruit, yet the origin of the fruit is also that of the buds.

Remarks.

1. Feeling and sensations are as little the origin or ground of thinking, as buds and blossoms are the origin of fruit. The fruit depends on them as a condition, but its origin precedes blossoms and buds, and is moreover also *their* origin. Thinking, however, *commences* as feeling, and develops itself from it gradually till it reaches its height. Human feeling and that of the animal must consequently differ from their very commencement, for the one contains thinking according to its possibility, in its latent state, the other not. Sensations and conceptions are related to thinking and its development as conditions; for without them it could not exist in man.

2. There is a difference between the expressions *I think*, and *I have a thought*. The words " I have," express a being, but one, which is not itself, what it possesses. " To have a good thought," and " to think well," is, therefore, not exactly the same. The thought I have may be *borrowed*, but when I think well, the thought being the product of my own thinking, is the same with it. Yet this must not be understood, as if a man might have a thought without thinking; he may have a word without the thought it contains; but to have a thought merely handed by another would be no better than to have another eat and digest for him.

SECTION II.

ON WILL.

CHAPTER I.

§ 1. GENERAL NATURE OF WILL.

It is usual to consider Reason and Will as wholly different activities, and to speak of mental and moral faculties. But the mind is one, and reason and will are so inseparable, that the one includes the other. They have *one* principle and one life; and what is on the one hand *liberty* of will, is on the other *spontaneity* of thought. Man cannot *will* a thing, unless he *knows* of it; he cannot have any knowledge of it without the influence of will. Before he resolves on a thing, he must consider it, and again, he must resolve to consider it. The more clear and distinct our thinking, the more it will be pervaded by the will; and the more considerate, wise and correct our actions, the more the breath of understanding will penetrate them. I investigate a subject by my *will;* and my will is directed to it by the *knowledge* I have of it. Will and reason constantly determining each other, are one and the same—existing in different forms; or " *Reason is nothing else than will with prevailing consciousness,* and *will is reason with a prevailing practical tendency.*"

It must be remarked here, however, that *will* may be viewed in a twofold aspect, as nature and as moral will; in the latter respect it is to be viewed in the closest connection with *law, moral obligation, duties* and *rights;* in the former it manifests itself by *desires, inclinations, emotions,* and *passions.* Only the *morally good* is free; the merely natural will is wholly dependent on external objects or internal passions, it does not determine itself by its own nature, but by the nature of that which is different from itself. In the sphere of the natural will we can recognize nothing but *determinism*. It will, therefore, be understood, that here we shall examine the will of man, as it is by nature, and not as it is by grace or religious influence. The natural will then lives in all our desires, inclinations and passions; and these, after a preliminary remark, we shall try to define and distinguish from each other. We may here recollect what has been said on the nature of instinct. It is on the one hand a feeling of want, and on the other the direction to the object by which the want may be removed. There is a corresponding relation between the wants of all animated beings and the things which may relieve them, as there is a relation between negative and positive poles. The want is the negative, and the food intended for it, is the positive. As this relation is a natural one, the being feeling the want, is excited and restless, for the want is related to the thing desired, and cannot remain quiet; this excitement demands a certain direction, a direction to the means by which to satisfy the want, and it is instinct which gives it. Now if the feeling of want is *painful*, that of satisfaction is *delightful*, so that the mere sight of food is exhilarating. Again: whatever can feel itself must feel external influences, and receive from them pleasant or unpleasant impressions. The stone exposed to the sun, does not feel it; the flower may wither, but the *eye* looking into it feels the most severe pain. When now any external influence upon a being which feels itself, excites its self-activity, *pleasure* will be felt by its reaction; when this self-activity is weakened, and perhaps rendered in some degree impossible, *pain* is the result. *Pain* and *pleasure* are, therefore, the two extremes, between which the existence of man vibrates, and upon which the general character of all desires and inclinations, emotions and passions *rests*.

The nature of instinct proceeds, as we have seen, from self-feeling; for without feeling itself, a being cannot feel want. Self-feeling is its channel. It is no less determined by this self-feeling than it determines the whole life of a living being; it directs it with an inflexible determination to its proper food, so that no horse has ever yet been seen to eat flesh, even in its greatest hunger, nor a tiger to eat straw. While instinct, as long as it is in the sphere of mere self-feeling has no choice with regard to the direction which it takes, it loses all direction when it enters the sphere of consciousness in man. As a stream, that flowing smoothly along its course turns neither to the right nor to the left, is, on plunging into the broad, deep ocean, suddenly deprived of its direction, so is instinct, when received by consciousness. For now *feeling* and *consciousness* unite; the mere feeling of want becomes a consciousness of it, as likewise the feeling of pain; what we feel we become conscious of, and feeling entering into our consciousness, gives it warmth and life, and fills it with pain or pleasure. But consciousness will not suffer itself to be driven to its objects by an instinctive power; where it reigns choice and arbitrariness, reason and will prevail. Instinct grows dull, and loses its nature; but as man continues to have wants, *What must supply the place of instinct?*

The full import of this question will be perceived, when we observe, that we cannot desire the unknown; and again that we cannot know any thing unless we desire to know it. Hence a desire cannot originate *directly* in our knowledge, nor this in our desire. How is this contradiction to be removed? Instinct raises the animal above it; but instinct is not in man what it is in the animal. The contradiction in man must be removed by what may be called *appetency*. This is instinct which has lost its direction; for though the direction is lost, the activity *continues;* man continues to feel hunger and thirst, and a tendency of his nature to satisfy them. This tendency is instinctive, but as man is conscious of it, it is no longer instinct as such. He feels hunger, but the object by which to satisfy it, is not pressed upon him by instinct. He sees, however, many objects that are pleasant to his sight; he feels an appetency to unite them with himself, to eat them without as yet knowing whether they will be *agreeable* or *disagreeable*. He eats the apple and finds it good, and from this moment the remembrance of the pleasure derived from the assimilation of it will always call forth the anticipation of pleasure as often as he feels want, and perceives an apple or represents it to himself by fancy. By *appetency* then, we understand *the original activity of instinct, which having* lost its direction by entering the sphere of *consciousness*, attempts to give itself a new one. Or appetency in man is the anticipation of a pleasure. I see for the first time a plate of beautiful grapes; their transparency, their pure juice swelling beneath the skin, attract the eye. As yet I have not tasted them, they may taste sweet, or bitter, or acid, for all is not gold that glitters; I cannot yet say that I shall like them, but I make the attempt, I taste and find them good, and from that moment I desire grapes whenever I see them.

What then is a *desire?*

Desire.

It is the positive direction which we have taken by means of appetency to an object or objects, which agree with our natural wants. Two things then are necessary for the origin of a desire; a *natural want* and an *object to remove it.* The want and this object must be brought together, and that which unites them is not instinct as such, but what we have called appetency. This appetency would be impossible without sensation; but sensation has here no reference to theoretical but to practical knowledge, for as soon as I see the *pear* a feeling of pleasure connects itself with my perception, and I already anticipate the enjoyment of eating it. And so likewise I examine it only with reference to its taste. Sensation and knowledge, therefore, enter into the service of the desires.

Desires are either *positive* or *negative.* The positive desires are those the objects of which agree with our nature, and thus produce the feeling of pleasure. The negative desires on the other hand, do not find what they seek, an object corresponding with our wants, and pleasure resulting from its union with ourselves; but the object positively desired, is discovered to be injurious or to produce an effect opposite to what we expected, and hence we abhor it whenever we again see it. No negative desire is possible without a *positive* one preceding it; for we must become acquainted with the nature of all things around us by our own experience, and though the sheep selects safely sugar from arsenic, man must either have eaten the latter himself, or have seen it used by others, before he will avoid it.

The difference between positive and negative desires will appear more distinctly if we inquire: What is to be understood by the *satisfaction* of desire? The satisfaction of a positive desire is the assimilation of its object with ourselves, making it part of our own existence, and receiving pleasure by doing so. I desire an apple which I see hanging on a branch perfectly ripe and pleasant to the sight; I pluck and eat it, and my desire is satisfied. It exists no longer for itself, but becomes flesh of my body and blood of my blood; it is converted into an accidence of myself. So it is with every thing else. The piece of sugar is desired by the child; its desire is half satisfied when it receives it, and fully when it eats it. The satisfaction of desire then consists in this; the want, the restlessness from which the desire arises, is removed, and the anticipation of pleasure realized at the expense of the object desired, for it is destroyed.—Our negative desires, on the other hand, are satisfied when the thing we dislike is kept away from us, consequently does not come in contact with us. The manner in which we keep it at a distance, may be effected by our turning away from it, by fleeing it, or if necessary by annihilating it. Again, *negative* desires and *abhorrence* differ. Every negative desire bases itself upon a positive one, and this upon a knowledge of the object; abhorrence, on the other hand, is the immediate expression of instinct, and does not rest on knowledge, but on a sensation, especially on that of smell or sight. The horse abhors carcasses; man, any thing unclean in his food.

A *demand*, on the other hand, differs from a positive desire, by basing itself upon a *right;* while a wish is a desire for something, which we either know to be out of our reach, or which we make no attempt to get into our power.

Every desire, however, is *transient;* for every satisfaction of desire is like the pressure of an elastic body that rises as soon as the hand is removed from it. Like the phœnix, which ever rises anew from its own ashes, or the liver of Prometheus, which grew as fast as the vultures ate it, so desire rises always anew from its satisfaction. The life, spent in the sphere of desire is, therefore, without true satisfaction, and man cannot remain within it. He wills something permanent, and passes over into the sphere of

Inclination.

If our desires cannot be permanently satisfied, and if they are changeable, constantly passing from one object to another,—our inclinations select a single object, fix themselves upon it, and instead of destroying it by assimilation, preserve it; for an *inclination* is the desire to *remain in constant and permanent connection with a certain object*, and to effect this, it must be carefully preserved. From this preliminary definition it may be seen that the difference between desire and inclination is not merely in degree, as some have asserted in saying that inclination is a desire to which we have become accustomed; the difference is one of quality; inclination is something else than desire. When under the influence of desire, we want the objects to yield to us, to pass over into ourselves, and become accidents of ourselves; when we have an inclination to an object we yield to it, bend towards it, and our aim is to remain in connection with it. It is not the repetition of a desire, therefore, that makes it an inclination so that the latter would be the former, having only become habitual. We cannot have an inclination, without having had a desire, and yet the difference remains one of quality or kind. If one desires to learn a mechanical business merely for the purpose of gaining a livelihood by it, he will not care for a particular one, but be satisfied with any; but an *inclination* will be bent upon some one, and no other, and whatever may oppose this inclination, it will remain the same. A mere desire to drink when we are thirsty differs not a little from an inclination for a *specific* wine.

No desire can therefore pass over at once into an inclination, and we all know that it is impossible for us to love a thing, merely because we desire to love it. That which renders a natural inclination *possible*, is an innate *propensity*. The wants of man, and his feeling of them, are permanent; appetency is the attempt to give these feelings a direction to certain objects, by which they may be removed. These objects are various, but only one is desired at a time, and it may be *one thing* or *another*. Man needs food and drink; what this food and drink may be, is indifferent in the sphere of desire; but propensity is the innate *tendency* of our wants and feelings to a *certain particular* object; it is the *adaptedness contained in the knowledge of an object, and in the feelings connected with this knowledge, to our capacity of desiring it*. This adaptedness or relation between our knowledge of an object and the desire for it is innate, and therefore precedes both in their reality, and exhibits itself at the moment that we for the first time perceive the object. How many ladies had Dante seen without being affected by them? But when he saw Beatrice, his heart was at once hers. So it was with Petrarch when he saw Laura. This propensity is so strong that no one can alter it, because it is something as subjective in man, as instinct is in animals; it is instinct modified by the influence of reason. Yet while none can change or extinguish it, every one is expected to govern it. And again, as no one can have an inclination for what he has no natural propensity, so he cannot avoid feeling an inclination, when a propensity exists in his bosom. Upon such a propensity talents and genius are based. Inclinations have, therefore, propensity for a medium. They presuppose desires, and are *impossible* without them; they must have an object; this object must be known, and with the knowledge of it a feeling of pleasure must be connected, as in desires.

How then is *inclination* to be *defined*? *When as often as we think of an object, we desire a connection with it, we have a propensity to it, which, indulged, will become an inclination.* We must not imagine, however, that as we have different inclinations, so we must have different propensities. Propensity is a general activity, which may *individualize* itself, and produce the most various inclinations, as one and the same reason takes the most different directions to the various objects of knowledge. I have a propensity to the past, to reflect on it, on historical facts; but here by virtue of this general propensity, I may incline to heraldry, to chronology, to the ethical portions of history, to criticism, &c. An inclination is either positive or negative. As positive, it is love of a thing, as negative, dislike.

The character of inclination is calm, it does not storm like desire, it is not vehement like passion, and yet it is full of warmth and life. When, however, this calmness is disturbed, when the objects of an inclination render man subject to themselves, their slave, the inclination loses its character, and becomes something more, it becomes,

Emotion.

"An emotion" according to Kames, "is an internal motion or agitation of the mind, which passes away without desire." This definition of emotion is not altogether accurate, for mind is itself an internal motion, it is an uninterrupted motion, and an emotion must be something different from the usual state of the mind. *Emotion is a disturbance of the quiet, peaceful, and otherwise uninterrupted motion of the mind.* From this definition it follows at once that the animal having no mind, cannot have emotions. Every emotion is a strong feeling, yet not every feeling is an emotion. The feelings of hunger and thirst, of fatigue or vigor, are no emotions; but feeling connected with a clear thought of their origin may be emotions. By the thought of its cause a feeling becomes united with consciousness, gains a hold upon the mind; and if this hold is so strong, that the person loses self-control, that, as Kames says, no desire, no determined direction can take place in him, that he becomes confused—then the feeling is an emotion. A man who is quietly walking alone in a beautiful grove, engaged in meditation, suddenly sees a rattle-snake before him; he clearly perceives his danger, and a feeling of displeasure connecting itself with his perception, he is so frightened that at first he is neither able to defend himself nor to run away. This is an emotion which deprives him of the command of his mind. Such an emotion may be compared to the disturbance of the quiet mirror of a lake when a stone is dropped into it. The waters seem in perfect rest, yet they are in motion. The stone disturbs their quietude, and small circles form themselves which constantly enlarge as they recede from the centre. Desires and inclinations have a determined direction to certain objects, but emotions have no direction at all. For instance a person highly insulted by another, feels wroth; he clenches his fist, his eyes roll—but he is at first unable to act; the offender meanwhile runs off and the angry man exclaims, "if I had him here now I would give him what he deserves." But we have not yet fully understood the nature of an emotion. We must see its origin and foundation. We have said that an emotion is a disturbance of the activities of mind: What are these activities? *Thinking*, *willing* and *feeling*. When these three activities are of equal strength and in harmony, or when thinking freely prevails, then the mind is active, but in no emotion; when *desire* prevails, the activity of the mind having a direction, is likewise not agitated, but when the thinking activity is impeded by that of feeling, when thinking becomes clouded by it—then we have an emotion. The possibility that "thinking may prevail in us, and be at the same time impeded by our feeling," has been called *excitability*. The greater this is in a person the more will he be under the influence of emotions. The correctness of this definition of emotion will appear too from the expressions we use, when we recover from an emotion. "I was overcome;" "I was unmanned;" "I was led away;" "I was not myself;" "I forgot myself;" &c. Animals, as was said above, cannot have emotions, because the ground of every emotion is *thinking*, connected with *strong feeling*. Yet we know that they express pain and joy, fear and hope. This only *seems* so however. Their pain and pleasure, proceeding from the measure of an external influence upon them, is of an entire bodily character, *disconnected with any thought*, and what seems to be fear or hope, is nothing but a confused and dark anticipation of which they can give no account to themselves, neither while they are agitated, nor afterwards. Their fear does not proceed from the thought of danger connected with strong feeling; but like the bird charmed by a snake, they have but an unknown dim feeling, not even amounting to anxiety. Emotions are likewise either negative or positive, as their nature harmonizes with that of the person. All positive emotions are *strengthening*, as joy, delight, hope; all negative ones are

26

weakening, or of a melting character, as grief, melancholy, &c.

We have said, a little above, that instinct loses its *direction* in man, and we have just stated that emotions are without direction; What then is the difference between instinct that has lost its direction, and emotions? Emotions are more intellectual than instinct after it enters into man, and again instinct gains a direction by appetency, while emotions pass away without taking any certain direction. Emotions, however, are transient like desires; and cannot be recalled. The joy I felt at the reception of glad tidings, when once gone, is gone for ever, as an emotion, and to pretend to have it again in all its liveliness and freshness would be sheer affectation. Emotions being transient, they can gain permanency only by connecting themselves with an inclination; but thus neither the inclination nor the emotion remain pure, they are mixed, and in this mixed state, they are

Passsion.

The difference between inclination and passion is not always kept up very distinctly, and the reason is, that they have the same contents. For as we have love of *honor* and of *property*, so we have ambition and avarice, which are passions, the objects of which are likewise honor and property. Again, every inclination may become a passion, either transient or permanent, and hence it demands much knowledge of human nature to distinguish between an *inclination* and a *passion*. They do not merely differ in degree, so that an inclination losing its proper measure would become passion; in this case it would be difficult to ascertain this *proper measure*. Passion has elements, which inclination has not, and the relation of passion to its object is wholly different from that of inclination to *its* object. What then are the elements of passion, that are not met with in inclination? Passion in general is a vehement, immovable, and persevering inclination, that has received into itself either a *strong emotion* or another *inclination* or a *desire*. A higher or lower degree merely, cannot make the same state of mind, at one time an inclination, and at another a passion, but the difference is produced by their entirely different nature. In passion, *thinking* and *feeling*, are wholly subordinate to desire; hence passions are blind. Every passion is at the same time *negative* and *positive*, a complete contradiction. Avarice is *positive* as a determined desire for money; *negative* as a constant depriving ourselves of the most necessary sustenance. So again with reference to the relation of passion to its object, it may be said, that *passion*, as its name indicates, is wholly under its control; that the object so reigns in it, as to exclude every other *inclination* or *desire*. A few examples may be given:

1. When an emotion enters into an inclination, it causes a transient passion. The father, for example, loves his son; this love is quiet and undisturbed. But the father hears of some danger which threatens his son; the thought of this danger connects itself with a strong feeling and becomes fear, and this emotion entering his paternal love, changes it into a passion, that will last as long as the fear continues, and will disappear with it. The more *excitable* a person is, and the more determined in his propensity and inclination to a certain object, the more easily passions of this sort will arise in his mind. A man loves property; this love is of a tranquil character, and he does not lose his equilibrium. But war breaks out; it renders property insecure—he is excitable, fear enters into his love and converts it into a transient passion. When the war is over and property becomes safe, the passion subsides.

2. Again; passions originate, when one inclination enters into another, and thus strengthening it, changes it into a passion. This passion will be permanent and always ready to break forth, as often as an emotion draws it out. A man, for instance, loves war and honor equally; here are two inclinations and if he observes that his reputation may be increased by his love of war, he will make this subservient to the other, and instead of love of honor, he will have ambition.

3. And finally, when a desire enters into an inclination, it likewise becomes a passion. The nature of desire and that of inclination is different. The desire wants the object to yield to us; in inclination the person bends towards

the object. Desire, to satisfy itself, destroys its object by assimilation, inclination is determined to preserve it. When desire and inclination enter into each other, they form a shocking contradiction, which is the essence of passion. To illustrate this, we will take once more the example of the ambitious man. He loves honor, and hence is ready to devote himself, all his skill, all his knowledge, all his power and even life to it; at the same time, he desires honor to yield to him, to be *his*, and longs for it merely for his own sake. If it were not *his* honor, he would not take any interest in it. On the one hand, then, he gives himself up to *honor*, considering it the highest good; on the other he desires honor to become a mere accident of himself.

In conclusion we would define passion thus: "*It is a strong, persevering, blind desire, that is either connected with a strong emotion or an inclination, and deprives man of self-control, chaining all his thinking and willing.*"

§ 2. RELATION OF DESIRES, INCLINATIONS, EMOTIONS, AND PASSIONS, TO THE WILL.

Acts of the will and those of desire resemble each other, and hence are not always distinguished in common life. And yet their difference is considerable. The motive of an action, prompted by desire, is always the *anticipation of pleasure*, be this pleasure sensual, intellectual, or rational. An action that proceeds purely from will, on the other hand, has for its motive, the knowledge and love of the divine law, and the feeling of regard for ourselves. With this feeling also, it is true, a pleasure is connected, but this pleasure is of a moral nature, depending on notions of right and duty. Acts of the will always have reference to rights; I may demand what I will; acts of desire do not regard them, but we frequently desire what we have no right to long for. Our natural desires, are therefore indifferent to right and duty, and consequently have in themselves no elements of moral goodness. Again: the soul of desire is lust, pleasure; being under its influence, we are under that of pleasure, and if our life is confined to the sphere of desire, it will know of nothing higher than *pleasure* or Eudaemonism. In this case our will does not determine itself by the idea of the divine law, nor by its own power, but it is determined by the notion of pleasure, and consequently it is not free, but under the dominion of something different from itself. It is true that man, while under the dominion of desire, may turn from one object to another, so that no one enchains him, yet it is the power of pleasure alone, that controls him, even when he is prudent, like Epicurus.

In inclinations, it is different, and man is even less free in them than in desires. For when we have once formed an inclination, it is a particular object, one out of many, that fastens us to itself, and claims our interest, care, and attention, above all others. We can, therefore, no longer turn away from it, and bend to another, as we please, but this object enchains us. Hence one inclination excludes those that cannot harmonize with it, and draws a circle around us, within which alone we can move with a certain degree of liberty. Our mere curiosity, for instance, finds every knowable object equally interesting; but when we feel a strong inclination to a particular science, it will limit our interest in other sciences, and though we may speak in an animated manner of them, yet they will attract us in proportion as they approach the one that is our favorite. But if in our inclinations we are not free, if in them we are determined by the power of their objects and the pleasure we take in them,—passion makes us wholly their slaves. They deprive us of all self-control; they do not permit any other inclinations to exist by their side, they are vehement and importunate desires, insisting with might on their satisfaction. They are like internal diseases, working secretly, absorbing and poisoning all the healthy portions of the will, and subjecting it wholly to their control.

Passions, unless their objects are of a noble character, run a dagger through the heart of will; destroying it in the most direct way. Man in the state of nature is the creature of passion. The highest good for man is *liberty*, civil or moral, external or internal; yet moral and internal liberty only renders civil liberty, or the independence of nations on each other, and that of citizens on the nations, and liberty of thought, valuable or desirable. Only when morally free, we may say with right, the will of man is his happiness. To preserve liberty, laws and duties and rights surround man. Now, that which most immediately destroys will is passion, because it disregards all duties and all rights. Take, for example, ambition; it is undoubtedly the desire of having others possess a good opinion of our characters. This desire is so great that it darkens our reason with regard to every thing else. It becomes the principle and motive of all actions, it subordinates all inclinations. The ambitious man does every thing because it will increase his reputation, and not because it is honorable in itself; the highest good he knows of, is his own honor. This, however, is certainly a slavish dependence on the object of our desire. The ambitious man needs the influence of others to spread his reputation. Hence, he becomes dependent on them externally, as he is on his desire for honor internally; for whatever does not promote it, can gain no hold on him. Every permanent passion is a suicide *committed by our will and our reason.* The influence of passion on our will being so great, we add a remark with regard to the different classes of passionate men. In this respect we may divide them all into three classes:

1. Some men are only at times overpowered by passions, but generally free from them. They possess fine talents, the power to acquire much and solid knowledge; they readily take an interest in all that deserves attention; for they are left free from those deep impressions which monopolize the interest of man. Their thinking is no less extensive, than energetic and deep, and so their feeling is both deep and expanded over many objects. They lay plans and execute them with perseverance and steadiness, for they are not drawn off by any sudden and powerful stimulus. They may be less inventive and ingenious, but they are clear, deep and thorough, and their minds are principally active in the form of pure reason. They are fond of speculation and philosophy, for this science must

be carried on without prejudices or predilections, without passions or emotions.

2. The second class comprising those who are passionate, whose passions however are transient. They have many inclinations, and being highly excitable, emotions will be easily called up, and through them their inclinations will become transient passions. These of course will affect their character. Their thinking and feeling will not be of equal strength, as regards their *extent* and *energy;* but they spread over a large field and thus weaken themselves. Taking an interest in every object brought before them, they persevere in nothing, but pass from one thing to another, knowing something of all, but not much of any thing. Their desire for knowledge is mere curiosity. They rarely ask for the principles of the arts or sciences; satisfied with a few facts they have no idea of a systematic life that pervades all sciences. Again: passionate men may take a deep interest for a time in the objects of their passions, but their interest continues only as long as their passion lives; while at the same time it is confined to the sphere of their passion. They take an interest in their native country, but not in the whole world. They prefer the *useful* to the *good*, and *right* and *dutiful.*

3. The third class of men are those who are governed by one strong and permanent passion. Their thinking is strong and energetic, but limited as to its extent; and so it is with their feeling. The limitation of these activities renders it possible to be more energetic and powerful within the limits in which they concentrate themselves, upon some few objects. Persons of this character are thorough in their knowledge. The envious man will be a close observer, the avaricious a good arithmetician. So it is with feeling. The proud man will not care for the sons of his neighbor, but the more deep will be his interest in his own. The man, whose passions are permanent, may appear externally cool, deliberate and free from deep emotions; for one great passion controls all his feelings and movements. The ambitious despot, for example, knows how to gain the confidence of all, while none is permitted to pry into his secrets, or to see his weak side.—To one of these three classes every man belongs, and to know man, we must

study the nature of the passions. The study of the poets, especially of Shakspeare, will be found very fertile.

Finally, we have yet to consider the relations of emotions to will. Emotions, while they continue, render desire impossible. This shows itself, when we have lost a friend by death, we lose all desire for food or drink. Emotions sometimes strengthen desire, but then emotion enters into desire and puts forth all its energy in the direction which the desire has taken. Again: it has been observed that some persons speak better than they write, while others write better than they speak: How is this to be explained? Emotions either strengthen or weaken our thinking; they strengthen it when thinking draws their power into itself and thus gains their assistance. It becomes then enthusiastic and thoughts flow more clearly, more rapidly and fully; the thought of that which causes the emotions, and the emotions become inseparable and aid each other. Persons, on whose thinking emotions have this effect, speak better, because they are more easily excited in public, than in their private study. When, however, the emotion so grows together with our thinking, that it wholly fills the latter, becomes its soul and does not suffer it to turn to any thing else, mental derangement may take place. This is the case when all our thinking and feeling has become *one grief;* when whatever we look upon, seems to be a mirror, reflecting only what agitates us, and when all seems to be gloomy and dark as ourselves. But emotions more generally weaken our thinking, and then we cannot speak as well as write. Our judgment becomes slow and our perceptions obscure. A young man appears for the first time in the pulpit; he desires to do well, but the feeling of danger arising from the possibility of failure, impedes his desire, unmans his judgment, and becoming embarassed he does not know where he is nor what he is doing. Or a person who has not often been in company, reluctantly enters it; in the course of conversation some witty or cutting remark is made which he keenly feels, but in his embarrassment cannot find a reply.

Lastly, emotions weaken our will; when we are wroth and act in this state, we do not determine ourselves by will but by the power of an unpleasant feeling. Our will is the slave of it and wholly determined by it. There is, of course, no physical necessity in the emotions to compel man to act in accordance with the impulse received from them. When the cloud, filled with electricity, strikes a house, it cannot do otherwise; but when a man filled with wrath strikes another, he might have refrained, he might have restrained himself. But in the latter case the question would be, What induced him to refrain from discharging his wrath, on his fellow man; Was it a sense of duty, or some selfish desire? We have seen then, that in the sphere of our natural will, there is no liberty to be found, and that consequently what is called so, is arbitrariness, but not freedom.

We shall now offer a few remarks on each of the above subjects in particular, yet so that we shall include inclination and passion in one chapter, as their objects are the same.

CHAPTER II.

§ 1. ON DESIRES.

Desires may be divided according to their objects. These are either *sensual*, or *sensual-intellectual*, or *rational;* and hence we have so many different classes of desires.

Sensual desires.

The term sensual does not include any reproach whatever, for it has here no reference to morality. Such a reference it can get only by our will in its relation to the divine, which is here wholly left out of view. These desires are called sensual, because their object becomes known to us by our senses; and because our knoweldge of them is sensuous. Yet it must not be thought, that any knowledge could exists without some reflection, or thought; we mean only to say, that sensation is the condition, without which no knowledge of the objects of sensual desires would be possible. The desires under consideration are numerous as their objects, which extend from inorganic nature, as minerals, waters, to the organic—vegetables of all kinds and animals. Whether an individual has many or few of them depends on his own constitution, and on the nature surrounding him. The latter is conditioned by the influences of the sun and moon, and climate in general. If the region in which a person lives, is productive, if it exhibits to his eyes a great *variety* of fruits and vegetables, his desires will be many : if the region is barren, or if its productions, though rich and plentiful, are limited in *their kinds*, the desires of its inhabitants cannot be various, though they may be vehement. No man can desire that of which he has no knowledge; he who has never seen an oyster, or a turtle, cannot long for one, and he who has never tasted southern fruits, as oranges, pine-apples, &c., will not feel a desire for them. As regards the constitution of man, it is, as we have seen in Anthropology, modified by various causes. Age affects it, and hence we desire in youth that to which we feel indifferent in manhood. Sexual difference likewise produces a difference in our sensual desires: woman has more delicate, more refined desires; those of man are more vehement and more coarse. And so the number and variety of our desires depend further on the race to which we belong, on the tribe, the nation, the age in which we live, on the family in which we are brought up. The Germans are fond of *sauerkraut;* the English of *roast beef;* the French of *bouillon;* the Italians of *maccaroni,* &c. So is each family a small whole in its own, separated from others by a family-spirit, expressing itself in peculiar views and feelings, customs and habits. Here also members of one family will have desires, which those of another have not. Some feel an aversion to milk, and whatever is made of it; others again desire it more than any other food.

Sensual—Intellectual Desires.

The object of these desires are those that may be perceived by our senses, but become objects of desire by *reflection.* Of this nature are all the objects of property. As sensual objects they are perceptible to the eye, but their character of *being property* is only known to the understanding. For that which renders them property, is the *law:* this cannot be seen with the eyes, and though signs and landmarks may separate our property from that of another, it is only by thinking, by acknowledging the invisible law, that we perceive and acknowledge property. The sign is there for the animal as well as man; but for the former it is a mere stone, a mere post; for unless we see that something is indicated by a thing, it is no sign for us. Again: *desires* are intellectual when objects are not desired so much on their own account, as on account of something else, when they are therefore considered as useful more than merely agreeable. So we become conscious of duration of time, and through it of that of life; we desire a long life because we desire the pleasures and enjoyments life grants us. Life is here desired on account of that which it offers. Should we be sick, the desire of life would induce us to desire the most unpleasant medicine, if we hoped to recover by taking it. So we may desire life for the sake of gathering property, or of acquiring reputation. The objects of sensual-intellectual desires are, therefore not only *agreeable,* but *useful.* But the useful is worth more than the agreeable; an illuminated saloon may be agreeable, but a machine is useful, and the latter stands higher. If the number of sensual desires, depends on many accidental circumstances, that of intellectual desire depends on the cultivation of the mind; and as the objects of intellectual desires stand higher or lower on the scale of intellect, we desire most those that stand nearest to ourselves.

There are some desires which, while the above are natural, are wholly unnatural. Persons whose systems are weakened and incapable of any longer serving the desires which they once enjoyed, still remember them, and from remembrance desire them again; or seeing others enjoy themselves, they desire their pleasures. This is the case with old voluptuaries especially, and with persons who have exhausted their nature by excessive indulgence. An alderman who was importuned by a beggar, when on his way to a dinner, said; " I would give you five guineas for your appetite."

Rational Desires.

Their objects are those which are not at all perceptible to the senses, and which consequently can only be perceived by thinking. Truth, for instance, is nothing *sensual:* the numbers written on the blackboard have a sensual existence, but we may rub them off at any time. The relation on the other hand, in which numbers stand to each other cannot be rubbed off, but remains for ever the same. The number *two* cannot be less nor more than two under any circumstances, and *two* added to *three* must always make *five*. This relation is the truth of numbers. But it is not visible to the eye, it is only accessible to the understanding. So it is with beauty. Not the marble, not the canvass and the colours, are beautiful—they may be agreeable;—it is thought alone that is beautiful when it appears in a sensible form. If we acknowledge beauty in nature, we must also acknowledge a spirit addressing us from all the productions of nature. The material by which beauty is expressed may be destroyed; languages die and become extinct; the marble crumbles in the course of time; colors grow pale; but beauty in its nature is eternal, and as such it is only an object to thought and reflection.

Now we desire truth, beauty, and goodness, but as soon as we enter these spheres, we have entered the sphere of pure will, and our desires must assume a moral relation. The nature of truth, of beauty, and honour is such that they cannot become *means;* they are the final end of all that is. If any one, for example, should desire honor merely because it is useful, and not because it is intrinsically desirable, he would, as soon as this was known of him, be denied honor by every one, for such a desire is dishonorable in itself. The honorable man, on the other hand, will sacrifice property and life to honor. The same is the case with beauty, speaking here of the beauty of art. It has the power to silence all desires, to raise us above sensual feeling, so much that it has for this reason at all times been considered an excellent means of cultivation. For when our desires are at rest we are left free to examine a thing; but when the object of our investigation excites desires by its sensual life, we seek less for its true nature, than for the use we may make of it. In all the beauties of art, sensual life, being absent, desires cannot be awakened by them. We may, however, desire beauty for its own sake, but not as means for any thing else. What then is the object of a rational desire? It is one that is likewise desired on its own account, that in our view of it cannot be lowered to become a *mere* means for something else, while at the same time it is confined to the sphere of natural desires. That which cannot become means again, and which is infinite in its nature, is always rational, and the object of a rational desire is *happiness.* The idea of happiness is that of an uninterrupted well-being. Man flees what is painful, and seeks what is pleasant; he is anxious to reduce the pain, without which no life has yet been found, to the smallest, and increase pleasure to the highest amount. The better he succeeds in affecting this, the more will he approach the ideal of happiness. All other desires have to serve that of happiness; all other ends will become subordinate to it; all his other desires will be governed by it, and brought into harmony with it. Wherein then does this happiness consist? It is an *uninterrupted* well-being: well-being is the feeling of pleasure; pleasure proceeds from the satisfaction of wants, for though pain is the opposite of pleasure, and cannot be sought for on its own account, it becomes by its removal, the source of pleasure. To satisfy wants we must have the means, and the idea of happiness includes them. Happiness then consists in the possibility of satisfying all our possible wants, and the desires arising from them. But there are many desires; they cannot all be satisfied at once; a man cannot eat and drink, read and speak at the same time. And again there are sensual and intellectual wants, and desires which frequently interfere with each other, so that if we indulge the former, we shall weaken the latter, and so the reverse. Hence prudence must compare one with the other, lest we should indulge the less valuable desire, and deprive ourselves of one that might have given more satisfaction. Yet, however prudent man may be with regard to the preference he gives one desire over the other, and with regard to the means which he may collect, and the object of which may be his study, he will, after all, not find what he seeks in his state of nature, for one thing alone remains permanent in him, his thirst for happiness, while all the rest is constantly changing. Dante, in his celebrated Convito, has shown this beautifully in the following passage. "The original desire that draws us to every thing is implanted in us by nature, and this is the desire to return to God as our fountain. And as the pilgrim who walks on an unknown path, considers every cottage which he perceives at a distance as the resting-place, and when he discovers that it is not, directs his hope onward to another, and thus from cottage to cottage, until at length he reaches the harbor;—so it is with the soul: as it enters the new, yet unknown path of this life, it directs its eye to the object of its highest good and every thing which it perceives to contain any good, it takes for it. And as its insight is at first imperfect, and has neither experience nor instruction, a little good seems great to it, and hence its desire is at first bent upon it. Thus we see little children vehemently desire an apple, and when they grow larger they desire a bird, and when still larger beautiful dress, and afterwards a horse, and then a wife, and then riches, and so on. The reason of this is that the soul does not find in any one of these things what it seeks for, and what it hopes to find elsewhere. And thus we may see that one wish always stands behind the other in the eye of the soul, like a pyramid which increases more and more, and spreads towards the basis, and the last ground and the basis of all wishes, is God. In truth, as one loses his way on a path here on earth, so the soul often loses its way on that path on which our wishes wander. * * * * As we see that he who walks in the right way, attains the end, and fulfils his wish, and comes to rest after his labors; but he who enters the wrong path never attains his object, and never comes to rest, so it happens also in life. The correct pilgrim comes to the end and to rest, but he that misses the path can never reach it; but with much disappointment of soul he will look with a longing eye into an empty distance."

Remarks.

1. Goethe, in his Faust, has represented the nature of *desire* in a most terrible manner. It is probably the only tragedy in which *desire*, as such, is the *pathos* of the hero. Faust would like to have the whole universe serve him; he desires every thing, and is satisfied with nothing. He is never under the influence of emotion or passsion: it is *desire* that destroys him.

2. In the sphere of desire we may discover *prudence;* but not *wisdom.* Epicurus was a prudent man, a man that would not inconsiderately indulge desires; he was a useful man, whatever Cicero, *de finibus bonorum,* may say against

him, for he taught that to be happy ourselves, we must assist others in becoming happy. Man needs man and cannot live without him, and knowing this, none should be selfish, but every one ought to live for others, that they again may live for him. This is certainly *prudent*. But happiness within this sphere of desires is not the highest end of man, and however prudently it may be planned, however prudently all means may be procured—there is an end higher still, and this is the salvation of the soul. This cannot be converted into a means; it is the final destination of man. And that man *is wise*, who endeavours to secure it to himself.

CHAPTER III.

INCLINATION AND PASSION.

The general character of all positive inclinations is that of love; it lives in all of them, and hence it is that most are named from it, as love of honor, love of life, self-love, love of fashion, &c. Love is *the entering* the nature and being of something else;—loving a thing we unite ourselves with it, without expecting it to yield to us. The character of love however, greatly differs. There is a *moral* love which may be demanded of us: we ought to love all our fellow beings, even our enemies. "Be like the cinnamon tree that pours fragrance on him who hews it down." There is a *religious* love, it is the love of God, and to God, it is mercy towards those that deserve no love, and it is the love kindled in our hearts by the Holy Spirit. And there is finally a *pathological* love, or natural love, which does not rest on principles of our will, but on a kind of sympathy between ourselves and its objects, on what has been called propensity. Its distant analogy may be found in the animal world at the time when the old attend to their young. Yet all consciousness being absent, it is but animal sympathy, instead of love, that we observe there. Hence it is that one generation of animals knows nothing of another, for they neither remember, nor love each other, after the young are once able to take care of themselves. No one would say either, however dependent his dog may be on him, that he is loved by him. Such doggish love would be worth little. All pathological or natural love, arises from a natural propensity to certain objects, and pre-supposes some resemblance between ourselves and them. In nature it is true that *unlike* poles attract each other, but they are nevertheless the poles of the same power, and have it in common with each other, and it is the power itself that thus divided, unites itself with itself by attraction. The objects of our love modify its character. They are either *ourselves*, or something *inanimate*, *things* and *objects* in nature, or they are our *fellow-men*. When its objects are inanimate we cannot properly speak of *love*, or if we do, we must use the word in a *limited* sense. It would be strange to say that we love a certain food or drink, or love a house, a garden, a golden chain, a ring: but in all these instances we would rather say we *like* such things. Only the *like* can enter into the nature of the *like*, the spiritual that of spirit, the sensual that of sensation; but inanimate things have nothing that resembles any thing in ourselves, and hence they cannot be *loved*, properly speaking. But we may love ourselves, and love our fellow-men. Yet the basis of all pathological love, is self-love, and no man ever lived that loved any thing different from himself, but self-love was the open or secret source of his interest. Christ alone was free from all self-love: he loved as none before, or after him; he loved the world sinful as it was, and loved it having no scheme in view for himself, free from every calculation in his own favor. His love, the prototype of all, was not chained to his self, but free and pure; he loved the world for its own sake. Our love, whatever be its object, rests always on our *self-love*, and we love every thing else because it *pleases us*, because it has something which we love in ourselves. Yet though all love commences in self-love, it is not necessary that the latter should remain the prevailing soul of the former, but it may become so strong and so pure, that self-love disappears. This shows itself especially when love becomes mutual, when it exists between two persons. This love like every other commences with self-love. We love a quality, a trait in the character of another, because it *pleases* us, because it corresponds with our idea of nobleness, or because it is agreeable to our feeling. The other loves himself as much as we love ourselves, and the approbation of others is desired as much by him as by us. He perceives our liking to one of his qualities, and though he should find nothing else in us, that could attract his attention, he will certainly like our liking to him, and thus his self-love will make him incline to us. But if our love could not leave the other, in whom we discovered a pleasant quality, indifferent, his love to our liking will certainly strengthen our inclination to him; now, however, its object will no longer be a *quality* in him, but his *love*, so that our love will love his love, or that love will love itself, that love will have itself as its contents. Thus self-love is merged in love; and love hovering over two like a genius of peace and harmony, so unites them, that though two in space and time, they will be one in spirit. There is a difference, for there are two; and yet there is none, for they are *one*. They do not love, the one something in the other, as his money, his beauty, his character; but each loves the love of the other; and love thus divided between two, resting in each, and being the same in both, only closes itself together with itself. It finds itself, and rejoicing in having found itself, it keeps together with itself. As the soul, according to Plato, was divided in two, before it entered the world, and now each half seeks the other, and as they will be delighted when they meet again, and are drawn towards each other by a mysterious feeling of their belonging to each other, so it is with love between two persons. Such love may commence in self-love, but where it blooms and lives, self-love dies away.

All inclinations either have reference to man in his relation to himself as an individual, or to him, as he is related to his fellow-men, and hence we have two general classes:

---

§ 1. INCLINATIONS ARISING FROM THE RELATION IN WHICH MAN STANDS TO HIMSELF.

Self-love.

Self love being the mother of all other inclinations, demands an attention above all others. Its object is the person himself that loves. It is the only love in which the subject that loves, and the object loved, are the same, for loving myself, it is I that love, and it is I that am loved. It includes a consciousness of our existence, and of every thing that can render it comfortable and pleasant. Arising from our natural tendency to preserve ourselves, we not only desire a continuation of our existence in the present life, but also after death, and not only rejoice in our preservation, but especially delight in every new mode of existence, in every developement of our powers. We love ourselves as we are, and love what we find in ourselves. Self-love is the mother of all other inclinations, because unless we take an interest in ourselves, it will be impossible to take it in any thing else. The relation, however, in which we stand to ourselves, will render it impossible for us, to be indifferent to ourselves; for there is no other object of which we can be so immediately conscious, and there is none of which we are conscious, that we can desire as much, as we desire a continuation of our existence. Every desire includes a knowledge of its object, which here is the subject that has the knowledge and the desire: but where knowledge and desire are so inseparable, that if we have the one, we must have the other, there must be a strong propensity, or such a possibility for the origin of an inclination, that the inclination will certainly be formed. Hence no man can help loving himself, for it is as natural to him as to breathe.

The object of self-love, it has been stated, is our self, and all it contains. Its contents are its existence, the continuation of this existence, life, and all that constitutes a part of ourselves.—We can, however, only love ourselves as *living* beings, and in proportion as we love ourselves we shall love our life. This we love because it is ours, and because we love ourselves. Love of life is therefore next in importance, for unless we live we cannot love.

Love of life.

The mere tendency to live, and continue life, we have in common with the animal: the worm when trodden upon writhes beneath the foot, as if it were unwilling to die;

the ox when struck with the axe of the butcher moans and rages as if he resisted with all his might the attempt to deprive him of his life. But no animal can love its life, for to love a thing, we must be conscious of it, and be able to desire it. Man may love his life; because he can render the idea of life objective to himself, he can in his thoughts separate life from himself, and say, "*my life.*" But we love life on account of its contents, and these are the joys and pleasures of life. Hence these become objects of our love. There are two ways in which we may enjoy ourselves in life:—life is activity; every activity that feels itself oscillates between *rest* and *labor;* the change from the one to the other is pleasant. It is pleasant to recreate one's self after labor, and it is pleasant to muscles and nerves to be active again after rest. A desire for rest without labor is *indolence,* and desire for constant employment becomes an inclination to enterprise, business, and may degenerate into restlessness. If the former by its power of sloth, drags us down to matter; the latter destroys the vigor of our system. But as rest becomes tedious, and activity exhausts, and consequently either by itself, becomes unpleasant, man will try to unite them moderately, so that neither one prevails above the other. This is the origin of diversion and amusements of every kind. For every play demands, on the one hand, some attention, some activity, yet one that does not fatigue, and on the other, it permits us to rest ourselves. Hence there is in children an inclination to play. But adults may likewise incline to games. The constantly changing and always attractive manner in which this kind of activity employs the mind, is highly fascinating, the skill we have an opportunity of exhibiting; the attraction offered to the imagination by chance that prevails in games, and by tempting a dark and concealed fortune, all of them render this kind of entertainment pleasant. So it is with hunting. The elements of this pleasure are manifold. All uncertainty is exciting; the uncertainty of success is therefore among the first; we half fear, and half hope; fear and hope mingling produce the emotion of anxiety, which is pleasant if hope prevails over fear. The next elements are, the exercise of skill and judgment in discovering the haunts of the game;

presence of mind in seizing the opportunity quickly, and with confidence when it offers itself. It is delightful too, to rest under the green boughs of trees, to move from place to place in pursuit of an object we much desire; the fragrance of woods is invigorating, and the observation of the life of animals is interesting. This inclination to hunting was greater during the middle ages, than it was among the ancients, or that is now. Among the ancients we find that the Egyptians, Indians, and all the Asiatic nations, considered animals sacred, and rather protected than destroyed them. Among the Greeks, too, certain animals were consecrated to certain gods, and were used in sacrifices. Yet Hercules and other heroes hunted them, especially those that were inimical to man. Hercules kills the Nemean lion, the Lernean serpent, &c. Inclinations to war, to adventures, and other tendencies of our nature, rest on the same principle.

Closely connected with our life, are the means by which we support it, and if we love the former we must take interest in the latter. Hence we form an inclination to *eating* and *drinking*, and to *society*. A good dinner in a good company has its attractions for every one. The union of sensual with intellectual enjoyments during meals, was highly cultivated by the Greeks; their *symposia* are well known. It seems that by satisfying our sensual wants, we are left more free, and alive to those of the mind. Food has certainly a soothing influence upon the mind, and it is for this reason, that while we eat and drink we forget past troubles and listen less to the cares that either harass us for the present or for the future. Hence it is too, that what is said during a meal, was thought by many nations to be spoken in confidence and sacred; and that certain nations, as the Arabians, will not injure their enemy after they have eaten with him. The citizens of Moskau, gave their empress when visiting her, bread and salt, and she accepting it, declared that all her apprehensions were gone. And in modern times we do not invite every one to eat and drink with us; but like to feel at liberty during our meals, to say what we please. Kant has very ingeniously pointed out the course good conversation should take during a meal. Every thing unpleasant to any one, absent or present, should be avoided, and it should pass from the mere *narration* of the novelties of the day, the contents of newspapers, to *arguing*. For in speaking of novelties and of the news of the day, different views will be expressed, and as every one thinks well of his own he will politely defend them. Conversation thus becomes more lively and will finally end in *jesting*. Much reasoning fatigues, especially towards the end of a festival, since eating makes one feel inclined to rest. Mirth, laughing and pleasant allusions are useful to digestion, &c. Inclination to *dancing*, smoking, and fashion, likewise proceed from our love of life and its enjoyments.

Our inclination to fashion concerns more the *form* of objects, than the objects themselves. It extends not only to dress, but to furniture, style of building, literature, art, and every thing else of which we make use. The inclination itself rests on an innate tendency to give form to whatever comes into our hands; we are *free* in giving this form, and not bound, like the spider or the bee, to a particular one for every object. Hence forms are changeable, and this changeableness of form is what is called *fashion*. Many object to it because it is changeable; but every product of man is perfectible, and man seeking constantly for the best form for dress and every thing else, and never finding the absolute best, changes it without interruption. Some form our dress, our furniture &c., must have: placing no value upon any particular one leaves us morally more free, than if we either adhere to an *old* fashion, because we consider it best, or are always anxious to be foremost in every one. Kant therefore says correctly, that there are fools *in* the fashion and *out* of it. It is weakness to speak against fashion. Since our dress needs some form, and which of the many possible forms this may be, is wholly *immaterial*. Fashion may become *useful;* for as it extends over the productions of the mind, there are times when certain institutions, the study of certain languages and sciences become fashionable, when we feel inclined to imitate what is good in other nations.

The inclination to smoking seems wholly unnatural. It was unknown until the discovery of America, and thence spread over all Europe. It is an *ethereal eating*, soothing and passing time. Though unnatural, it no doubt had a very simple origin. Some think that the Indians who kindled fire with a great deal of trouble, tried to preserve it, by placing coals in the stem of a plant, and by putting this plant into the mouth whenever it became inconvenient to carry it in the hand. Others are of opinion that the Indians, in order to protect themselves from musketoes, made smoke around themselves, and at first putting smoking plants into their mouths for convenience sake, they become fond of them and so formed by degrees a habit of using them.

So is our inclination to dancing natural in its origin. The emotions of savages are few in number, but strong and vehement in energy. They became sometimes so agitated that they must open a vein to obtain relief. Generally, joyful occurrences cause them to jump and run about, and in these irregular motions, those which we call dancing and which keep time and rhythm, originated. Dancing is, therefore, the external representation of our internal emotions by the motions of the body. So soldiers have different marches for every military motion, and these marches accompanied by music have their effects upon them. In Liefland, the reapers in harvest keep time with music. With us, however, dancing does not proceed from an emotion, but we dance to excite one. The savage jumping about needs no music: he sings and claps his hands; that is enough for him; we must have music the melodies of which will inspire us and dispose us to dancing.

Manifold indeed are the inclinations that may arise from the natural tendencies of our nature, all of which have reference to man as an individual being. We have desire for knowledge; when this desire is satisfied by any one, when we observe his willingness and zeal to aid us, we love him, and this love is that of the scholar to the teacher. We have a desire for health; if we are sick and recover through the aid of a skillful physician, we again cannot but feel attached to him. And so it is with the *ward*, who unable to defend his own rights, will, as he becomes conscious of their value, strongly incline to his careful, attentive, and disinterested guardian. We shall now consider self-love in its negative form, in which it is

Self-hatred.

By hatred in general, we understand here a constant dislike to whatever could interfere with our self-love. The object of this hatred may either be something *external*, or the *person* who hates himself so that he is himself the object of his own displeasure. Hating himself, man desires to direct his thoughts away from himself; filled by the highest displeasure, he would forget himself. Self-hatred seems wholly unnatural, and the question is, What is its origin? *Nothing but self-love.* This is paradoxical. Self-love seems to be the principle of self-hatred, and this certainly is no better than to say: a man hates himself because he loves himself. The object of self-hatred is man himself, yet not the whole of man, but some one of his qualities, closely and inseparately interwoven with his whole character and being. Man loves himself and would like to be as perfect in every respect as possible. The interest he takes in himself induces him to sketch an ideal of what he ought to be: he then compares himself as he is, with this ideal, and finding that he is not by any means like it, he receives pain from the result of this comparison. Instead of making a resolute attempt to improve his character, his will seems diseased and is inactive, and the displeasure mingling with his feelings of self-love, he avoids thinking of himself and hates himself. Thus *self-hatred* originates only in self-love. When in addition to this, man becomes weary of life, either because he has spent his physical powers in the excessive indulgence of sensual pleasures and hates their constant and monotonous repetition, or because he has suffered misfortunes without sufficient firmness to support himself properly under them—then it is possible he will commit suicide. And in the commission of it we may see that man hates himself because he loves himself. For what can be the reason, for which he should desire to make an end to his own life? Either he must desire to withdraw himself from an activity to which he would have to attend in order to live as is the case with many persons who have lost property or honour, or to free himself from suffering like Mirabeau or Clavier, or to obtain an imagined happiness like the Indian philosopher Calamus. In all these instances however, we must say that if the self-murderer did not love himself, he could not care for life or death, but taking interest in himself, he kills himself to be free from something that is painful to him, or obtain that which he much desires. With some flattering hope the self-murderer embraces death. The correctness of these remarks are corroborated by the fact, that persons who are particularly concerned for their life and its preservation, very often have an irresistible tendency to commit suicide. This has been observed by Gall. Suicide committed in such an instance, is certainly the fruit of an irregular self-love.—Nothing leads, however, more quickly to the aversion to life than inactivity. When a gradual transition from rest to labor is wanting, time is stript of interest and we fell oppressed with its tediousness. The mind hates emptiness, it feels a horror, a void: it desires to fill its life with deeds and actions. Hence many, as has been remarked, hang themselves, because time rests too hard on them.

Aversion is the negative, not of self-love as such, but of a modification of it. When we do not love our *self* as a whole so much as one of its qualities, say personal beauty, or art, science, or anything that belongs to it, then our inclination should be called "*love of our qualities, or of that which is ours and not self-love.*" This love of what is our own, is principally found among children, who love their *hand* or their *eye*, or something belonging to themselves, but cannot yet form a notion of themselves as a whole. It is met with among women, and characterizes some nations as the Athenians of ancient, and the French in modern times. In proportion as we love every thing belonging to ourselves, we feel an aversion to all that may interfere with it. I love, for example, health, and as soon as I hear of a prevailing disease I feel a strong aversion to it; I love wealth and hate to see poverty wrapped in rags: we love truth and in proportion as we feel inclined to it, we shun ignorance. Here, likewise, suicide may be committed. The honor of a person is not the person; yet it is a high quality of his character, and he loves it more than himself. If honor is wounded, and he despairs of recovering it, he kills himself. So a lady loves her beauty; she is seized with the small-pox; her face is covered with marks and she is ready to die.

Self-love as a Passion.

Self-love as a passion, is *selfishness*, and originates when a desire enters our self-love. The desire is that every thing shall serve us, and exist only for us to the exclusion of every one else. Every desire the end of which does not lie out of the sphere of him who desires, is selfish; and when such a desire enters into an inclination, it converts the latter into a passion. Passion renders the origin of other inclinations, if not impossible at least difficult; hence the selfish man cannot take interest in any thing unless it has some reference to himself. The man who loves himself may love others, but the selfish man is incapable of loving from disinterested motives. Truth and beauty have value for him as far as they are useful to him; if he cannot see their immediate use, they leave him indifferent. The selfish man expects the devotion of all, he expects every one to be active for him; but feels little inclined to do any thing for others. If he is disappointed in his expectation he feels unhappy. He is incapable of forming friendship because he can only take interest in himself. He will break any connection if it comes in collision with his interest. Selfishness either concerns our whole self or only parts of it. When the latter is the case, passions arise, when a desire draws itself into an inclination, which we have formed to something, belonging to ourselves, to an attribute of our character, to skill in art or knowledge, science, &c. I love a science because by labour and application, I have acquired considerable knowledge in it and have made it my own. Now I desire that every one else shall love it as I do, and if I discover that it is not generally favored, I become passionate. Or I am strongly inclined to some practical object which I have in view; I desire the assistance and interest of every one, and try to gain it by all means and ways. My inclination will thus become a passion, and force me to sacrifice rest and frequently honor to it. For to gain the interests of others, I shall if my inclination has become passion, accomodate myself to every one, agree with every one's views and nowhere show my own in opposition to those of others.

Another form of selfishness is *passion for enjoyment.* When our inclination to pleasure is pervaded by the desire for every thing that may serve it, when this desire makes us hunt for pleasures, then our inclination is a passion. As such, it renders all other inclinations subordinate to itself, and takes interest in nothing unless it can be eaten or drunk, or made in some way subservient to our pleasures. Works of art and literature, sciences and all intellectual productions, have worth only when they can be enjoyed by way of a refined pleasure. This passion exhibits itself also thus. When we love life and are willing to labor in order to enjoy it, our love is an inclination. But when we desire enjoyments independent of labor, when we desire to enjoy what others have gained by their labor, or when we desire others to labor that we may enjoy the fruits of their labors, then our inclination to life and its enjoyments is a passion.

There is, finally, a *theoretical* egotism or selfishness which we will merely mention here. It is that egotism, which has either laid down certain rules and maxims for practical pursuits and for intercourse with men, all of whom it considers selfish and under the influence of the same selfish rules which it has adopted, and on the execution of which it insists with a singular perseverance. Or it is egotism in theory, science, which considers its judgments and views and hypotheses to be infallible, and expects all others to yield to them.

Self-love as passion in its negative form.

Here it is self-hatred, as represented above, that becomes a terrible passion, in which man constantly tortures and vexes himself; for he is not satisfied either with himself or with any thing in himself, and this passion may be compared to the bodily disease called epilepsy. In this disease every nerve touches and wounds the other, and every muscle affects the other with pain; the whole body seems to be in conflict with *itself,* and seems to be determined to ruin itself by its own remaining strength. The individual is sick through his own nerves and muscles; nerves and muscles are not attacked from without, but they afflict each other mutually. So it is with self-hatred when it is kindled into a *passion*. The dissatisfaction of man with himself is a permanent one and he cannot think of himself without the greatest pain. He consumes his life in bitterness, for in all he does and undertakes, he will perceive frailties, and these will so attract his attention that he cannot see the good mingled with them. If he could do the latter, he would mend what is imperfect and go joyfully from one degree of improvement to another. The artist while he finishes a work, may notice its frailties, but having finished it, he has improved himself and commences a new work with a determination to execute it, as much more skillfully as his own power has been raised, and so he advances himself by every work and with himself all his productions. The man dissatisfied with himself finds all his thoughts constantly drawn to his frailties and weaknesses, and cannot turn them away from them. It seems as if every possible pleasure in life or that man could take in himself was suddenly suppressed, because the higher idea which man has of himself, and of genuine pleasure cannot enter on such pleasures as being beneath it. This discord like an electric spark passes through every feeling of pleasure that man might derive from his productions or life, or any thing that life offers. For once at war with himself he is so with every thing else, and finds fault with whatever comes from the hand of man. Every thing human is imperfect; but it has likewise something good; the man dissatisfied with himself and the world, will every where see only the faults and not the beauties. He is morose, and as the proverb says, finds fault with the fly crawling on the wall. There is no innocent pleasure, no work, no science in which he does not find something to censure.

And finally, our aversion to life may become a passion and then it may be called *ill humor*. In it man desires every thing, and is satisfied with nothing. No joy and no hope, no knowledge and no skill is equal to his anticipations. Dissatisfaction alone is permanent, but its objects are in a constant flow. This *ill humor* differs widely from the humor of the poet. He is likewise conscious of the infinite and great, and of the deficiencies of every human work and pursuit. But instead of finding fault with these deficiencies and becoming morose, the poet by his power of language represents the contrasts between the infinite and the trifling anxiety, and solicitude expressed by man for the finite and the stress laid on little things, and thus renders the trifling cares of man ridiculous, yet without bitterness or satire. He uses the infinite as a mirror, and making the pursuits of man reflect themselves in it, he effects all he desires.

§ 2. INCLINATIONS ARISING FROM THE RELATION OF MAN TO HIS FELLOW-MEN.

Love of property.

The notion of property pre-supposes a relation of men to each other, in which they are united at least for the purpose of protecting each other and what they possess. In this relation every one must have something, a bow or a net, a staff or a herd of cattle. Separated from all the rest, isolated like Robinson Crusoe on a distant island, a man could not have property, for though the whole island might be his by the law of taking first possession, there would be no law to protect him in his property. Only when many are united so that one has a property from the possession and use of which every one else is excluded, we speak of property and not until then. If love of property is impossible without a relation of the possession to other men, it is impossible likewise without a notion of property and its value. There are animals that in collecting a small provision for the inclement seasons seem to have an idea of *time* as something future, for they lay up for future wants, and of *property*, for they attempt to defend it when it is attacked. So the bees guard their honey, cows on the

Alps of Switzerland seize certain objects, and defend them vehemently from others. The German rat gathers in a great quantity of wheat, and many poor persons seek its holes and take the fruits of its labors. Yet no one would seriously say that animals truly have property, or else man would steal, as often as he makes use of their provisions without their permission. They have no idea of property nor of time, and they defend what they instinctively gather from an impulse of their nature and not from a feeling of *right*. The *idea* of property is therefore necessary, to form an inclination to it. Where it is wanting there is no inclination. Children of rich parents, may have a great deal of property, yet they have no idea of it. They know not the value of wealth and hence do not care for it. If their parents are dead we place them under the care of guardians, when they grow and become of age, they generally form a strong inclination to property, for they have then become conscious of its value. As an inclination to property is impossible without an idea of it, so we must have an idea of time, and its duration; for property is to be permanent, to endure in time. The apple when eaten, is no longer the property of any one; but the tree, from which it was plucked will bear apples again. The child, however, will give the whole tree for a single apple.

The love of property pre-supposes therefore *an object, from the possession and use of which every one else is excluded, a notion of time and the value of property as a means of support in all time.* The less persons are accustomed to look ahead, the less strong will be their love of property. Savages have no clear idea of time in its three great divisions, the past, the present, and future; their social life is not well-regulated, and their love of property is consequently weak. They live by fishing, and the chase, and their unerring shafts easily make the wild bird or the stag their property. But such property is of no duration; the bow and the arrows, the net and the trap are the only permanent property of savages. The momentary want demands their labor, but the want being satisfied they do not trouble themselves any further. The property of Nomades stands on somewhat higher ground. Their social life is more close and settled, and their notion of time is more accurate. Living on the milk of animals, they must raise and protect them. Yet their property is still movable, like that of savages. Cain kills Abel; the farmer supplants the wandering herdsman. Where agriculture prevails, the notion of time becomes strong and clear, for the farmer depends on seasons. Farms cannot be moved; the object of property is therefore permanent. But while thus the character of property becomes permanent and immovable, it is not wholly adapted to the changeableness of time and to *our own* mutability. The farm, the house, the garden, will always remain on the same spot, though we may desire to change our residence. Now it might be that two, either of whom would desire the property of the other, might make an exchange. Such instances would, however, be rare. It will be more frequently the case that, one anxious to relinquish his estate for the purpose of seeking another residence, might find one willing to *sell* his, but not to *exchange* it, and then a medium would be required, by which to represent the respective value of each property. This representative of property is found even among savages, and consists principally in some thing rare, as rare feathers, shells, or birds. In the Old Testament, however, money is mentioned. It is the representative among all civilized nations, and the question is; What is the reason that gold and silver are used for this purpose?

The hypotheses on this subject are different, as they take into consideration one or the other quality of property. One of its qualities is that it must have been gained by labor. The apple I eat, plucking it from the tree of another, is not mine in the sense in which I call the fruit of that tree mine, which I have grafted, and upon which I have bestowed much care. Hence they say that silver and gold, and the precious metals are only to be brought forth from the bowels of the earth by much labor, and for this reason they are well qualified to represent property, for it must also have been earned by diligence, if not directly by our own, by that of those from whom we inherited it. They are *rare* too, not very abundant, and consequently their value will place a proper estimate on property in general. Yet property may be gained without labor; a thing belonging to no one becomes mine by my mere will to take possession of it, for *res nullius cedit primo occupanti.* Others, therefore, have directed their attention to the use to be made of property, and said, the representative of property ought to be something which cannot itself be used for any thing else. The design of property is, *to be used;* if that which represents it, can be used, then it becomes a part of property, and not its mere representative. It might effect exchanges, but not sales. Yet we have innumerable articles made of gold and silver, and this hypothesis is not therefore fully correct. Hence we must keep a different quality of property in view, and this is its *permanency* and *duration.* Of all bodies the precious metals are the most durable; gold and silver retain their nature in all the changes they may have to undergo; lead, iron, and copper are destructible. Again; precious metals cannot be imitated, and if mixed with inferior substances, it is easy to detect it. It is remarkable that many persons love its representative more than property itself; they prefer money to that, the value of which it represents. The reason perhaps is, that money is more movable, that it is the same every where.

The elements of the pleasure we take in the possession of property are many, and among them are the following: Property in general, the possession of earthly objects, increases the feelings of our existence; for what we possess attaches itself to us. Hence the possession of property gives us a feeling of greater importance, influence, and security. Again: all property is to serve as means, either for the satisfaction of *bodily,* or *intellectual,* or *moral* wants and activities, and if the satisfaction of these wants is pleasant, the possession of the means must be so. Property secures to us a certain degree of independence. It is pleasant to be able to follow out and execute one's own plans. But to do this demands property. In proportion as any one has wealth, he will feel inclined to think that he can do what he wills, and this again is pleasant. Some love the *acquisition* of property, more than property. Activity is pleasant in itself and is the soul of life; if the activity which we employ for something that we may call our own is successful, it may become the object of our inclination. And as the acquisition, so the *preservation* of property may be the object of an inclination, which may be called *economy*. Property has reference to the future, and every one who is wise will be impressed with the necessity of preserving the means of support after they have once been acquired, and of maintaining the balance between one's income and expenses, lest the fruits of labor be overbalanced by the pleasures of enjoyments. This inclination is found in all classes of men, yet the higher classes are much more frequently inclined to spend freely. Artists, poets, and persons of the same or similar employments are frequently poor. Socrates had little or nothing; Luther died, leaving his estate involved in debt; Melancthon knew not how to preserve what he earned, or what was presented to him, and Calvin left nothing of note. Nevertheless the inclination to the preservation of property is a useful one, and if exercised in the proper spirit is a virtue.

Love of property as a passion.

All property is to be considered as means for some end, it is to be used, to be consumed, for it has no value whatever, unless it is employed. But when one's love to property has degenerated into a passion, our relation to it has been changed, and while before we considered it *means*, we now regard it as the *end* of all our activity and of our life. It is generally said that *too great inclination* to property or a *desire for too great an amount* becomes a passion; but both definitions are wrong. My inclination to property may be very great, and I still may feel at liberty to use it for my bodily support, for my pleasures, or the promotion of benevolent objects, and as long as I can do so, I am not under the dominion of a passion. And again it is wrong to say that where a *too large amount* is desired, we have yielded to a passion. For what is *much* or *little* in the scale of wealth? We call him well off who has as much as he needs. But the rational man needs not much to live on, for nature is satisfied with little,—*Natura paucis contenta;* yet another needs an amount which some would call much. The ideas of riches are, therefore, relative, and from them we cannot derive a definition of *avarice* or *cov-*

etousness. It cannot be the *object* of an inclination either that converts it into a passion; it remains the same, though its quantity should be greater or less. Nor can it be the *idea* we form of this object; for this may be infinite as the object itself, and still not force us to form a passion for it. When a man would rather lose his life than his property, when he would rather starve himself and his family, than use his money as means, when consequently his property is his idol for which he labors and lives, when he is no longer free but the slave of his idol, then instead of an inclination to property he has a passion for it. The relation of the person to his property has been changed; the difference between this inclination and its corresponding passions is *one relating to quality* and not merely *one to quantity.* Passions pervert what is originally correct. What is means becomes an end, and what ought to be the end becomes means. Money becomes the end, and the persons the means for its acquisition and preservation. It is not *he* that *has* the money, but the money has him. Money is the substance and being of his life, he is its accidence. This appears clearly from the manner, in which the man whose idol is money, treats himself and all others. He that has nothing is *worth* nothing in his view; *property* and not *personality* makes with him the man! When he holds intercourse with men, his motive is the anticipation of some benefit or advantage which he may derive from such an intercourse. If he cannot gain *something*, he will not seek the society of any one. Again, he frets himself in the same way. If he loses what he possesses, his joys are gone, and life being stripped of its highest good for him, he kills himself.

Love of property, as a passion, presents itself under two different forms, for we either delight in the acquisition of property, and then it is *covetousness* or *self-interest;* or we delight in its preservation and then it is *avarice.*

1. *Covetousness* is the passion that desires constantly to add to the stock we already have. The covetous man knows of but one good,—property, or money—he therefore indulges not any other passion that might interfere with this. He desires an *infinite* increase of his wealth, and yet knows of no end, for which to use it. He does not

care very particularly how he obtains his possessions if he has only a legal title to them. "He removes landmarks, seizes every thing his debtor has, lest he should lose interest, demands the reward before he assists the sufferer, and will rather see the corpse of the stranger exposed by the way-side than bury it without being certain of his fee." It is not necessary, however, that the covetous man cheat, and make use of immoral means to obtain his possession. He may be the prudent, cool, calculating arithmetician who well knows that *honesty* is the best means of attaining his grand object. The covetous is always the self-interested. For in all he does, says, and undertakes, he has only his own advantage in view; and nothing else can move him to do any thing.

2. *Avarice* has for its objects the preservation of its property. The avaricious, mistaking its true value, will not suffer himself to use it for any purpose, not even for the necessaries of life. The miser who stumbled against a stone and hurt his toe, exclaimed, "it was well that I had not on my shoe, or else I should have torn it." "The avaricious man denies himself every pleasure, lest he should receive detriment in that which is so dear to him. He knows of no greater happiness than to count his guineas again and again. He conceals them with the most anxious care, and returns alarmed to see if he has left the slightest clew that might lead to the discovery of his heart's treasures. The English millionaire dressed in the rags of a beggar, and on a famished horse travels from province to province in search of his idol; he feeds his horse upon hedges, dips his hard bread in water and returns with a full purse, concealing the guineas thus gained in the torn hangings of a distant room, where his son-in-law, to whom he had given his daughter empty-handed, after much seeking finds them." This is the true character of the avaricious man. Yet he must live, he must eat and drink, and must spend something; but he will try to get every thing for the lowest price and of the cheapest kind. He is cold and hard as the metal that he loves, selfish in the highest degree, unwilling to give or lend, or assist in any way; hence he is hated by all, loved by none.—The conditions required for the origin of covetousness or avarice, may be

the idea a person entertains of the influence which wealth gives, and its power to grant access to gratifications of every kind; an avaricious man of this character will be anxious to have the full extent of his wealth known. Or the idea of the usefulness of money is lost, especially when no other desire keeps it alive, and the avaricious man *loves* money for its own sake and finds his sole pleasure in hoarding it. Such a one will wish to appear poor to the world. Others fear poverty in the midst of plenty, like the Duke of Buckingham, who though possessed of immense wealth, feared he would die poor as a church mouse.

Prodigality is the opposite of *avarice*. The prodigal spends what he has without thought of the future. His desire is to live and enjoy life. "He loses self-control and stability of character, and is influenced in all his resolutions by the allurements of sensuality. He purchases what is offered and pays double interest to get the money. Every whim that strikes his fancy is indulged, and every duty neglected; while his family is suffering from want, he feasts his associates in pleasure. He very generously pays those who assist him in the execution of his wishes, but leaves his faithful servants who labor for his real benefit, unrewarded. Louis XV., of France, spent 2,000,000 of francs a week on his profligacy, and suffered his most faithful officers to starve. The spendthrift makes presents when he cannot redeem his notes. He must come to a miserable end, for his expenses are sufficient to swallow up the greatest fortune. He will then drown his cares in increased dissipation, in gambling and drinking, and finally terminate his career by suicide." The spendthrift may be amiable, the miser is always detestable; the spendthrift loves society and shares his pleasures with others, the avaricious loves none but himself. He is *proud* and haughty to those who ask his assistance, *hard* to his nearest relatives who depend on him; and prepared to encounter even contempt if he can gain by it. The object of the *covetous* man may be enjoyment and a splendid style of living, but he is ever careful lest he should injure his estate by his expenditures, and makes every effort to increase his wealth at the same time that he appears to spend it freely. It is said in the Bible that it is more difficult for a rich man to enter the kingdom of God, than for a camel to go through the eye of a needle. The question here offers itself; Why is this so? Is there any thing in property itself that renders it impossible to preserve purity of heart or to become a christian? This cannot be, for the Bible admonishes us to gather property, by saying: "Let him that stole, steal no more, but rather let him labor, working with his hands the thing which is good, *that he may have to give to him that needeth.*" It is said by some, that riches expose to many temptations, that they fill man with too great a love of earth, &c.;—but poverty and want are no less trying and tempting, for if riches may lead to pride, haughtiness, vanity and sensual pleasures, poverty may lead to flattery, falsehood, fraud, theft and murder. The possession of property is necessary, and the greater or less amount is here of no consequence. And yet the Bible declares riches a great obstacle in the way of our salvation. It is not riches but the *value* we place upon them, that causes this difficulty. When we consider it as the highest good, when our desire for it makes us forget our duties to God and man, when we are covetous and avaricious, then it is more difficult for us to enter the kingdom of heaven than for a camel to go through the eye of a needle. And to be rich in this sense, it is not necessary that we should have great possessions; the man who has but a cottage may value wealth as much as he who possesses millions; he may be tortured day and night by his thirst for wealth. Again: covetousness and avarice destroy all morality. As passions they regard nothing that is in their way; but every impediment only serves to increase their energy and power and makes them more violent. The avaricious man expects to become rich without God, and does not hesitate to use any means that may lead to his favorite object. Not faithful to his God, he cannot be expected to be so to his fellow-men. His honor is to gain his object by craftiness, his happiness to increase his wealth. And from the abundance of his heart, his mouth speaks. What does not bring him gold is unworthy of his attention. He will violate his duty to parents and children, friends and benefactors if it comes in contact with his passion; nothing is too sacred to be sacrificed to money, even his honor has a price. No pledge is inviolable to him, no contract will he keep unless forced by law or self-interest; he will betray his friend as Judas betrayed the Savior. Thus he sunders the nerve of human society, poisons the fountains of social life, destroys confidence and good faith, and substitutes in their place suspicion and distrust.

But there is another characteristic of covetousness and avarice to be considered. It is *cold* and *deliberate*, and unlike other passions, increases with age. The lower the flame of life burns, the weaker the fire of imagination grows, the stronger and more exclusive it becomes. With great care the avaricious man extinguishes all *nobler* emotions, lest they should lead him off from the great object of his desires, lest a kindly feeling should in a moment of weakness cause him to overlook his advantage and to commit an inconsiderate action, as he would call it. With age the ardor of our feelings decreases, and avarice that had before to contend with them, increases in proportion as our understanding becomes more cool, more calculating. With most other passions this is the opposite; Dante, in his Divina Comedia, meets the avaricious in the seventh circle of hell, and represents them as having a purse hanging around the neck, on which they look with childish delight.

The idea of property itself leads to great selfishness, for property is exclusive; and if instead of endeavoring to ennoble ourselves, we yield to low passions, riches must become a teeming source of selfishness. The correct view on the subject before us is that all property takes its rise in the will of God; for the earth and all that it contains, is his. Before the fall there was no *mine* and *thine*, but all was common to those that could use it. With the fall selfishness rose in man, absorbing by its bitter root all healthful juice. Now, each sought for the centre of his existence in himself, and forgetting the common origin of all, he no longer recognized a brother in a fellow-man, but saw in him a stranger. In this selfishness man grasped after all around him: without an intervening law the stronger of our race would have deprived the weaker ones of the most necessary means of sustenance. But God, from eternal love, appointed the right of property, lest men fighting for possessions destroy each other. Now, every right imposes a duty, and the enjoyment of all rights depends on the fulfillment of our duties; so that one can preserve his property only by abstaining from that of others. It was for this purpose that God permitted men to divide the earth and its productions, that those who in their sinfulness were inclined to say; "*all* is mine!" might learn to say, "these *things are not mine!* from them I must abstain, however great my desire to possess them." Property was intended not to *strengthen* our selfishness, but to *bridle* it, to break and subdue our selfish will. As rich and poor must live together, a great variety of duties of love and kindness, originate in their mutual relation, which only become possible by the possession of property. But the avaricious man perverts all this, and makes wealth the source of rude, resistless selfishness: of quarrels and law-suits, of enmity and hatred.

It may be well to remark, in conclusion, that the term *riches* does not refer solely to that property, the representative of which is money, but to every thing, science, honor, skill, or whatever it may be, in the possession of which man feels himself rich, and which he desires as the highest good. The objects of our riches may be different, the power exercised over us by them will be the same. Is honor the object of our passion? the tie that fastens us to earth, and draws us away from God, is *ambition*. Is the object beauty? the tie is *vanity;* is it *knowledge?* the tie is literary fame. In each of them we are fettered by sin, for truth alone, that comes from Christ, can make us free. Taking the term *avarice* in this extensive sense, it may be justly said, that it is the root of all evil. Christ demands our *whole* affection, and whatever we love on earth must have a reference to his kingdom, and we must love it only because of this its relation. No *rich* man, none that feels rich in any thing out of Christ, can therefore enter the kingdom of heaven.

Love of Honor.

Personal honor was as little known among the ancients as personal liberty. The honor and liberty of the nation was that of each individual citizen, and Cato living wholly in the thought of national liberty, kills himself, when he considers it lost, because he knows of none belonging to himself, as an individual. "In the Iliad it is the wrath of Achilles, which is the moving principle on which all the rest becomes dependent, but it is not what we in modern times understand by honor. The offence felt by Achilles does not concern his honor, but he is grieved because Agamemnon has taken away his portion of the spoils, his γέρας an honorary reward for his bravery. The violation concerns something *real*, a gift, into which it is true some preference, some acknowledgment of bravery and glory is placed; and Achilles is enraged, because Agamemnon meets him in an unworthy manner, and declares that he will not regard him among the Greeks—yet the true feeling of honor is no where perceptible in Achilles. This appears too from the fact, that he is fully satisfied, when he receives back the portion, taken away from him, with some additional presents; and also from the circumstance, that Agamemnon is ready to make this reparation, though both, according to our views, have rudely abused each other. They roused their anger by abusive words, but not their feelings of honor." Our principal question here of course must be: What do we understand by honor? By *external* honor we understand the good opinion which our fellow-men have of our qualities, of our character, or of ourselves. Honor is therefore not any thing tangible or material like property, it is wholly ideal, and love of honor is but the value we place upon the opinion, which others form of us or of our qualities. A man that does not care for this opinion, will not care for honor. Our fellow-men will in general value what is calculated to promote the general welfare, and it will consequently receive their good will and good opinion. Hence, whatever is of this general character, whatever is generally desirable, will also be honorable, and bring honor to him, who either *has* or *acquires* it. Some honor is innate, as for example, that of being man, of being possessed of genius, of talents; other honor is inherited, as for example, the honor to be born of honest parents, or descended from an old and honorable family. From this latter honor, that of nobility arose, which was confined to a certain separate rank, but which is now passing away, as civilization dispels the remaining clouds of darkness. The noble ancestors of some old families, had served their country by their bravery, and the generous sacrifices which they willingly made for its sake, and thus had gained the good opinion of their contemporaries in a high degree. By distinguishing themselves above others by lofty deeds, they were raised above them. Yet what belonged exclusively to their own merit, was appropriated by their sons, as if virtue could be inherited like a piece of ground, or like property, and so the most degenerate sons frequently enjoyed that of which they were wholly unworthy.

Honor, in the second place, may be gained by *acquiring* whatever is of general value in the opinion of men. Here then a man's honor depends on his will and natural capacities. The means by which it is to be acquired, are *skill* in the use of our limbs, especially for the production of such works, as will benefit the community. This is the case with the soldier, who knows how to manage his horse, and to wield his sword. The honor of the soldier differs however from the mere reputation of the juggler, whose skill has no reference to the general welfare. Honor may be acquired by skill in realizing useful designs and purposes, the invention of new machines, or the construction of such as were already known; by works of the fine arts, and by science. The scientific man enjoys a more lasting honor than the artist, though the latter may be more honored during his life. Sciences are free from the peculiarities of a national spirit, art is under its influence. The Aphrodite of Apelles, and the Madonna of Raphael, differ more than the logic of Aristotle and that of Whateley. Among the scientific, those again are most highly honored, whose sciences are most closely related to practical pursuits. Honor may be acquired by every occupation, that has reference to the satisfaction of our wants. Every one, who while he is active for himself benefits the community at the same time, receives honor. So the farmer has honor, for on his occupation the basis of the whole government rests. The mechanic labors indeed for himself, but if he is skilful he will benefit the whole community in which he lives, and will be honored. Honor is higher in proportion as the occupation by which it is acquired, has less the welfare of the individual than that of the whole community in view. The honor of a valuable justice of the peace is greater than his, who lives entirely to himself; yet the justice of the peace may labor at the same time, for the support of his family; he may be a carpenter, a farmer, or a merchant: hence, the honor of the minister or the judge is still greater, for they devote themselves wholly to the welfare of the public. This external honor may be indicated by orders and insignia; but it ceases to be honor, if it has no relation at all to morality, and thus becomes mere *reputation.*

We now pass over to the consideration of *internal* honor.

Internal or subjective honor is the idea which a person has of himself, of his qualities or character. The person is, however, free to seek for honor in any thing he possesses or is; for the notion of honor is his own creation and he may place in it what he pleases. It is, therefore, not the object, which is honorable in itself, but the notion of the subject, on which honor is dependent. The contents of honor may be high virtues, such as *honesty, faithfulness, courage, bravery,* the *exact fulfilment of duties:* these are honorable in themselves; but with regard to subjective honor, they become so only, when the person raises them into the sphere of honor by his own determination, when he resolves to seek his honor in them. The question is not whether a thing is honorable in itself, but whether it agrees with our notions of honor. Hence a man of honor, in this sense of the word, may neglect many duties and still remain an honorable man in his own opinion, and again, he will often perceive obligations, and insist on their most exact fulfilment, when others can see none. He creates his obligations by the principles of his own honor, and considers it a point of honor to lead them out. It is this kind of honor, which may lose all true substance and become wholly whimsical, a mere form without any true life. In this case, trifling and insignificant notions are frequently brought in connection with our honor; and we insist on having them regarded as if they were really of great importance. We see then, that it is wholly left to the arbitrary choice of a person to extend *his* honor as far and over as many of his personal qualities as he pleases, and it is therefore natural that such subjective honor, the limits of which it must be difficult to ascertain, is easily wounded; especially when we consider that honour is something so subjective and that the notions of it differ so widely, that no general rule can be given as to what is offensive or not. What leaves one cold, rouses another into passion. And as no one is willing to have his honor estimated by another, but claims the right to be his own judge in such matters, every one will when offended on so delicate a point, himself seek for satisfaction, for he alone knows how much or little is required to make a sufficient reparation. This goes so far that unless the offender is himself a man of honor he is neither able to give nor take away the honor of another; hence unable either to offend or to give satisfaction. For satisfaction consists in seeing honor acknowledged by another, but if he does not appear honorable to me his opinion cannot be of any value to me.

But neither the external nor internal honor is the true honor. True honor can only be acquired by virtue, by moral conduct, by a correct relation to the divine law. The love of this honor is the root of many good traits in the character of man; it ennobles, and without it, it must be difficult to fulfil our other duties; since this honor alone can gain for us the true confidence of our fellow-men, without which we could not enjoy a sphere of conscientious activity. This honor may be acquired by every one; women by chastity and her other domestic virtues; man by what he does and effects by faithfulness to a given promise, by scorning undignified actions, by works of art and of science:—all may acquire moral honor which alone can render any other honor valuable. Moral honor alone is permanent. " Like a hymn it is always attractive, while the mere objective or subjective honor is like a street song, which wearies the ears." The honor of Napoleon and that of Washington, differs as essentially as that of Robespierre and Luther. " Moral honor cannot be taken from us. Luther was stripped of his titles by the council of Orlamuende during his contest with Carlstadt, but he nevertheless remained the honorable Martin Luther. A panegyric on Cromwell, on the other hand, is like a false coin, it will not become current. It is most injurious to him, in whose mouth or hand it is last found."

Love of honor as a passion.

When the love of honor becomes a passion, it is either *ambition*, and thus stands connected with external honor; or it is *pride* and is founded on internal honor. Ambition is the vehement and blind desire for the good opinion of our fellow-men; this desire is blind and vehement, because honor is not desired on its own account, not because it is noble and good, but on his account who desires it. The ambitious constantly thinks of increasing his honor and hence is always bent upon something future, the execution of which seems arduous and demands power and strength of mind, but in all he does he has his own reputation in view, and he could do any thing, right or wrong, if his honor would be advanced by it. The truly honorable man will everywhere do what is good and right, and so he is determined to avoid what is dishonorable in itself. The ambitious man only asks: Will it bring honor in the opinion of others? for this opinion alone sanctions in his view what is honorable, and without it there is no honor. He longs to see every thing acknowledged that is his, while the truly honorable man is satisfied with knowing that what he does is honorable in itself, and that he is worthy of honor. He will, therefore, perform what is honorable and not look for applause. External honor has its expressions in society; rank, offices of different kinds, &c., include an honor in themselves which they confer on any one, who occupies them whether he deserves it or not. Hence the ambitious desires prominent positions in public life, he will strive to be at the head of affairs; he cannot bear to have any one above him, and would rather be the first in a village than second in Rome. Ambition leads to many vices. It courts public opinion and consequently must yield to it and become unfaithful to its own principles, if it has any. It will distinguish itself, and seeks originality and pretends to what it has not. It leads to *hatred* and especially to *envy*, for it cannot avoid drawing comparisons between itself and others, and perceiving that others have the same or more than it has, and at the same time desiring to have the sole title to honor, it enviously asperses the qualities of others. Envy consists in the strange opinion, that we alone ought to have, what others nevertheless have likewise; that others ought not to make any pretensions to it, because we are superior to them; that because others are *in our way*, therefore we are not *first in rank*, and that nothing is wanting to our elevation but their removal.—It will be generally found connected with ambition, for the ambitious will always meet his equal, and this he cannot endure. Envy is not excited by the dead. Byron did not envy Shakspeare, nor Napoleon, Alexander or Cesar; *nascitur in vivis livor, post fata quiescit*,—Envy rages among the living, after death it dies away. It is for these reasons that it is honorable to be called a man of honor, but despicable to be charged with ambition. Though an ambitious man stands higher in public opinion, than an avaricious one, because the object of the former is *ideal* that of the latter wholly *material*.

Pride, as was stated, is founded upon internal honor, and differs consequently from ambition, as the internal from external honor. Ambition endeavors to gain the good opinion of others and possess it, whether right or wrong; pride is satisfied with *its own*. It does not, like ambition, yield to the opinions of others or court them, but rather expects all to look up to it. When others do not feel and express by their actions this subordination to the proud, he either grows cold or becomes distant. If the ambitious desires to be foremost and first every where, the proud will demand it in a much higher degree, and jealousy will be more incident to his character, than to that of the ambitious; for nothing but the highest of all can satisfy him. The ambitious may acknowledge some weakness and frailty in his character, but the proud makes the highest pretensions in every respect, does not acknowledge any frailty, insists on unlimited admiration, raises himself above all others, and expects them to be humble in his presence. The ambitious is constantly in search of honor, the proud considers himself in possession of it, and would not be willing to appear to be seeking for it. Pride differs from *haughtiness*. The haughty man expects others to consider themselves a mere nothing in his presence, and to feel happy if he calls upon them for their services. When this haughtiness grows still more excessive, it becomes *superciliousness*, which desires others to despise themselves, when they perceive its splendor and greatness.—We have repeatedly had occasion to remark, that passions include extremes, that they are *living contradictions*. This remark may again be made here. For the proud, the haughty, the supercilious, while they expect all others to bow before them, will themselves bow before others and do homage if the occasion requires it. This is expressed by Tacitus, in his forcible manner; *Aliis humiliter inserviunt, dum aliis crudeliter superbiant*,—They serve some in humility, while they make their pride felt by others. Pride may be divided into as many classes, as there are objects of pride. There is a pride of learning, which easily passes over into vanity; there is a pride of virtue, which is the fruit of self-righteousness; there is a pride of piety, that humbly acknowledges human depravity, while at the same time it thinks well of itself, as having left behind the mass of conception; there is a pride of nationality, when we consider our nation superior to all others; there is finally, a pride of genius, originality, money, property, a pride of rank from the soldier to the prince, including every rank and condition of men. One kind of pride we must mention here, as arising from the true and genuine honor, from that honor which can alone be acquired by *virtue*. This pride is correct and moral, and is felt, when any one suggests to us any thing base, and when we reject such a suggestion with scorn. It consists in our own conviction that our honor has *no* price, that it cannot be bribed either by money or any thing else, and that we cannot be induced to do wilfully any thing mean. If, nevertheless, any one approaches us with sinister intentions, we feel indignant at him.

Finally, it is necessary to distinguish *vanity* from pride. By vanity we do not understand here the transitoriness and perishableness of all things, but the disposition which induces man to place a high value upon every thing that is his, and because it is his. The man is vain in a somewhat different respect, that expects the finite and transitory to be permanent, and seeing himself disappointed, exclaims: all is vain! while in fact his imagination alone is vain. For transitoriness does not make things, the nature of which it is to be finite, vain. They go and come again. Youth, beauty and understanding are valuable, and not vain, though youth decays, beauty fades, and understanding loses its vigor. But why should we not enjoy these things, though they are transitory? Have they no value in reference to our higher duties? Things are not vain because they are transitory, but *we* are vain, when we place our affections upon the transitory, and expect it to remain the same for ever. We transfer our own vanity into the things of the world and pronounce it *their* quality, while in fact it is *ours*. The vanity we here speak of is the desire for the immediate notice of our qualities, and an expression of a good opinion. It is a modification of ambition, and it enters more into the *retail sale* of honor. It is therefore little, and differs by this *littleness* from pride. It either places particular stress on things, that must be wholly indifferent to public opinion, as for instance, on the day on which we were born, on dress or personal beauty, or on such, as are of more general value, as wit, language, skill. The latter objects may easily lead to vanity; for as they please the person who has them, so they are attractive to all. The vain person noticing their general attractiveness desires that they shall please others, because they are **his**, and so his interest in any object is not immediately derived from the object itself, but from the impression it makes upon others. Hence, the vain person will constantly contrive to have an object that impresses others favorably seen by them. Perhaps a lady is vain of her beautiful hand, and she will certainly know how to exhibit it with a full appearance of modesty. As honor is a high good, but is abused by ambition, so are beauty, talent, genius, much to be desired; but when we love them, not because we consider them high and noble, but because they are ours—because we possess them—when we could not take any interest in them, in case we were deprived of them, then our love of them is *vanity*. This vanity is closely connected with the one before described, and the only difference is that it is more *selfish*. It is right to love all things that God has created, but it is wrong to expect of them, what God has not given them; and so it is right to love our personal qualities and that which belongs to us, but it is wrong to believe them good, because they are connected with *us*. Both kinds of vanity may pervade the spirit of whole ages. About the middle of the last century, a melancholy feeling, of the vanity of all things, spread itself over the world. Young's Night Thoughts, Sterne's Sentimental Journey, and Werther's Sorrows, induced or encouraged that silent consumption of mind and energy. And so again whole ages may be diseased with vanity as a modification of ambition; especially such as are without a determined character. Much depends too upon the character of individuals and nations. The English, for instance, are inclined to pride, the French to vanity.

The inclinations which we have had under consideration thus far, as arising from the relation of man to his fellow-men, had for their contents objects, that could neither understand nor answer them. These inclinations rest, therefore, solely in him who has them, and cannot be reciprocated. The inclinations we now have to examine are divided between at least two persons. They are, therefore, mutual inclinations, and social in the highest sense of the word, and the first among them is

Love.

Love, in general, is the devotion of one person to another. In it we surrender the independence of our existence, and desire to become self-conscious, not in ourselves only, but especially in the consciousness of another. In him we seek ourselves, by him we desire to be acknowledged and received with our whole personality and all connected with it. His consciousness we desire to penetrate, to fill with our person all his will and knowledge, all his desires and wishes. Then the other lives only in us, as we live in him. Thus both are identical, and each lays his whole soul into this identity. Love is therefore, ennobling; for loving we do not belong to ourselves, but to him whom we love, as he belongs to us. Thus our selfishness is broken; we forget ourselves as isolated beings, and seek and find ourselves only in each other; we do not exist and live for ourselves alone, but at the same time for him, whom we love, and principally for him; for in him the root of our joys and pleasures rests, in him we possess ourselves wholly, out of him the world is dreary and dead to us. Whatever cannot be drawn within this circle of our love, leaves us indifferent. "Especially in female characters is love most beautiful; for with them this devotion, this surrender is the highest point, as they center their intellectual and real life upon this feeling of love, in it find their only hold on life, and if misfortune touches it, they disappear like a light which is extinguished by the first rough breath. In this subjective tenderness of feeling love is not found in the classic art of Greece, where it appears only as a subordinate element for representation, or only in reference to sensual enjoyments."

In Homer, either no great weight is placed upon it, or love appears in its most worthy form, as marriage in the domestic circle, as, for instance, in the person of Penelope, or as the solicitude of a wife and mother in Andromache, or in other moral relations. The tie, on the other hand, which attaches Paris to Helen, is acknowledged as immoral, and is the cause of the terrors and misfortunes of the Trojan war, while the love of Achilles to Briseis has little depth of feeling, for Briseis is a slave, and at the disposal of his will. In the odes of Sappho, the language of love is raised to lyric inspiration, yet it is more the lingering, consuming fire of the blood that is expressed, than the warmth of feeling and the emotions of the *heart*. In another respect, love, as expressed in the delightful little songs of Anacreon, is a cheerful, general enjoyment, which without suffering, without struggles, and without the resignation of an oppressed and longing heart, joyfully seizes the immediate pleasure, not regarding it as necessary to possess *this* object of affection, and no other. Neither does the noble Tragedy of the ancients know the inclination of love in its romantic significance. Especially with Æschylus and Sophocles it does not claim any particular interest. For though Antigone is destined to be the wife of Hæmon, though Hæmon defends her before his father, and even kills himself because he cannot save her—he speaks before Creon only of objective relations, and not of the power of subjective passion, which in fact he did not feel in the sense of a modern passionate lover. Euripides makes use of love as an essential pathos in his Phedra, yet there it is represented as a criminal aberration of blood, as a passion of sense, as instigated by Venus, who desires the destruction of Hippolytus, because he will not bring sacrifices to her. So we have in the Venus de Medici a beautiful image of love, and nothing can be said against its neatness and plastic execution, but the expression of internal warmth and life, as modern Art demands it, is wholly wanting.

The same is the case in the Roman poetry, when after the dissolution of the republic, and of the rigidity of moral life, love degenerated more or less into sensual enjoyment. Petrarch, on the other hand, though he wrote his sonnets for amusement only, gained his immortal reputation by the fancies of his love, which under the warm Italian sky, connected itself in the depths of his heart with religion. Dante's exaltation also proceeded from his love of Beatrice, which rendered sublime in him, became a religious love, while his boldness and bravery was transformed into a religious intuition of art, in which—what no one else would venture —he made himself the judge of all men, and consigned them to hell, to purgatory, or to heaven. As a contrast to this exaltation, Bocaccio represents love, partly in vehemence as a passion, partly as stripped of all morality, making in his various novels the morals of his age and country pass in review before our eyes.

In the German *minnesong*, love is full of piety, tender, without richness of imagination, playful, melancholy, monotonous; with the Spaniard, it is full of imagination in its expression, knightly, subtle in seeking and defending its rights and duties as a matter of honor, and fanatical in the time of its highest splendor. With the French, especially in latter times, it becomes gallant, inclining to vanity, a forced feeling created by sophistry, a kind of sensual enjoyment without passion, or passion without enjoyment, a feeling and sentimentality full of *reflection*.

From the above it will be seen that at present we have under consideration

Sexual Love.

This is founded on a tendency of nature, which, divided between two of different sexes, draws them irresistibly, yet mysteriously towards each other, and makes each feel, that it cannot find its completion in itself, and must seek for it in another. This love is pure and noble, when it is called forth by love. " The purest love is the effect of the most perfect, external beauty in its union with an equally perfect internal beauty of the heart. It calls forth noble and delightful feelings in ourselves, silences every desire, and renders us happy by its presence. It is a perfect union of the most beautiful in us with the most beautiful out of us. Its removal leaves a void in the heart; we are drawn after it." This is the case with all lovers. Every one considers his love the fairest, most beautiful, and most virtuous of all that ever lived. If personal beauty is wanting, other charms will compensate for it, or make the lover overlook the deficiency. Sexual love is the bloom of our intellectual and bodily life, and as the flower reveals by its color and fragrance the life of the plant, so love will render manifest the ideal of beauty and loveliness, and the kind of life which a person conceals within himself. Again: love is the intellectual and physical development of youth, for it is the joint product of imagination and fancy, and of bodily vigor and freshness of nerves and muscles, all of which have arrived at the stage of maturity. If love induces us to seek for all that is noble and beautiful in order to adorn with it the object of love; if we desire to seek for honor and every virtue, to lay it at the feet of the beloved one; if we long for nothing more than the entire union of soul with soul,—then our love is noble, and the being of whom it is the blossom must be so likewise. Such love excites us to virtuous and magnanimous actions, and many a youth of amiable qualities, but who was exposed to dangers, has been rescued by love, and raised by it into the sphere of beauty and nobleness, from that of sensual enjoyments. In sexual love now, if it is to be pure, love must be the only object desired, not money, not mere external beauty. Such love will desire its preservation, and this it can obtain only by a permanent union, which is marriage. *Marriage* is the external representation of the internal union, produced by love between two persons of different sexes, and sanctioned by the usual ceremony. Husband and wife are truly one. The interests and wishes of the one are also those of the other; they enter so wholly and entirely into each other's feelings, views, and desires, that they seem to have but one thinking power. Genuine marriage cannot, therefore, be produced by a mere ceremony, but must have its possible existence in love. Yet what is once joined together, let no man put asunder, and hence the choice is short, and the regret is long.

From the above it must follow that true love renders Monogamy indispensable, and that Polyandry or Polygamy are wholly unnatural. We can exchange our *Self* but once, and receive but one *Self* in exchange for it. And here is the point too, on which it must appear possible, that love may become a passion. For, as we cannot love every one, but must naturally be limited in our choice, the idea may take hold of our mind after we think we have found the person, that she and no other in the world is the one whom we can love. Centreing our affections upon her, it seems wholly impossible to us, that we should be able to love any other. If now impediments are thrown in our way, if we fear the loss of our love, and know that no reparation can be made to us, our love will be changed into a transient or permanent passion.

Sexual Love as a Passion.

The impediments laid in the way of love, are either external, or they are contained in one of the lovers, and may be termed internal. The external impediments proceed from the world around us, from its manners and views, from the family spirit, its interests, from laws and prejudices, and the prose of life. The lovers think of nothing but their love; they are satisfied with it. Yet man is not to live to his feelings only, he has duties to perform, and to honor the many relations, in which he finds himself.

Thus a collision between his love and his duties may easily take place. Among these possible collisions none is more frequent than that of honor. This may demand the resignation of love, merely because the two are not of equal rank. This opposition, however, will only strengthen the power of love, and instead of yielding to the suggestions of honor, it becomes so irresistible as rather to sacrifice life than yield to any obstacles. Again: the will of parents, family duties, duties towards the country, or faithfulness to a vow, may interfere with love, and here again it will become passion. Now it may be that this passion overcomes all difficulties, and effects its final union, or that the person acknowledges the power of these objective rights and duties, and struggles silently with himself and the power of his own passions. On the latter passion the play of the Maid of Orleans, by Schiller, rests. Very often, as we have said already, it is the *prose* of life—intrigue, prejudices, and the like, that oppose love, determined to destroy the fairest prospects. In this case, also, love becomes a passion, and makes every sacrifice to conquer difficulties. If the difficulties will not yield, if all daily grows darker, love may be driven to suicide, or terminate in insanity.

The internal impediments are always to be sought for in the lovers themselves. Here it may be, that love on the part of one has never fully developed itself. When now the other demands the exclusive possession of the love of the first, and when he feels that this is not fully given, that, perhaps, a third receives as much attention as himself, he will become passionate, and his passion will be *jealousy*. When love is pure on both sides, all fear is banished. It is often a feeling of weakness, a feeling that we do not deserve the possession of the love of the other, that causes this fear. So Othello is certain of Desdemona's love; he fears nothing. Iago cannot succeed at first in filling his heart with suspicion, until he mentions his age, his dark color, &c. From that moment suspicion is ripe in Othello's breast.

Love may become a transient passion, when the greatness of the new feeling, the darkness of the relations, that are yet indistinct, the late youthful pride, which is now to surrender, to confess itself conquered, embarrass: love would not betray itself, and betrays itself by this very wish for concealment. It desires to meet the beloved, and trembles or flees when he approaches. It seeks solitude to give free course to its tears, and keeps secret from others what moves the heart. It does not venture to pronounce the name, but it finds circuitous routs to hear from the beloved object.—So love may become a transient passion in a moment, when after we have secretly anticipated a kind reception from the person in whom we are interested, we receive a distinct and marked sign of it, one that can no longer be misinterpreted.

The passion of love is one of the most painful. The object appears to him who is under its influence as the only possible one he could choose; a certain fatality, a necessity against which he strives in vain, chains him to this one, which is in his eyes the most perfect. Without him or her the passionate lover does not expect to enjoy life or to become happy in any way. Hence the most bitter feeling of an irreparable loss constantly agitates the breast, and presents nothing but misery. Love, as was alluded to above, may mitigate and even expel other passions, but when once a passion, it cannot itself be rendered less strong by any other inclination. It is too certain of its loss, it feels that no reparation can be made, that it must carry its grief with it for ever.

After these remarks on love as a passion, we shall now approach some inclinations which spring from sexual love, and the first among them is

Parental and filial love.

All love between parents and children commences in the love of the mother to the children and father. The mother in loving the newly born child loves herself, for its life is hers. She nourishes it with her milk, it comes from her and lives through her. She attends to it because she loves it. The child grows and observes; its wants are satisfied by the mother, from whose eyes love and sympathy stream into its own. It loves the mother and this love remains the same throughout life. "A true son will cling to his mother, and never part with her. For that which enters most deeply into the heart of man and his whole character is his love of the mother, who loved him first. Coriolanus suffered himself to be conquered only by his love to his mother, and there has, probably, never been a great man who did not speak of his mother, when she was alluded to, with the most heartfelt love, as did Frederick I,. Napoleon, &c." It is the love of the mother to the child that calls forth that of the father to it; for the father loves it because he loves the mother. The child, on the other hand seems to love the father because it loves the mother, and she loves the father. And so again it is with the love of the children to each other. The mother loves all, and all love the mother; but when all are loved by the mother to the same extent, then all loving the mother will love what she loves, and consequently love each other. This family love will be ruined when one of the children is made a pet by the mother, as in that case jealousy and envy will be generated. When all is right the love of the mother will be the center of all the members of the family; all will incline towards her and again spread from her, but like the branches of a well-proportioned tree, that, while they each turn away from the trunk, only do so to form a more beautiful and perfect crown. One needs only to watch a little family to perceive the correctness of the above remarks. Children will constantly quarrel with each other, but the mother reigns among them, commands peace, reconciles, quiets, and silences them, and makes them love and indulge each other. Thus it may be truly said that all the moral relations in the family and government, have their strong hold in the love of the mother, and that she is the basis on which the whole fabric rests.

Fraternal love.

This is the love between sisters and brothers, and its character is of the brightest purity. There are, however, some differences in it, for it is either love between two sisters or two brothers, or it is love between sister and brother. As love between two sisters or between two brothers, it is not so fine and strong; for one sister is what the other is, and one brother what the other; the attraction is not so irresistible, and if a desire should arise in both for one and the same object, as is often the case in the division of property, or if, for instance, two brothers should fall in love with the same lady, as was the case in Schiller's celebrated Bride of Messina, the fraternal love might easily turn into hatred. There are other causes from which hatred may arise between brothers. The relation of the members of a family to each other is not one resting immediately on duties and rights like that of citizens to each other. One brother may, therefore, make demands on the other as if he had really a right to them. If the other declines fulfilling these demands, he may charge him with want of love. This might occur when the one of two brothers is a spendthrift, and the other a prudent man. No hatred can be more bitter or more terrible than that between two sisters or two brothers; and the reason is that when they love each other, it is in the purest and warmest manner; that during the time of their love neither has a secret from the other, neither thinks of concealing his frailties and weaknesses, as one stranger would from another; hence when they hate each other, each feels himself betrayed and consequently fraternal hatred is more bitter than any other, unless principles of honor and morality restrain it. The warmer the love, the more intense the hatred: this is a general law. There can be no purer love, on the other hand, than that between the brother and sister. For the sister loves the brother, as she cannot love any one else. She cannot love mother or father as she may love her brother, for the difference of age, and the dependence upon them, makes her feel under some restraint; the same is the case with her love to aunt and uncle. Her love to her husband, however pure it may be, is already more selfish. But her love to her brother is free from all selfish emotions, is perfectly pure. This love was called by the Greeks a divine love, resting upon a divine law, and when in Sophocles it comes in contact with the human statute of Creon, Antigone fulfils the former, violating the latter. In modern times we are much inclined to seek for its ground merely in the *blood*, but love does not cling to the blood, it rests in spirit, and family love has its ground in family spirit. In this spirit all incline to each other, and to their common trunk; all are constrained by it to love each other, and hence, every family forms a whole, that excludes every one not belonging to it, not pervaded by that spirit which produces a resemblance of feeling and views, of desires and inclinations in all the members of the same family. It is remarkable, however, that among the members of a family, grandparents and grandchildren feel more attraction for each other, than children and parents. To what is this owing? The parents standing between grandparents and grandchildren, as the present between the future and the past, are full of vigor, strength, and insist on the execution of their plans, on discipline, &c. The grandparents are, on the other hand, losing their vigor, the root of their existence is in the past, they better remember early impressions, those of their childhood, than those they received in more advanced age. They can, therefore, enter more easily into the feelings and life of children, than parents. Children receiving more indulgence from them, will, of course, incline more strongly to them.

But if each family is a whole that does not admit anything from without, then selfishness must be its character, and all intercourse between the members of different families must be rendered impossible. The question is: How may this selfishness be broken? In two ways: First, by intermarriage, and secondly, by the common love of all citizens to their native country.

National Love.

The love of all families to each other is, therefore, first effected by the love of their different members to each other. The love between son and daughter, as bride and bridegroom, will unite two families; and their children again will unite others, until all the families of a nation grow together by sexual love, and form one great whole. If the love of the mother to her children and theirs to her, may be compared to a tree, the branches of which, while they spread, bend nevertheless back to the common trunk; the love of one family to another may also be compared to a tree the full grown branches of which sink themselves into the soil, send forth roots and form new trees, remaining nevertheless connected with the parent-tree. The thus connected families again form a whole, and this is the nation—*nanciscor*. And here, secondly, *national* love develops itself. All the citizens of a nation have the same objects of affection, one country, one language, one manner of thinking, the same customs and morals. Every one that loves them will love those who agree with him in their inclinations. Hence it is that when two citizens of the same country, who while at home took no notice of each other, meet in a distant foreign land, they will form an immediate acquaintance. Hence too, we delight to hear our native tongue again after we have for a long time spoken the language of other nations. But the country also, its soil, its valleys and mountains, its rivers and streams, its productions, its skies, its villages, towns and cities, its public roads and canals, and in short all belonging to it become the objects of our love, and this love is that to the *Fatherland*. "Yet I know nothing more sweet than home," says Homer. The love for the Fatherland was stronger in ancient times than in modern. The Christian religion, has taught us to consider every stranger as a friend and brother, and civilization has rendered manners and customs more similar to each other among all nations.

Love of Mankind.

As every family is at first exclusive, so every nation again forms a whole, kept together by a national spirit, and thrusting out whatever does not proceed from it. Thus our nation stands opposed to another, and all are enemies to each other. This is proved by history; for all intercourse among nations commenced in *wars* rather than in mutual *love*. Each nation, as a whole, is selfish; considers its own productions in art and science, its heroes and victories, its laws and institutions superior to those of other nations and expects them to be acknowledged thus, and as the same pretensions are made by each nation, and none is willing to do what the other demands,—all will feel opposed to each other. How is this general dislike to be removed? It might at first sight seem that commercial intercourse and general cultivation would effect this, but when more closely examined, it must be acknowledged that such intercourse rests on national selfishness and close arithmetical calculation, and that it may for this reason often lead to ruptures, from which the most bitter hatred and wars may proceed. Science and art on the other hand, as long as national prejudices exist, cannot penetrate all nations in a perfectly free form, and their power is consequently limited to a national form, and in it they become a matter of national pride, and consequently an object of national jealousy and quarrel. The only power left to remove national enmity and produce peace among all nations is the christian religion, which teaches us, to "*love all men.*" We cannot love the whole race as a mass, but we may love every one whom we meet with, and take an interest in every nation and tribe of mankind on the face of the earth. This is the spirit of Christ and of missions; this ought to be the spirit of every man. The general possibility of loving all men becomes a *duty*, and this duty is the crown of all pathological inclinations. It commences with sexual love; it passes over to connubial love and refines itself still more in the paternal and filial love, in fraternal, family, and national love, until it appears in its highest beauty, in the love to all men. As the model of this love we have Christ, who persecuted by all, by the Jews, and Romans, and Greeks, surrounded by malice, voluptuousness, faithfulness, standing alone in the midst of enemies, *loved all, and hated none.*

Remarks.

1. It is usual to consider *friendship* as an inclination, a view that is wholly erroneous. It is not founded on the relations of our organism, but rests on the affinity of two souls, on the perception of an internal quality, and its pillars are *unlimited confidence*, and as *unlimited faithfulness.* Friendship is therefore a *virtue*, and though it may commence in an inclination, and may include love, it goes far beyond it. Frankness and openness, communication and participation, are indispensible to it. The beautiful poem of Schiller, entitled Die Burgershaft, represents the nature

of friendship in a masterly and a most impressive manner. Friendship is impossible without mutual regard, but we may *love* without it; we may say, "I love thee, but I cannot respect thee!" friendship rests on a moral respect for each other; on principles and needs no love, though it may have it.

2. Family love and national love may easily pass over into passions. The former may then be called *Nepotism.* This passion makes us prefer whatever is connected with our families to anything that proceeds from other families. It is a family pride that is ready at all times to defend the meanest actions of its relatives, to praise beyond measure what is good in them, and if power and influence allow, to raise them to rank and positions of honor, whether they deserve it or not. Nepotism will not benefit but ruin a government; it is Despotism on a small scale, and will become one on the largest if permitted to take its own course. So national love may become a passion, but always in the form of a disinclination. Two nations dislike each other; they have the same common object in view; only one of them can obtain it, and hence this collision arouses their dislike, and converts it into a passion, which has for its desire mutual destruction. Such a passion may more easily originate between two particular nations than between others. The French and English dislike each other; the Germans and English love each other. It will be more difficult for the latter than the former to become arrayed against each other.

3. A nation is an organized body; it has therefore different ranks, as it has different activities. Members of different ranks may dislike each other, and this dislike may break forth into passion in times of revolution. This dislike may seem very insignificant at its commencement, and continue so for a long time. It then is a mere indifference of the persons to each other. One man discovers an inclination in another which he has not; he is therefore wholly indifferent to it. The other notices this indifference, and feels chagrined.—A merchant, for instance, loves money; to acquire it demands a certain amount and a certain kind of knowledge. The learned man on the other hand, inclines to knowledge for its own sake, and he will feel as

indifferent to the money of the merchant, as the merchant to what he thinks useless knowledge. If they become acquainted with each other, they will at first leave each other cold, and by degrees dislike each other. This dislike will express itself thus: they either avoid each other, or when brought together are polite, while each is aware of the dislike of the other.—Such a dislike for a long time existed between Cuvier and Geoffrey St. Hilaire, both of whom labored in the same sciences, and in the same institution, but carried out different views. This dislike may, however, increase till it becomes hatred, which desires the destruction of the object hated, and ends in open hostility. For these are the three degrees of all disinclinations: First, *Dislike*, which is a mere indifference, and desire to have nothing to do with him, whom we dislike. Secondly, *Hatred*, or a desire to injure him whom we hate. And thirdly, *Enmity*, or a determination to hurt, destroy, and injure him whose enemy we are. This dislike takes place principally, as was said, between persons of different ranks and occupations, as between the nobility of a country and the farming class, between philosophers and clergymen; but it takes place also between members of the same profession, between lawyers or physicians. So Plato and Xenophon are said to have secretly disliked each other, yet this has never been fully ascertained. *Party hatred* is likewise found among the members of a nation. The cause is the partial inclination of some to a common object, to common principles, and their prominent representatives. This inclination will attract those that cherish it to each other, and unite them in proportion, as it separates them from all those that have it not, and have perhaps a similar and equally strong predilection of other objects and principles. It is not love to each other that unites the members of a party, but love to the same inclination, harmony of views and feelings, of desires and efforts. The separation of the different parties includes *indifference;* this indifference may become *hatred*, and in times of revolution *enmity*, as that between Loyalists and Democrats. As these parties in the government may rage against each other, so the different sects in religion. The Catholic hates the Protestant; the Jew the Christian; the Turk the Persian,—and among the

Protestants again, there was a time, when Lutherans and the Reformed hated and persecuted each other.

4. All disinclinations have the same conditions, that positive inclinations pre-suppose for their origin. They are the dislike on the part of one to something on that of the other; as, for instance, the dislike of one to the slow tedious manner of speaking of the other. The other perceives this dislike, and dislikes it. The former now will dislike in addition to the slow speaking, this dislike of the other, and so both will at first be cool in their intercourse, but soon hate and become hostile to each other.

CHAPTER IV.

EMOTIONS.

"Emotions are like water, that breaks away the dam; passions like a stream, that digs its bed constantly deeper. Emotions affect the health like apoplexy; passions like consumption. Emotions are like intoxication that passes over in sleep, but leaves its traces in the headache that follows; passion is like a disease arising from swallowed poison, and it needs a physician of the soul, who after all cannot prescribe radical, but only palliative medicine." Emotions have been divided into two classes, the one of which comprises those that are *strengthening*, as cheerfulness, joy, hope; and the other, those that are *weakening*, as fear, anxiety, grief. This division, as will be seen, is taken from the effects which emotions have upon us, and though correct in this respect, it is not founded on emotions, as they are in themselves. Another division, founded wholly upon the nature of emotions, has therefore been adopted, which we shall follow in its whole arrangement without attempting to make any essential changes. According to this view, emotions are either *simple, mixed,* or *compound*.

§ 1. SIMPLE EMOTIONS.

They are *pleasure* and *pain;* both as emotions are feelings connected with a thought, and differ thus from mere bodily pleasure and pain. They neither of them require any other emotion or feeling for their existence except that of agreeableness or disagreeableness. This may be connected with a perception or sensation; but here it is the feeling that attaches itself to the *knowledge* of an object. They are called *simple* or pure emotions, because they are the same, whatever may be the object in the knowledge of which they originate, not depending as a condition on an additional feeling, neither in their energy, nor in their duration. He that for the first time enjoys the view of a beautiful landscape, will experience the emotion of pleasure in which all desires are silenced. This pleasure arises from the agreeable feeling, accompanying the examination of the landscape. It is *simple* and *pure*, though the scenery is variegated and our reflections on it are manifold. We rejoice in nature, and are satisfied with this pleasure, as long as it continues, desiring nothing for the time being. Or a friend unexpectedly visits us; our pleasure is so great, that at first we do not think of asking him how long he will stay with us.—So the emotion of pain is simple and pure, not a bodily or sensual pain, but like pleasure, a feeling, arising from our knowledge of an object, and always the same, though the objects of our knowledge may be different. Like the emotion of pleasure, it exists independent of the organs of sense, sensual pain and pleasure always demand organs, the physical ability of which is either raised or depressed by some external influence upon them. Their energy and duration differ, their nature is the same. There is an emotion of pain " that thrusts its long proboscis into the heart, and draws forth tears in streams. The whole heart swells and flows, and convulsively compresses its inmost fibres." Such pain dissolves itself in tears, it is an infinite feeling, but pure and simple. In it the sufferer does not feel or desire to injure or remove the object by which the pain is caused.—The purity of the emotions of pain and pleasure, expresses itself too, by their relation to the present. The object which they concern may be in the past, the emotion rests wholly and entirely in the present. Thus these emotions are contained wholly in themselves, need nothing else for their existence, and are therefore both simple and pure.

§ 2. MIXED EMOTIONS.

Here, also, we have but two, *fear* and *hope;* and if pain and pleasure had only reference to the present, these refer to the *future.* They are called mixed, because they cannot originate without the former two, but pre-suppose them for their existence. Again: fear and hope having reference to the future, are impossible without the idea of time, and demand, therefore, much reflection. Hence they are of a higher character, than *pleasure* and *pain.* The thought of the future draws out the soul of man and renders him great, that of the immediate present contracts his mind. Jean Paul is therefore right in saying: "Neither pleasure nor pain, but only hope can give us rest."

Hope.

This is a pleasure in the present, strengthened by the expectation of pleasure in the future, or it is a pleasure connected with the anticipation of some future occurrence that will be agreeable to us. Its element is pleasure, but pleasure on the one hand as felt in the present, and pleasure on the other as anticipated in the future. This two-fold reference of hope to the present and future, gives it a mixed nature. Every thing future is only *possible;* the degree of the probability of an occurrence will condition the energy of *hope.* The beggar who hopes to become a king, is insane; the impediments that may seem to be in the way of a future good must be such as can be surmounted, and there must be a high degree of probability that this will give way, or there can be no hope. So when we perceive all impediments yielding to the approach of the hoped for good, our hope will become *confidence.* Hope, as the expectation of something future, is indispensable to enterprise and activity. The farmer sows his seed, hoping that it will germinate and grow; the sailor leaves his native shore, hoping he shall see it again laden with wealth; hope of victory accompanies the soldier in war, and hope that the seeds of truth will find their appropriate soil, and bring forth fruit, if not now, after his death, encourages the teacher to persevere in his arduous work. Who would be eager to endeavor and act, to advance and improve himself and all around him, were not hope playing in his bosom? Every person, from the child to the aged, hopes; but as imagination and understanding, are more or less developed or naturally more or less energetic, hope will correspond with them. The hope of the child is but an uncertain, dark and confused anticipation, or a wish; the hope of the youth needs little *probabilily;* imagination loves to calculate on the favor of fortune. The hope of manhood is of a general character; its objects are better times and the benefit of posterity; it rests on cool understanding, and a knowledge of the present and its elements, and is firm, strong and persevering, even when surrounded by misfortunes or preyed upon by disease. The old man, submissive and resigned, continues to hope though near the grave, but his hope is directed to another world, and if of any value, it must rest on *faith.*

One who has been frequently disappointed, will find it difficult to hope; yet no one is entirely without hope. When all hope disappears, *despair* takes its place. Despair is that situation of mind, in which fear and grief no longer give room to hope, in which sadness consumes every joy, and neither present nor future good can find any access to us. A willing resignation of the world differs from despair; such a resignation is blessed with internal peace and rest, and while it hopes nothing for itself, it may hope for others. Resignation is the result of character, of principle, of views which we have formed of life and the value of its enjoyments; it is a principled limitation of our wishes and desires.

Fear.

This is the opposite of *hope;* a feeling of strong displeasure connecting itself with the thought of a future evil or of an unpleasant occurrence, that in all probability will take place. The future evil, the occurrence of which is not very probable, cannot alarm us. We all believe that there will be a time, when the earth shall be no more, but every one of us expect to be gone before it arrives. Hence we do not fear it. No one is ashamed of hope, but many dislike to have it known that they can fear, and yet fear is older and more powerful than hope. It is natural to man, for dependent as he is on powers that are not under his control, it would be foolish to pretend to be above fear.— Fear has its different degrees, and much may depend on age, experience, constitution, and temperament to which of these degrees we are principally subject. These degrees are: First: A mere feeling of *uneasiness*, when we have to exercise our strength to avert an impending evil, and feel uncertain of success, or when the danger is indefinite. Secondly: It becomes *terror*, when it is suddenly excited, and when it deprives us of all presence of mind; then we grow pale and tremble. This is the case when we at once perceive a destructive power of nature threatening us and see no possibility of escape. Thirdly: It may become *stupefaction*, when the evil feared falls upon us and really harms us.

There must of course, always be an object in which we take an interest, and whose existence we consider endangered. These objects of fear may be manifold; and as they differ, so fear differs in its character. We may fear *physical* evils, or moral crimes and their punishments, the reproaches of conscience, the violation of *honor* or of that which is sacred and inviolable. *Reverence* is a fear, the object of which is Beauty, Holiness, Truth, God. And so again with the fear that our honor might be violated, a feeling of shame and confusion is connected. Of these many species of fear, we shall consider only two: *Reverence* and *Shame*.

Reverence is the regard we feel for the true value contained in a thing, and the fear to approach or abuse it. Regard or respect is the beginning of reverence, and he only who can perceive the true value of a thing is susceptible of regard and reverence. In proportion as a man is truly cultivated, in proportion as he can discern an eternal and indestructible value in nature, in beauty, and truth, he will revere them, and the more will *reverence* be the bloom of all his cultivation. This fear is therefore delicate; its object is not the occurrence of a physical evil, but that of an ideal, a moral misfortune. Such would be the violation of any thing sacred to him whose mind is truly cultivated. The barbarian destroys whatever comes in his way; not having the most distant idea of the value of beauty, he ruins the finest works of art. In times, when all fear of laws, and the fear of all that is sacred is gone, as in those of revolutions, no monument of former greatness however grand, is protected from the hand of destruction. It is easy to *fear*, but difficult to *revere*. Reverence, then, is the tender fear which we feel in the presence of persons, or in handling things, the value of which has become known to us, and which we fear, to injure or abuse.—*Shame*, on the other hand, is the fear felt by us of losing the good opinion of others, by a mistake or error which we have committed, that would offend decorum, morality, or custom, &c., it has reference to sexual relations, and in this respect is the fear that others might consider us *impure* in our feelings. This feeling may be very painful and pervade our whole mind. It may be called forth suddenly when any thing which we desire to conceal from the world is exposed; when a weakness is detected, or a frailty noticed. Goethe has represented this emotion by a most beautiful likeness. He says in his Notes on his West-Oestliche Divan; "In countries where they have no layers of lime, the shells of muscles are used for the preparation of a very necessary building material, and piled up between dry branches, they become glowing hot, with the flame which is kindled beneath them. The beholder cannot resist the feeling, that these creatures a short time before full of life, growing and thriving in the ocean, enjoyed in their way the general pleasure of existence and now, not burned to ashes, but penetrated by the fire, retain their full form, while all life is extinguished in them. Suppose that night comes on and that these organical remnants really appear glowing to the eye of the spectator; no more appropriate image of the pain of the soul can be placed before our eyes. If any one desires a perfect picture of this, let him ask the chemist to put oyster shells into a state of phosphorescence when he will confess with us, that the glowing hot feeling which pervades man, when a just reproach meets him unexpectedly in the midst of the self-conceit of confident self-feeling, could not be more terribly expressed." Thus shame penetrates man and the blood rushes to the face, till it glows like the shells that are penetrated by fire.

Remarks.

1. Fear and hope cannot exist at the same time in the same breast, for they exclude each other as a pleasure and pain. And so again pain and hope exclude each other as pleasure and fear. When we deeply mourn, it is difficult for us to hope, and it is wholly wrong to endeavor to excite hope in the mourner during the time that his grief is greatest. The best consolation is to mourn with him, to sympathize with his grief. So we cannot enjoy ourselves fully, when in the midst of our pleasure we fear poison. It is therefore equally imprudent to introduce tidings of misfortune, by first exciting a cheerful mood in him whom they concern.

2. If the animal can feel sensual pleasure and pain, and thus may have something similar to the two corresponding emotions, it is wholly deprived of *hope* and *fear*, for these are impossible without a full and clear idea of futurity, and this idea is impossible without understanding. Now it is well known that the animal flees from certain objects, and this might seem to resemble fear; but the cause of flight is not a knowledge of the danger; it is only a feeling of displeasure instinctively connected with the sight of the object. The perception of such an object has the same effect upon the animal that lightning has upon the eye of man.

§ 3. COMPOUND EMOTIONS.

These emotions are called compound, because their elements are not simple, but always partake of the nature of two other emotions. These two emotions do not constitute a third one in an *external* manner, but receive each other so, that their elements grow together and form internally one. The sap of a plant consists likewise of many different substances, and is after all but one in its nature. The compound emotions may be divided into *depressing* and *invigorating* affections of the mind; the former being founded on *pain* and *fear*, the latter on *pleasure* and *hope*.

Depressing Emotions.

Melancholy or *Sadness*. Pleasure and pain, as was said above, exclude each other, and where the one is, the other cannot be. And yet we find them united in *melancholy*. But they exist in it as mere elements and not as emotions; neither is any longer what it originally was, but each has entered into the other and exists in an impure state. Melancholy is, therefore, both painful and pleasant. The union of pain and pleasure depends on our remembrance of the past—hence it is, that melancholy is not found among children, for their remembrance is either weak or as yet they have none at all. The remembrance of the past is connected with a feeling of pleasure, for it in some degree recalls past enjoyments. But at the same time the past with its enjoyments cannot be revived, so that it is again *real;* the remembrance, therefore, includes the knowledge of a loss and with it a feeling of pain. This enters into the pleasure and both become sadness. This emotion, which is at the same time both sweet and bitter, joyful and sorrowful, expresses itself in three different ways:

First, In old age, when man looks back upon his youth. Then he was strong and vigorous, then little was required for his joys and yet they were full of life and of warmth. Cares were strangers to him, and the future smiled upon him like a balmy May day. Such recollections are delightful, but they are not without sadness, for those days of youth are gone, and never will return. No power on earth can bring back even a single hour. Nor were they without their labors and sorrows, which will likewise enter into our recollection, and pain will mingle with pleasure. So Goethe says of himself in advanced age: " they have called me a child of fortune, nor have I any wish to complain of the course of my life. Yet it has been nothing but labor and sorrow, and I may truly say that in seventy-five years, I have not had four weeks of true comfort. It was the constant rolling of a stone that was to be always lifted anew." At another time he said, "I should not like to live my life over again; as the mature plant could not desire to return again to the contracted state of buds and seeds." At another. "When I look back upon my earlier and middle life, and consider how few are left of those that were young with me, I am reminded of a summer visit to a watering place. On arriving one makes the acquaintance of those who have been already some time there and leave the week following. This loss is painful. Now one becomes attached to the second generation, with which one lives for a time and becomes intimately connected. But this also passes away and leaves us solitary with the third which arrives shortly before our own departure, and with which we have no desire to have much intercourse." In such words deep sadness breathes.

Secondly, The recollection of our home likewise calls forth this *sad delight* or *delightful sadness.* Our fancy carries in itself the scenery of our native country to which a part of our life, of our feelings and desires were once closely linked. As these images emerge from the depths of our mind and present themselves to us, our numerous connections, friends, relatives, the happy hours spent in the circle of sisters, brothers and parents, will likewise appear before the eye of the mind, and when we consider that we are far off from parents and home, when then our thoughts are constantly bent upon the scenes of our infancy—we feel sad and though unhappy, nevertheless desire to retain this feeling of sadness, because it is the only consolation remaining to us.

Thirdly, The remembrance of a friend, whose loss is not recent, but of by-gone-days. If recent, we feel grief and mourn. But when at a distance and when the first bitterness of grief is over, we delight in the remembrance of the hours we spent with him, and at the same time feel sorrowful because they will never return. So Victor in Jean Paul's Hesperus, exclaims of his friend. "O! that I could once more speak to thee, good, dear and noble friend of my youth." It is not necessary, however, that we should have suffered a loss which we bewail, but the *beautiful* and *divine* may make a sorrowful impression upon us, and we may become melancholy by it. Music heard at a distance has this effect. Hence Plato said, that it reminds us of a better home.

These feelings of desire, and longing, of pain and pleasure, constitute the theme of *elegiac* poetry. In it grief either prevails over pleasure, as for instance, in the noble Elegy in a Country Church-Yard; or pleasure over grief, as in Goethe's Elegies. And again, this poetry sings either of the sadness called forth by the consideration of the vanity of all things, by the sight of ruins, the standing, but broken remnants of the life of by-gone ages; or it sings the grief caused by our own disappointments. In the former case, its character is noble, in the latter selfish. Yet the mouth of the poet is blessed, for in his grief melody and speech are granted him to mourn in the deepest fullness of his distress, and if man in his sadness grows silent, God has permitted him to tell what he suffers.

Anxious Expectation.

This likewise belongs to the depressing emotions, for as the person can do nothing whatever with regard to the object expected, its long delay must weary and exhaust; what we possess we can no longer expect, but what is yet at a distance from us, we may expect. The object of expectation is, therefore, always something future; but that which is entirely future is only possible, and hence uncertain. Expecting a thing, we *hope* and *fear* at the same time. We hope that our expectation will be realized, and we fear that we may be disappointed. The more intense our interest in the object, the more fear and hope will mingle in our breast. This is beautifully illustrated in the poem of Schiller called Die Erwartung, *Expectation*, where hope prevails over fear, and yet cannot entirely free itself from the latter. A lover sits in a garden expecting his beloved. Every rustling leaf makes him imagine that he hears her approaching footsteps, and he looks anxiously around for her whose presence he desires; every motion startles him, and his heart is divided between hope and fear.—*Anxious* expectation is always caused or depends on a doubt entertained by the person; if the possibility, that an occurrence will take place is great, we have *hope* in the place of anxious *expectation;* or, if the occurrence be of an unpleasant nature, *fear*. For example, we watch the disease of a friend: if his danger is uncertain and his disease yet undeveloped, we are constantly under the influence of *anxious expectation;* if the danger be great, we *fear*, if it seems diminishing, we *hope*.

Despondency.

This emotion arises from the union of *fear* and *pain*, and is the opposite of cheerfulness. It may be produced when we see a friend suffer; the sight of this suffering is painful; we perceive at the same time the danger threatening him, and fear for him. This fear uniting itself with our pain, makes us *despondent*. If our fears are realized, our despondency becomes *grief*. This becomes *mournfulness* when grief continues, and it becomes still more bitter if the grief is not softened by a single ray of hope. Despondency is increased by the recollection of former pleasures, or by the sight of the happiness of others. Hence it loves solitude.—The emotion of despondency manifests itself in different ways. It unnerves the system, fills the eyes with tears, makes us silent, solitary, and reluctant to take an interest in any thing. It extends time, for "sad hours seem long." *Weeping* is an interesting phenomenon; it is the effect of the influence and power exercised by the emotions of the mind upon the body; all weakening emotions strongly affect the glandular system, and especially the muscles of sight and respiration; when these are weakened, sighing and tears will be the natural consequence. These effects are however not only produced by such emotions as naturally tend to relax the system; those that are in themselves strengthening, become the opposite, when their measure exceeds our capacity to receive them. So violent laughter brings tears into the eyes. The extreme of a strengthening emotion becomes weakening. The deepest grief is silent and tearless; weeping would relieve the breast.— The emotion of despondency likewise weakens the soul;

it discourages, renders us indifferent to the world, even to life, and makes the sight of cheerfulness painful to us. Its effects on the soul and body may ruin the constitution, and not only attract disease, but render medicine ineffectual.

Patience.

This is the deep feeling of a present evil or misfortune, connected with the hope of overcoming it by yielding; or it is pain combined with the hope, that by enduring and giving way to it for a time we may obtain relief. This emotion does not excite, but weakens. In courage, the hope of overcoming an evil by resistance, excites our activity; in patience, no desire to resist is felt. The courageous man suffers the pain, hoping to remove it by his own power and strength; the patient man bears it, hoping to be freed from it in the course of time. To resist disease or misfortune would avail nothing; they come from a higher hand, and it would be childish to clench the fist, and grind the teeth, or attempt to overcome them by a sinful obstinacy. Patience may be exercised as a virtue, and is then the result of will, and not an emotion. As such it is an ornament of the Christian, and assumes the character of an entire resignation of our own will in misfortune, and a readiness to leave all with God; or it is the resignation we feel, when we must suffer wrong, and cannot obtain justice; we then prefer suffering to doing wrong. A different species of resignation, not in any way a virtue, is sometimes manifested by warriors, who seeing themselves surrounded by a host of enemies, throw away their weapons, speak not, move not, ask for no favor, but suffer themselves to be hewn down, or taken captive. Such resignation is an expression of pride, a pretended fortitude. Patience may also be exercised in public life, and here as an adjunct to courage, it may be cultivated by soldiers. Fabius Cunctator effected more by tiring out Hannibal than if he had impatiently met him in battle.—The greater irritability of man renders *courage* more natural to him, than inactive patience, while the greater sensibility and inclination to retirement, and a feeling of dependence will cause patience to be more common in woman. Yet women may be as courageous as men, and there have been some who have showed more presence of mind, and greater determination in executing a plan, than many men would have done. A young girl who could repeatedly venture upon the strong billows of a raging river to rescue her beloved friends from danger; a woman that in the moment of the highest danger, thrusts the dagger into the bosom of an ill-fated seducer; sufficiently prove, that woman may be courageous.—Patience is not the opposite of courage, but its opposite is cowardice.

Awe.

This is an emotion, that arises either from our relation to the *supernatural* or to the *natural*. Man stands in a relation to the *supernatural*, by his reason and will, and the pillars of this relation are faith on the one hand, and morality on the other. When we believe that God is just and holy, that nothing sinful can endure his presence, the feeling connected with this belief will be a religious awe; when we are convinced that the divine will is sacred and inviolable, and that all duties are imposed upon us by it, the feeling will be a moral one. But man may enter into a relation to the supernatural by his imagination; the supernatural world would then be filled by his imagination, with good or evil spirits, who in his opinion may exercise either a benevolent or malicious influence upon this world in accordance with their natures. This is the origin of the fear of spectres; they are the products of a diseased imagination and a corrupt conscience; and man in fearing spectres, fears himself, his own thoughts and fancies. When this fear reigns, the emotion of *secret awe* may easily make its appearance. When a man really believes that he may see spectres, *fear* will seize him, and the emotion will not be that of *awe*. But when we ourselves feel safe, when instead of seeing spectres, we read well-written stories of them, the fear and pleasure will mingle in our breast, and the emotion in question will result from them. So children will cluster around their nurse in the hour of twilight, and listen with delight to her stories, but at the same time they will approach more and more closely to her, and would not for the world leave the room, without a light. If they felt only fear, they could take no pleasure in these stories.—The emotion of secret awe presupposes, however, several conditions : First, A belief in the possibility that supernatural beings can make their appearance in the world and affect us. Secondly, A particular time ; night, twilight: when the light illuminates and defines the forms of all things around us, we do not fear spectres. When during the day we become interested in the stories of spectres and supernatural apparitions, it is the poetical manner in which they are represented, that interests us, and our feeling is that of the sublime.—The other form of secret awe, arises from the relation in which man stands to nature. Whatever be the power man may exercise by his ingenuity over nature, there are some powers before which he must recede. Such are the elements of water and fire, earthquakes, hurricanes, and storms. When a conflagration breaks out in a large city, and in a part of it filled with merchandize, when we see the flames spread with the swiftness of the wind, and rise high into the air, when we hear the report of exploding powder casks, and see hundreds of persons endeavoring to combat the flames: we are at the same time penetrated by fear and apprehension, and rejoice to see man oppose the elements of destruction. Or when we see a courageous person venture upon a boisterous river, when we see him struggle and gain his object by ingenuity and presence of mind, we feel fear and pleasure mingle, and their union forms what we have called an emotion of awe.

We may here remark that a few emotions are yet to be mentioned, which may be ranked among the compound emotions:—The first of these is *astonishment*. It arises when either the opposite of that which we feared, or of that which we expected takes place. Another is *surprise or wonder:* it is the emotion that takes place in us, when, we see a power, with which we believed ourselves to be intimately acquainted, produce effects, for which we could not have looked. When on the other hand, man compares his own power with that which he sees producing actions in another that would seem wholly impossible to him, and for which his energy would not in any way be sufficient, he will *admire* it. No man on earth, unless he be stupid and sluggish, can avoid the emotion of admiration, for every one will find a power far exceeding his own, and Horace's "*Nil admirari*," is incorrect. Who would not look with admiration upon a Shakspeare, or Calderon, or Goethe? We nowhere read in the Bible, that Christ, when he was on earth, was under the influence of admiration, but we read that once or twice he expressed surprise: what power could exceed his, and deserve his admiration? The other class of compound emotions next demands consideration and this is that of

Strengthening emotions.

And first among these we may mention *courage*. This is grief, connected with the hope of overpowering it by resistance. Courage demands, therefore, as its conditions: First; An evil, future or present, and a feeling of pain derived from an apprehension of this evil. Secondly; A prospect of removing it by our own efforts. Hope, one of the constituent parts of courage, is pleasant, and if connected with a feeling of strength, it produces a desire to encounter danger and to seek opportunities for exhibiting courage. Courage may, however, be a virtue, and is then not an emotion, but the product of moral principles, of a morally good will, and of a conviction, that the object in danger, demands our assistance.—Courage as an emotion becomes *bravery*, when a feeling of honor inspires to action; it becomes *rashness*, when the danger is not only very great, but seems to require a greater amount of power than is possessed by him who braves it. It demands a strong inclination for action, much confidence and a lively imagination. Courage becomes *temerity*, when the object of bravery or courage is not promoted but frustrated by it. The object of courage is victory; this, temerity loses, for it is passionate and blind. Courage is considerate and self-possessed, while temerity is wholly devoid of prudence. It may be called forth by disgust with life; in this case the person meets his foe in combat wishing to lose his life in the encounter; or it is produced by intoxicating drinks, or by physical means, by religious notions, as among the Turks who believe that whatever is allotted to man, will seize him, whether he be at home or in war, active or indolent.—*Boldness*, finally, is courage that ventures to say or express what others would hesitate to convey in such language.

Wrath.

The strong feeling of displeasure accompanying the idea that others have injured us either wilfully or without design, may excite wrath, as likewise the perception of wrong, inflicted upon others. Wrath itself is a suddenly excited feeling of displeasure, with the sudden hope, either to resist, or to destroy the cause of the evil. The greater our bodily excitability, the more easily we are brought under its influence. While it continues, the offending object absorbs our whole attention, puts us off our guard, and deprives us of due consideration, so that we say what we afterwards regret, injure the innocent, and even inflict an expression of our displeasure on inanimate objects, like the boy who stumbling against a stone vents his rage upon it. Modifications of wrath are *refractoriness*, which we feel, when anything is urged upon us against our will, or when it is suggested to us that we ought to love what we dislike ; *indignation*, when we perceive anything offensive to good-breeding, to politeness, or to justice and equity ; *obstinacy*, when others insist on our changing our views and opinions, without showing sufficient reasons for our doing so. This is the kind of wrath, the absence of which in a man Aristotle considers a sign of a slavish disposition. *Anger* is the dissatisfaction we feel with ourselves, when we have committed an error. *Chagrin* pre-supposes a purpose, an end, which we feel ourselves justified in endeavoring to attain, but which we cannot execute. While under its influence, we become discouraged from attempting anything else; and take an interest in nothing. We consume ourselves in silent anger. *Malice* is the pleasure we take in destroying, or seeing destroyed that which is the favorite enjoyment of others, or which we envy them. Wrath, in general, was more common with the ancients than it is with us. To conquer it shows more greatness of mind, than to express or cherish it. Children and rude persons express their displeasure by using offensive language.

Joy.

This emotion differs from that of mere pleasure. The latter has only reference to the present, joy always more or less to the future, and *hope* is one of its necessary constituents. Joy is therefore pleasure, strengthened by the hope of future happiness. Without this hope no one can be really joyful, since the prospect of future misfortune would make us unhappy. Joy rests on a *pleasant present*, and a *smiling future*, it is the union of pleasure and hope, of the present and the future. Joy becomes *delight* when the long-wished-for occurrence takes place as we expected, and when at the same time a new hope arises in our breast so that care and trouble can gain no hold upon us. In such cases the emotion of joy has often proved fatal; for hopes suddenly realized while the mind is again drawn powerfully into new future prospects, distract the mind and by its connection with the body, cause the entire derangement or destruction of the physical system; as wrath is said to make every thing appear blue to us, and as fright dulls the hearing. The degrees of joy are very numerous, beginning with *satisfaction* and terminating in *rapture*. *Cheerfulness* is a lively joy; *mirth* a joy connected with mischief, &c.—Joy expresses itself externally by a cheerful countenance, by *singing* and *laughing*. Its peculiar songs are lyric poems, *dithyrambi*, in which the poet either fully or significantly expresses what moves and agitates him. It may also express itself without words by merely humming a melody. Birds likewise sing and express their peculiar state of self-feeling, their feeling of sensual pleasure or pain, but man alone can *laugh*, and hence many have considered laughing the peculiar distinction between man and animals. This definition that man is an animal that can laugh, has been laughed at, and yet it is correct in one respect, unless the definition of laughing, by Kant, is wholly wrong. " Whatever is to excite hearty laughter, must contain something contrary to reason. Laughing is the transformation of an excited expectation into nothing." This definition, as will be seen, has reference to *understanding*, to *thinking*. It presupposes an *expectation*, and this expectation, highly excited, sees what is expected result in *nothing*. The nothing here is that which is *contrary to reason*, hence either the physical impossible or the logical impossible. When a father has high expectation of his son, and this expectation is changed into nothing, he will not laugh, but feel pain; his expectation is, therefore, properly speaking, not changed into nothing, but into pain. Or when we expect great results from the convention of a public body or from the operations and effects of a law, and find our expectation deceived, we do not feel like laughing, for our expectation has resulted in grief. The expectation in these instances is not changed into *nothing*, but into the opposite of what was expected; instead of the law benefiting the community, it injures it. Animals cannot have any clear expectation, nor an idea of what is to be understood by the term "*nothing*," they cannot laugh, for laughing, according to Kant, is an expression of intellect. A few examples will make this definition of laughing more clear: A person relates, that an Indian when at the table of an Englishman in Surat, saw him open a bottle of ale, which burst forth in a torrent of foam. The Indian expressed his astonishment with many exclamations, and when asked by the Englishman what he found so amazing, he answered; I do not wonder at its coming out, but I wonder how *you got it in*. Of course we expected a good reason for the astonishment of the Indian and instead of it we get *nothing*, for what he says is itself impossible, since no one would be able to get the spreading foam of ale into a bottle. Again: A rich merchant gives us an account of the distress and anxiety he suffered on his return from India; he states every thing circumstantially, how he had to cast much of his wealth overboard, and how he was penetrated and overcome by the deepest despondency; and finally, directs our attention to the effect the misfortune had upon him; we, full of sympathy, anxiously listen to hear what it was, and when our expectation is raised to the highest pitch, he informs us that: "the effect of these troubles was so great, that during the night following all the hair on my wig became gray." This is physically impossible, for this hair has no life, and is not in any way connected with the life of the person. So when it is asked, why Hudibras wore but one spur, we shall certainly laugh if we are directed to look in the poem for the answer, and find the following:

> For Hudibras wore but one spur,
> As wisely knowing could he stir,
> To active trot one side of's horse
> The other would not hang.

This answer of course changes our expectation into nothing, for it gives no reason, but what it states may be understood of itself. The definition of laughing by Kant, agrees in part with that of Aristotle, who says, that the absurd or incongruous excite laughter; it explains, however, but one kind of laughter, for there are other kinds that cannot be included in it. Laughter, in general as to its causes, is a real Proteus; they cannot be reduced to a single and common class—and all attempts to do so, have as yet proved vain.

CONCLUSION.

ON RELIGION.

§ 1. GENERAL NATURE OF RELIGION.

We have now considered man in his different relations to nature, to himself, and to his fellow-men; yet *one* we have omitted, that to his Creator. This relation, if it is to be pure, must rest on faith, and faith is the gift of God. The soul in its state of nature is selfish in all its feelings, words and actions; it is blind and corrupt, it poisons whatever it touches, and all its notions of right and wrong, of equity and justice, have for their measure the selfishness of man. Hence constant wars and litigations, deceptions, theft and murder: courts of justice, police, prisons, punishments and even executions. *Self-interest* and selfish desires move the mass of mankind. There is nothing good in man from which pure religion or a knowledge of divine things might proceed, and hence as long as man is in a state of sinfulness, God is *veiled* from him, and though he might see the divine wisdom and power of the *teleological* relations and grand phenomena of nature, he could not discover in them the *holiness* of God. But what is a religion without the idea of holiness? What is a knowledge of God if this is not included in it? *Deus a diabolo differt castitate*, says Melancthon. Yet, I hear it stated, that there were religions independent of a revelation: Whence are these? Did they not grow forth from something in man? —To answer this question satisfactorily, we must agree on what we understand by religion. And here we shall have at once to reject a host of views, but particularly the following:

1. Religion is not the mere knowledge that there is a God. Such knowledge may be the source of much philosophical speculation, but it leaves the heart cold, and does not animate the will to good actions. The devils know that there is a God and tremble, they know what they hate to know, and what they cannot love. Again: If religion consisted in knowledge it would necessarily follow, that the most learned divines must be the most devoted and religious; that the degree or amount of knowledge must also be that of godliness; which is by no means the case. On the contrary the same amount of knowledge may be found in persons who have very different degrees of piety; and so piety may be the same, though the knowledge of different persons should differ widely.

2. Religion is not mere morality, so that our will driven by the conviction of a future state of retribution, desires every where to fulfill the will of God, and the manifold duties imposed upon us. Word and actions are mere empty sounds and forms; that which is their soul is the motive producing them. Motive and design exist before action, and are the offspring of our sanctified or depraved disposition. That which renders an action good or evil, lies not in the deed itself, but in the will, and the power that sanctifies the will. The same action performed by the religious and irreligious has an entirely different value as to its moral goodness. An unsanctified will can only lead to stoic pride.

3. Religion does not proceed from a feeling of dependence in man. This feeling in its lowest stage, it is is said, is a mere feeling of dependence on nature, its productions, its terrible or benign phenomena. While feeling dependent on nature in these respects, man feels free as regards his will and moral actions and does what he pleases. But when the original feeling is cultivated, it becomes a feeling of dependence that will leave nothing perfectly free in man, but will include his will also, so that he is and feels wholly dependent on the *Infinite*. This feeling includes the other, that there is a progressive union of man with God, and this is the germ of all religion, whether Feticism or Polytheism, only that Monotheism is the purest of all religions.

This view on the origin of religion is one that seems highly plausible, and to refute it we shall consider for a moment the nature of *feeling*.—We understand by it "*the general susceptibility of pleasure and displeasure.*" Activity whether physical or organic, has its limitations; these limitations have different degrees, and the notice we take of these degrees of limitation is that which we call feeling, and this is either pleasant or painful. Every activity of man has a certain capacity to receive impressions, and cannot receive any beyond it; if excited beyond measure it is destroyed. The stone lying in the heat of the sun, does not suffer, because it remains what it is though broke in pieces, and because it cannot feel though it is burning hot to our sensation. The plant cannot receive the rays of the sun in every degree, but only in one commensurate to its life or strength; exposed to too great a degree of heat, it withers yet it cannot feel. But the eye looking into the light of the sun, feels pain and may become blind. We say now that when any activity of man is promoted by any cause whatever, a feeling of pleasure is experienced, when impeded, that of displeasure. And as the activity differs, so the feeling. Our bodily activity, when the different functions are harmonious and regular, is accompanied by a feeling of pleasure, of hilarity, and this is a feeling of health; when these functions are impeded, when digestion is sluggish and heavy by a feeling of displeasure, of a tendency to rest, of sickness. So feelings accompany our thinking power, as those of pleasure, when we find what we seek for in the sphere of truth without great labor, and when the difficulties in our way yield, and those of pain, when we meet with different results from what we expected, or when we do not find at once what we seek; this is so with feelings connecting themselves with the sight of beauty, when we see the infinite in the finite, the thought represented is a sensible form in an image. These feelings are not merely physical, not merely in the nerve, but their ground is the *soul*. Every merely sensual feeling is in a particular nerve, local; the feelings under consideration are spread throughout the whole inner man; and again the feeling of beauty cannot arise from a sensual impression, but must finally rest in an act of judgment.

Neither have the feelings of which we speak any external objects; but they are wholly *subjective*, the *most subjective* possessed by man. This can easily be shown by comparing them with sensation. When I feel the heat of the sun, warmth is the object of my feeling; when I hear the voice of a person, sound is the object of my feeling; when I feel the smoothness of a surface, I feel with my hands or fingers, and the object is the thing felt. But when a feeling of pleasure is connected with the hearing of the voice of a friend then this *pleasure* has no object that is felt; it arises from the *recognition* of a friend, and the object of the feeling is pleasure. Or when the feeling of pleasure unites with that of smoothness, this has not for its object smoothness, it has no relation whatever to it, but merely to ourselves. All feelings are either *agreeable* or *disagreeable* when they have merely reference to our sensuality; or when they refer to form and contents, their expression is that of the *beautiful, sublime,* or the opposite. Now I may say, the lily is *beautiful;* or the fragrance is *agreeable*, in all these instances the predicates express feelings, which have in reality no *object*. For the predicate beautiful, is not continued in the rose, nor that of agreeable, in the fragrance: these predicates are my feelings which I transfer and place into these objects, pronouncing these their qualities. When on the other hand I say, the lily is a bulbous plant, then the predicate is a constituent part of the lily, a predicate resting in its logical subject. The rose will remain a rose whether I declare it to be beautiful or not; but it will no longer remain a rose if it is not a flower or a plant.

The first objection then to be made to the assertion, that religion originates in a feeling of dependence on the Infinite is this:—Feeling is without an object and a mere feeling of dependence leaves the object on which we depend, wholly undefined; it demands therefore knowledge from some other source, but knowledge is more than feeling. Feeling without knowledge is blind.

Again: This feeling of dependence on the Infinite is not found everywhere; on the contrary we find in its place a slavish feeling of dependence on nature, on the finite, on animals, vegetables, stones, &c. If this feeling of dependence on the finite, is the feeling of dependence on the Infinite but in its rude state, it demands cultivation, and can be found only among the cultivated, since it would be impossible to cultivate feeling alone, and independent of the other activities of the mind. But religion is not merely intended for the cultivated, it is for all, for the rich and the poor, for the learned and the ignorant. Nor is it true, that the most cultivated are always the most religious.

And in the third place: *Feeling* and *thinking* are inseparable. There is a feeling connecting itself with the thought of the *Infinite*, but it is not the origin of this thought; it only accompanies it, as a feeling of respect accompanies our morally good actions. The feeling of regard may act as a *motive*, but it is not the principle of our actions, since to know whether they are good or not, we must compare them with the law, and every comparison is an act of *judgment* and not of *feeling*. And this feeling of *self-regard*, or respect, while originating in the most different actions, will nevertheless be the same. So it is with the feeling of despondency, of joy, of grief; they all may have various causes and still be the same feeling.—Feeling being without a *definite object*, demanding knowledge for its very existence, is even not a sure sign of truth, much less its origin. Or in other words, feeling may give *certainty* to him that has it, but not *truth*. Heathen whose religions are superstitions, the systems of sin and wickedness, have as much feeling as Christians, as much zeal, and as much fervor. How many are willing to sacrifice themselves for the supposed truth of their religion, how many desirous of becoming martyrs! All mysticism and superstition take their rise in feeling, when connected with fancy and imagination. Feeling without knowledge is blind, mystical, dark, inexpressible and unintelligible; its contents may be the highest or lowest, right or injustice, joy or grief, wrath or hatred, hope or fear, the royal flower or the most noxious weed. All feeling is changeable; now it raises our zeal and interest, and now again it leaves us cold and indifferent; now it elevates us to heaven, and now again it suffers us to sink down to despair.

§ 2. TRUE RELIGION.

What then is true religion? It is a *peculiar* activity of God, which announcing itself to the *heart* of man, changes it, converts it, and restores man to peace with himself, with the world, and with God. A few words on this definition will render it perfectly clear.—The object of religion is the restoration of *peace;* this can be restored only by an union of man with his Creator, through whom alone he can perceive the true value of every thing created by him, and estimate it properly. This union is to be produced by a peculiar activity of God upon the heart of man. This activity is *peculiar*, because it differs from every other divine agency, and announces itself as such to the heart, so that it needs no further proof, but is its own authority : as the light of the sun needs no other light to make itself seen or manifest, so this activity of God, directed upon the heart, makes it certain of its nature. It is the *heart* upon which it acts, purifying and converting it. Feelings and knowledge are changeable, the heart is *permanent.* Again : It is the centre of man, uniting in itself thought and will and feeling, for from it good and evil thoughts proceed ; it is according to the Bible the source of desires and passions, the seat of consciousness, of the conscience, and of our whole inner man. It being changed, the whole man is changed ; it being converted from the world to God, from sin to holiness, all the activities of which it is the seat will be turned contemporaneously and for ever. Hence, while in the state of nature the different activities of mind were at war with each other—while thinking delighted perhaps in abstract, cold and useless speculations, in generalizing every thing so that no form in reality could any longer correspond with it ; or while imagination would suppress thinking, and beget, as in India, the most fantastical and shapeless productions, or while will wholly directed to the sensual, was entirely absorbed by desires and passions ;— they are now brought into harmony pervaded by one spirit, by one love, and by one object, so that man having God in his heart, will have him in his thoughts, in his will, his actions and his feelings, so that none of these mental activities will feel healthy and joyful without this reference to God. Religion then is always based upon a communication of God to man, and where this communication is wanting, where the regenerating power of the Spirit is absent, there cannot be true religion. We must, therefore, consider all heathenish religions as superstitious; they rest on a faith created by themselves, and not produced by God in them; they do not free man from sin by converting him, but lead him deeper into it. A glance at them must prove this, and especially prove too, that the activities of the soul, while man is in the state of nature, are at war with each other. For all religions are either the productions of *desire* to the exclusion of the other activities, or of *imagination*, or of cool *reflection* and *understanding*.

§ 3. RELIGIONS OF DESIRE.

1. The lowest of all superstitions, and one spread among the numerous tribes of Africa, is that of *enchantment* or *feticism*. It is wholly produced by desire and a feeling of want. By his immediate will man expects to effect what he desires, to exercise power over nature and its elements, to conjure storms, diseases, and death. "Enchantment is in itself nothing else than the expression that something opposes the purposes of man, and that it ought not to be." This opposition is pronounced without the use of any means in a direct manner, or means are called in aid, and the enchantment is indirect. The principal thing is, that man by his mere will, here and there, desires to coerce nature to be at his disposal. Again: Whatever may injure or benefit man, receives his adoration; whatever may serve as remedy or means, all stones, and herbs, and animals, deserve his devotion, for each is possessed of a peculiar power, and each good for something. Gold differs from copper, the hare from the stag, the fur of the former from that of the latter; each has an efficacy different from that of the other,

&c. The deity is the *fetish;* it has no universal form, no unchangeable existence, but now it is a *stone,* which the negro carries about with him, and which he worships until he gets tired of it. Then he chooses something else for his deity, and so on. Now it is the water, that attracts his curiosity, by its transparency, penetrableness, liveliness, murmuring; now the stormy wind, now the fire, which is no less destructive than beneficial. Or it is a plant, a tree, —as it grows forth, spreading and clothing itself in a lovely green, on the top of which the flower in all its splendor makes its appearance—which attracts his admiration, and to which he ascribes a power, it does not possess; or it is the animal which moves freely about, seeks its food, and resembles the savage in its actions, yet is mute, mysterious, and hence a wonder to him.

2. The second form of superstition, in which desire is still perceptible, is *Buddhism,* as met with among the Mongols, Birmans, and Chinese in the west. In it desire is controlled, for the individual recedes before the one, indistinct and unknown substance, which all in all, is unconscious of itself; the individual retiring into itself, grows mute and silent. This superstition teaches that all has proceeded from *nothing;* this is the deity, and does not mean an abstract absence of being, but an undefined, incomprehensible, shapeless *being,* a being so vague, and so without contents, that if we are asked what it is, we must say *nothing* of all that we can know. All will return to *nothing*. *Silence, obedience, resignation,* are the highest virtues. The silence of the grave is the element of eternity. Cessation of all motion, both in body and soul, is the highest happiness of man; when once reached, man is the same with Fo or Buddha. Buddha himself stands in a position of deep meditation; feet and hands cross each other, and one of his toes is placed in his mouth, indicating that he feasts on himself, on his own meditations. The highest end man may attain is to connect himself by meditation and silence with *nothing;* then he will be the same with God, not to be distinguished from him.

The belief in the metamorphosis of the soul causes the worship of animals, for which they erect temples. Even hospitals for diseased cows are met with. A missionary relates the history of a dying Chinese, who sent for him and complained, that a *bonze* had told him, that as he was in the service of the emperor, so he would remain in it after his death, for his soul was to pass into an imperial post-horse, and he ought then to attend faithfully to his service, not kick nor bite, nor stumble, and be satisfied with little food. This religion, however, worships its deity in the form of living men, called Lamas. There are especially three of them, that receive the honor of being considered gods; the one is Dalai Lama, in Lassa; the other is Lama, in Thibet, and the third in Tartary.

§ 4. RELIGIONS OF IMAGINATION.

1. *Brahminism.* This is a fantastical wild production. Imagination is not bridled in it by reason, its form is shapeless, without measure or proportion, and hence, though symbolical, by no means beautiful. It is pantheistic, for it makes no distinction between the free activity of God and that of the world and man. "The whole world is Brahma, grew forth from Brahma, consists in Brahma, and will finally be absorbed by Brahma." The creation of the world is rather an *emanation*, for the deity flows forth in innumerable gradations, down to the being and existence of finite things, which are the being of the *deity* itself. The whole world is the result of a desire in the deity for change. Hence, all is *divine*, a part of deity; every flower and every star, every leaf and every twig. Yet the Indians have not *one* idea only of the creation, but many, and these differ essentially. In the Vedas we find the following account.— Brahma sits in solitude, another being higher than himself, tells him to extend himself and beget himself. But Brahma was not capable during a thousand years, to comprehend his extension, and hence he returned into himself. Cosmogonies in the law-book of Menu, in the Vedas, and Puranas differ, hence nothing can be said with certainty. The Brahmins are the existence of Brahma; they came

forth from his mouth; but every one may become Brahma by great rigor of life, especially by remaining for ten years inactive, by living on leaves and dried grass, by standing on one leg, crossing the arms above the head, &c. Great phenomena of nature, the Ganges, the sun, the Himmalehs, are identified with Brahma; every activity being divine, imagination personifies all, and hence an innumerable host of gods, at the head of whom stands Indra. Finally, sin is nothing but a limitation of Brahma, for infinite in himself, he exists in the finite; to conquer these limits by asceticism is conquering sin.

2. *The Persian Religion.* In this we perceive the deity divided in itself, a dualism that is *external* as to its origin. In the Christian religion we have likewise the kingdom of Satan, opposing that of God: but Satan is a created being, and God is in himself *one*; again, Satan is conquered, but Ahriman and Ormuzd are continually at war. The ancient Persians revered the sun or fire as the highest *being*. Zervane Akerene or eternity is the original ground of all. As nature does not produce any thing *pure*, as all in it is of an impure and mixed nature, there must be *two* principles and not *one* that is like a tavern keeper, who pours out of two casks, mixing the drink. These are contained in Zervane Akerene, and are Ormuzd or the light, and Ahriman or darkness. Light and darkness are consequently not mere *symbols*, but the one *is* the good and the other the evil. The difference between physical and moral evil is destroyed. The good is the light itself; whatever contains light and life, contains therefore good and is Ormuzd. Mithra stands between them, assists Ormuzd, and desires the destruction of Ahriman. The latter is sometimes called the first-born of light, but is said to have forsaken it.

The kingdom of light is unshaken above the solid sky in heaven; also on the mountain of Albordi; the kingdom of darkness was below the earth until it broke forth into the world of bodies of Ormuzd. Hence it is that the space between heaven and earth is divided by night and day. Before this corruption, Ormuzd had a kingdom of spirits of light, and Ahriman one of spirits of darkness. But afterwards the two kingdoms oppose each other. Those that believe the lies of Ahriman will, however, be thrust into darkness after death, while those, faithful to Ormuzd, will be received into the kingdom of light. This then is the religion which makes God fight with God.

3. The *religion of enigma* or the religion of the Egyptians. In it we meet first with the God *Hermes*, the personification of mind, the god that invented language, writing and science; the spirit of light that lives in heavenly bodies. Osiris, however, is the god that was most adored by the people. His sister was Iris, the goddess of the earth and the moon. Osiris, the god of goodness, the principle of all life, like Ormuzd, has an enemy in Typhon. Osiris dies by his hand, the god himself is killed. *Death*, this great enigma of human life, is the principal theme of the Egyptian religion. Even their god dies, and the highest happiness of man is to be buried near his tomb, to slumber near him after a life of care and disappointment. But Osiris rises again, becomes the judge of all the dead and thus Typhon is conquered. Ahriman continues to oppose Ormuzd, but Typhon's power is destroyed by the death and resurrection of Osiris. As Osiris is principally honored as the god of the dead, as their judge, so the Egyptians seem to have paid more attention to the dead, than the living. The palaces of their kings and nobles are crumbled to dust, but the monuments and tombs erected to the dead, are not injured by the tooth of time. Grottos destined for their reception extend many miles; and the pyramids attract our attention at present, as they have gained the admiration of thousands long before us. This religion is certainly full of seriousness, it seems to have discovered that all is vain, to have a full idea of the immortality of the soul—for Herodotus expressly states, that the Egyptians had been first in believing the soul to continue after death—and yet they adored cats and dogs, birds and monkeys, and especially Apis.

The religion of the Egyptians, deserves to be called enigmatical; its hieroglyphics, the symbolical character of art among them, in which every thing is significant, even the number of pillars, of steps, of pots set around the tomb of Osiris, has meaning and is not decided on from considerations of proportion. But Oedipus, a Greek, solved the enigma of the Sphinx, thrust her down the precipice and slew her. As we approach the religion of Greece, we perceive every thing grow clear and transparent, enigmas recede ; stones and rocks as mere *signs* are no longer sufficient; in the place of *symbols*, we have *mythi* and the productions of an art, that renders the most dark and difficult lucid, and sets forth all that may move the breast of man.

4. The religion of *Beauty*, or the religion of Greece. The gods of Greece were persons, whose will was free, and who were not subject to any power of nature, nor limited to it. The highest among these gods was Jupiter ; he had given the laws of justice, was himself justice, and both gods and men had to obey it, yet without being forced by necessity, but freely and willingly. But there was an iron necessity, αναγκη, reigning over gods and men, of which it was unknown, whether it was blind or intelligent, possessed of will, or a power that could neither determine itself, nor could be determined by any thing else, but could not be otherwise than it was. This power allotted to every god his portion of power, and the manner of his existence, and if men sought counsel from the gods through their oracles and attempted to discover the future, the gods could tell them only what this blind fate had granted them to know. Yet Zeus had given the law and Sophocles sings beautifully : " Be it the lot of my life, to preserve holy purity in word and deed, faithful to eternal rights that came down from above, born in ether's space, which no earthly being, no mortal man begot ; Olympus is their father ; never will they sleep in forgetfulness, for a god lives powerfully in them, never growing old." " There is nothing that is not Zeus, and Zeus is justice." Thus justice, right, the *law* is acknowledged and man is willing to obey it. But at the same time there is the incomprehensible, irresistible *Fate*, against whose decisions mortal man can do nothing, and through whose power he may be forced against his will, to violate the law. Laius for instance receives the oracle, that he will be killed by a son, not yet born ; to prevent this misfortune, he exposes the infant child on the mountain *Cithaeron*, and considers himself safe. But Oedipus taken up by a shepherd, fell into the hands of the king of Corinth, was educated by him at a dis-

tance from home, and when grown up being offended, he consults the oracle concerning the truth of the insult and receives the answer, that he was fated to marry his mother. Believing Corinth to be his home, he leaves it, lest the oracle should be fulfilled. On his wanderings he meets Laius, whom he does not know; insulted by him he strikes and kills him. Thus Laius falls by the hand of his son, who commits parricide, without having any idea of it. He arrives at Thebes, the home of his birth, but not known to him as such; here he solves the enigma of the Sphinx and receives the publicly promised reward, the hand of the widowed queen Jocasta. She was the wife of Laius and the mother of Oedipus. Thus Oedipus violates two divine laws against his will, being guided by fate. And here we must remark, that the Greek heroes imputed all the consequences of an action, all that connected itself with it, to themselves, whether these accidental circumstances were included in their resolutions or not. In modern times, we hold ourselves responsible only for as much as our resolution and calculation, our intention and design contains and all that accidentally attaches itself to our actions, we exclude from the amount of guilt.—So again in another tragedy of Sophocles, in Antigone, we see the divine law of family love enter into a collision with the civil law or human statutes of the king Creon. Both laws are to be kept sacred, but Antigone, seeing the corpse of her brother unburied, finds herself in the dilemma, that she must either break the one or the other law. The family law was considered divine in Greece, the civil, human; she therefore resolves at the peril of her own life to offend the civil and obey the divine law. This, that she knowingly and by a resolution of her will must break one of two laws, was her fate. Here we may remark, that before the Greek religion, there was no distinction made between divine and human laws, and that at present the possibility of a collision of duties is no longer admitted.

This dependence on fate rendered it impossible for the Greeks to feel perfectly free; but instead of forming resolutions of their own, and from the elements contained in their own self-consciousness in important undertakings, they took refuge in the oracles, as the Romans in their *auguria, auspicia,* and *haruspicia.* The uncertainty whether their undertakings would meet the approbation of the gods, and their feeling of an entire dependence on them made them seek their counsel in every public or private affair.— We have called the religion of Greece that of beauty; thus far it has exhibited itself only as that of *necessity.* It is beautiful, however, in the following respects:—The gods of Greece are free and intelligent beings; as such they were to be represented. Nothing in nature was sufficient to be this representative, hence it was to be produced by art. All beauty has the following elements. First; *Sensation,* that of seeing or hearing. Secondly; A pure *thought.* Every sensation is finite, limited; but a thought is infinite. Here is a contradiction, and it is removed by the artist, who unites *thought* and *sensation* in Thirdly; An *image.* The more this image seems to exist only for the purpose of exhibiting the thought of the artist, the more it seems only the transparent body of this idea, which is the soul, the more it deserves to be called beautiful. The Greek artist, creating by his imagination in his soul an idea of the being and nature of his gods, felt an irresistible urgency to represent this idea of others by an external form, so that they also might possess it. The idea of Apollo was that of a being, free from care, cheerful in itself, vigorous, and powerful, that of intellect personified. Such an idea is infinite in itself; the artist possesses the power to represent it by an image, in a sensible form, and the god appears before us, creating in us the idea, which inspired the artist.

§ 5. THE RELIGION OF UNDERSTANDING OR COOL REFLECTION.

This was the religion of the Romans. It was Eudaemonism, a religion of usefulness. Cicero praises the Romans on account of their piety, because they desired the approbation of their gods in all their undertakings. But the truth is, that the Romans honored their gods because they stood in need of them, for they had their designs, which they expected by honoring the gods to induce them to execute. When the old gods were not favorable to them, they created new ones. It is known that neither the Greeks nor the Romans had a doctrinal part of religion; festivals, the theatre, were the only means of preserving religion in public. In Greece it was principally the tragedy, which unlike that of Shakspeare, did not mingle mirth with sadness, but was serious throughout. Its themes were justice, purity of disposition and action, the holiness and the inviolability of the divine law. If these laws were offended, man had to atone for the offence, and it was only by submitting patiently and humbly to the punishment inflicted by the gods, that he could become reconciled with them, and with the law. This is beautifully exhibited in Oedipus in Colonna. The Romans received their tragedies from Greece, and the only entertainment of the kind, which grew forth on *Roman* soil and was *peculiar* to the Romans, was the butchering of *animals* and *men*. Hundreds of men, four or five hundred lions at a time were killed, or forced to destroy each other before a delighted public. In such entertainments we cannot discover any moral worth, any thing that could refine or cultivate. So the whole religion of the Romans was mean and worthless. A religion that has its roots in the idea of *usefulness*, is contemptible. In it the notion of gain or the apprehension of loss, hope and fear for himself, determine man to be pious; love is not to be met with where *usefulness* is the ground of religion; here the question is: *What is the end?* and again: Is it a *private* or *public* one? If that of a whole government, is it *dominion*, as it was with Rome? Whatever be the object and end, the followers of such a religion look to their gods for the satisfaction of some interest, and thus make them mere tools, means for the purposes of man. Man may honor them, but in doing so he hopes that they will pay him for his trouble, that his designs and purposes will fill their breast, and make them willing to promote his wishes. Such creeping humility is hypocrisy.

The end, the Romans had in view, and for the sake of which they desired the favor of their gods, was to conquer all nations, and enrich themselves with the spoils of war. Hence, their highest god was Fortuna Publica; *Roma* is a governing, a divine, holy being, and in the form of a god it is *Jupiter Capitolinus*, the highest of all the gods. Other gods had to preside over the fertility of the earth, the skill of man. There was a *Jupiter Pistor*, who presided over the art of baking. *Fornax* was the oven, in which the grain was dried. *Vesta* the fire, over which the bread was baked.—Comparing a single god of Greece with one of Rome, we shall find a striking difference. "Athena was the goddess of Athens; she had not to *serve* Athens or its inhabitants, was not their tool, but their *Spirit*, and Athens was only the external existence of this spirit. *Jupiter Capitolinus*, on the other hand, is not the *Roman spirit*, but he is a god that has to serve it."

Having thus touched upon the most important forms of superstitious religion, we must come to the conclusion, that man left to himself, is wholly unable to restore a proper relation between himself and God, to restore harmony and peace. Sin has its root in the will; unless it is sanctified, *Holiness*, the soul and substance of religion will and must be absent. But this will can only be sanctified by the regenerating power of the Holy Spirit. Yet corrupt as these religions were, they were a faint echo of the knowledge of Divine things, that man received in paradise, a dark and confused remembrance, held down by sin, and not able to emerge from the depth of corruption, it being itself pervaded by sin. The knowledge of death, however, the fear of evils of every kind, the perception of the vanity of all things, the urgent warnings of conscience even in its state of depravity—roused this dim remembrance, which in connection with a sinful imagination, with desires and evil concupiscence, produced idolatry, the worship of animals, sacrifices, and all other parts of superstitious belief.—The correctness of this view appears from the fact that the remembrance of the flood, and a hope of the restoration of man to the favor of God, run throughout all nations more or less clearly. This remembrance and this hope include the idea, that there was once a state of mankind purer, and better than the present, and that the present is not what it ought to be. This is indicated too, by the great number of sacrifices.

If we see on the one hand, that man cannot create a religion of his own, and on the other, that he is anxious to worship a higher being, we should expect nothing less, than that he would seize with joy upon a revelation, made to him by God himself. And yet the opposite of this is true. Man without religion is incomplete; a plant, that has not flowered; a bell, without a tongue, which cannot give a clear and distinct sound; a planet, that having wandered from its sun, is without light; a ship, without a compass, a stranger, without a home. And though this is so, his sin veils the light of revelation as a cloud that of the sun. Revelation is there, but he cannot see it, because the eye of his soul is filled with the darkness of sin, satisfied with its state, it feels pain, when looking into the light of revelation. We cannot withhold from our readers an extract from the beginning of the seventh book of Plato's Republic, which though written by a heathen, expresses the relation of the sinner to the gospel in a masterly manner. Perhaps it may have more weight with some, than if it were written by a distinguished divine of modern times:—

"See men in a subterraneous, cavernlike dwelling, which has an opening along the whole cavity towards the light. Suppose that from their infancy they were chained by the neck and limbs, so that they must remain on the same spot and can only look *forward* but are unable on account of the fetters to turn their heads around. A fire burning above, and at a distance behind them, gives them light. Between the captives and the fire, a road passes; along it runs a wall, like one which jugglers erect before the spectators, from behind which they exhibit their skill. Along this wall men are carrying all kinds of vessels, which overtop the wall, and statues and other stone and wooden images of all kinds of art. Some of these men speak, others are silent. This whole comparison now applies to us. For in the first place these chained persons see nothing of themselves and of each other, except the shadows cast by the fire upon the opposite wall of the cavern. And so of all that is carried along the wall, only the shadows are seen. Now if they can speak with each other, they certainly name what they see. And if their prison had an *echo*, they would, when one of the passers by should speak, imagine the fleeting shadows were speaking. Hence they would not consider anything else to be true than the *shadows* of those works of art.—Let us then consider the cure and redemption from their chains and ignorance; how it will be, if they should meet with the following things:— Suppose one was unchained and forced to walk up, and to look into the light, and in doing so, he felt pain and could not on account of the dazzling splendor perceive those things, the *shadows* of which he saw before; if then any one should assure him, that before he saw only vanities, but now, nearer to reality and turned to that which truly is, he saw more correctly, and if he showing him all that passed by, should ask him, what each is and force him to answer, he certainly would be confused and would believe, that what he formerly saw, was more real, than what now was shown him. And if he were urged to look into the light, his eyes would pain him, he would flee it and return to that, which he is able to look at, firmly convinced that it was more true than what was shown him last. Suppose too, some one would violently lead him up the rough and steep ascent and not release him, until he had brought him to the light of the sun; he will feel much pain, and be dragged up against his will. And when he now comes to the light, and has the eyes full of rays, he will be unable to see any thing of all that is shown him, as being real and true. In order to see, what is above, he must become accustomed to the light, at first he would most easily perceive shadows; then the reflections of men and other things in the water, and at length men themselves. And thus he would prefer contemplating what is in the sky, and the sky itself at night, and seeing the light of the moon and stars to looking at the sun and the light in the day. But after some time he will be able to view the sun itself instead of the image in the water, and then he will find out, that it is he, that causes the revolutions of time and years, and disposes all in the visible space, and is also the cause of what the captives saw in their cavern. And if he should now remember his first dwelling and his fellow captives, he would certainly consider himself happy and pity them,—

if they were in the habit of giving honor, praise and rewards to him who could most accurately see the passing shadows and remember best what came first, what last, and what at the same time, and who could best foretell what will come next, he would no longer desire this reward, nor envy those in power and honored among them. He would much rather like Achilles in Hades, prefer cultivating the land of a poor man and enduring every thing else, to having such notions and living there again. And this we will consider yet, that if he should go down again and sit in his place, his eyes would be full of darkness, coming directly from the sun. And if he should again emulate those who had always been captives there, in the examination of those shadows, while there was yet a glimmer before his eyes, and while they had not yet accustomed themselves again to darkness:—he would be laughed at, and they would say, that he had come down with spoiled eyes, and that it was not worth while to ascend; but that every one ought to be killed, that would attempt to force them and take them up to the light of the sun." [The Jews really did so.]

"The whole picture must now be applied thus: The region, which becomes manifest to us by sight, is the *cavern;* the power of the sun is the light of the fire in the prison, the act of ascending and the view of the things above, is the elevation of the soul into the region of knowledge. Now my belief is this, [Plato speaks] and God knows whether it is correct. What I know is this, that *last* of all, that may become known, and only with great pains the *idea of the good* is perceived; but when *once perceived*, it is acknowledged as the power of all the good and beautiful, wherever it be met, of the light and the sun from which it flows forth, in the visible; of truth and reason in all knowable things, so that every one must see this idea, if he will act rationally either in private or public affairs."